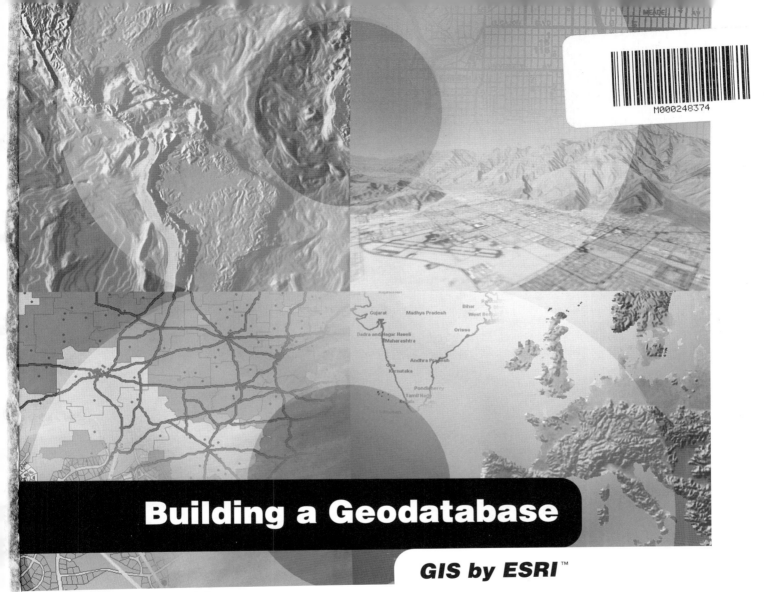

Building a Geodatabase

GIS by ESRI™

Andrew MacDonald

M000248374

CONTRIBUTING WRITERS

Tom Brown, Julio Andrade, Erik Hoel, and Jonathan Bailey.

U.S. GOVERNMENT RESTRICTED/LIMITED RIGHTS

Contents

1 Introduction 1

Before you create your geodatabase 3
Three ways to create a geodatabase 4
Geodatabases and ArcCatalog 8
The first step: creating your database 9
Tips on learning how to build geodatabases 14

2 Quick-start tutorial 15

Exercise 1: Organizing your data in ArcCatalog 18
Exercise 2: Importing data into your geodatabase 20
Exercise 3: Creating subtypes and attribute domains 24
Exercise 4: Creating relationships between objects 29
Exercise 5: Building a geometric network 31
Exercise 6: Creating annotation 36
Exercise 7: Creating layers for your geodatabase data 41
Exercise 8: Editing your geodatabase 44

3 Creating new items in a geodatabase 55

Geodatabase items 56
Creating tables 61
Creating feature datasets 65
Creating feature classes 71
Creating indexes 79
Granting and revoking privileges 82

4 Migrating existing data into a geodatabase 83

How data is converted 84
Importing shapefiles 96
Importing coverages 102
Importing tables 109
Importing a geodatabase feature class 111

Importing a CAD feature class 114
Importing rasters 115
Copying geodatabase data 121
Loading data into existing simple feature classes and tables 123
Registering ArcSDE layers and tables with the geodatabase 127
Analyzing geodatabase data 128

5 Subtypes and attribute domains 129

What are subtypes and attribute domains? 130
Working with attribute domain properties 134
Browsing the attribute domains of a geodatabase 135
Creating new attribute domains 137
Modifying and deleting attribute domains 140
Associating default values and domains with tables and feature classes 141
Creating subtypes 142
Modifying and deleting subtypes 145

6 Defining relationship classes 147

What is a relationship class? 148
Relationship classes in ArcCatalog and ArcMap 152
Creating a simple relationship class 154
Creating a composite relationship class 158
Creating an attributed relationship class 161
Creating relationship rules 163
Managing relationship classes 165
Exploring related objects in ArcMap 166
Using related fields in ArcMap 169

7 Managing annotation 171

Annotation in the geodatabase 172
Annotation and ArcCatalog 175
Creating annotation classes 176

Converting labels to annotation   181
Converting coverage annotation to geodatabase annotation   183

8   Dimensioning   185

Dimensions in the geodatabase   186
Dimensions and ArcCatalog   189
Creating dimension feature classes   190
Creating and managing dimension styles   195

9   Geometric networks   205

What is a geometric network?   206
Geometric networks and ArcCatalog   210
Creating geometric networks   211
Creating a new geometric network   216
Building a geometric network from existing simple feature classes   220
Adding new feature classes to your geometric network   228
Network connectivity: defining the rules   231
Establishing connectivity rules   232
Managing a geometric network   234

10 Geocoding services   235

Geocoding services   236
Geocoding services in ArcCatalog and ArcMap   238
Preparing reference data for a geocoding service   240
Creating a geocoding service   245
Maintaining geocoding indexes   248
Maintaining geocoding indexes   250
Preparing address data for geocoding   256

11 Building geodatabases with CASE tools 259

What are CASE tools? 260
Creating UML packages and static structure diagrams 271
Setting tagged values 272
Creating feature datasets 273
Creating feature classes 274
Creating relationship classes 278
Creating domains 283
Creating subtypes 288
Creating relationship rules 294
Creating geometric networks 296
Creating connectivity rules 298
Extending classes with custom behavior 303
Exporting your UML model to the repository 309
Checking your model for errors 311
Generating schema from the repository 312
Selecting feature datasets 316
Setting properties for object classes (tables) 317
Setting properties for feature classes in a feature dataset 320
Setting properties for relationship classes 323
Creating the schema 325

12 Editing your geodatabase 327

Editing in ArcMap and your geodatabase 328
Managing the edit cache 332
Editing with default values and attribute domains 334
Editing relationships 341
Editing relationships and related objects 346
Editing annotation 365
Editing network features 374
Editing dimension features 395
Loading objects from other feature classes 428

13 Working with a versioned geodatabase   435

Integrating versioning with your organization's work flow   436
Registering data as versioned   438
Creating and administering versions in ArcCatalog   439
Working with versions in ArcMap   446
Editing and conflict resolution   449
Editing a version   454
Versioning scenarios   458

Glossary   461

Index   471

Introduction

IN THIS CHAPTER

- **Before you create your geodatabase**

- **Three ways to create a geodatabase**

- **Geodatabases and ArcCatalog**

- **The first step: creating your database**

- **Tips on learning how to build geodatabases**

The *geodatabase* supports a model of topologically integrated *feature classes*, similar to the *coverage* model. It also extends the coverage model with support for complex networks, *relationships* among feature classes, and other object-oriented *features*. The ESRI® ArcGIS™ applications (ArcMap™, ArcCatalog™, and ArcToolbox™) work with geodatabases as well as with coverages.

The ArcInfo geodatabase model is implemented on standard relational databases with the ArcSDE™ application server. ArcSDE defines an open interface to database systems for our users. It allows ArcInfo to manage geographic information on a variety of different database platforms including Oracle®, Microsoft® SQL Server™, IBM® DB2®, and Informix®.

The geodatabase model defines a generic model for geographic information. This generic model can be used to define and work with a wide variety of different user- or application-specific models. By defining and implementing a wide variety of *behavior* on a generic geographic model, we provide a robust platform for the definition of a variety of user data models.

The geodatabase model supports an object-oriented vector data model. In this model, entities are represented as *objects* with properties, behavior, and relationships. Support for a variety of different geographic object types is built into the system. These object types include simple objects, geographic features (objects with location), network features (objects with geometric integration with other features), *annotation* features, and other more specialized feature types. The model allows you to define relationships between objects, together with rules for maintaining the referential integrity between objects.

This book describes how to take your geodatabase design and implement it with ArcInfo 8. ArcCatalog has various tools for creating and modifying your geodatabase *schema*, while ArcMap has tools for analyzing and editing the contents of your geodatabase.

Successfully implementing a multiuser GIS system with ArcInfo and ArcSDE starts with a good data model design and database tuning. How the data is stored in the database, the applications that access it, and the client and server hardware configurations are all key factors to a successful multiuser GIS system. Designing a geodatabase is a critical process that requires planning and revision until you reach a design that meets your requirements and performs well. Throughout this book, guidelines for good data modeling of each aspect of the geodatabase are discussed to help you implement a successful multiuser GIS system with ArcInfo, either with ArcSDE or with a personal geodatabase.

A critical part of a well-performing geodatabase is the tuning of the database management system (DBMS) in which it is stored. This tuning is not required for personal geodatabases; however, it is critical for ArcSDE geodatabases. For more information on tuning your database for ArcSDE and the geodatabase, see the *Configuration and Tuning Guide for <DBMS>* PDF file.

Once you have a design, you can create the geodatabase and its schema by loading existing shapefile and coverage data, creating new database items with ArcCatalog, using Unified Modeling Language (UML) and Computer-Aided Software Engineering (CASE) tools, or a combination of all three.

Before you create your geodatabase

One of the most important steps in creating an effective database is designing its schema. The same is true for any geodatabase. When designing a geodatabase, you should consider questions like:

- What kind of data will be stored in the database?
- In what *projection* do you want your data stored?
- Do you want to establish *rules* about how the data can be modified?
- How do you want to organize your *object classes* and subtypes?
- Do you want to maintain special relationships between objects of different types?
- Will your database contain networks?
- Will your database store custom objects?

Once you have answered these and other questions, you are ready to begin creating your geodatabase design. You can use the data modeling guidelines in this book to help you design a geodatabase which both meets your requirements and also performs well. This book will then guide you through the process of physically implementing your geodatabase design.

Three ways to create a geodatabase

Once you have designed your geodatabase, you can employ any of three methods to create a new geodatabase. The method you choose will depend on what the source of your geodatabase data is, whether you will store custom objects in the geodatabase, or whether you intend to create a new geodatabase from scratch. In practice, you will often use a combination of all or some of the methods outlined.

The three methods of creating a geodatabase are discussed briefly here. Subsequent chapters will outline how each task is performed.

Three Methods to Create a Geodatabase

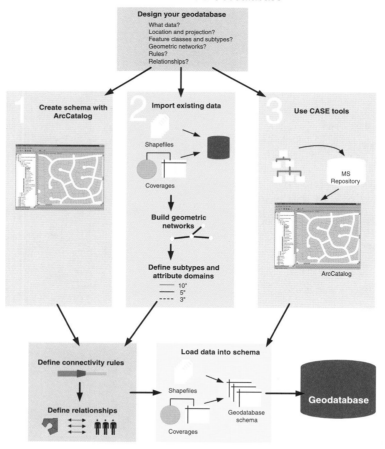

The first step is always to design the geodatabase. This book and the book *Modeling Our World* are guides to help you design your geodatabase. Once this design is complete, you can proceed with the method that best suits your situation.

Design your geodatabase

What data?
Location and projection?
Feature classes and subtypes?
Geometric networks?
Rules?
Relationships?

Creating a new geodatabase from scratch

In some cases, you may not yet have any data that you want to load into a geodatabase, or the data you have to load only accounts for part of your database design. In this case, you can use the tools provided in ArcCatalog to create the schema for feature datasets, tables, geometric networks, and other items inside the database.

ArcCatalog provides a complete set of tools for designing and managing items you will store in the geodatabase.

Migrating existing data into the geodatabase

It is very likely that you already have data in various formats—shapefiles, coverages, INFO™ tables, and dBASE® tables—that you want to store in a geodatabase. You may also have your data stored in other multiuser geographic information system (GIS) data formats such as ArcStorm™, Map LIBRARIAN, and ArcSDE.

Through ArcCatalog, you can convert data stored in one of these formats to a geodatabase by importing it. A series of dialog boxes will guide you through the conversion process. Once you have become familiar with this process, more advanced batch data converters can be used to perform these operations more efficiently.

When converting data from one of these formats into the geodatabase, both the spatial and nonspatial component of each object is translated. For example, when converting a *shapefile* to a feature class, both the shapes (geometry) and attributes are stored in the geodatabase. Attributes can be left out or renamed. Shapefiles of the same spatial extent can be imported into the same feature dataset. All or some of the feature classes from a coverage can be imported into an integrated *feature dataset*.

Converting ArcStorm and Map LIBRARIAN data is done using tools that are similar to those used for importing coverages. However, you must use ArcSDE for Coverages before ArcCatalog or ArcToolbox can access and display ArcStorm and Map LIBRARIAN data.

If you already have your data in an SDE® 3.x database, you do not need to reload your data. ArcCatalog contains tools that allow you to register the existing data with the geodatabase. Once registered, you can also use ArcCatalog to reorganize that data into feature datasets.

ArcInfo 8 and geodatabases do not support multiple feature types in a single feature class (for example, points and lines in the same feature class). If any of your SDE 3.x layers contain multiple-entity types, those must be reorganized into single feature type layers before you can view them in ArcInfo or register them with the geodatabase.

Annotation stored with SDE 3.x is read only in ArcInfo 8. If you want to use ArcMap to edit this annotation, you must convert it to geodatabase annotation. See Chapter 7, 'Managing annotation', for more information on converting SDE 3.x annotation to geodatabase annotation.

Once you have imported your data into the geodatabase, you can then use ArcCatalog to further define your geodatabase. ArcCatalog contains tools for building *geometric networks* and for establishing *subtypes*, *attribute domains*, and so on.

To learn how to move your existing data into the geodatabase, see Chapter 4, 'Migrating existing data into a geodatabase'.

Building geodatabases with CASE tools

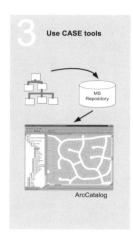

Computer-Aided Software Engineering (CASE) consists of tools and techniques that automate the process of developing software systems and database design. You can use CASE tools to create new custom objects and generate a geodatabase schema from a UML diagram.

Object-oriented design tools can be used to create object models that represent the design of your custom objects. Based on these models, the CASE tools' Code Generation Wizard will help you create a component object model (COM) *object* that implements the behavior of the custom object and the database schema where these custom objects are created and managed.

The steps for creating custom objects are:

1. Design the object model using UML.

2. Export the model to the Microsoft repository.

3. Generate stub-code and implement behavior.

4. Create a geodatabase schema for the custom object.

For details on steps 1 and 3, see *Modeling Our World* and the *Creating custom behavior with the UML* PDF file. Step 4 will be discussed in more detail in Chapter 11, 'Building geodatabases with CASE tools'.

Further refining the geodatabase

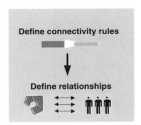

Whether you load data manually or use ArcCatalog to create the geodatabase schema, you can continue to define your geodatabase by establishing how objects in the database relate to one another.

Using ArcCatalog, you can establish relationships between objects in different object classes and *connectivity rules* for objects participating in geometric networks. These relationships and rules may be part of the schema that CASE tools generate, but often you will want to further refine what is generated by CASE to meet your geodatabase design. You can continue to use the geodatabase management tools in ArcCatalog to refine or extend a mature database throughout its life.

Loading data into a geodatabase schema

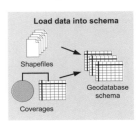

Once you have generated your schema using one of the methods described, you will want to insert data into that schema. This is a different process than importing data. You can do this by editing the database in ArcMap to create new objects, or you can load objects from existing shapefiles, coverages, CAD feature classes, INFO tables, dBASE tables, ArcStorm, or Map LIBRARIAN.

Data creation and maintenance may involve managing version and topology information. ArcCatalog and ArcToolbox have wizards to help you with this—Simple Data Loader and Object Loader—that will be discussed in Chapter 4, 'Migrating existing data into a geodatabase'.

Geodatabases and ArcCatalog

ArcCatalog is the manager for your geodatabase. With ArcCatalog, you can easily view and modify the contents of your geodatabase. ArcCatalog contains a full suite of utilities to create and manage a geodatabase.

Accessing geodatabases in ArcCatalog

In ArcCatalog, you can automatically access data in several formats such as shapefiles and ArcInfo coverages. You can also automatically access any personal geodatabase that is stored on a disk.

You can access remote ArcSDE geodatabases by creating a connection to the database. Database connections to remote geodatabases behave in a similar way as personal geodatabases, with one important difference: when you delete a personal geodatabase, the database itself is deleted from the disk. When you delete a remote geodatabase connection, however, only the connection is deleted—the geodatabase and its data are unaffected.

Spatial database connections

Using data stored in a DBMS such as Oracle requires a database connection. There are two methods for connecting to a spatial database from ArcInfo. One method is to connect to an ArcSDE service that spawns a process on the server to broker the connection between ArcInfo and the database instance.

The second method is to use a *direct connection* to the database. In this case, ArcInfo connects directly to the database server. The functionality that is managed by the server process in the first connection method is transferred to the client, thus eliminating the middle tier. The direct connect method is a two-tiered architecture, rather than three tiered.

You can use the direct connect method to connect to your geodatabase if it is stored in Oracle8*i*™ or SQL Server. If connecting to SQL Server, you do not require any additional software to connect to the database. If direct connecting to Oracle8*i,* the Oracle client software needs to be installed on your machine, and you need to provide an Oracle service name for your server.

For more information about direct connect, see ArcSDE *Configuration and Tuning Guide for <RDBMS>* PDF file.

When you add a new connection to an ArcSDE geodatabase service, or a direct database connection in ArcCatalog, it creates a connection file on disk. This file contains the information needed to establish a connection. The username and password can be included in the connection file and are encrypted for security.

You can set up connection files for your organization and distribute these such that end users will not require any information about the geodatabase server to which they are connecting.

The first step: creating your database

The first step in creating your geodatabase is to create the database itself using ArcCatalog.

There are two kinds of geodatabases: personal geodatabases and ArcSDE geodatabases. Creating a new personal geodatabase involves creating a new .mdb file on disk.

Before you can create data in an ArcSDE geodatabase, you must do some setup first. Setting up the database for use as an ArcSDE geodatabase is described in *Managing ArcSDE services* and in the *ArcSDE installation guide* PDF file, located in the documentation folder of the CD–ROM installation media. For direct connections only, please see the ArcInfo installation guide for setup instructions.

Several *versions* of an ArcSDE geodatabase can exist, although not every table or feature class in the geodatabase must be versioned. Feature editing in ArcMap requires a versioned feature class in a geodatabase.

New connections will automatically access the ▶

Creating a new personal geodatabase

1. In the ArcCatalog tree, right-click on the location where you want to create the new personal geodatabase.

2. Point to New.

3. Click Personal Geodatabase.

   ArcCatalog creates a new personal geodatabase in the location you selected and sets its name to edit mode.

4. Type a new name for this personal geodatabase.

5. Press Enter.

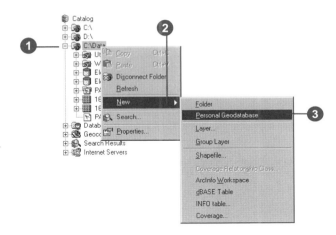

DEFAULT version of the database. To connect to an alternative version, you must provide your *username* and *password* along with the version name. If you do not specify the version, ArcCatalog connects to the DEFAULT version.

Tip

Testing the connection
Clicking OK in the Spatial Database Connection dialog box does not actually connect to the database but creates the connection file on disk. To make sure that the connection parameters you entered are correct, you can click Test Connection.

See Also

For more information on how to use ArcCatalog to browse your file system, see Using ArcCatalog.

Adding a connection to an ArcSDE geodatabase service in ArcCatalog

1. Double-click Database Connections.

2. Double-click Add Spatial Database Connection.

3. Type either the name or the *IP Address* of the *server* to which you want to connect.

4. Type either the name or the TCP/IP *port number* of the ArcSDE service to which you want to connect.

5. Type the name of the database to which you want to connect if your DBMS supports it; otherwise, skip to step 6.

6. Type the username and password with which you will connect to the ArcSDE geodatabase.

7. Check the check box to save the username and password in the connection file so that you can connect to the database without being prompted to log in.

8. Click OK.

9. Type a new name for the spatial database connection.

10. Press Enter.

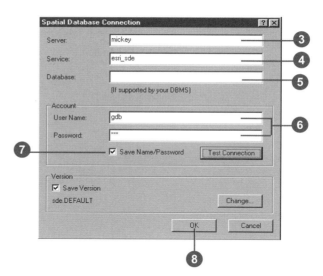

Adding a direct connection to an Oracle8*i* geodatabase in ArcCatalog

1. Double-click Database Connections.

2. Double-click Add Spatial Database Connection.

3. Type "sde:oracle".

4. Type the username.

5. Type the password followed by "@<oracle service name>".

6. Check the check box to save the username and password in the connection file so that you can connect to the database without being prompted to log in.

7. Click OK.

8. Type a new name for the spatial database connection.

9. Press Enter.

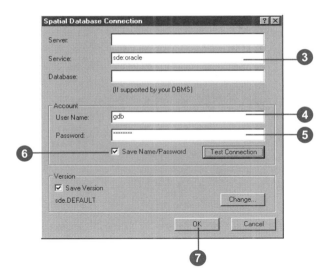

Adding a direct connection to an SQL Server geodatabase in ArcCatalog

1. Double-click Database Connections.

2. Double-click Add Spatial Database Connection.

3. Type "sde:sqlserver:<name or the IP Address of the server>". In this example, the server name is "fabio".

4. Type the name of the database you want to connect to.

5. Type the username and password.

6. Check the check box to save the username and password in the connection file so that you can connect to the database without being prompted to log in.

7. Click OK.

8. Type a new name for the spatial database connection.

9. Press Enter.

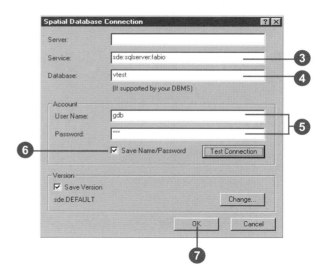

See Also

For more information on geodata-base versions, see Chapter 13, 'Working with a versioned geodatabase'.

Connecting to an alternative version of the database

1. Follow steps 1 through 7 for adding a connection to a spatial database geodata-base service or direct connect in ArcCatalog.

2. Click Change.

3. Click the Version dropdown arrow and click the version you want to access.

4. Click OK.

5. Click OK in the Spatial Database Connection dialog box.

6. Type a new name for the spatial database connection.

7. Press Enter.

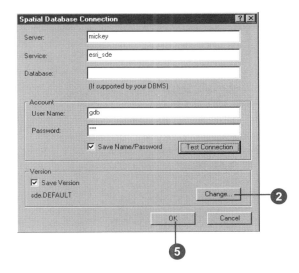

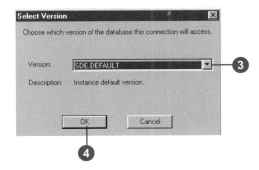

Tips on learning how to build geodatabases

If you're new to GIS, remember that you don't have to know everything about ArcCatalog and geodatabases, or know how to extend the ESRI data model, to get immediate results. To learn how easy it is to import data and create geodatabases with a variety of behavior, see Chapter 2, 'Quick-start tutorial'. ArcGIS™ comes with the data used in the tutorial, so you can follow along step by step at your computer. You can also read the tutorial without using your computer.

Finding answers to questions

If you are like most people, your goal is to complete your tasks while investing a minimum amount of time and effort on learning how to use the software. You want intuitive, easy-to-use software that gives you immediate results without having to read pages of documentation. However, when you do have a question, you want to be able to find the answer quickly so that you can complete your task. That's what this book is all about—getting you the answers you need when you need them.

This book describes how to get your existing data into a geodatabase; how to create new items in your geodatabase; and then, once created, how to add a variety of behavior to that data. Although you can read this book from start to finish, you will likely use it more as a reference. When you want to know how to do a particular task, such as creating a geometric network, just look it up in the table of contents or index.

What you will find is a concise, step-by-step description of how to complete tasks. Some chapters also include detailed information if you want to learn more about the concepts behind the tasks. Refer to the glossary if you come across any unfamiliar GIS terms or need to refresh your memory.

About this book

This book is designed to introduce how to build a geodatabase using existing data or by using a schema implemented with ArcCatalog or CASE tools. While this book does have some conceptual content about the different aspects of the geodatabase, it assumes that you already have a schema design that you are trying to implement. If you have not yet designed your schema or need more information on how to make the best schema design decisions, please take some time to read *Modeling Our World*, which you received with ArcGIS.

Getting help on your computer

In addition to this book, the ArcGIS online Help system is a valuable resource for learning how to use the software.

Contacting ESRI

If you need to contact ESRI for technical support, see the product registration and support card you received with ArcGIS or refer to 'Contacting Technical Support' in the 'Getting more help' book of the ArcGIS Desktop Help system. You can also visit ESRI on the Web at www.esri.com and www.arconline.esri.com for more information on the geodatabase and ArcGIS.

ESRI education solutions

ESRI provides educational opportunities related to geographic information science, GIS applications, and technology. You can choose among instructor-led courses, Web-based courses, and self-study workbooks to find education solutions that fit your learning style and pocketbook. For more information, go to www.esri.com.

Quick-start tutorial

2

IN THIS CHAPTER

- **Exercise 1: Organizing your data in ArcCatalog**

- **Exercise 2: Importing data into your geodatabase**

- **Exercise 3: Creating subtypes and attribute domains**

- **Exercise 4: Creating relationships between objects**

- **Exercise 5: Building a geometric network**

- **Exercise 6: Creating annotation for your data**

- **Exercise 7: Creating layers for your geodatabase data**

- **Exercise 8: Editing your geodatabase**

It is easy to create a *geodatabase* and add *behavior* to it, and it requires no programming when you use the data management tools in ArcCatalog—the application for browsing, storing, organizing, and distributing data. When querying and editing the geodatabase in ArcMap—the application for editing, analyzing, and creating maps from your data—you can easily take advantage of the data and behavior in your geodatabase without any customization.

In this tutorial, you will use ArcCatalog to create a geodatabase that models a water utility network. You will add behavior to the geodatabase by creating *subtypes*, *validation rules*, *relationships*, and a *geometric network*. You will use ArcMap to take advantage of the behavior by editing some of the existing *features* in the geodatabase and adding some additional features.

The study area is a portion of the City of Montgomery, Alabama. A geodatabase that contains most of the data, a *coverage* representing water laterals, and an INFO table representing parcel owner data are provided with the software. You will import the coverage and INFO table into the geodatabase and then modify its properties to give it behavior.

This tutorial lets you explore the capabilities of the geodatabase using ArcCatalog and ArcMap. You can complete this tutorial at your own pace without the need for additional assistance. This tutorial includes eight exercises. Each exercise takes between 10 and 20 minutes to complete.

You will use several *datasets* throughout this tutorial. The following tables provide descriptions of these datasets:

Coverage	Description
Laterals	Water laterals

INFO table	Description
Owner.dat	Parcel owners

Geodatabase	Description
Montgomery	Database that contains most of the City of Montgomery data you will use

Feature datasets	Description
Landbase	Land base data
Water	Water network data

Feature classes	Description
Parcels	Parcel polygons
Road_cl	Road centerlines
Road_eop	Road edge of pavement
RoadNames	Annotation for Road_cl
Dimensions	Dimension features
Distbmains	Water distribution mains
DistmainDiam	Annotation for Distbmains
Fittings	Water network fittings
Gatevalves	Water gate valves
Hydrants	Water hydrants
Pipencasement	Water pipe encasements
Prodwell1	Production wells (polygon)
Prodwell2	Production wells (point)
Pumpstat	Pump stations
Sysvalves	Water system valves
Tanks	Water tanks
Transmains	Water transmission mains
TransmainsDiam	Annotation for Transmains
Trtplant	Water treatment plant
Vaults	Water meter vaults

The datasets were provided courtesy of The Water Works & Sanitary Sewer Board of the City of Montgomery, Alabama. They have been simplified by ESRI. The City of Montgomery cannot guarantee the reliability or suitability of this information. Original data was compiled from various sources, and the spatial information may not be accurate. This information may be updated, corrected, or otherwise modified without notification.

Exercise 1: Organizing your data in ArcCatalog

Before you begin the tutorial, you must first find and organize the data that you will need. This can be done using ArcCatalog.

Connecting to data

In ArcCatalog, data is accessed through folder connections. When you look in a folder connection, you can quickly see the folders and data sources it contains. You will now begin organizing your data by creating a folder connection to it.

1. Start ArcCatalog by either double-clicking a shortcut installed on your desktop or using the Programs list in your Start menu.

2. Click the Connect To Folder button and navigate to the BuildingaGeodatabase folder on the local drive where you installed the tutorial data (the default installation path is C:\arcgis\ArcTutor\BuildingaGeodatabase). Click OK to establish a folder connection.

Your new folder connection— C:\arcgis\ArcTutor\BuildingaGeodatabase—is now listed in the Catalog tree. You will now be able to access all of the data needed for the tutorial through that connection.

Exploring your data

Before you begin modifying the geodatabase, explore the datasets provided for the tutorial.

1. Click the plus sign next to the C:\arcgis\ArcTutor\BuildingaGeodatabase folder connection to see the datasets contained in the folder. Click the Preview tab and click the laterals coverage to see its geometry.

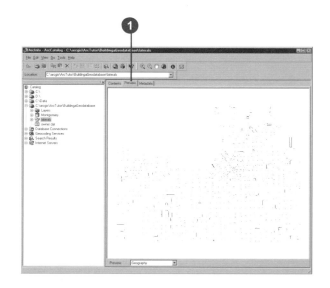

2. Click the plus sign next to the Montgomery geodatabase and double-click each *feature dataset* to see the *feature classes* and *relationship classes* it contains. Click each feature class to preview its geometry.

3. Click the owner.dat INFO *table*. Notice how the Preview Type automatically changes to Table and displays the table's records. This table contains the owner information for the Parcels feature class in the Montgomery geodatabase. In the next part of this exercise, you will import this table into the geodatabase and create relationships between the parcels and their owners.

You will perform most of the tasks for modifying the Montgomery geodatabase schema with ArcCatalog. Later, you will use ArcMap to create *annotation* and edit the geodatabase.

Now that you have found and organized your data in ArcCatalog, you are ready to start the first task in the tutorial: importing data into the geodatabase.

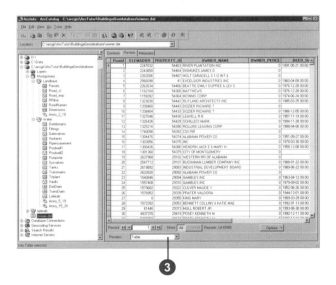

3

Exercise 2: Importing data into your geodatabase

Before you can start adding behavior to your data, you must get it into a geodatabase. You will import two datasets into the Montgomery geodatabase—laterals and owner.dat. The laterals coverage contains water laterals for the Montgomery water dataset, and the owner.dat INFO table contains owner information for the parcel features already in the geodatabase.

Importing the coverage

1. In ArcCatalog, right-click the Water feature dataset in the Montgomery geodatabase, point to Import, and click Coverage to Geodatabase.

You will use the Coverage to Geodatabase tool to import the arcs in the laterals coverage into the Water feature dataset.

This tool is used to specify your input coverage, input feature class, and output feature class. Because you opened this tool by right-clicking a feature dataset, the output geodatabase, Montgomery, and feature dataset, Water, are already filled in for you.

There are several ways to set the input and output datasets. You can also drag a dataset or datasets from the ArcCatalog tree or Contents tab and drop them on the text box. Alternatively, you can click the Browse button to open the ArcCatalog minibrowser and navigate to your dataset, or you can type the full pathname to the dataset in the text box.

Tutorial instructions will simply ask you to type dataset names and their paths into the appropriate text boxes. However, feel free to use any of the techniques just described to make the entry.

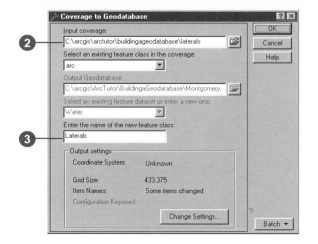

2. Type "C:\arcgis\ArcTutor\BuildingaGeodatabase\laterals" for the input coverage.

3. The default input feature class is arc, indicating that the arcs from the coverage will be imported. You can accept the defaults. Type "Laterals" for the name of the new feature class.

4. Click OK.

A message appears showing the progress of your data import operation. All geodatabase data importing tools and wizards display such a message or a progress indicator. When the tool or wizard is finished, the

message disappears, indicating that all of the features have been imported.

Your new Laterals feature class is now in the Montgomery geodatabase in the Water feature dataset.

5. In the ArcCatalog tree, navigate to and click the Laterals feature class. Click the Preview tab to see the features.

6. Right-click Laterals and click Properties.

The names of feature classes and tables in a geodatabase are the same as the names of the physical tables in the relational database management system (RDBMS) in which they are stored. When you store data in an RDBMS, the names for tables and fields are often very unclear, and you need a detailed data dictionary to keep track of what data each table stores and what each field in those tables represents.

The geodatabase lets you create *aliases* for *fields*, tables, and feature classes. An alias is an alternative name to refer to those items. Unlike true names, aliases can contain special characters such as spaces because they don't have to adhere to the database's limitations. When you use data with aliases in ArcMap, the alias name is automatically used for feature classes, tables, and fields. However, in ArcCatalog these items are always represented by their true names.

You will now create aliases for your new feature class and its fields.

7. Click the General tab.

8. Type "Water laterals" for the alias for this feature class.

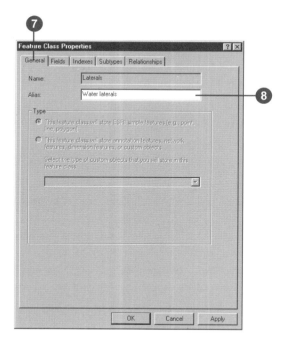

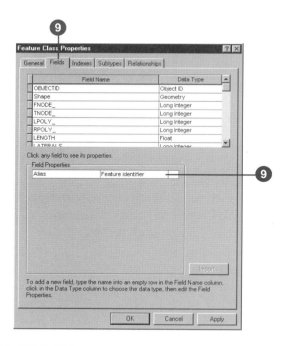

9. Click the Fields tab. Click the **OBJECTID** field and type "Feature identifier" for its alias.

10. Repeat step 8 for the following fields:

Field	Alias
Shape	Geometry field
DEPTH_BURI	Depth buried
RECORDED_L	Recorded length
FACILITY_I	Facility identifier
DATE_INSTA	Installation date
TYPECODE	Subtype code

11. Click OK.

Now that you have imported your Laterals feature class into the geodatabase and added some aliases, you are ready to import the owner.dat INFO table.

Importing the INFO table

The owner.dat INFO table contains owner information for the parcels in the Parcels feature class in the Montgomery geodatabase. To be able to create relationships between the parcels and their owners, the owner information must be imported into the Montgomery geodatabase. You will use the Table to Geodatabase tool to import the owner.dat

INFO table into the Montgomery geodatabase. You will then create aliases for the table.

1. Right-click the Montgomery geodatabase, point to Import, then click Table to Geodatabase. You'll use the Table to Geodatabase tool to import the owner.dat INFO table into the Montgomery geodatabase.

2. Type "C:\arcgis\ArcTutor\BuildingaGeodatabase\ owner.dat" for the input table.

3. Type "Owners" for the name of the output table.

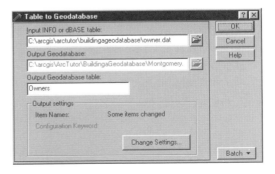

4. Click OK. A message informs you of the progress of the operation.

5. In the ArcCatalog tree, click the Owners table in the Montgomery geodatabase. Click the Preview tab to see its rows.

6. Right-click the Owner table and click Properties to see the table's properties.

7. Type "Parcel owners" for the alias for this table.

8. Click the Fields tab and type the following field aliases:

Field	Alias
OBJECTID	Object identifier
OWNER_NAME	Owner name
OWNER_PERCENT	Percentage ownership
DEED_DATE	Date of deed

9. Click OK.

The data in the laterals coverage and owners.dat INFO table is now in the Montgomery geodatabase. Now you can take advantage of the geodatabase by applying behavior to your data. You will begin this task by creating subtypes and *attribute domains*.

Exercise 3: Creating subtypes and attribute domains

One of the advantages of storing your data in a geodatabase is that you can define rules about how the data can be edited. In Exercise 2, you will define these rules by creating a new attribute domain for lateral diameters; creating subtypes for the Laterals feature class; and associating the new domain, existing domains, and default values with fields for each subtype.

Attribute domains are rules that describe the legal values of a field type. Multiple feature classes and tables can share attribute domains stored in the database. However, not all the objects in a feature class or table need to share the same attribute domains.

For example, in a water network, suppose that only hydrant water laterals can have a pressure of between 40 and 100 psi, while service water laterals can have a pressure of between 50 and 75 psi. You would use an attribute domain to enforce this restriction. To implement this kind of validation rule, you do not have to create separate feature classes for hydrant and service water laterals, but you would want to distinguish these types of water laterals from each other to establish a separate set of domains and default values. You can do this using subtypes.

To learn more about subtypes and attribute domains, see Chapter 5, 'Subtypes and attribute domains'.

Creating an attribute domain

You will use ArcCatalog to create a new coded value attribute domain. This new domain will describe a set of valid pipe diameters for your new Laterals feature class.

1. Right-click the Montgomery geodatabase and click Properties.

2. Click the first empty field under Domain Name and type "LatDiameter" for the name of the new domain. In the description field, type "Valid diameters for water laterals" for the domain's description.

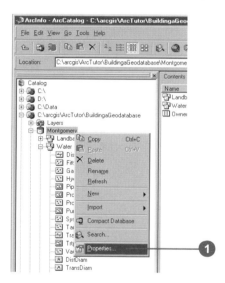

You will now specify the properties of the domain. These properties include what type of field this domain can be associated with, what type of domain it is (range or coded value), the split and merge policies, and what the valid values for the domain are.

A range domain describes a valid range of numeric values, while a coded value domain describes a set of valid values. In this case, you will create a new coded value domain.

All domains also have split and merge policies. When a feature is split or merged, the ArcInfo system looks to these policies to determine what values the resulting feature(s) have for a particular attribute.

3. Click the Field Type to get a dropdown list and click Float for the field type for this domain.

4. Click the Domain Type to get a dropdown list and click Coded Values for the domain type.

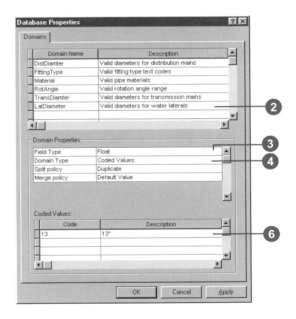

5. Click the *Split policy* to get a dropdown list and click Duplicate for the split policy for the domain. The *Merge policy* will default to Default Value.

You'll type the valid values, or codes for the coded value domain, and for each code you will provide a user-friendly description. As you will see later in the tutorial, ArcMap uses the user-friendly description, not the code, for values of fields that have coded value domains associated with them.

6. Click the first empty field under Code and type "13" for the code; then click the Description field beside it and type "13"" for the code's description.

7. Add the following coded values to the list:

Code	Description
10	10"
8	8"
6	6"
4	4"
3	3"
2.25	2 1/4"
2	2"
1.5	1 1/2"
1.25	1 1/4"
1	1"
0.75	3/4"
-9	Unknown

8. Click OK to add the domain to the geodatabase.

Your attribute domain is now part of your geodatabase. In the next part of the tutorial, you will associate this domain with a field in a feature class.

Creating subtypes and associating default values and domains

Using the properties of the Laterals feature class, you will create subtypes and associate default values and domains with the fields for each subtype. By creating subtypes for the Laterals feature class, not all of the water lateral feature need have the same domains, default values and, as you will see later in the tutorial, connectivity rules.

1. Right-click the Laterals feature class and click Properties.

2. Click the Subtypes tab.

You will now specify the subtype field for the Laterals feature class. The subtype field contains the values that identify to which subtype a particular feature belongs.

3. Click the Subtype Field dropdown arrow and click TYPECODE.

You will now add subtype codes and their descriptions. When you add a new subtype, you will assign default values and domains to some of its fields.

4. Click the Description field next to subtype code 0 and type "Unknown" for its description.

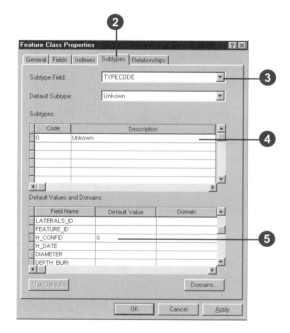

5. Click the Default Value field next to **H_CONFID** and type "0" for its default value. Do the same for **DEPTH_BURI** and **RECORDED_L**. For the **WNM_TYPE, PWTYPE** fields, type "WUNKNOWN" as the default values.

6. Click the Default Value field next to **DIAMETER** and type "8" for the default value. Click the Domain dropdown list and click LatDiameter to set it as this field's attribute domain for the Unknown subtype.

7. Repeat step 6 for the **MATERIAL** field, typing "DI" for the default value. Click Material in the Domain dropdown list.

8. Add the following additional subtypes and set the default values and domains the same as for the Unknown subtype, except for the **WNM_TYPE** and **PWTYPE** field default values.

Code	Description
1	Hydrant laterals
WNM_TYPE, PWTYPE	default value = WHYDLIN
2	Fire laterals
WNM_TYPE, PWTYPE	default value = WFIRELIN
3	Service laterals
WNM_TYPE, PWTYPE	default value = WSERVICE

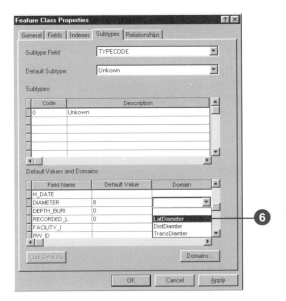

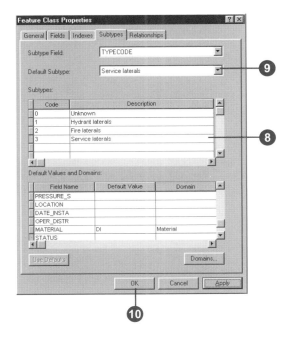

When adding new features to a feature class with subtypes in the ArcMap editing environment, if you don't specify a particular subtype, the new feature will be assigned the default subtype. Once you have added all the subtypes for this feature class, you can set the default subtype from those you just entered.

9. Click the Default Subtype dropdown arrow and click Service laterals to set it as the default subtype.

10. Click OK.

You have now added behavior to the geodatabase by adding domains and creating subtypes. In Exercise 8, you will see how ArcMap behaves with subtypes and domains. First, though, you will add some additional behavior to the geodatabase by creating relationships.

Exercise 4: Creating relationships between objects

In Exercise 2, you imported an INFO table containing owner objects into the Montgomery geodatabase. The geodatabase already has a feature class called Parcels that contains parcel objects. You will now create a *relationship class* between the parcels and the owners so that when you use the data in ArcMap you can easily find out which owners own which parcels.

1. Right-click the Landbase feature dataset, point to New, then click Relationship Class.

The New Relationship Class wizard should now be open. The first panel of the wizard is used to specify the name, the origin, and the destination feature class or table for the new relationship class.

2. Type "ParcelOwners" as the name of this relationship class.

3. Click Owners for the origin table.

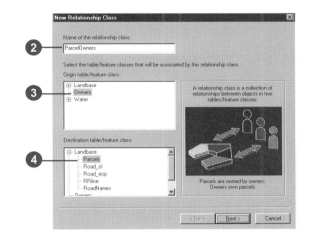

4. Double-click Landbase and click Parcels for the destination feature class. Click Next.

   This next panel is used to specify the type of relationship class you are creating. You are creating a simple relationship class since owners and parcels can exist in the database independent of each other. You can therefore accept the default type—simple relationship class.

5. Click Next.

   You must now specify the path labels and the message notification direction. The forward path label describes the relationship as it is navigated from the origin class to the destination class—in this case, from Owners to Parcels. The backward path label describes the relationship when navigated in the other direction—from Parcels to Owners.

The message notification direction describes how messages are passed between related objects. Message notification is not required for this relationship class, so accept the default of None.

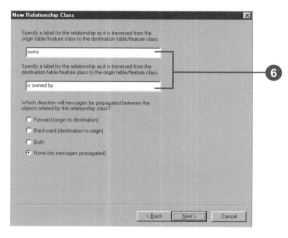

6. Type "owns" for the forward path label and type "is owned by" for the backward path label. Click Next.

You will now specify the cardinality of the relationship. The cardinality describes the possible number of objects in the destination feature class or table that can be related to an object in the origin feature class or table.

7. Click 1-M (one-to-many) to specify that one owner may own many parcels. Click Next.

You must now specify whether or not your new relationship class will have attributes. In this example, the ParcelOwners relationship class does not require attributes, which is the default.

8. Click Next.

The next step is to specify the primary key in the origin table (Owners) and the embedded foreign key field in the destination feature class (Parcels). Owners and Parcels that have the same value in these fields will be related to each other.

9. Click the first dropdown arrow and click PROPERTY_ID for the origin table primary key.

10. Click the second dropdown arrow and click PROPERTY_ID for the embedded foreign key in the destination feature class.

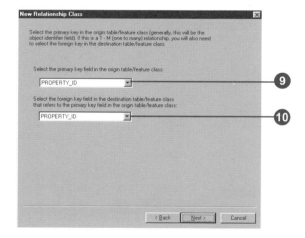

11. Click Next. A summary page appears. Once you have reviewed the summary, click Finish.

You have now added a second kind of behavior to the geodatabase—relationships. In exercise 8, you will see how ArcMap behaves when editing relationships, but first you will continue to add behavior to the geodatabase by creating a geometric network and defining connectivity rules.

Exercise 5: Building a geometric network

Feature classes stored in the same feature dataset can participate in a geometric network. Geometric networks model network systems such as water networks. In this part of the tutorial, you will build a geometric network from the feature classes in the Water feature dataset in the Montgomery geodatabase. You will then create connectivity rules to define which features can connect to each other in the network.

Creating the water network

1. Right-click the Water feature dataset in the Montgomery geodatabase, point to New, then click Geometric Network.

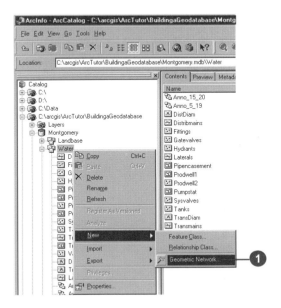

The Build Geometric Network Wizard should now be open. You can use this wizard to either build a geometric network from existing feature classes or to create an empty geometric network. In this case, you will be building a network from the existing feature classes in the Water feature dataset.

2. Click Next.

The second panel is used to specify whether to build a network from existing feature classes or to create an empty one. You want the default—Build a geometric network from existing features.

3. Click Next.

You must now select which feature classes in the feature dataset will participate in the geometric network and what the name of the network will be.

4. Check all of the feature classes in the list.

5. Type "WaterNet" for the name of the geometric network. Click Next.

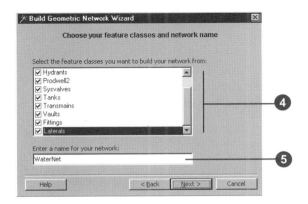

You must now specify which line feature classes will become complex edge feature classes in the geometric network. By default, all line feature classes become simple edge feature classes.

6. Click Yes to specify that some of the line feature classes will become complex edges.

7. Check Distribmains and Transmains to make the water distribution and transmission mains complex edges.

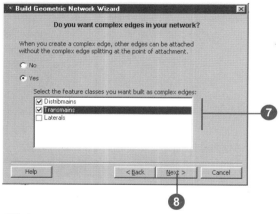

8. Click Next.

Features in a geometric network must be precisely connected to one another. The feature's geometry in the input feature classes can be adjusted to make the connectivity through snapping. You must now specify whether these features need to be adjusted to snap to one another in the network-building process.

9. Click Yes to specify that some of the features need to be adjusted. Type "1.0" for the snapping tolerance.

10. Check all of the feature classes to indicate that the features stored in each one can be adjusted.

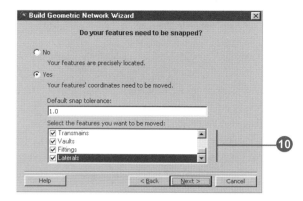

11. Click Next.

You must specify which, if any, of the junction feature classes can act as sources and sinks in the network. ArcInfo uses these sources and sinks to determine the flow direction in the network.

12. Click Yes to indicate that some of the junction feature classes will act as sources or sinks.

13. Check the Tanks feature class to indicate that tanks can be sources or sinks in the network.

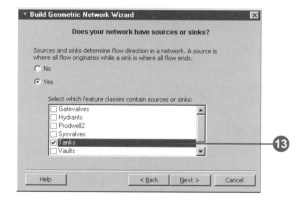

14. Click Next.

Now you can assign network weights. A network weight describes the cost of traversing an element in the logical network such as the drop in pressure as water flows through a pipe. This geometric network does not require weights, which is the default.

15. Click Next. A summary page appears. Once you have reviewed the summary, click Finish.

A progress indicator appears, displaying the progress for each stage of the network-building process.

Your new geometric network, WaterNet, has been created in the Montgomery geodatabase. Next, you'll establish *connectivity rules* for your water network.

Creating connectivity rules

Network connectivity rules constrain the type of network features that may be connected to one another and the number of features of any particular type that can be connected to features of another type. By establishing these rules, you can maintain the integrity of the network connectivity in the database.

1. Right-click WaterNet and click Properties.

The Geometric Network Properties dialog box should now be open. The dialog box provides information about feature classes participating in the network and a list of the network weights. You can also add, delete, and modify connectivity rules using this dialog box.

2. Click the Connectivity tab.

This tab lets you add and modify connectivity rules for the geometric network. You will first create a new *edge–junction rule*, which states that hydrants can connect to hydrant laterals; it also indicates that when a hydrant lateral is created, a hydrant junction feature should be placed at its free end.

3. Click the dropdown arrow and click Laterals.

4. In the list of subtypes in the feature class, click Hydrant laterals.

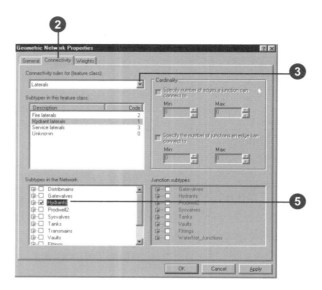

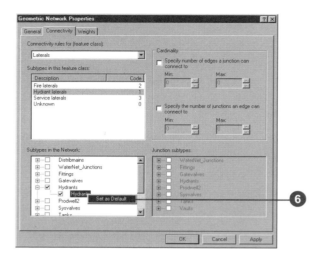

You will now click the types of junctions that hydrant laterals can connect to in the network. For purposes of simplicity, hydrant laterals can only connect to hydrants.

5. Check Hydrants in the list of subtypes in the network.

You should also specify that when you create a hydrant lateral, if an end of the lateral is not connected to another edge or junction, then a hydrant is placed at that end.

6. Click the plus sign next to Hydrants, right-click Hydrants under it, then click Set as Default. A blue "D" will appear next to the hydrant subtype, indicating that it is the default junction for this edge subtype.

You will now create a new *edge–edge rule* that states that hydrant laterals can connect to distribution mains through taps, tees, and saddles. The default junction for connections between hydrant laterals and distribution mains will be taps.

34

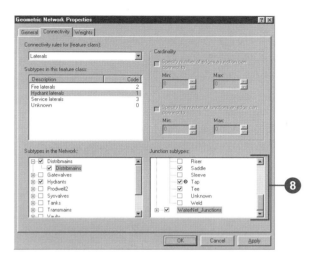

You have now added additional behavior to your geodatabase by defining connectivity rules. You would normally define many more connectivity rules for a network. However, for the editing section of this tutorial, you only need to define the connectivity rules specified here. In the next part of the tutorial, you will create feature-linked *annotation* for your new hydrant lateral feature class.

7. In the network subtypes list, click the plus sign next to Distribmains and check Distribmains under it.

   Because you have checked an edge in the network subtypes list, the list of junction subtypes in the network becomes active. In this list, you can specify which junction types hydrant laterals and distribution mains can connect through.

8. In the junction subtypes list, click the plus sign next to Fittings and check Tap, Tee, and Saddle in that order. Notice that Tap has a blue "D" next to it; this means that Tap is the *default junction*. Check WaterNet_Junctions, which is the generic, or default network junction type.

9. Click OK.

Exercise 6: Creating annotation

In Exercise 1, you browsed through the existing feature classes in the Montgomery geodatabase. Some of these feature classes contained annotation that was linked to features in the Distbmains and Transmains feature classes. You then imported the water laterals from a coverage into the Water feature dataset. Now, you will create an annotation class to store feature-linked annotation for the water laterals.

Creating the annotation class

You'll create the annotation class in the Water feature dataset in the Montgomery geodatabase.

1. Right-click the Water feature dataset, point to New, then click Feature Class.

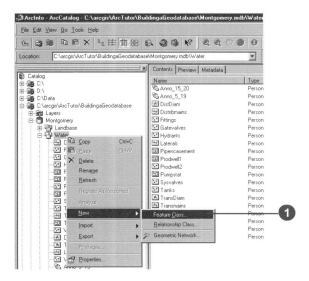

The New Feature Class Wizard should now be open. This wizard can be used to create new simple, network, custom, or—as in this case—annotation feature classes in a geodatabase. The first panel lets you specify the name of the new feature class and its alias. It also gives you the option of storing nonsimple features in the feature class (network, annotation, etc).

2. Type "LateralDiam" in the Name text box.

3. Type "Water lateral diameter annotation" in the Alias text box.

4. Click the second Type option to store annotation objects. Click the first dropdown arrow and click ESRI Annotation Feature.

5. Check Link the annotation to the following feature class.

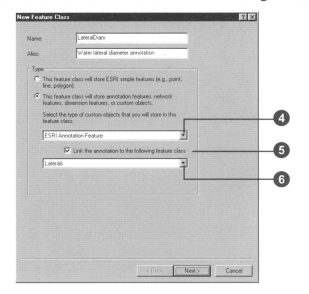

6. Click the second dropdown arrow and click Laterals to link the annotation to the water laterals.

7. Click Next.

Use this panel to specify how the features to which this annotation class is linked will be annotated. You can choose a field in the linked feature class or a combination of fields. You can also specify some advanced symbology and placement options.

You'll specify an expression involving a number of fields on the Laterals feature class to derive the annotation.

8. Click the Label Field dropdown arrow and click DIAMETER.

9. Click Expression to specify an annotation expression.

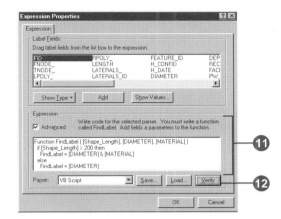

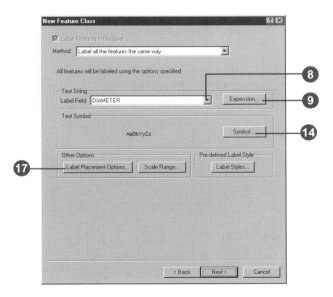

The Expression Properties dialog box should now be open. Using this dialog box, you can derive labels from multiple fields in the linked feature class and use logic to derive labels from those fields. In this case, you will specify that all laterals greater than 200 feet in length must be annotated with their diameter and their material type; those that are less than 200 feet in length should be annotated with their diameter only.

10. Drag Shape_Length and MATERIAL from the Label Fields list and drop them on the Expression text box.

11. Check Advanced and modify the expression to make it the following:

```
Function FindLabel ( [Shape_Length],
[DIAMETER], [MATERIAL] )

    if [Shape_Length] > 200 then

      FindLabel = [DIAMETER] & " " & [MATERIAL]

    else

      FindLabel = [DIAMETER]

    end if

End Function
```

12. Click the Verify button to ensure that you typed the expression correctly. If you get an error, try retyping the expression.

13. Click OK.

14. Click Symbol.

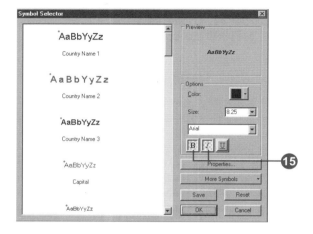

The Symbol Selector dialog box lets you set the font, color, and size of the text used to annotate your features.

15. Click the Bold and Italic buttons.

16. Click OK.

17. Click Label Placement Options.

The Placement Options dialog box opens. Here you will specify the default placement of the annotation relative to its feature.

18. Click the second option to specify that a single annotation feature is created for each lateral feature.

19. Click OK.

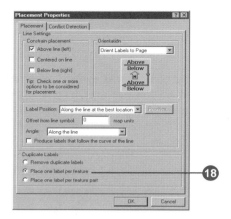

20. Click Next on the wizard.

Use this panel to specify at what scale your annotation will be displayed with the font size you specified in the Symbol Selector dialog box. If you zoom in to a larger scale, the annotation will appear larger, and if you zoom out to a smaller scale, the annotation will appear smaller.

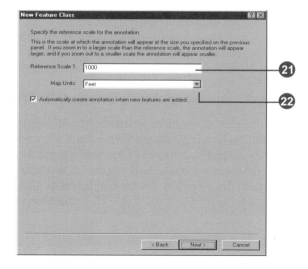

21. Type "1000" for the reference scale.

22. Click the Map Units dropdown arrow and click Feet for the map units. When a new feature is created in the linked feaure class, you want a new annotation feature to also be created. Be sure the box is checked to include this default. Click Next.

    This panel is used to specify storage parameters for the database to store this feature class. No special storage parameters are required, which is the default.

23. Click Next.

    This panel lets you add additional fields to those required fields that already appear in the panel. This feature class does not require any additional fields.

24. Click Finish.

You have created a new annotation class that is linked to the Laterals feature class. This new annotation class does not yet contain any annotation features. You will now use ArcMap to create the annotation features for all of the features in the Laterals feature class.

Generating the annotation features

To create annotation for the laterals features and store them in the feature-linked annotation class that you just created, you will need to use ArcMap.

1. Start ArcMap by clicking the Launch ArcMap button in ArcCatalog. You can also start ArcMap by either double-clicking a shortcut installed on your desktop or using the Programs list in your Start menu.

2. Click the Add Data button to add the Laterals feature class and the LateralDiam annotation class to the *map*.

   The Add Data dialog box appears.

3. Navigate to the Water feature dataset, select the Laterals and LateralDiam feature classes, and click Add.

The data is added to your map. You will now annotate the annotation features.

4. Click the Select Features button on the ArcMap Tools toolbar.

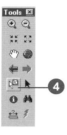
④

5. Select all of the laterals by dragging a box around them on the map.

6. In the ArcMap table of contents, right-click the Laterals layer, point to Selection, then click Annotate Selected Features.

⑥

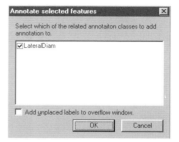

The Annotate selected features dialog box appears. Use the defaults for this operation.

7. Click OK.

8. Close ArcMap.

You have populated the annotation class by deriving text from fields in the linked feature class. The links, stored in the geodatabase as relationships, are automatically created between the features and their annotation. In Exercise 8, you will see how annotation responds to changes in the feature it is linked to. First, however, you will create new *layer* files for the Laterals and the LateralDiam feature classes.

Exercise 7: Creating layers for your geodatabase data

To make browsing for and symbolizing data more convenient, you can create *layers* from your geodatabase data and use these layers in ArcMap. Most of the layers you will need have been created for you; they are stored in the Layers folder in your tutorial directory. In this exercise, you will create new layers for the Laterals and the LateralDiam feature classes.

Creating the Laterals layer

1. In ArcCatalog, right-click the Laterals feature class and click Create Layer.

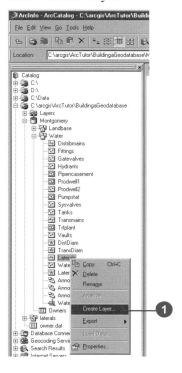

2. Browse to the Layers folder under your tutorial directory and type "Water laterals" for the name of the new layer.

3. Click Save.

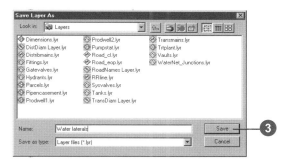

The new layer is created. You will modify the properties of the layer to add symbology.

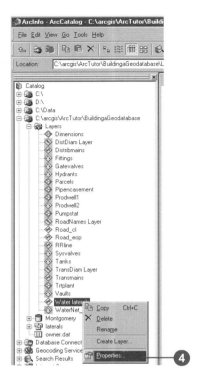

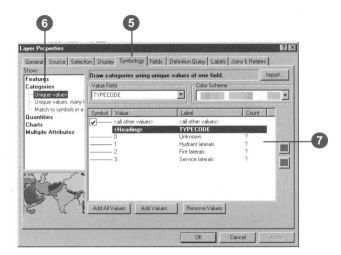

By default, the Unique values classification based on the subtype field is used to symbolize the layer. This is the setting you want, but you must modify the symbology of each subtype.

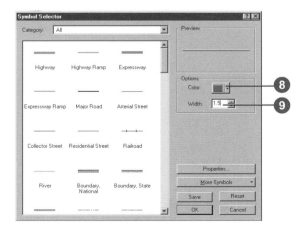

4. In the ArcCatalog tree, open the Layers folder, right-click the Water laterals layer, then click Properties.

You can use the Layer Properties dialog box to modify many aspects of a layer, such as its visible scale and its transparency. In this case, you will modify its symbology.

5. Click the Symbology tab.

6. Click Categories.

7. Double-click the colored line next to Hydrant laterals.

    The Symbol Selector dialog box appears. You will use this dialog box to set the symbol properties for the laterals.

8. Click the Color dropdown arrow and click purple to make the line color purple.

9. Type "1.5" in the width text box to give the line a width of 1.5.

10. Click OK.

11. Repeat steps 7 through 10 for the Fire laterals, making the symbol a red line with a width of 1.5.

12. Repeat steps 7 through 10 for the Service laterals, making the symbol a dark blue line with a width of 1.5.

13. Click OK to close the Properties dialog box.

    Your Water Laterals layer is complete. You can now create the annotation layer for the water laterals.

Creating the LateralDiam layer

1. Right-click the LateralDiam feature class and click Create Layer.

2. Navigate to the Layers folder and type "Water lateral diameter annotation" for the name of the new layer.

3. Click Save.

    The new annotation layer is created. Since this layer points to an annotation feature class, the symbology is a property of the annotation and therefore does not have to be set in the layer.

You have successfully imported coverage and INFO data into your geodatabase and created subtypes, rules, a geometric network, and feature-linked annotation. The exercise takes you through some editing tasks. These include modifying existing features and their attributes and creating new features. The editing portion of this tutorial will show you how the behavior you added to the geodatabase makes editing your spatial data easy.

Exercise 8: Editing your geodatabase

The previous exercises have guided you through the process of importing data into your geodatabase. Using that imported data, you created rules about how the data could be edited, related objects in the imported table to objects in a feature class, created a geometric network, and created feature-linked annotation. You will now learn how easy it is to edit your geodatabase.

In this exercise, you will add all of the layers from the tutorial directory to your map. Once the data is on your map, you will perform the following edits:

- Update the owner information for a parcel.
- Move an existing fire hydrant 50 feet further back from the edge of the road.
- Create a new hydrant lateral.

Updating the owner information for a parcel

1. Start ArcMap by either double-clicking a shortcut installed on your desktop or using the Programs list in your Start menu.

2. Click the Add Data button to add the geodatabase layers to the map.

The Add Data dialog box appears.

3. Navigate to the Layers folder, select all the layers, and click Add.

   The data is added to your map. You're ready to begin editing.

4. Notice that the Editor toolbar is still displayed from the last time you used ArcMap.

5. Click the Editor menu and click Start Editing.

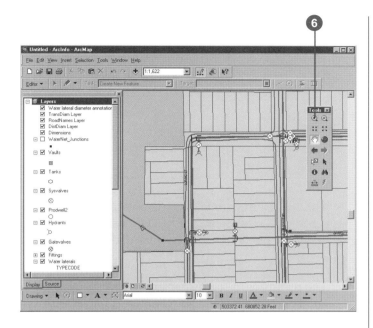

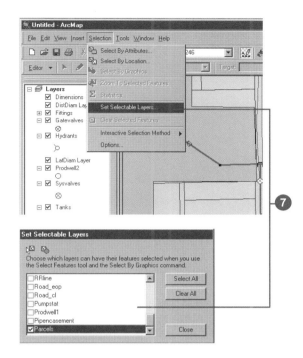

6. Click the Zoom In button and drag a box around an area with some distribution mains and parcels. You can now see the features more clearly.

   You will begin by editing the parcels. To make it easier to select only parcel features, you'll set the parcels as the only selectable layer.

7. Click Selection and point to Set Selectable Layers. This will open the Set Selectable Layers dialog box. Uncheck all layers except the Parcels layer, then click Close to close the Set Selectable Layers dialog box.

8. Click the Edit tool.

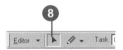

9. Select a group of parcels by dragging a box around them.

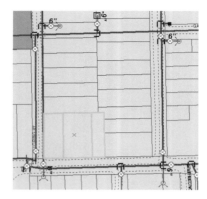

10. Click the Attributes button on the Editor toolbar.

The Attributes dialog box now appears with a list of the selected parcel's PARCEL_ID values. The attribute values of the first selected parcel are displayed on the right panel. Each parcel has a plus sign next to it; click it to get the related owner objects.

11. Click the plus sign next to the first parcel.

The backward path label—"is owned by"—that you typed when you created this relationship class, is visible under the parcel in the Attributes dialog box.

12. Click the plus sign next to "is owned by".

The identifier of the owner object (presented by a number) that is related to (owns) this parcel is displayed under the relationship path label.

13. Click the owner identifier value.

The attributes of the owner of this parcel are listed on the right panel. Notice that the field name aliases you entered earlier for the owner table are displayed instead of the true field names. You can edit the values for this owner's attributes easily using the aliases.

14. Click the value for Percentage ownership and type "100".

15. Press Enter.

16. Click the Close button to close the Attributes dialog box.

You have used the ParcelOwners relationship class that you created to find the owner for a parcel and edit its attributes. To see how network connectivity is automatically maintained during the editing of network features, you are now going to edit some network features.

Moving an existing fire hydrant

Your first edit will be to move a fire hydrant away from a street edge of pavement. Fire hydrants are network features and participate in the network with the water lateral features. You will see that network connectivity is maintained when the hydrant feature is moved.

1. Click the Selection menu and click Clear Selected Features to deselect the parcels you selected in the previous task.

2. Click Selection, point to Set Selectable Layers, uncheck the Parcels layer, check the Hydrants layer, and close the window.

3. Zoom in to an area with a fire hydrant.

4. Click the Edit tool and drag a box around the fire hydrant you want to move. The fire hydrant should now be selected.

 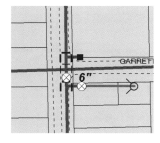

5. Click and drag the selected hydrant away from the distribution main. Notice that the lateral between the hydrant and the valve stretches as the hydrant is moved.

6. Drop the hydrant into its new position.

Notice that when the hydrant was moved, the lateral rubber-banded to maintain its connectivity with both the hydrant and the valve. This is an example of how ArcGIS 8 maintains network topology during interactive editing.

Creating a new hydrant lateral

In this exercise, you will use a combination of network editing, connectivity rules, attribute rules, and feature-linked annotation to add a new hydrant lateral off a distribution main in your water network.

1. Click the Selection menu and click Clear Selected Features to deselect the hydrant you selected in the last part of the tutorial.

2. Click the Selection menu and point to Set Selectable Layers. Uncheck the Hydrants layer, check the Distribmains, Water laterals, and Fittings layers, and close the window.

3. Zoom to an area with a distribution main.

4. Click the Task dropdown arrow and click Create New Feature.

5. Click the Target dropdown arrow. You will see a list of the layers currently on your map. The Water laterals layer has a plus sign next to it. The plus sign indicates that this layer has subtypes. Click the plus sign to see the list of subtypes that you added after you imported the laterals coverage.

6. Click Hydrant laterals. The new feature will be created in the Water laterals layer and will be assigned the Hydrant Lateral subtype.

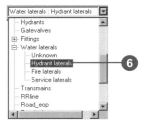

In order to establish network connectivity when you add your new hydrant lateral, you must snap it precisely to the distribution main.

7. Click the Editor menu and click Snapping.

The Snapping Environment window appears. When you add the hydrant lateral, you will add it to some point along a distribution main. So, you must set snapping to the edge of distribution mains.

8. Check the Edge check box next to Distbmains and close the Snapping Environment window.

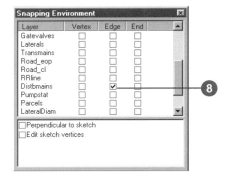

9. Click the Sketch tool.

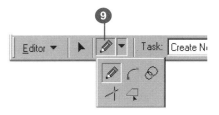

10. Move the pointer over one of the distribution mains. The pointer snaps to the edge of the distribution main.

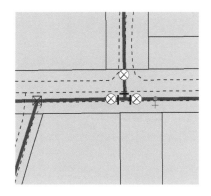

11. With the pointer snapped to the main, click once to start the new hydrant lateral. You have just started an *edit sketch*.

In this example, you want to constrain the hydrant lateral to be perpendicular to the distribution main.

12. While the edit sketch is still active, right-click the distribution main. On the Sketch tool context menu, click Perpendicular.

As you move the pointer, you can see that your sketch of the hydrant lateral is constrained to be perpendicular to the distribution main. You will now create a lateral 65 feet long.

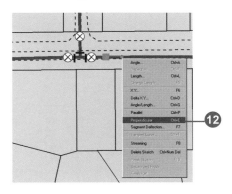

13. Right-click on the sketch and click Length. Type "65" and press Enter.

A new vertex is added to the lateral, perpendicular to the distribution main and 65 feet away.

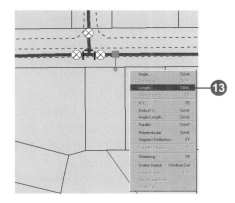

14. Right-click and click Finish Sketch to finish the edit sketch and create the new hydrant lateral.

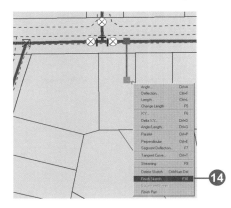

When the new hydrant lateral is created, a number of things happen. First, a junction between the distribution main and the hydrant lateral is created and they are topologically connected in the network. Since you established a connectivity rule between these feature types with a default junction when you created the network, the junction type is the default junction—tap.

A junction is also added to the other end of the new hydrant lateral. Since you created a connectivity rule between water laterals and hydrants where hydrants were the default junction, the junction created is a hydrant.

Now drag the hydrant lateral; you will see that the distribution main rubber-bands to stay connected with the lateral. Click the Undo button to undo the move. If you click the distribution main, you will see that it remains as one complete feature. This is a complex edge—it is split in the logical network but remains a single feature in the geometric network.

When the new hydrant lateral was added, its annotation was also added. Since this lateral is less than 200 feet in length and the default value for diameter is 8 inches, the annotation text is "8"".

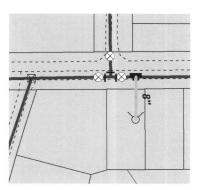

To see how the annotation feature responds to changes in the hydrant lateral, you will change the value for the diameter of the lateral.

15. Click the Edit tool and select the new hydrant lateral if it is not already selected.

16. Click the Attributes button.

    The new hydrant lateral's attributes are displayed in the right panel of the dialog box. Notice the default values you entered earlier in the tutorial appear in the attributes table, while other fields have null values.

17. Click the Diameter value.

    You created a coded value domain and associated it with the diameter field for hydrant laterals. Notice that you are given a dropdown list of the values' description to choose from.

18. Click 6".

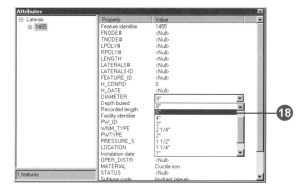

Since the annotation for laterals is derived in part from the value of the Diameter field, when you clicked the new value for the diameter the annotation was automatically updated to reflect that change.

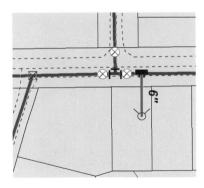

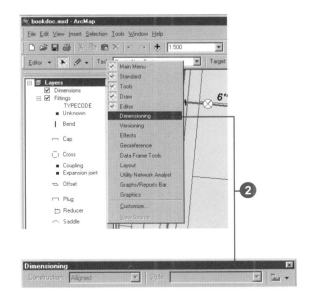

Creating a new dimension feature

In this part of the exercise, you will create a new dimension feature to display the distance between two fire hydrants in your water network. You will create this new dimension feature in the Dimensions feature class in your geodatabase.

1. Zoom to an area with two or more hydrants.

   When creating dimension features, a special toolbar called Dimensioning is required that contains a set of dimensioning construction methods and the list of styles that can be applied to your new dimension features.

2. Right-click one of the toolbars displayed in the ArcMap window. A dropdown list of all the toolbars available to you are listed. Those that have already been added to your map have check boxes next to them. Click Dimensioning and the Dimensioning toolbar will appear.

3. Click the Target layer dropdown arrow on the Editor toolbar and click Dimensions. The Dimensioning toolbar will become active.

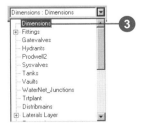

You will use the Aligned construction method to construct an aligned dimension feature, which is the default. Since you are dimensioning features in your water network, you will use the Water dimensions dimension style.

4. Click the Style dropdown arrow; a list of the dimension styles in the Dimensions feature class is listed. Click the Water dimensions style.

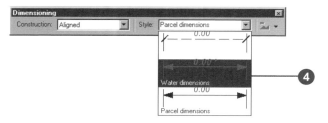

5. Click the Editor menu and click Snapping.

   The snapping environment window appears. Since you are creating a dimension feature to display the length between two hydrants, you need to set your snapping to the vertices of hydrants.

6. Check Vertex next to Hydrants, then close the Snapping Environment window.

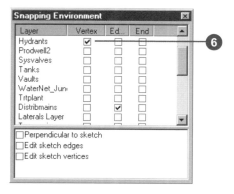

7. Click the Sketch tool.

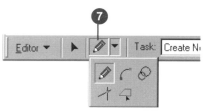

8. Move the pointer over one of the hydrants. The pointer snaps to the hydrant.

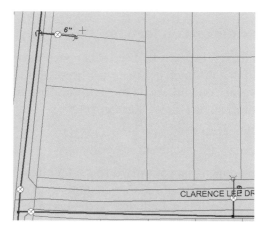

9. With the pointer snapped to the hydrant, click once to start an edit sketch.

10. Move the pointer over the other hydrant.

    As you move the pointer, you will notice that the edit sketch dynamically draws a preview of the first part of the dimension feature and updates its length.

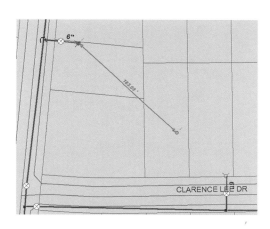

11. With the pointer snapped to the second hydrant, click once.

12. Move the pointer away from the hydrant.

    As you move the pointer, you will notice that the edit sketch dynamically shows how the dimension feature's height changes as you move the pointer.

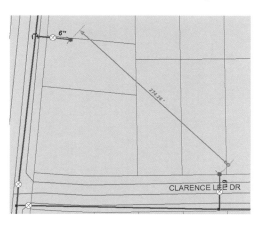

13. When you have the dimension at the height you want for your dimension feature, click once.

    Since you are using the Aligned construction method, the sketch is automatically finished after the three points are input and your dimension feature appears as it was previewed in the edit sketch.

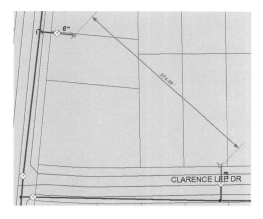

Congratulations! You have just performed edits on your geodatabase.

Using ArcCatalog, you created a geodatabase and added behavior to your features. Using ArcMap editing functions, you took advantage of the geodatabase's behavior to make your editing tasks easier. Experiment with some of your own edits to this geodatabase and try to create your own geodatabase with behavior that meets your needs.

There are many features of the geodatabase yet to discover and tools in ArcInfo to create, manage, and query it. In the next few chapters, you will learn about the features that make the geodatabase a complete, smart way to store and manage your GIS data.

Creating new items in a geodatabase   3

IN THIS CHAPTER

- **Geodatabase items**

- **Creating tables**

- **Creating feature datasets**

- **Creating feature classes**

- **Creating indexes**

- **Granting and revoking privileges**

The first step in creating any database is to design the *tables* it will contain. A good design will ensure that data retrieval is fast and efficient. *Modeling Our World* discusses the considerations to take into account when you build a geodatabase.

When your design is complete, you can start creating the database using ArcCatalog tools. You can create tables, feature datasets, and feature classes in a *geodatabase*. After adding data to tables and feature classes, you can build *indexes* for the appropriate *fields* to improve *query* performance. You can also grant and revoke privileges on your table, feature class, or feature datasets for another database user.

After creating feature classes, tables, and feature datasets, you can refer to further chapters in this book to create more advanced items such as *geometric networks*, *relationship classes*, and so on.

Geodatabase items

Geodatabases organize geographic data into a hierarchy of data *objects*. These data objects are stored in feature classes, object classes, and feature datasets. An *object class* is a table in the geodatabase that stores nonspatial data. A *feature class* is a collection of features with the same type of geometry and the same attributes.

A feature dataset is a collection of feature classes that share the same *spatial reference*. Feature classes that store simple features can be organized either inside or outside a feature dataset. Simple feature classes that are outside a feature dataset are called standalone feature classes. Feature classes that store topological features must be contained within a feature dataset to ensure a common spatial reference.

ArcCatalog contains tools for creating object classes (tables), feature classes, and feature datasets. Once these items are created in the geodatabase, further items such as subtypes, relationship classes, and geometric networks can also be created. These geodatabase items are covered in subsequent chapters.

Spatial reference

When creating a new feature dataset or standalone feature class, you must specify its spatial reference. The spatial reference for a feature class describes its coordinate system (for example, geographic, UTM, and State Plane), its spatial domain, and its precision. The spatial domain is best described as the allowable coordinate range for x,y coordinates, m (measure) values, and z-values. The precision describes the number of system units per one unit of measure. A spatial reference with a precision of 1 will store integer values, while a precision of 1,000 will store three decimal places. Once the spatial reference for a feature dataset or standalone feature class has been set, only the coordinate system can be modified—the spatial domain is fixed.

All feature classes in a feature dataset share the same spatial reference. The spatial reference is an important part of geodatabase design because its spatial domain describes the maximum spatial extent to which the data can grow. You must be careful to choose an appropriate x, y, m, and z domain. For example, if you create a feature dataset with a minimum z-value of 0 and a precision of 1,000, none of the features in the feature dataset can have z-values that are less than 0, and all z-values will be stored to three decimal places. The same rule applies to x- and y-values. The exception to the rule is m domains; feature classes within the same feature dataset can have different m domains.

The spatial domain for a feature class or feature dataset cannot be changed. If the required x-, y-, m-, or z-value ranges for your database change, the data has to be reloaded into feature classes with a spatial reference that accommodates the new value range.

A collection of predefined geographic and projected coordinate systems is installed with ArcInfo. You can create custom coordinate systems, or you can import a coordinate system from an existing feature class, feature dataset, coverage, or shapefile. You can read more about spatial references and spatial domains in *Managing ArcSDE Services* and *Understanding Map Projections*.

Spatial index grid size

Each feature class has a spatial index that is automatically generated and maintained by the ArcInfo system. The spatial index is used to quickly locate features in a dataset that might match the criteria of a spatial search. The spatial index is calculated based on parameters that are provided when the feature class is created.

For most database management systems (DBMSs), the spatial index is a two-dimensional grid system that spans a feature class such as the locator grid you might find on a common road map.

For most data, only a single grid size is required. Because feature size is an important factor in determining an optimum grid size, data that contains features of very different sizes may require additional grid sizes so that larger features can be queried faster. Feature classes may have up to three grid sizes. Each grid size must be at least three times the previous grid size.

If the spatial index of the feature class is a grid, then it can be changed at any point in its lifetime. For a more detailed discussion of spatial indexes and grid sizes, see the *ArcSDE configuration and tuning guide for <DBMS>* PDF file.

Field properties

When you use ArcCatalog to create a new table or feature class, you can specify any number of fields to be included. You can also specify settings for fields such as the field type and the maximum size of the data that can be stored in it.

Each field type has special properties. All fields have properties default value, *domain*, *alias*, and allow *nulls*. The field alias property will be discussed in the next section. You can set the allow nulls property to "No" if you do not want the field to store null values. If you set the allow nulls property to "Yes", then the field will allow null values.

Use the default value property if you want the field to be automatically populated with a default value when a new feature or object is created with the ArcMap editing tools. You can set a domain, which is a valid set or range of values that can be stored in the field by using the domain property. Default values and domains are discussed in detail in Chapter 5, 'Subtypes and attribute domains'.

The exceptions are fields of type ObjectID, binary large object (BLOB), and Geometry. ObjectID, BLOB, and Geometry type fields do not have a default value and domain property. Alias is the only property of an ObjectID field you can modify, while BLOB and Geometry fields have special properties you can modify.

The properties of a Geometry field describe the kind of features that can be stored in a feature class, the size of the spatial index, and the spatial reference for the features.

Field precision and scale

The precision and scale of a field describe the maximum size and precision of data that can be stored in it. The precision describes the number of digits that can be stored in the field, while the scale describes the number of decimal places for float and double fields. When creating a new field in a geodatabase feature class or table, you can specify the field's type, precision, and scale. When the field is actually created in the database, the field type may be changed based on the precision and scale values you specify.

Use the following guidelines for choosing the correct field type for a given precision and scale:

- When you create a float, double, or integer field and specify 0 for precision and scale, the geodatabase will attempt to create a binary type field if the underlying database supports it. Personal geodatabases support only binary type fields, and precision and scale are ignored.

- When you create float and double fields and specify a precision and scale, if your precision is greater than 6, use a double; otherwise, use a float. If you create a double field and specify a precision of 6 or less, a float field is created in the database. If you create a float field and specify a precision greater than 6, a double field is created.

- If you specify a scale of 0 and a precision of 10 or less, you should be creating integer fields. When creating integer fields, your precision should be 10 or less or your field may be created as double.

Required fields

All tables and feature classes have a set of required fields that are necessary to record the state of any particular object in the table or feature class. These required fields are automatically created when you create a new feature class or table and cannot be deleted. Required fields may also have required properties such as their domain property. You cannot modify the required property of a required field.

For example, in a simple feature class, OBJECTID and Shape are required fields. They do have properties such as their aliases and geometry type that you can modify, but these fields cannot be deleted.

Some types of feature classes have a number of required fields; for more information, see Chapter 7, 'Managing annotation', and Chapter 9, 'Geometric networks'.

Field, table, and feature class aliases

The names of feature classes and tables in a geodatabase are the same as the names of the physical tables in the DBMS in which they are stored. When storing data in a DBMS, often the names for tables and fields are very cryptic, and you require a detailed data dictionary to keep track of what data each table stores and what each field in those tables represents. For example, your database may have a feature class called "Pole" that has a field called "HGT". Without consulting your data dictionary, you may have a difficult time determining that Pole stores utility poles and HGT has values for pole heights.

The geodatabase provides the ability to create aliases for fields, tables, and feature classes. An alias is an alternative name to refer to those objects. Unlike true names, aliases do not have to adhere to the limitations of the database, so they can contain special characters such as spaces. In the above example, you may set the alias for the "Poles" table to "Utility Poles" and the alias for the "HGT" field to "Height". In ArcMap, when using data with aliases, the alias name is automatically used for feature classes, tables, and fields. However, in ArcCatalog these objects are always represented by their true names. You can view the alias for feature classes, tables, and fields by examining their properties.

Aliases can be specified when creating a feature class or table and can be modified at any time. Similarly, when creating new fields, the alias is set as a property of that field and can be modified at any time.

Tracking properties of geometry

Often when working with spatial data, you may want to query your data based on properties of the geometry. For example, you may want to query the water mains feature class for all mains that are more than 50 feet in length. Doing this by examining each geometry and calculating its length can be a slow process, especially if there is a large number of water mains in the feature class. To make this more efficient, the feature class has special fields that track this kind of information about the geometry of your features.

Line feature classes have a field that tracks the features' length, while polygon feature classes have fields that track both its features' area and perimeter. When changes are made to the geometry, the values in these fields are automatically updated. These fields behave like other fields, except that you cannot delete them, assign default values and attribute domains to them, and assign values to them while editing in ArcMap.

When you create a new feature class in a personal geodatabase, these fields will not be displayed in the fields panel of the wizard. However, when you open the properties dialog box for a polygon feature class, you will see fields named Shape_Area and Shape_Length that store the area and perimeter of the geometry. When you open the properties dialog box for a line feature class, you will see a field named Shape_Length that stores the length of the geometry. Point and multipoint feature classes do not have either field.

When you create a new feature class in an ArcSDE geodatabase, these fields will be called SHAPE.AREA and SHAPE.LEN, respectively.

In ArcMap, these fields behave as any other field in the identify window, the layer properties dialog box, the attribute table dialog box, and the query builder. For more information on these aspects of ArcMap, see *Using ArcMap*.

Feature datasets

Feature datasets exist in the geodatabase to define a scope for a particular spatial reference. All feature classes that participate in topological relationships with one another (for example, a geometric network) must have the same spatial reference. Feature datasets are a way to group feature classes with the same spatial reference so that they can participate in topological relationships with each other.

To most users, feature datasets also have a natural organizational quality, much like a folder on a file system. Since for many geographic information system (GIS) applications the majority of the data for a particular database has the same spatial reference, the temptation to group large numbers of feature classes into feature datasets is irresistible.

Feature datasets, however, have a cost associated with them. Updates to a feature class in a feature dataset can potentially ripple to other feature classes within the feature dataset that participate in topological relationships. For example, when using the shared editing tools in ArcMap to maintain shared geometry in an integrated feature dataset, it is assumed that all of the simple feature classes in a feature dataset participate in the topological association. Therefore, when you edit the features within the feature dataset with the shared editing tools in ArcMap, all simple feature classes within that dataset are affected.

Use feature datasets to group classes that have topological relationships with each other (that is, geometric networks and planar topology). Beyond that, don't overload feature datasets with lots of feature classes. Having standalone feature classes (at the database level) is perfectly acceptable. If you do want to group your classes into feature datasets, try to group feature classes based on those that are used together in your applications.

Integrated feature datasets

Most vector datasets have features that share boundaries or corners. Editing a boundary or vertex shared by two or more features updates the shape of each of those features. This is called a topological association.

A topological association means that some parts of the features' shapes share the same location. In addition, different feature classes in a feature dataset often share geometry between them. For example, moving a slope boundary in one feature class would also update a forest stand in another feature class.

Topologically associated feature classes in a geodatabase are stored in an *integrated feature dataset*. You can use the topological editing tools in ArcMap to maintain the topological associations of features in an integrated feature dataset.

You create an integrated feature dataset by running the Integrate command in ArcMap. All simple feature classes in an integrated feature dataset are treated as part of the topological association. So, it is important when modeling integrated feature datasets to include only those simple feature classes that are part of the topological association.

To learn how the Integrate command works, see *Editing in ArcMap*.

For more information about topology in general, see *Modeling Our World*.

Schema locking

In multiuser databases, more than one user may be reading and editing the same data at the same time. To be able to work with data in a geodatabase for applications such as ArcMap, the application must assume that the *schema* for that data is fixed while it is working with it.

For example, when you add a feature class from a geodatabase to your map, its schema cannot be altered by you or another user. Once you have removed the feature class from your map and no other users are querying or editing that feature class, its schema can be altered.

ArcMap, ArcCatalog, and other applications written with the ArcInfo 8 Component Object Model (COM) components will automatically acquire a shared lock when editing or querying the contents of a geodatabase feature class or table. Any number of shared locks can be acquired on a single feature class or table at one time. When using ArcCatalog to modify schema—add a field, alter rules, and so on—the application will attempt to acquire an exclusive lock on the data being altered.

An exclusive lock can only be acquired if no other locks—shared or exclusive—are already on the data. If there are already other locks on the feature class or table, ArcCatalog will not be able to establish its exclusive lock and the schema will not be editable. Once an exclusive lock has been acquired, no shared locks can be applied, so the data will not be accessible in ArcMap or ArcCatalog by another user.

Exclusive locks can only be acquired by the owner of the feature class or table being modified and, therefore, only the owner can ever modify the schema of an item in a geodatabase. Some of the items that exist in a geodatabase—which are discussed in further chapters—such as geometric networks, relationship classes, and so on, have special schema-locking behaviors. Each of these is discussed in its own respective chapter.

Schema locking in personal geodatabases works in much the same way except the locks are databasewide. Once an exclusive or shared lock is acquired on an item in a personal geodatabase, that lock applies to all items in the geodatabase.

Creating tables

You can create tables in a geodatabase with an easy-to-use table designer. If you accept the designer's defaults, you will create a table that uses simple row objects to represent each row in the table.

When defining a table's fields, be aware that each database has its own rules defining what names and characters are permitted. The designer checks the names you type using a set of common rules, but each database is slightly different. If you want more control over a field's data types or structure, create the table directly in the database.

If you have custom row objects registered on your system, you can choose to create a table in which to store these objects. Custom objects usually have a set of required fields that are necessary to record the state of any particular object in the table. ▶

See Also

For details about using configuration keywords with ArcSDE, see the ArcSDE configuration and tuning guide for <DBMS> *PDF file.*

Creating a table to store simple objects

1. In the ArcCatalog tree, right-click the database in which you want to create a new table.

2. Point to New.

3. Click Table.

4. Type a name for the table. To create an alias for this table, type the alias.

5. Click Next. ▶

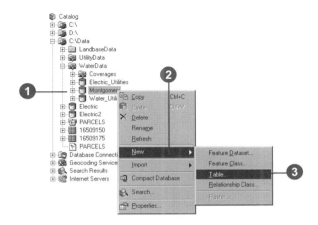

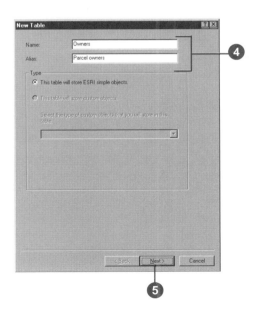

These required fields are automatically prepopulated in the table wizard. You will be able to see these fields on the fields panel, but you will not be able to delete or modify them. You will only be able to add additional fields.

In the simple row table, the OBJECTID field is an example of a required field.

Tip

Using another table as a template

When creating a new table, you can use another table as a template. Click Import, navigate to the table whose field definitions you want to copy, then click OK. Now you can edit the field names and their data types.

Tip

Deleting a field

If you have entered a field that you do not want to include in the new table, select it by clicking its tab in the grid, then press Delete.

If your geodatabase does not use ArcSDE, skip to step 8.

6. If you want to create the table using a custom storage keyword, click Use configuration keyword and then type the keyword you want to use.

7. Click Next.

8. To add a field to the table, click the next blank row in the Field Name column and type a name.

9. Click in the Data Type column next to the new field's name and click its data type. ►

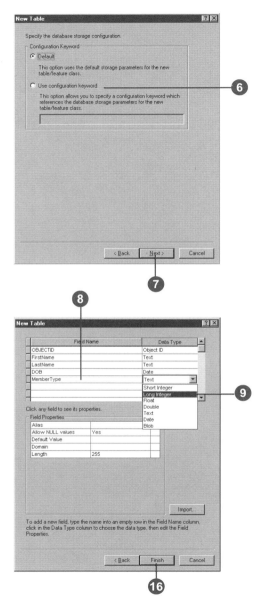

Tip

OBJECTID field

All simple tables in the geodatabase require an ObjectID type field. The ObjectID field uniquely identifies each object stored in the table in the database. The default ObjectID field will not be deletable in this wizard.

10. To create an alias for this field, click the field next to Alias and type the alias for this field.

11. To prevent nulls from being stored in this field, click the field next to Allow nulls, click the dropdown arrow, and click No.

12. To associate a default value with this field, click the field next to Default Value and type the value.

13. To associate a domain with this field, click the field next to Domain, click the dropdown arrow to see a list of the domains that apply to this field type, and click the domain.

14. To set other properties specific to the type of field, either click the property in the dropdown list or type the property.

15. Repeat steps 8 through 14 until all the table's fields have been defined.

16. Click Finish.

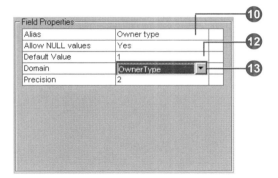

Custom objects

If you do not have any custom objects registered on your system, the option to specify one when creating a table will be unavailable.

Creating a table that stores custom objects

1. Follow steps 1 through 3 for creating a table to store simple objects.

2. Type a name for the table. To create an alias for this table, type the alias.

3. Click the second option to store custom objects in the table.

4. Click the dropdown arrow to see a list of available custom row objects and click the object you want to store.

5. Click Next.

6. Follow steps 6 through 16 for creating a table to store simple objects.

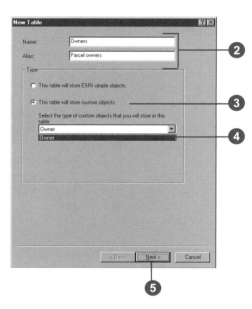

Creating feature datasets

When creating a new feature dataset, you must define its spatial reference. This includes its coordinate system—either geographic or a specific projection—and the coordinate domains—the minimum x-, y-, z-, and m-values and their precision. All feature classes in the dataset must use the same coordinate system, and each coordinate of every feature in all feature classes must fall within the coordinate domains. The exception to the rule is m domains; feature classes in the same feature dataset can have different m domains.

When defining the coordinate system, you can choose a predefined coordinate system, use an existing feature dataset or standalone feature class as a template, or define a custom geographic or projected coordinate system.

Creating a feature dataset with a predefined coordinate system

1. In the ArcCatalog tree, right-click the database in which you want to create a new feature dataset.

2. Point to New.

3. Click Feature Dataset.

4. Type a name for the feature dataset.

5. Click Edit to define the feature dataset's spatial reference. ▶

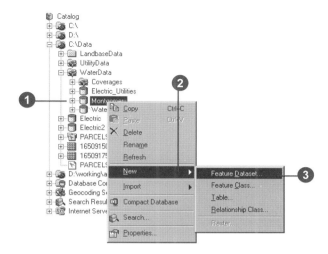

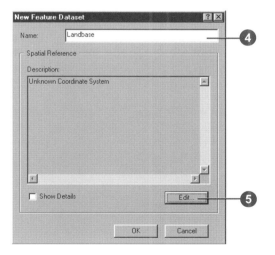

Tip

Saving the coordinate system

You can click Save As to save the coordinate system as a .prj file.

6. Click Select or Import to set the feature dataset's spatial reference.

7. Navigate to the spatial reference you want to use, or navigate to the feature class or feature dataset whose spatial reference you want to use as a template.

8. Click Modify if you want to change any parameters in the coordinate system you have chosen. Edit the coordinate system's parameters and click OK.

9. Click the X/Y Domain tab.

10. Type the minimum x-, minimum y-, maximum x-, and maximum y-coordinate values for the dataset and type the required precision for the coordinate values. ►

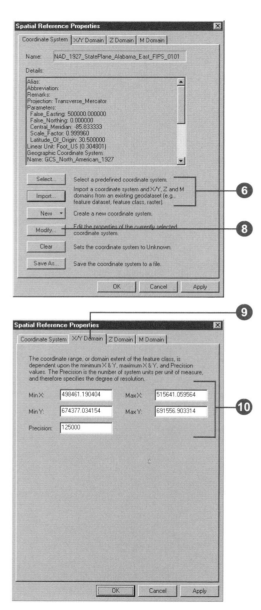

Precision

Since the size of the spatial domain is dependent on the value of precision, when the precision is changed, the maximum m- or z-value will change to fit within the size of the spatial extent. Similarly, when the maximum m- or z-value is changed, the precision will also change to fit the domain extent.

11. Click the Z Domain tab.

12. If any feature class in the feature dataset will have z-values, type the minimum z-value and maximum z-value for the dataset, then type the precision required for the z-coordinates.

13. Click the M Domain tab.

14. If any feature class in the feature dataset will have measures, type the minimum m-value and maximum m-value for the dataset and then type the precision required for the m-values.

15. Click OK. ▶

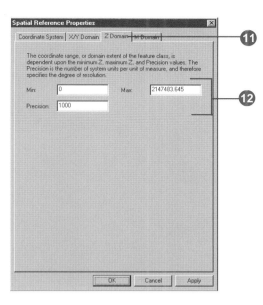

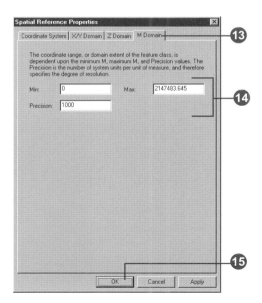

16. To see the details of your new dataset's spatial reference, check Show Details.

17. Click OK.

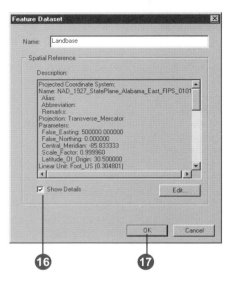

Editing predefined parameters

You can easily create variations of a predefined coordinate system. For example, choose a predefined datum from the dropdown list; the text boxes now contain the selected datum's parameters, and their contents are read-only. Now choose <custom> from the datum dropdown list. The contents of the text boxes do not change, but you can now edit their values. Type a name for your datum in place of <custom>.

Saving the coordinate system

You can click Save As to save the coordinate system as a .prj file.

Defining new geographic coordinate systems

1. Follow steps 1 through 5 for creating a feature dataset with a predefined coordinate system.

2. Click New and click Geographic.

3. Type a name for the coordinate system.

4. Type the parameters for a custom datum or choose a predefined datum from the dropdown list.

5. Type the angular unit or choose a predefined angular unit from the dropdown list.

6. Type the degrees, minutes, and seconds defining the prime meridian's longitude or choose a predefined prime meridian from the dropdown list.

7. Click OK.

8. Follow steps 9 through 16 for creating a feature dataset with a predefined coordinate system.

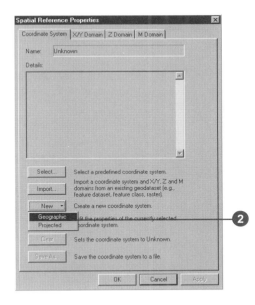

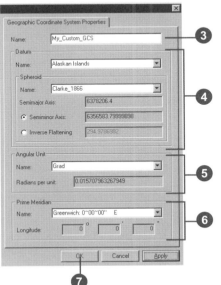

See Also

For information about which parameters are appropriate for which projection, see Understanding Map Projections.

Defining new projected coordinate systems

1. Follow steps 1 through 5 for creating a feature dataset with a predefined coordinate system.

2. Click New and click Projected.

3. Type a name for this coordinate system.

4. Choose a projection from the dropdown list and type the appropriate parameter values for that projection.

5. Type the linear unit or choose a predefined linear unit from the dropdown list.

6. Click Select or New to set the geographic coordinate system.

7. Navigate to the geographic coordinate system or navigate to the feature class or feature dataset whose geographic coordinate system you want to use as a template.

8. Click Modify if you want to change any parameters in the geographic coordinate system you have selected.

9. Click OK.

10. Follow steps 9 through 16 for creating a feature dataset with a predefined coordinate system.

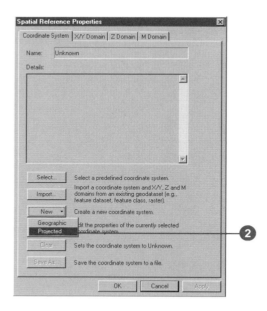

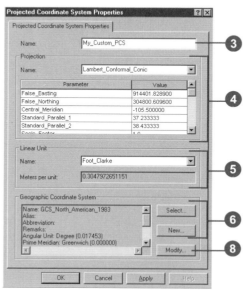

Creating feature classes

You can create feature classes in a geodatabase with ArcCatalog. If you accept the wizard's defaults, you will create a feature class that uses simple feature objects—points, lines, or polygons—to represent its features. You can also create features with custom behavior.

When creating a feature class, you must define the geometry field's properties such as its spatial index and the geometry type. When creating a standalone feature class, you must define its spatial reference. All feature classes in a feature dataset must use the same spatial reference, which was defined when the feature dataset was created. The exception to the rule is m domains; feature classes in the same feature dataset can have different m domains. ▶

See Also

For details about using configuration keywords with ArcSDE, see the ArcSDE configuration and tuning guide for <DBMS> *PDF file.*

Creating a feature class in a feature dataset

1. In the ArcCatalog tree, right-click the feature dataset in which you want to create a new feature class.

2. Point to New.

3. Click Feature Class.

4. Type a name for the feature class. To create an alias for this feature class, type the alias.

5. Click Next. ▶

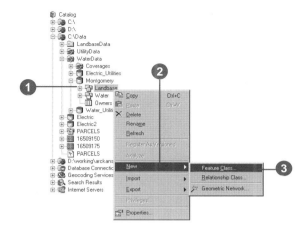

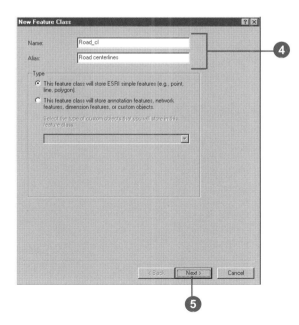

If you have custom features registered on your system, you can choose to create a feature class in which to store these objects. Custom features usually have a set of required fields that are necessary to record the state of any particular feature in the feature class.

These required fields are automatically prepopulated in the feature class wizard. On the Fields panel, you will be able to see these fields, but you will not be able to delete or modify them. You will only be able to add additional fields.

In the simple feature class, the OBJECTID and Shape fields are examples of required fields.

Tip

Using another feature class as a template

When creating a new feature class, you can use another feature class as a template. Click Import, navigate to the feature class whose field definitions you want to copy, and then click OK. Now you can edit the field names and their data types.

If your geodatabase does not use ArcSDE, skip to step 8.

6. If you want to create the table using a custom storage keyword, click Use configuration keyword and type the keyword you want to use.

7. Click Next.

8. To add a field to the feature class, click the next blank row in the Field Name column and type a name.

9. Click in the Data Type column next to the new field's name and click its data type. ▶

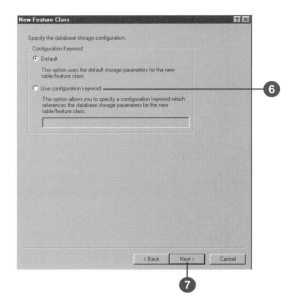

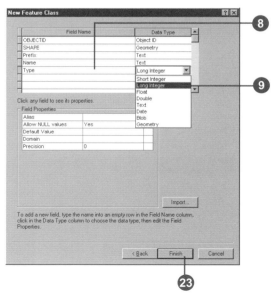

OBJECTID and Shape fields

All simple feature classes in the geodatabase require an ObjectID and geometry type fields. The default ObjectID and geometry fields will not be deletable in this wizard.

10. To create an alias for this field, click the field next to Alias and type the alias for this field.

11. To prevent nulls from being stored in this field, click the field next to Allow nulls, click the dropdown arrow, and click No.

12. To associate a default value with this field, click the field next to Default Value and type the value.

13. To associate a domain with this field, click the field next to Domain, click the dropdown arrow to see a list of the domains that apply to this field type, and click the domain.

14. To set other properties specific to the type of field, either click the property in the dropdown list or type property.

15. Repeat steps 8 through 14 until all the table's fields have been defined. ▶

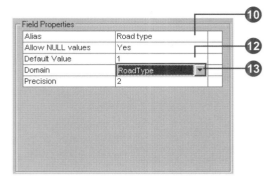

16. Click the name of the geometry field in the Field Name column.

17. To create an alias for the geometry field, click the field next to Alias and type the alias.

18. To prevent null shapes from being stored, click the field next to Allow nulls, click the dropdown arrow, and click No.

19. Click the field next to Geometry Type, click the dropdown arrow, and click the type of features you want to store in this feature class.

20. To set the spatial index grid parameters for the feature class, click the fields next to the grid size you want to specify, and type the grid value.

21. If you want the shapes in this feature class to store z-values, click the field next to Contains Z values, click the dropdown arrow, and click Yes.

22. If you want the shapes in this feature class to store m-values, click the field next to Contains M values, click the dropdown arrow, and click Yes.

23. Click Finish.

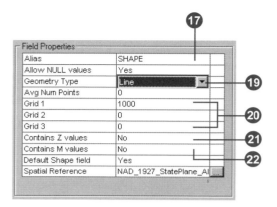

Field Properties	
Alias	SHAPE
Allow NULL values	Yes
Geometry Type	Line
Avg Num Points	0
Grid 1	1000
Grid 2	0
Grid 3	0
Contains Z values	No
Contains M values	No
Default Shape field	Yes
Spatial Reference	NAD_1927_StatePlane_Al

Tip

Saving the coordinate system

You can click Save As to save the coordinate system as a .prj file.

See Also

For examples of how to define new geographic and projected coordinate systems, see 'Creating feature datasets' in this chapter.

Creating a standalone feature class

1. Follow steps 1 through 22 for creating a feature class in a feature dataset.

2. Click the Spatial Reference Properties button to define the feature class's coordinate system.

3. Click Select or Import to set the feature dataset's spatial reference.

4. Navigate to the spatial reference you want to use or navigate to the feature class or feature dataset whose spatial reference you want to use as a template. Click Add.

5. Click Modify if you want to change any parameters in the coordinate system you have chosen. Edit the coordinate system's parameters and click OK. ►

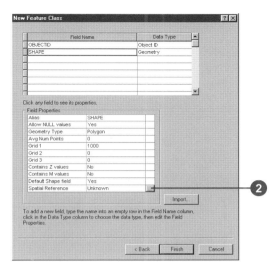

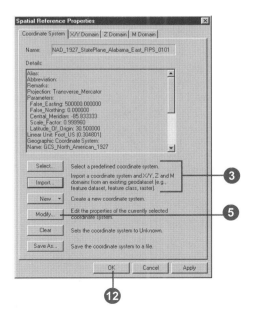

6. Click the X/Y Domain tab.

7. Type the minimum x-, minimum y-, maximum x-, and maximum y-coordinate values for the dataset and type the required precision for the coordinate values.

8. Click the Z Domain tab, if present. If your feature class does not store z-values, skip to step 10.

9. Type the minimum z-value and maximum z-value for the dataset, then type the precision required for the z-coordinates. ▶

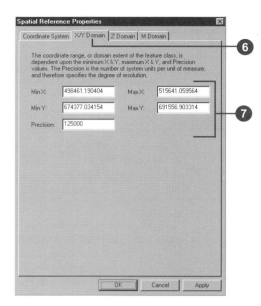

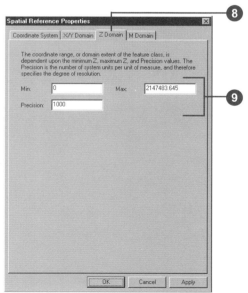

Tip

Precision

Since the size of the spatial domain is dependent on the value of precision, when the precision is changed, the maximum z-value will change to fit within the size of the spatial extent. Similarly, when the maximum z-value is changed, the precision will change to fit the domain extent.

10. Click the M Domain tab, if present. If your feature class does not store m-values, skip to step 12.

11. Type the minimum m-value and maximum m-value for the dataset and then type the precision required for the m-values.

12. Click OK.

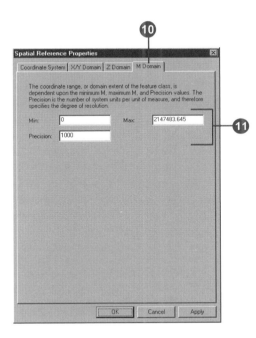

Creating a feature class that stores custom features

1. Follow steps 1 through 3 for creating a feature class in a feature dataset.

2. Type a name for the feature class. To create an alias for this feature class, type the alias.

3. Click the second option to store custom objects in the feature class.

4. Click the dropdown arrow to see a list of available custom features, then click the feature you want to store.

5. Click Next.

6. Follow steps 6 through 23 for creating a feature class in a feature dataset.

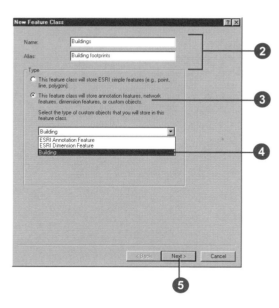

Creating indexes

Once you have data in a table or feature class, you may want to create attribute indexes to make your queries faster. Spatial indexes increase the selection speed of graphical queries on spatial features. An attribute index is an alternate path used by the DBMS to retrieve a record from a table. It is much faster to first look up the index and then go to the appropriate record than to start at the first record and search through the entire table.

Attribute indexes can be created for single or multiple fields on the feature class and table property pages. Once an index has been added, it can be deleted and readded at any point in the lifetime of the feature class or table.

You can use the same property page to delete a spatial index from and add a spatial index to your feature class.

You can modify the spatial index for an ArcSDE feature class by deleting the index and reading it. You cannot access the features stored in an ArcSDE feature class if it doesn't have a spatial index. ▶

Creating a new attribute index

1. In the ArcCatalog tree, right-click the table or feature class for which you want to create an index.

2. Click Properties.

3. Click the Indexes tab.

4. Click Add.

5. Type the name for the new index.

6. Check the Unique check box if your field values are unique. Check the Ascending check box to create an ascending index. Data in an ascending index is returned in ascending order.

7. Click the field or fields for which you want to build this index.

8. Click the arrow button to move the fields to the Fields selected list.

9. Use the up and down arrows to change the order of the fields in the index.

10. Click OK. ▶

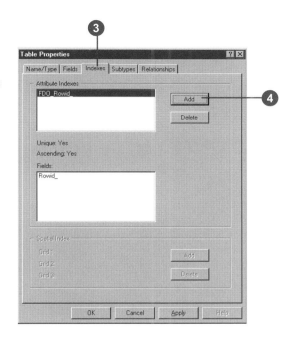

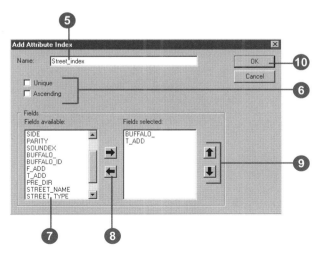

Building a new spatial index for an ArcSDE feature class is a very server-intensive operation—it should not be done on very large feature classes when a large number of users are logged in to the server.

Deleting an index

You can delete an index by clicking it in the Attribute Indexes list and clicking Delete.

11. Click Apply to build the index and close the property page.

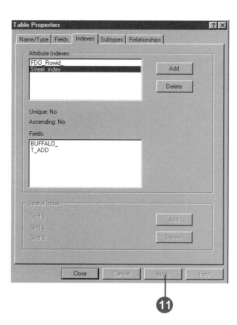

ArcSDE spatial indexes

For more information on what it means to have an ArcSDE feature class with no spatial index, see Managing ArcSDE Services.

Modifying the spatial index

1. In the ArcCatalog tree, right-click the feature class whose spatial index you want to modify.

2. Click Properties.

3. Click the Indexes tab.

4. If there is already a spatial index, you must first delete it. If there is no spatial index, skip to step 6.

5. Click Delete.

6. Click Add.

7. Type new index parameters if you do not want to use the ones already in the settings for this feature class.

8. Click OK.

9. Click OK to build the spatial index and close the property page.

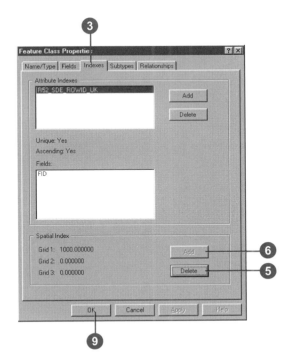

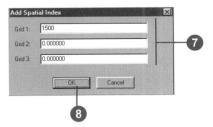

Granting and revoking privileges

If you want to let other database users view and/or modify the contents of any items, you must grant them the privilege to do so. The same tool for granting privileges can also be used to revoke privileges from a particular database user.

You have several options when granting privileges. You can specify that a user has no privileges. You can grant "select" privileges, meaning that they can view, but not modify, the contents of an item. Alternatively, you can grant a user full privileges (Select, Update, Insert, and Delete) to both view and modify the contents of an item.

Granting or revoking privileges on a feature dataset causes all of its contents to have the same privilege changes. When you add new items to a feature dataset or build a geometric network (see Chapter 9, 'Geometric networks'), you will need to grant privileges on the feature dataset again.

1. In the ArcCatalog tree, right-click the item or items for which you want to grant privileges.

2. Click Privileges.

3. Type the name of the user whose privileges you want to change.

4. Click the privileges you want them to have. UPDATE, INSERT, and DELETE will only be active if SELECT is clicked, and these work as a unit. If you leave all options unchecked, the user will have all access privileges revoked.

5. Click Apply to change the privileges.

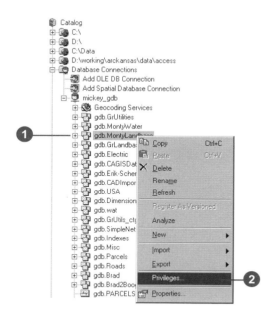

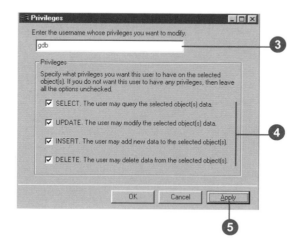

Migrating existing data into a geodatabase

4

IN THIS CHAPTER

- **How data is converted**

- **Importing shapefiles**

- **Importing coverages**

- **Importing tables**

- **Importing a geodatabase feature class**

- **Importing a CAD feature class**

- **Importing rasters**

- **Copying geodatabase data**

- **Loading data into existing simple feature classes and tables**

- **Registering ArcSDE layers and tables with the geodatabase**

- **Analyzing geodatabase data**

With ArcCatalog, you can import and load *shapefiles*, *coverages*, computer-aided design (CAD) data, and INFO and dBASE *tables* into a *geodatabase*. ArcCatalog also lets you move data between personal geodatabases and ArcSDE (formerly SDE) geodatabases. All of these data import, data loading tools, and wizards are accessible from ArcCatalog and ArcToolbox.

If your existing data is stored in a format other than one listed above or those discussed in this chapter (such as TIGER® files), ArcToolbox has the tools you need to convert that data into a format that can be imported or loaded into the geodatabase.

How data is converted

ArcCatalog and ArcToolbox each contain tools to import spatial *data* from coverages, shapefiles, and CAD feature classes into a geodatabase. They also contain tools for importing nonspatial data from INFO and dBASE tables. Tables, coverages, and shapefiles can also be imported in other ways. However, it is recommended that you use these tools or a custom application written with the ArcInfo COM components to import data into a geodatabase for the following reason:

When a shapefile, coverage, or CAD feature class is imported using an ArcCatalog or ArcToolbox tool, a geodatabase *feature class* is created to store the *features*. This feature class stores both the geometry and *attributes* from the input data. The feature class is automatically registered with the geodatabase system tables so that it can participate in *relationships* and *geometric networks*, have *validation rules*, and so on. Similarly, when a table is imported, a table is created in the geodatabase and automatically registered with the geodatabase system tables. Coverages, shapefiles, and CAD feature classes are imported into ESRI simple feature classes. INFO and dBASE tables are imported into ESRI simple row tables.

Any table, shapefile, coverage, or CAD feature class that is imported by some other mechanism will not be registered with the geodatabase system tables and will therefore not be a true geodatabase feature class or table. The ArcInfo system has tools to register these feature classes and tables with the geodatabase; these tools will be discussed later in this chapter.

There are some basic rules about loading data into a geodatabase that are discussed later in this chapter. Briefly, these rules are:

- Try to do all your data loading before versioning your data.
- Try to load all your data before building geometric networks.
- If you load lots of data into a versioned geodatabase, run compress to reduce the size of the delta tables.

Spatial reference

When you import shapefiles, coverages, and CAD feature classes, you create a new standalone feature class, a new *feature dataset* and feature class, or a feature class in an existing feature dataset. In the first two cases, you have to define a *spatial reference*.

If your coverage, shapefile, or CAD feature class has a defined projection, the import tools will automatically create the new feature class with the same *projection*, unless you specify otherwise. If you do choose to import the data into a different projection than the source data is in, the features will automatically be projected.

Because all feature classes in a feature dataset share the same spatial reference, you must only specify a new spatial reference when loading the first feature class or when creating the feature dataset in ArcCatalog. For more information about spatial references, see Chapter 3, 'Creating new items in a geodatabase'.

Spatial index grid size

Each of the data importing tools suggest a grid size based on the spatial reference, average feature size, and number of features in the input shapefile or coverage. The suggested grid size is only an approximation. You can determine the optimum grid size for any feature class by examining the data and the needs of the application querying it.

Data mapping

When you convert data from one format to another, a question arises about how data of a specific type maps from one format to the other. Importing data into the geodatabase is no exception. In this case, how both the spatial type and the *attribute field* type map from one data type to another must be considered. For each geodatabase field type, the field itself is persistently stored in the database differently depending on which database management system (DBMS) stores the geodatabase.

All feature class and attribute item types in coverages are mapped to geometry and field types in the geodatabase. More than one feature class type in a coverage will map to the same geometry type in the geodatabase. For example, points, tics, and nodes all map to geometry type point. Table 1 illustrates the mapping of feature class type to geodatabase geometry type between coverages and the geodatabase.

Coverage and INFO table items are mapped based on a combination of their type and their width. For example, an item of type I can map to a short integer, long integer, or double, depending on its width. Table 2 summarizes the item to field type mapping between coverages and the geodatabase.

Table 1: Coverage feature class to geodatabase geometry type mapping

Coverage feature class	Geodatabase geometry
point	point
arc	line (polyline)
polygon	polygon
node	point
tic	point
region	polygon
route	line (polyline) with measures
annotation	annotation*

*Annotation in the geodatabase is not a geometry type but is implemented as a feature type. For more information on annotation feature classes in the geodatabase, see Chapter 7, 'Managing annotation'.

Table 2: Coverage, INFO item to geodatabase field mapping

Item type	Item width	Geodatabase field type
B	4	long integer
C	1–320	text
D	8	date
F	4	float
F	8	double
I	1–4	short integer
I	5–9	long integer
I	10–16	double
N	1–9	float
N	10–16	double

Like coverages, all feature and attribute types in shapefiles are mapped to geodatabase geometry and attribute types. Shapefile feature types are very close to the different geometry types stored in a geodatabase, so their mapping is more straightforward. This is illustrated in Table 3.

Table 3: Shapefile to geodatabase geometry type mapping

Shapefile	Geodatabase geometry
point	point
point M	point with measures
point Z	point with Zs
polyline	line (polyline)
polyline M	line (polyline) with measures
polyline Z	line (polyline) with Zs
polygon	polygon
polygon M	polygon with measures
polygon Z	polygon with Zs
multipoint	multipoint
multipoint M	multipoint with measures
multipoint Z	multipoint with Zs

Each different shapefile and dBASE field type maps to a single geodatabase type independent of field size. The exception is the Number type field, which will map to a long integer if its number of decimals is zero and to a double if its number of decimals is greater than zero. The shapefile and dBASE field type to geodatabase field type mapping is summarized in Table 4.

Table 4: Shapefile, dBASE field to geodatabase field mapping

Field type	Field width	Geodatabase field type
date	-	date
string	1–255	text
boolean	-	short integer
number	1–4 (decimals = 0)	short integer
number	5-9 (decimals = 0)	long integer
number	10–19 (decimals = 0)	double
float	1–13	float
float	14–19	double
number	1–8 (decimals > 0)	float
number	9–19 (decimals > 0)	double

When converting *CAD feature classes* from AutoCAD® DWG, MicroStation® DGN, and Drawing Interchange File (DXF) formats to geodatabase feature classes, the geometric features found in the CAD drawing are mapped to geodatabase geometry. This mapping is summarized in Table 5.

Table 5: CAD to geodatabase geometry type mapping

CAD feature class	Geodatabase geometry
point	point
polyline	line (polyline) with Zs
polygon	polygon with Zs

The properties that are inherent to CAD features are preserved in the output feature class's attribute table. These attributes include entity type, layer, color, and linetype, as well as complex information, such as tag data, block attributes, and database linkage values. The CAD field type to geodatabase field type mapping is summarized in Table 6.

Table 6: CAD field to geodatabase field mapping

Field type	Geodatabase field type
string	text
integer	long integer
double	double

Importing a geodatabase feature class

You can use the Feature class to Geodatabase tool in ArcCatalog and ArcToolbox to import feature classes from one geodatabase to another or to import features from one feature class into a new feature class in the same geodatabase. This tool creates simple feature classes only and does not preserve object identity.

Therefore, when you use this tool to import a custom or network feature class, a new simple feature class is created and the geometry and attributes of each feature are imported. If the input feature class has any subtypes (Chapter 5), default values (Chapter 5), relationships (Chapter 6), and so on, they are not imported along with the features.

Analyzing geodatabase data

If your geodatabase is stored in a DBMS, such as Oracle, SQL Server, DB2, or Informix, the Analyze command in ArcCatalog can be used to update the DBMS statistics on your datasets. The Analyze command updates the statistics of business tables, feature tables, and delta tables and the statistics on those tables' indexes.

The type of DBMS that your geodatabase is stored in will dictate which statistics the Analyze command updates. For more information on your DBMS, see the ArcSDE online documentation. For more information on when you should run the Analyze command on your data and which tables should be analyzed, see Chapter 13, 'Working with a versioned geodatabase'.

Copying and moving geodatabase data

In addition to the Feature class to Geodatabase tool, ArcCatalog contains tools to directly move and copy data between geodatabases while preserving object identity, subtypes, relationships, network connectivity, and so on. With this method of copying data, you can copy entire feature datasets or individual feature classes between geodatabases.

When the data is copied, the copy has all the behavior of the original data; any attribute domains referenced in the original geodatabase are copied along with the feature class or table. If the feature class or table participates in a relationship class, then that relationship class, along with the feature class or table it is related to through that relationship class, is also copied. As an example, if you copy a feature class with feature-linked annotation, the feature-linked annotation class is automatically copied with the feature class.

If you are copying a feature class into an existing feature dataset, either in the same geodatabase or in another geodatabase, then the spatial reference of the feature class and the feature dataset must match. If the spatial references do not match, you will not be able to copy the data.

You can move feature classes and relationship classes in and out of, or between, feature datasets in the same geodatabase by dragging and dropping them in ArcCatalog. When moving a feature class into a feature dataset, the feature class and the feature dataset must have the same spatial reference.

If you copy or move a network feature class, all the feature classes that participate in the network, and the geometric network itself, are also copied or moved with the feature class.

Coverage annotation

In the geodatabase, *annotation* is not a geometry type but a feature type. Coverage and shapefile features are imported into feature classes that store ESRI simple features with geometry types of point, line, or polygon; annotation is stored in feature classes that store annotation features.

You cannot import a coverage annotation feature class into the geodatabase using one of the data loading tools or wizards. A different process exists for converting coverage annotation to the geodatabase. This process is described in Chapter 7, 'Managing annotation'.

Data conversion versus data loading

The tools and wizards for importing coverages, shapefiles, and INFO and dBASE tables into the geodatabase require that each shapefile and coverage feature class be loaded into a new feature class and each INFO and dBASE table be loaded into a new table.

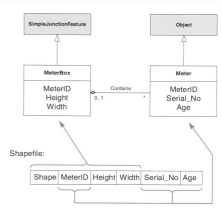

This diagram shows how you may use the Object Loader or Simple Data Loader to populate a geodatabase schema from a shapefile with different schema.

The feature class or table cannot exist before you begin the import process.

Because an existing feature class or table can be in any number of states, a separate data-loading tool is required to load data from a shapefile, coverage feature class, INFO table, or dBASE table into an existing geodatabase feature class or table.

A feature class can be in one of two states:

- Nonversioned simple data

- *Versioned* simple, network, or custom *object* data

In the case of nonversioned simple data, an *edit session* is not required to insert new features or rows into the table or feature class. Once loaded, all data is visible in all versions of the database. This data-loading operation is performed with the Simple Data Loader Wizard in ArcCatalog. For information on how to use this wizard, see 'Loading data into existing simple feature classes and tables' in this chapter.

In case of versioned simple, network, or custom objects, an edit session is required to insert new records into the table or feature class to ensure that the network connectivity and version information is managed correctly. This data-loading operation is performed with the Object Loader Wizard in ArcMap. For more information on the Object Loader, see Chapter 12, 'Editing your geodatabase'.

As an example of when you might use the Simple Data Loader or the Object Loader, consider the following:

You have generated your schema using the CASE tool Schema Generation Wizard (see Chapter 11, 'Building geodatabases with CASE tools'), and you have a simple junction feature class called MeterBox and a table called Meter. MeterBox and Meter participate in a one-to-many relationship class (see Chapter 6, 'Defining relationship classes'). MeterBox has the attributes MeterID, Height, and Width. Meter has the attributes Serial_No and Age and the embedded foreign key MeterID, which relates the meter to its meter box.

In your shapefile database, you have maintained your meter boxes and meters in a single shapefile that has the attributes MeterID, Height, Width, Serial_No, and Age. You can use the Object Loader to take the data in that shapefile and split it between the MeterBox feature class and the Meter table while maintaining the relationships between the meter and its meter box.

Use the Object Loader to load the shapefile into the MeterBox feature class, matching the MeterID, Height, and Width fields from the shapefile with those in the feature class. Repeat the process, loading the shapefile into the table (only the attributes will be loaded), matching Serial_No, Age, and MeterID. Since the objects in MeterBox are related to objects in Meter by the embedded foreign key MeterID, the relationships will be maintained during the data-loading process.

Importing ArcStorm and Map LIBRARIAN data

ArcMap and ArcCatalog display and query ArcStorm and Map LIBRARIAN data that is served by ArcSDE for Coverages. ArcSDE for Coverages layers are treated in the same way as ArcSDE 8 layers in that they can be displayed and queried, but they can't be edited. To import ArcStorm and Map LIBRARIAN data into a geodatabase, use the Feature Class to Geodatabase tool described in 'Importing a geodatabase feature class' later in this chapter.

Loading data into an existing schema

One of the ways to design your geodatabase data model is to use Unified Modeling Language (UML) and Computer-Aided Software Engineering (CASE) tools. When you do this, you use the Schema Wizard in ArcCatalog to translate your UML design into an empty geodatabase schema—that is, a set of feature classes, tables, relationship classes, geometric networks, and rules (see Chapter 11, 'Building geodatabases with CASE tools'). You may want to start directly editing that schema to build your database, or you may want to populate that schema with existing data. When loading data into a geodatabase schema, you must consider how your database's performance will be impacted, especially when working with network data.

There is more than one strategy for loading data into an existing database schema. Each strategy has its limitations and affects performance of the database. The strategies and performance considerations of each are outlined below.

If you have generated your schema using CASE tools, there are two strategies you can use to load your data:

Strategy 1: Using the Simple Data Loader:

1. Use the Schema Generation Wizard to create the empty geodatabase schema from your UML model in your database.

2. Delete any networks that were created. This will also delete any associated connectivity rules and class extensions.

3. Load all of your data into your database using the Simple Data Loader in ArcCatalog.

4. Build any required networks using the Build Geometric Network Wizard in ArcCatalog or ArcToolbox.

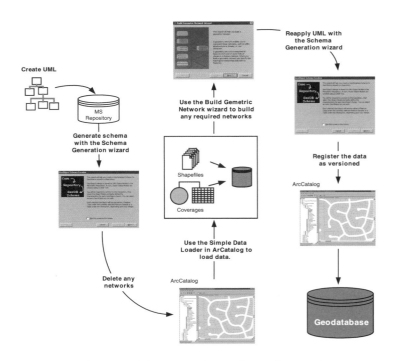

Loading data into an existing geodatabase schema: Strategy 1

5. Use the Schema Generation Wizard to reapply the UML to the existing data to re-create the network connectivity rules and to assign any class extensions.

6. Register your data as versioned.

This strategy has a number of advantages. Without a network, your data will load much faster. Since the data is not versioned, all of the data will be loaded directly into the base tables, and you won't be required to compress your database. If your data model includes geometric networks, deleting the network in step 2 will automatically delete all connectivity rules associated with that network, and all of its participant feature classes will revert to simple feature classes. By reapplying the UML model after the network is built, your connectivity rules are reapplied and any class extensions described by the model are also reassociated with their corresponding classes.

This method's only limitation has to do with custom objects that have custom object creation behavior. Using this strategy, custom creation behavior will not be executed. In this case, you may want to do a combination of the first and second method (see below): load all noncustom features, build networks, apply your model from which to create the custom object classes, then version your data and use the Object Loader to populate the custom classes.

To learn more about geometric networks and connectivity rules, see Chapter 9, 'Geometric networks'. To learn more about versioning, see Chapter 13, 'Working with a versioned geodatabase'. To learn more about class extensions, see *Exploring ArcObjects*.

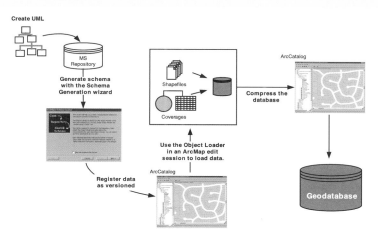

Loading data into an existing geodatabase schema: Strategy 2

Strategy 2: Using the Object Loader:

1. Use the Schema Generation Wizard to create the empty geodatabase schema in your database.

2. Use the Simple Data Loader in ArcCatalog to load your existing data into your simple feature classes and tables.

3. Register your data as versioned.

4. Use the Object Loader in ArcMap to load your existing data into your network feature classes. This step automatically builds network topology within an edit session.

5. Run compress to compress the database (you should always run compress after large data loads into versioned classes).

6. Use the Analyze command in ArcCatalog to update the database statistics for each feature class into which you loaded data.

This strategy has a number of disadvantages. First, loading data into network feature classes is a slow process—up to several seconds per feature—that can make using this method impractical for loading a large number of network features. Since it is versioned, all of the data loaded will be in the delta tables, not the base tables for the feature classes. If you use this method to load your data, then once it is loaded you should run compress on your database to push all the records from the delta tables to the base tables. Having your data in the base tables will result in better query speed than having large amounts of data in your delta tables. For more details on base tables, delta tables, and compressing your database to improve performance, see Chapter 13, 'Working with a versioned geodatabase'.

Appending data to a geodatabase

Once your database is built and your data is loaded and in production, you may want to append another area of data to your existing database. If you don't have any network data in your geodatabase, the process is straightforward:

1. Use the Object Loader in ArcMap to load the new data into your feature classes.

2. Run compress to compress the database (you should always run compress after large data loads into versioned classes).

3. Use the Analyze command in ArcCatalog to update the database statistics for each feature class into which you loaded data.

All object behavior is executed such as creating linked annotation for feature classes that have a linked annotation class.

If you are appending data to network feature classes, then the above method will work. However, since the entire network cannot be cached when using the Object Loader to load data into

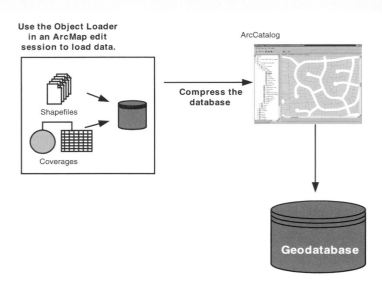

Appending data to a geodatabase using the Object Loader

network feature classes, it will be a very slow process—up to several seconds per feature, depending on the number of feature classes in the network. This method may be slow, but it executes any necessary object behavior.

This method will work fine for simple features. If you are appending a large amount of data into a network (more than a few thousand features), then this method may be too time-consuming to be practical. When working with networks, there is an alternative, faster method to appending data.

This method involves unregistering the data as versioned and dropping the network for the duration of the data-loading operation. The fact that the data must be unregistered as versioned is very important. When unregistering data as versioned, all edits that have been made on the data that are not in the base table will be lost. The following outlines the steps to take for this method to ensure no data will be lost:

1. Reconcile and post each outstanding version in the database against the DEFAULT version. After posting, delete each version.

2. Run compress to compress the database.

3. Unregister the data as versioned. Note: If you have not completed steps 1 and 2 before unregistering your data as versioned, then you will lose any edits that those versions contain.

4. Delete the geometric network.

5. Use the Simple Data Loader in ArcCatalog to load the new data to your existing feature classes.

6. Rebuild the geometric network using the Build Geometric Network Wizard in ArcCatalog or ArcToolbox.

7. If you created your geodatabase schema using CASE tools, use the Schema Wizard to reapply the UML to the existing data in order to re-create the network connectivity rules and to assign any class extensions. If you are not using CASE tools, then you will need to use ArcCatalog to re-create your connectivity rules.

8. Register your data as versioned and continue with production. Registering the data as versioned automatically updates the database statistics for the feature classes.

There are a number of limitations to this method that may make it necessary for you to use the first method:

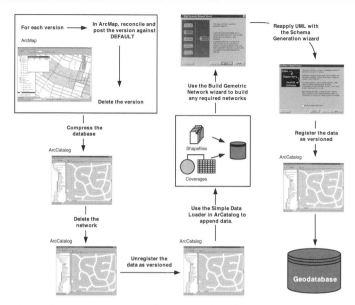

Appending data to a geodatabase using the Simple Data Loader

- You cannot use this method if your network has any complex junction features with connection points and custom topology since the process of batch rebuilding the network will not re-create the custom topology.

- The process of rebuilding the network will reconnect all network features you may have disconnected from the network.

- If any of your network feature classes have feature-linked annotation, you cannot use the Simple Data Loader to load features into it. In this case, you must use the Object Loader so that all annotation features will be created along with the new network features.

To learn more about geometric networks, complex junctions, enabled and disabled network features, and connectivity rules, see Chapter 9, 'Geometric networks'. To learn more about reconcile, post, compress, and versioning, see Chapter 13, 'Working with a versioned geodatabase'.

ArcSDE 8 layers and tables and the geodatabase

In the ArcInfo system, ArcSDE 8 layers and tables are treated as geodatabase feature classes and tables; they can be displayed, queried, and edited. However, these layers and tables participate in other functionality such as validation rules and relationship classes.

ArcSDE 8 layers and tables as defined here were created with applications other than those that use the ArcInfo COM components to manage the database. This includes ArcSDE layers that were created with the ArcSDE administration tools and existing SDE layers from an SDE 3 database. All of these layers and tables can be displayed and queried in ArcInfo 8, and if versioned, they can also be edited.

In order for ArcSDE layers and tables to participate in the more advanced functions of the geodatabase, they must be registered as feature classes and object classes (tables) with the geodatabase system tables. Once they are registered with the geodatabase, they can have subtypes, default values, validation rules, and participate in relationship classes. You can drag and drop these feature classes into feature datasets that have the same spatial reference. ArcCatalog contains tools to register an ArcSDE layer or table with the geodatabase; these tools are discussed further in this chapter.

Importing rasters

Raster data can be loaded into a geodatabase using the Raster to Geodatabase tool or Raster to Geodatabase Wizard in ArcCatalog

and ArcToolbox. When raster data is stored in a geodatabase, it is converted from its original format into a new format for storage in a DBMS. In the DBMS, the raster is stored as many small binary large objects (BLOBs). Reducing the amount of data transferred between the client and the server optimizes performance. Storing multiple resolutions of the raster, cutting the raster into tiles that become the BLOBs, and spatially indexing the raster does this. Each time the raster is queried, only the tiles necessary to satisfy the query are returned instead of the whole dataset. This makes it possible to store very seamless raster datasets (tens to hundreds of gigabytes) and serve them quickly to a client for display.

There are several storage parameters that you can use to tune your raster data: pyramids, tile size, and data compression.

Pyramids are reduced resolution representations of your dataset, which are used to improve performance. Pyramids can speed up display of raster data because the server returns only the data at a specified resolution that is required for the display. Pyramids are created by resampling the original data. The resample methods instruct the server how to resample the data to build the pyramids. Nearest neighbor should be used for nominal data or raster datasets with colormaps such as land use data, scanned maps, and pseudocolor images. Bilinear or cubic should be used for continuous data such as satellite imagery or aerial photography.

The tile size controls the number of pixels you want to store in each BLOB and therefore the size of the BLOB. This is specified as a number of pixels in X and Y. A good guideline is to use a tile size that is one quarter the size of the data you plan to serve. For example, if you plan to serve data to a client whose display window will normally be 500x500 screen pixels, use a tile size of 250x250 pixels.

Data Compression compresses the blocks of data before storing in the geodatabase. The compression used is LZ77, which is a lossless compression, meaning the values of cells in your raster dataset will not be changed. The amount of compression will depend on the data. The fewer values and more homogeneous the data, the higher the compression ratio.

The primary benefit of compressing your data is that it requires less storage space. An added benefit may be improved performance of up to 20 percent because you are transferring smaller packets of data from the server.

A set of geographically continuous raster datasets can be loaded into the geodatabase and managed as individual rasters, a raster catalog, or one seamless raster. A raster catalog is a collection of individual rasters in the geodatabase. You can work with a raster catalog such as a single raster. The server manages the tiling of the individual rasters. Alternatively, you can mosaic your rasters into one seamless raster. A single raster will always perform better than many rasters, so to optimize performance it is best to mosaic spatially continuous raster datasets.

For more discussion of raster data, see *Modeling Our World*.

Importing shapefiles

A wizard lets you easily import shapefiles into new or existing feature datasets in the database or into the database as standalone feature classes. The wizard calculates default values, which can be used to import the shapefile. However, you can also customize those parameters. After using the wizard a few times, try using the Shapefile to Geodatabase tool in ArcCatalog, which lets you import several shapefiles into the database at once.

The wizard and tools for importing shapefiles into a geodatabase are also accessible from ArcToolbox.

See Also

For more information on using tools to perform operations on multiple shapefiles, see Using ArcToolbox.

Importing shapefiles using default values

1. In the ArcCatalog tree, right-click the shapefile you want to import into your geodatabase.

2. Point to Export.

3. Click Shapefile to Geodatabase Wizard.

   The wizard appears with the input shapefile field already populated with the shapefile you selected in ArcCatalog.

4. Click Next.

5. Navigate to the database or database connection into which you want to import the shapefile or type its path.

6. To import the shapefile into an existing feature dataset in the database, click the first option and then click the feature dataset's name from the dropdown list.

   Click the second option and type the new feature dataset's name to import the shapefile into a new feature dataset.

   Click the third option to import the shapefile as a standalone feature class.

7. Type a name for the new feature class.

8. Click Next. ►

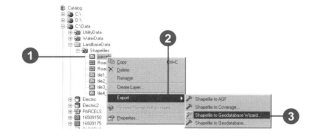

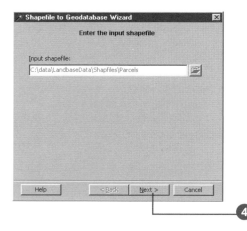

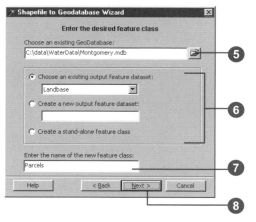

9. Click the first option to accept the default parameters.

10. Click Next.

11. Review the options you specified for your data import operation. If you want to change something, you can go back through the wizard by clicking the Back button.

12. When satisfied with your options, click Finish to import the shapefile into the database.

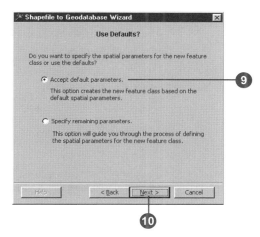

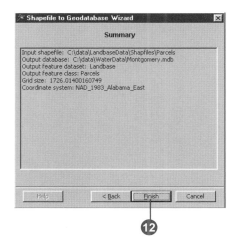

See Also

Managing ArcSDE Services *explains in detail the spatial index grid and how its values should be calculated.*

Importing shapefiles using custom values

1. Follow steps 1 through 8 for importing a shapefile using default values.

2. Click the second option to import the shapefile defining custom parameters.

3. Click Next.

4. Type custom spatial index grid values if you do not want to use the defaults. (Only one index grid is used in Personal geodatabases, while ArcSDE geodatabases use up to three.)

5. Click Next. ▶

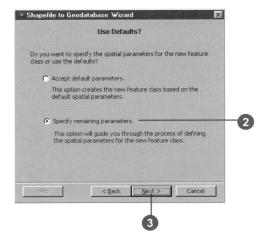

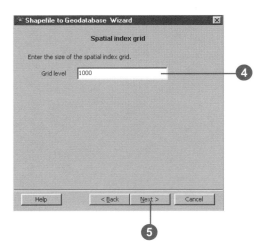

Corrected field names

Changes to the field names are proposed on invalid field names. For example, when a field name contains an invalid character such as a hyphen, the hyphen is replaced by an underscore in the corrected field name. An error message indicating why the original name was corrected appears in the Original Error column.

Undoing field name edits

You can click the Revert button to change the corrected field names back to their original values, as automatically corrected by the Import Wizard.

Changing the spatial reference

All the feature classes in a feature dataset must use the same spatial reference. Therefore, once a feature dataset has been created, you cannot change its spatial reference. The spatial reference panel will only appear when you are importing the shapefile into a new feature dataset or into a standalone feature class.

6. Review the names in the Corrected Fields column. Click a name and type a new one if you do not want to use the default.

7. Double-click in the Delete field column and then click Yes if you do not want to include one of the original fields in the new feature class.

8. Click Next.

   If you are importing the shapefile into an existing feature dataset, skip to step 16.

9. Review the summary of the coordinate system that will be used.

10. Click Change if you want to modify any of the shapefile's coordinate system parameters.

   Otherwise, skip to step 15. ▶

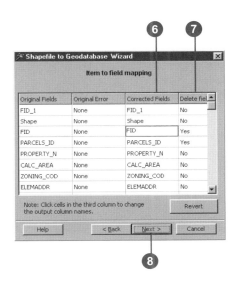

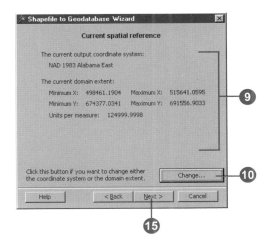

See Also

For details on how to create a new coordinate system and for important information about spatial reference and how it affects your data, see Chapter 3, 'Creating new items in a geodatabase'.

11. Click one of the buttons to change the default coordinate system by one of the following methods: selecting a preexisting one; importing a coordinate system from a shapefile, coverage, or feature class; defining a new one; or modifying the default coordinate system's parameters.

12. Click the X/Y Domain tab and modify the default parameters.

13. Repeat step 12 with the Z Domain and M Domain tabs, if present.

14. Click OK. ▶

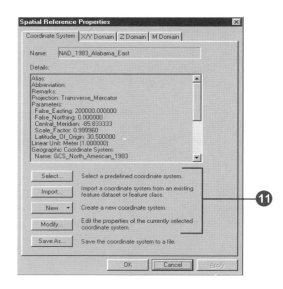

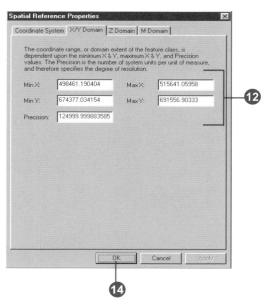

15. Click Next.

16. Review the summary of the parameters used to import the shapefile.

   To change a parameter, navigate back to the appropriate panel by clicking Back.

17. Click Finish.

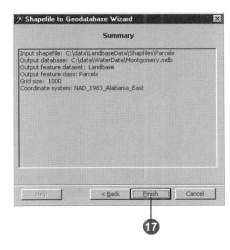

Importing coverages

You can use a wizard to import a coverage's feature classes into new or existing feature datasets in the database or into the database as standalone feature classes. You can choose which feature classes you want to import. The wizard calculates default parameters, which can be used to import the feature classes; you can customize those parameters for each feature class. When you choose to customize the parameters, you will cycle through a series of wizard panels, once for each feature class.

After using the wizards a few times, try using the Coverage to Geodatabase tool in ArcCatalog, which lets you import several coverages into the database at once.

You can also access the wizards and tools for importing coverages into a geodatabase from ArcToolbox.

Importing coverages using default values

1. In the ArcCatalog tree, right-click the database or feature dataset into which you want to import the coverage.

2. Point to Import.

3. Click Coverage to Geodatabase Wizard.

4. Navigate to the coverage you want to import into the database or type its path.

5. Check the boxes next to the feature classes you want to import.

6. Click Next. ▶

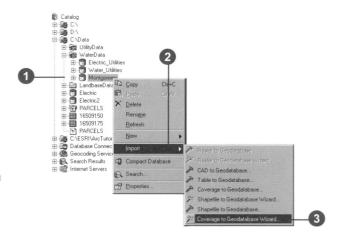

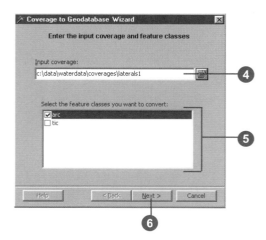

7. The geodatabase will be prepopulated with the one clicked in the ArcCatalog tree. Had you evoked this wizard by clicking export on the coverage, then you would have to browse for, or type in, the database.

8. If you right-click on a feature dataset, then the dataset will be prepopulated. If not, click the first option to choose an existing feature dataset and then choose the feature dataset's name from the list.

   Click the second option to create a new feature dataset, then type in the new feature dataset's name.

   Click the third option to create a standalone feature class.

9. Click Next.

10. Click the first option to import the feature classes using the default parameters.

11. Click Next. ▶

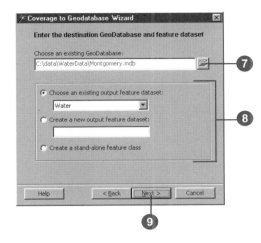

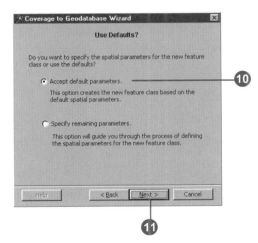

Importing multiple feature classes

If you have chosen to import multiple coverage feature classes into a geodatabase, each will be imported into a separate feature class.

A progress bar will be displayed for each coverage feature class imported.

12. Review the options you specified for your data import operation. If you want to change something, you can go back through the wizard by clicking the Back button.

13. When satisfied with your options, click Finish to import the coverage into the database.

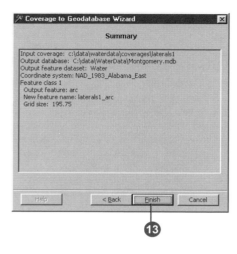

Importing coverages using custom values

1. Follow steps 1 through 9 for importing coverages using default values.

2. Click the second option to import the coverage defining custom values.

3. Click Next.

   If you are importing the coverage into an existing feature dataset or into a standalone feature class, skip to step 11.

4. Review the summary of the coordinate system that will be used.

5. Click Change if you want to modify any of the coverage's coordinate system parameters.

   Otherwise, skip to step 10. ►

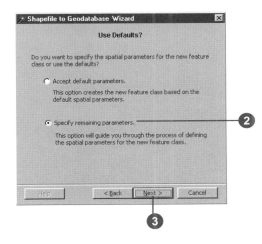

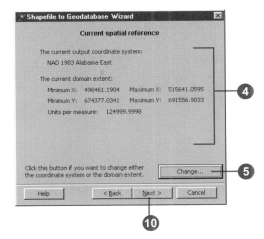

6. Click one of the buttons to change the default coordinate system by selecting a preexisting one; importing a coordinate system from a shapefile, coverage, or feature class; defining a new one; or modifying the default coordinate system's parameters.

7. Click the X/Y Domain tab and modify the default parameters.

8. Repeat step 7 with the Z Domain and M Domain tabs, if present.

9. Click OK.

10. Click Next. ▶

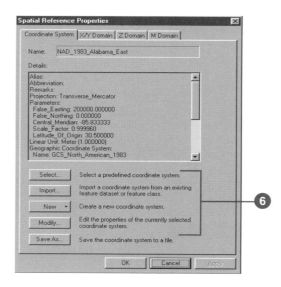

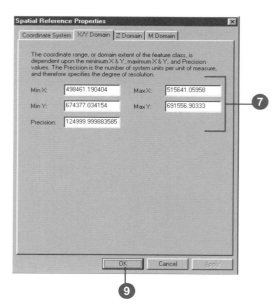

Tip

Naming a feature class

Each feature class in the database must have a unique name.

11. Review the names in the Output feature class column. Click a name and then type a new one if you do not want to use the default.

12. If you want to define custom parameters for loading a feature class, double-click in the Edit defaults column and click yes.

13. Click Next.

    If you are not defining custom parameters for any feature classes, skip to step 21.

14. Type custom spatial index grid values if you do not want to use the defaults. (Only one index grid is used in personal geodatabases, while ArcSDE geodatabases use up to three.)

15. Click Next. ▶

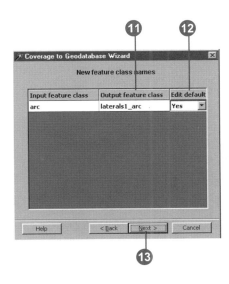

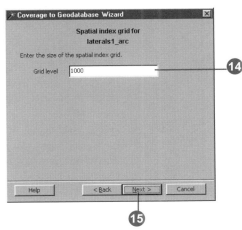

16. Review the names in the Corrected Fields column. Click a name and type a new one if you do not want to use the default.

17. Double-click in the Delete field? column. Click Yes if you do not want to include one of the original fields in the new feature class.

18. Click Next.

    If you are importing the coverage into a feature dataset, skip to step 20.

19. Review the summary of the coordinate system that will be used to create the standalone feature class. To modify the coordinate system, follow steps 5 through 10 in this task.

    Repeat steps 14 through 19 for each feature class whose parameters you chose to customize.

20. Review the summary of the parameters used to import the coverage's feature classes.

    To change a parameter, navigate back to the appropriate panel by clicking Back.

21. Click Finish.

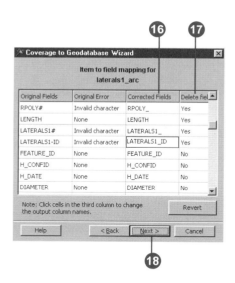

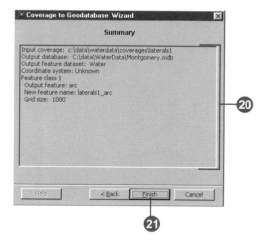

Importing tables

The Table to Geodatabase import tool lets you easily import your dBASE and INFO attribute tables into a geodatabase.

The tool will automatically correct any illegal or duplicate field names and will also allow you to specify how these corrections are made.

This same tool can also be used to import multiple INFO and dBASE tables in the database. For more information on using the batch capabilities of this tool, see *Using ArcToolbox*.

You can also access the tools for loading tables into a geodatabase from ArcToolbox.

Tip

Batch loading

If you select multiple tables from the contents view of ArcCatalog and click Import to Geodatabase, the tool is automatically set in batch mode with all of the input tables prepopulated.

1. In the ArcCatalog tree, right-click on the INFO or dBASE table you want to import.

2. Point to Export.

3. Click Table to Geodatabase.

4. Navigate to the geodatabase or ArcSDE geodatabase connection into which you want to import the table or type in its path.

5. Click Change Settings to manually modify illegal and duplicate field names or to specify a configuration keyword.

   If you want the tool to autocorrect the field names and you want to use the default storage configuration, skip to step 9. ▸

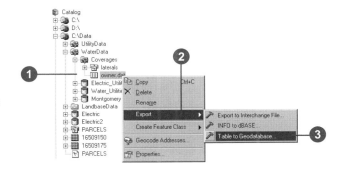

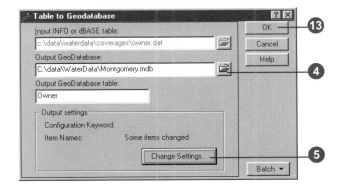

Undoing field name edits

You can click the Revert button to change the corrected field names back to their original values as automatically corrected by the Import tool.

6. Click Item Names to manually modify illegal and duplicate field names.

7. Review the names in the Corrected Fields column. Click a name and type a new one if you do not want to use the default.

8. Double-click in the Delete field? column. Click Yes if you do not want to include one of the original fields in the new table.

9. If you are importing this feature class into a personal geodatabase, skip to step 12.

10. Click Keyword to specify a configuration keyword.

11. Click Use configuration keyword if you want to create the table using a custom storage keyword and type the keyword you want to use.

12. Click OK.

13. Click OK to import the table.

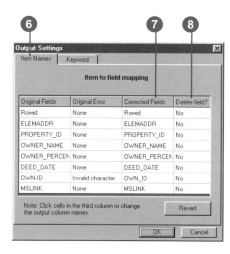

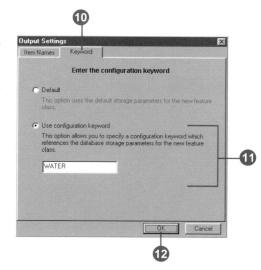

Importing a geodatabase feature class

The Geodatabase to Geodatabase data import tool lets you easily import a feature class from one geodatabase into another. You can also use this tool to import a feature class into a new feature class in the same geodatabase.

This process does not preserve object identity and always results in a simple feature class that contains no subtypes, default values, and so on (see Chapter 6, 'Defining relationship classes').

Like the other import tools, you can change the spatial reference and modify the output fields and field names. These tools are accessible from either ArcCatalog or ArcToolbox.

Tip

Batch loading

If you select multiple feature classes from the contents view of ArcCatalog and click on Import to Geodatabase, the tool will automatically be set in batch mode with all of the input feature classes prepopulated.

1. In the ArcCatalog tree, right-click the feature class you want to import to a new geodatabase feature class.

2. Point to Export.

3. Click Geodatabase to Geodatabase.

4. Navigate to the geodatabase or ArcSDE geodatabase connection you want to import the feature class into or type its path.

5. If you want to import the feature class into an existing feature dataset, click the dropdown arrow to see a list of available feature datasets and click the feature dataset.

   If you want to create a new feature dataset, type its name.

   If you want to create a standalone feature class, then leave this blank.

6. Type the name for the new feature class.

7. If you want to load the data with all of the default settings, skip to step 21.

8. Click Change Settings if you want to change the output spatial reference, grid size, or field names. ▶

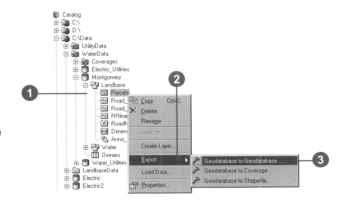

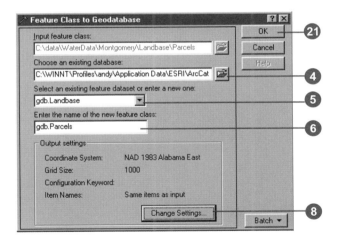

9. Click the Spatial Ref tab if you are importing this feature class into a standalone feature class or into a new feature dataset and want to change the output spatial reference.

10. Click Change. Otherwise, skip to step 13.

11. Follow steps 11 through 13 for importing shapefiles with custom values to change the spatial reference.

12. Click the Grid size tab to change the grid size.

13. Type custom spatial index grid values. (Only one index grid is used in personal geodatabases, while ArcSDE geodatabases use up to three.) ▶

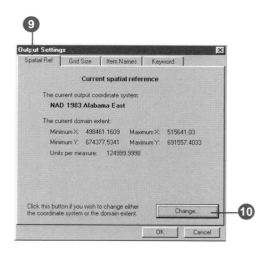

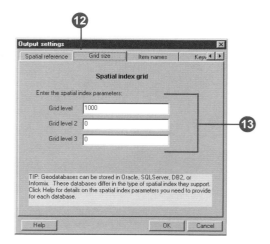

14. Click Item Names to manually modify illegal and duplicate field names.

15. Review the names in the Corrected Fields column. Click a name and type a new one if you do not want to use the default.

16. Double-click in the Delete field? column and then click Yes if you do not want to include one of the original fields in the new feature class.

17. If you are importing this feature class into a personal geodatabase, skip to step 20.

18. Click Keyword to specify a configuration keyword.

19. Click Use configuration keyword if you want to create the table using a custom storage keyword and then type the keyword you want to use.

20. Click OK.

21. Click OK to import the feature class.

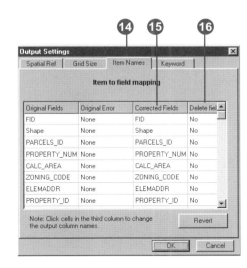

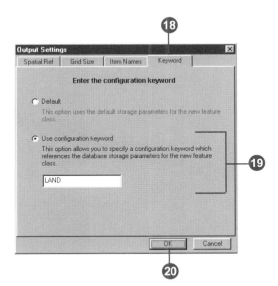

Importing a CAD feature class

The CAD to geodatabase data import tool lets you easily import a feature class from a CAD dataset to a geodatabase. You can use this tool to import CAD feature classes from AutoCAD DWG, MicroStation DGN, and Drawing Interchange File (DXF) formats.

Like the other import tools, you can change the spatial reference and modify the output fields and field names. These tools are accessible from either ArcCatalog or ArcToolbox.

Tip

Batch loading

If you select multiple feature classes from the contents view of ArcCatalog and click on Import to Geodatabase, the tool will automatically be set in batch mode with all of the input feature classes prepopulated.

1. In the ArcCatalog tree, right-click the CAD feature class you want to import to a new geodatabase feature class.

2. Point to Export.

3. Click CAD to Geodatabase.

4. Navigate to the geodatabase or ArcSDE geodatabase connection you want to import the feature class into or type its path.

5. If you want to import the feature class into an existing feature dataset, click the dropdown arrow to see a list of available feature datasets, then click the feature dataset.

   If you want to create a new feature dataset, type its name.

   If you want to create a standalone feature class, then leave this blank.

6. Type the name for the new feature class.

7. Follow steps 7 to 21 for Importing a geodatabase feature class.

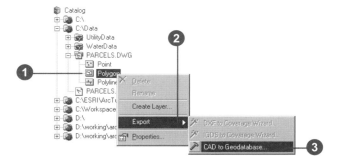

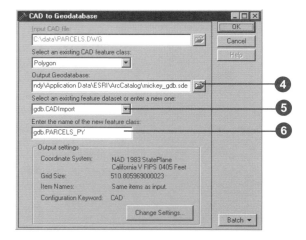

Importing rasters

Raster data can be loaded into a geodatabase using the Raster to Geodatabase tool or Raster to Geodatabase wizard in ArcCatalog and ArcToolbox.

There are several storage parameters that you can use to tune your raster data: pyramids, tile size, and data compression.

Importing rasters using default values

1. In the ArcCatalog tree, right-click the raster you want to import into your geodatabase.

2. Point to Export.

3. Click Raster to Geodatabase Wizard. The wizard appears with the input raster field populated with the selected raster.

4. Click Next. ►

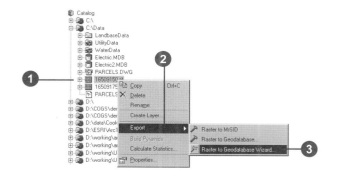

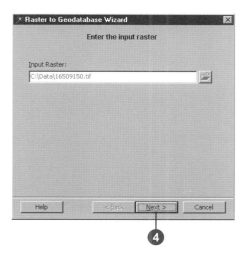

5. Navigate to the database connection into which you want to import the raster or type its path.

6. Click the first option to import and mosaic the raster into an existing raster in the database or to update an existing raster, then click the raster name from the dropdown list.

   Or click the second option and type the new raster name to import the raster into a new raster.

7. Click Next.

8. Click the first option to accept the default parameters.

9. Click Next. ▶

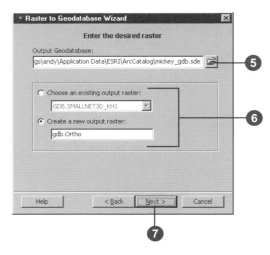

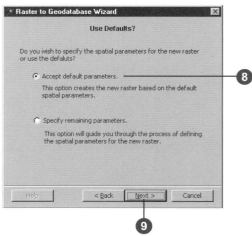

10. Review the options you specified for your data import operation. If you want to change something, you can go back through the wizard by clicking the Back button.

When satisfied with your options, click Finish to import the raster into the database.

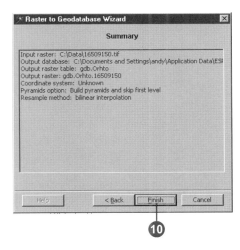

Defining custom values

1. Follow steps 1 through 8 for importing rasters using default values.

2. Click the second option to import the raster defining custom parameters.

3. Click Next.

4. Check the Append to existing data check box if you import to existing raster and want to mosaic the rasters.

5. Check the Build statistics check box if you want to build statistics for the raster in the database.

6. Click the Compression dropdown arrow and click none for no compression or click LZ77 to compress the raster.

7. Type the tile width and tile height if you want to change them.

8. Click the first option if you don't want to build pyramids after importing the raster into database. Or click the second option to build pyramids and skip the first level for the raster imported into database. Or click the third option to build pyramids and not skip the first level. ▶

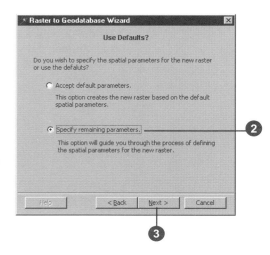

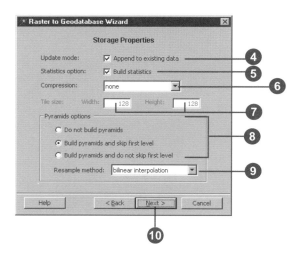

9. If you choose build pyramids, click the resample method from the dropdown list.

10. Click Next.

11. Review the summary of the coordinate system that will be used.

12. If you are importing the raster into existing table, skip to 15.

    Click Change if you want to modify any of the raster's coordinate system parameters.

13. Follow steps 11 to 14 for importing a shapefile with custom values.

14. Click Next.

15. Click Use configuration keyword if you want to create the table using a custom storage keyword and type the keyword you want to use.

16. Click Next. ▶

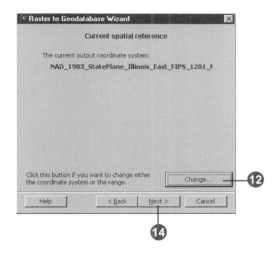

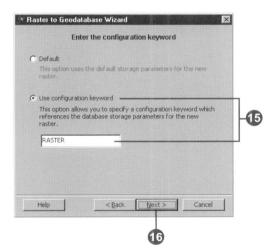

17. Review the summary of the parameters used to import the raster.

To change a parameter, navigate back to the appropriate panel by clicking Back.

18. Click Finish.

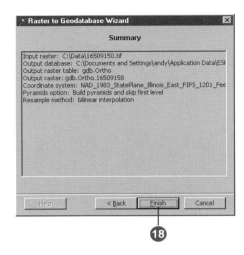

Copying geodatabase data

ArcCatalog contains tools that directly move and copy data between geodatabases while preserving object identity, subtypes, relationships, network connectivity, and so on. Using these tools, you can copy entire feature datasets or individual feature classes between geodatabases.

When the data is copied, the copy has all the behavior of the original, and any attribute domains it referenced in the original geodatabase are also copied along with the feature class or table. If the feature class or table participates in a relationship class, then that relationship class, along with the feature class or table it is related to through that relationship class, is also copied. As an example, if you copy a feature class with feature-linked annotation, the feature-linked annotation class is automatically copied along with the feature class.

If you are copying a feature class into an existing feature dataset, either in the same geodatabase or in another geodatabase, then the ►

1. In the ArcCatalog tree, right-click the dataset you want to copy. This can be a feature dataset, feature class, or table.

2. Click Copy.

3. Right-click the geodatabase to which you want to copy the data.

4. Click Paste. ►

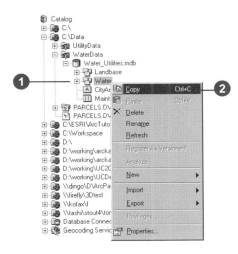

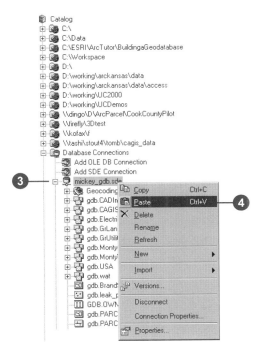

spatial reference of the feature class and the feature dataset must match. If the spatial references do not match, you will not be able to copy the data.

You can move feature classes and relationship classes in and out of, or between, feature datasets in the same geodatabase by dragging and dropping them in ArcCatalog. When moving a feature class into a feature dataset, the feature class and the feature dataset must have the same spatial reference.

If you copy or move a network feature class, all the feature classes that participate in the network, and the geometric network itself, are also copied or moved along with the feature class.

When you Paste data into a geodatabase, a dialog box appears. It allows you to see exactly what data is being copied, resolve any name conflicts, and assign configuration keywords for each object being copied.

A dialog box appears that indicates what data is being copied. Any name conflicts are automatically resolved and highlighted in red.

5. Type over the target name to change any of the resolved names.

6. If you want to use a configuration keyword for any of the objects being copied, type it under Config. Keyword for that object.

7. Click OK.

   A progress indicator will appear to indicate the progress of the data copy.

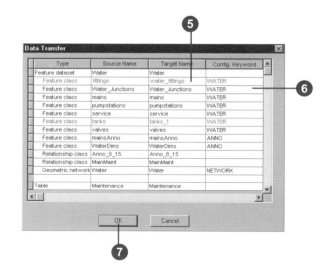

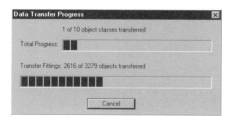

A progress indicator will appear to indicate the progress of the data copy.

Loading data into existing simple feature classes and tables

The tools and wizards for importing coverages, shapefiles, and INFO and dBASE tables into the geodatabase require that each shapefile and coverage feature class be loaded into a new feature class and each INFO and dBASE table be loaded into a new table. The feature class or table cannot exist before you begin the import process.

Because an existing feature class or table can be in any number of states, a separate data-loading tool is required to load data from a shapefile, coverage feature class, INFO table, or dBASE table into an existing geodatabase feature class or table.

In the case of nonversioned simple data, an edit session is not required to insert new features or rows into the table or feature class. Once loaded, all data is visible in all versions of the database. This data loading operation is performed with the Simple Data Loader Wizard in ArcCatalog. ▶

1. In the ArcCatalog tree, right-click the table or feature class that you want to load data into and click Load Data.

2. Click Next on the introductory panel.

3. Browse to the input feature class or table.

4. Click Add to add the table of feature class to the list of source data.

5. Repeat steps 3 and 4 until you have specified all of the source data.

6. Click Next. ▶

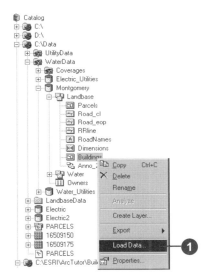

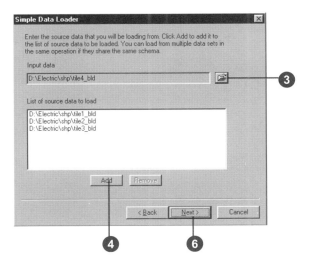

The wizard will allow you to specify a number of source tables and feature classes, provided their schema match. It also allows you to specify which fields in the input data are loaded into which fields of the target feature class or table.

The wizard also gives you the option to load all of the source data into a specific *subtype* of the target and lets you specify a query to limit the features loaded.

This wizard will only be available if the target stores simple, nonversioned data. For loading objects into nonsimple or versioned data using the Object Loader, see Chapter 12, 'Editing your geodatabase'.

Tip

The subtype field

If you choose to load data into a specific subtype, you will not be able to match a field from the source data to the subtype field in the target data; the subtype field will be automatically populated.

7. If you do not want to load data into a specific subtype of the target, click the first option, then skip to step 10.

8. If you want to load data into a specific subtype, click the second option.

9. Click the dropdown arrow and click the subtype into which you want to load the source data.

10. Click Next.

11. To match a source field with a field in the target feature class or table, click the dropdown arrow in the Matching Source Field list and click the field from the source data that you want to match to the target field.

    If you do not want data from a field in the source data to be loaded into the target data, leave the Matching Source Field blank.

12. Repeat step 11 until you have matched all the fields you want to load from your source data to the target fields.

13. Click Next. ►

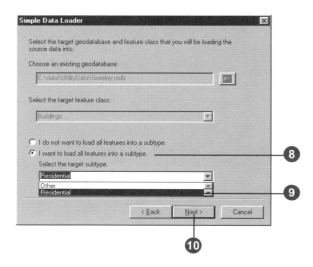

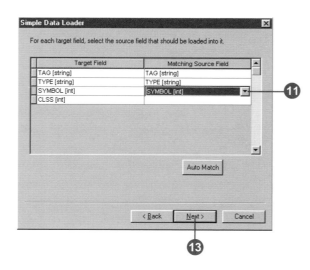

Tip

Source data

When matching fields, you can browse the source data's field values to help you correctly match the source and target fields.

Tip

Relationships

If the feature class or table you want to load data into participates in a relationship class with messaging (such as a composite relationship class), the data is considered nonsimple and the Load Data command will be grayed out.

To load data into these feature classes and tables, you can either delete the relationship, or use the Object Loader.

See Chapter 6, 'Relationship classes', and Chapter 12, 'Editing your geodatabase', to learn more about relationship classes and the Object Loader.

See Also

To learn more about using the Query Builder to query your data, see Using ArcMap.

14. Click the first option and skip to step 19 if you want to load all of the source data.

15. Click the second option if you want to limit the features from the source data loaded into the target using an attribute query.

16. Click Query Builder to open the Query Builder dialog box.

17. Use the query builder to create a query to limit the features or rows from the source data that are going to be loaded into the target.

18. Click OK.

19. Click Next. ▶

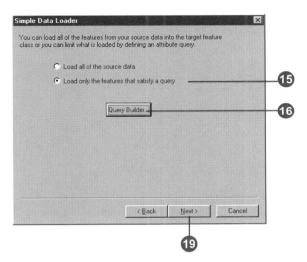

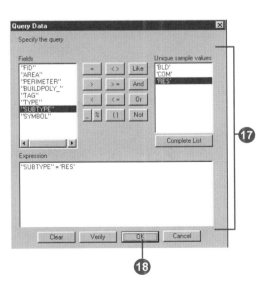

20. Review the options you have specified for loading your data. If you want to change something, you can go back through the wizard by clicking Back.

21. When satisfied with your options, click Finish to load your data.

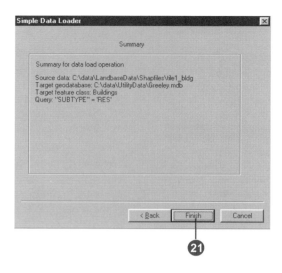

Registering ArcSDE layers and tables with the geodatabase

ArcSDE 8 layers and tables that were created with applications that were not written using the ArcInfo 8 COM components are not registered with the geodatabase system tables. These ArcSDE layers and tables still appear in the ArcCatalog tree as feature classes and tables; however, they cannot have subtypes, default values, or domains or participate in relationships and geometric networks.

You can use ArcCatalog to register these ArcSDE layers and tables with the geodatabase. This operation will promote ArcSDE layers to geodatabase feature classes and ArcSDE tables to geodatabase object classes.

Tip

ObjectID column

If the ArcSDE layer or table is not already registered with the ArcSDE table registry, then this operation will register it and add an ObjectID field to the table. This field will be called OID for tables and FID for layers. If a field called OID or FID already exists on the table or layer, then another name is chosen.

1. In the ArcCatalog tree, right-click the table or feature class you want to register with the geodatabase.

2. Click Register with Geodatabase.

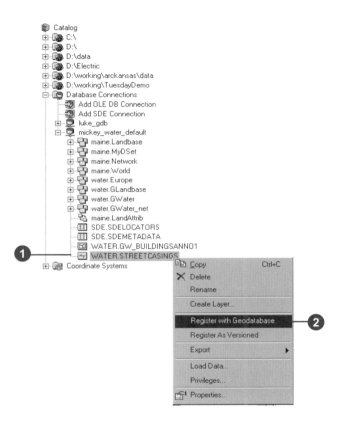

Analyzing geodatabase data

If your geodatabase is stored in a DBMS, such as Oracle, SQL Server, DB2, or Informix, the Analyze command in ArcCatalog can be used to update the RDBMS statistics on your datasets. The Analyze command updates the statistics of business tables, feature tables, and delta tables, along with the statistics on those tables' indexes.

Tip

Analyzing feature datasets

When you analyze a feature dataset, all of the feature classes contained in that feature dataset are analyzed. If the feature dataset contains a geometric network, then the network tables are also analyzed.

See Also

For more information about which of your feature classes' tables should be analyzed and when, see Chapter 13, 'Working with a versioned geodatabase'.

1. In the ArcCatalog tree, right-click the dataset you want to Analyze. This can be a feature dataset, feature class, or table.

2. Click Analyze.

3. Check those tables you want analyzed.

4. Click OK.

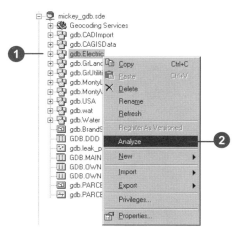

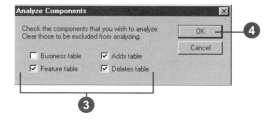

Subtypes and attribute domains

5

IN THIS CHAPTER

- **What are subtypes and attribute domains?**

- **Working with attribute domain properties**

- **Browsing the attribute domains of a geodatabase**

- **Creating new attribute domains**

- **Modifying and deleting attribute domains**

- **Associating default values and domains with tables and feature classes**

- **Creating subtypes**

- **Modifying and deleting subtypes**

When maintaining your geographic *database*, care must be taken to ensure that when you edit the *data* you do so in a manner that is consistent with the system you are modeling. The *geodatabase* together with the ArcMap Editor provides mechanisms to ensure that the data you store in your geodatabase is consistent with your data model.

The geodatabase has several data integrity and data management capabilities including *validation rules*, *subtypes*, *relationship classes*, *geometric networks*, and so on. Each of these capabilities and how you use them are covered throughout this book. This chapter describes the subtypes and the first class of validation rules—*attribute domains*.

What are subtypes and attribute domains?

The geodatabase stores *objects*. These objects may represent nonspatial real-world entities such as manufacturers or they may represent spatial objects such as pipes in a water network. Objects in the geodatabase are stored in *feature classes* (spatial) and *tables* (nonspatial).

The objects stored in a feature class or table are organized into subtypes and can have a set of validation rules associated with them. The ArcInfo system uses these validation rules to help you maintain a geodatabase that contains valid objects. This chapter outlines how to create subtypes for your feature classes and tables and how to establish *attribute* validation rules for the objects stored in them.

Subtypes and validation rules

Tables and feature classes store objects of the same type—that is, that have the same *behavior* and attributes. For example, a feature class called WaterMains may store pressurized water mains. All water mains behave like water mains and have the attributes ReferenceID, Depth, Material, GroundSurfaceType, Size, and PressureRating.

You may be modeling a system in which water mains can only be made of cast iron, ductile iron, or copper. They can only be a certain size based on their type, and there are four possible ground surface types. When you create a new water main object using ArcMap, you may want these attributes to take on certain default values. Similarly, when ArcMap changes values for an attribute, you may want to make sure that only legal or valid values are inserted into the attributes for that lateral.

When an object in a feature class or table has valid values for all of its attributes, it is considered to be a valid object. If one of its attributes contains an invalid value, it is considered to be an invalid object. When designing your geodatabase, you can specify what makes any particular object in a feature class or table a valid feature by establishing one or more validation rules.

There are four broad classes of validation rules: attribute domains, *connectivity rules*, relationship rules, and custom rules. Connectivity rules are discussed further in Chapter 9, 'Geometric networks'; relationship rules are discussed further in Chapter 6, 'Defining relationship classes'; and custom rules are discussed further in *Exploring ArcObjects*. This chapter focuses on attribute domains.

Attribute domains are a rule that describes the legal values of a *field* type. Multiple feature classes and tables can share attribute domains stored in the database. Therefore, the water mains feature class can use the same domain for the ground surface type field as can a feature class that stores water laterals.

Although all objects in a feature class or table must have the same behavior and attributes, not all objects must share the same attribute domains. For example, it may be true in a water network that only transmission water mains can have a pressure between 40 and 100 psi, while distribution water mains can have a pressure of between 50 and 75 psi. You would use an attribute domain to enforce this restriction. To implement this kind of validation rule, you do not have to create separate feature classes for transmission and distribution water mains, but you would want to distinguish these types of water mains from each other to establish a separate set of domains and default values. You can do this using subtypes.

Feature classes and tables can contain subtypes. An object's subtype is determined by its subtype code value. The subtype code is stored in an integer field in the feature class or table. Each subtype can have its own set of default values and attribute domains for a given field and (as described in Chapter 9, 'Geometric networks') different connectivity rules associated with it.

Features in the geodatabase have behavior, geometry, a system-managed unique identifier, attributes, and can also have subtypes. Different subtypes can have different sets of valid values for their attributes.

When to use subtypes

An important geodatabase design issue arises when you must decide where it is appropriate to use subtypes and where additional feature classes are required. When you are trying to distinguish objects by their default values, attribute domains, connectivity rules, and relationship rules, it is recommended that you create separate subtypes for a single feature class or table.

When you want to distinguish objects based on different behaviors, attributes, access privileges, or whether the objects are multiversioned (see Chapter 13, 'Working with a versioned geodatabase'), you must create additional feature classes.

Attribute domains

Attribute domains are used to *constrain* the values allowed in any particular attribute for a table, feature class, or subtype. Each feature class or table has a set of attribute domains that apply to different attributes and/or subtypes. These attribute domains can be shared across feature classes and tables in a geodatabase.

There are two different types of attribute domains: range domains and coded value domains. Each domain has a name, a description, and a specific attribute type to which it can apply.

A range domain specifies a valid range of values for a numeric attribute. In the water mains example, you could have subtypes transmission, distribution, and bypass water mains. Distribution water mains can have a pressure between 50 and 75 psi. For a distribution water main object to be valid, its pressure value must be some value between 50 and 75 psi. A range domain specifies this range of values.

A coded value domain can apply to any type of attribute—text, numeric, date, and so on. Coded value domains specify a valid set of values for an attribute. The GroundSurfaceType field on the water mains feature class stores the type of material above the water main. Water mains may be buried under different types of surfaces: pavement, gravel, sand, or none (for exposed water mains). The coded value domain includes both the actual value that is stored in the database (for example, 1 for pavement) and a more user-friendly description of what that value actually means.

When editing your feature classes and tables, you can enforce these rules by validating individual or sets of objects. For details on editing objects with subtypes and validation rules, see Chapter 12, 'Editing your geodatabase'.

Attribute domains do not have a property that allows or disallows *null values* in an associated field. When a table or feature class is created in a geodatabase, each field has a property that indicates whether or not null values are permissible values. The database itself will not permit null values to be inserted into columns that do not support them. Therefore, all domains treat null values as valid values.

Splitting and merging features

Often when editing data, a single *feature* is split into two features, or two separate features are combined, or merged, into a single feature. For example, in a land base database, a land parcel may be split into two separate land parcels due to rezoning. Similar zoning changes may require two adjacent parcels to be merged into a single parcel.

While the result of these types of edit operations on the feature's geometry is easily predictable, their effects on the attribute values are not. The behavior of an attribute's values when a feature is split is controlled by its *split policy*. When two features are merged, an attribute's value is controlled by its *merge policy*.

Each attribute domain has both a split policy and a merge policy. When a feature is split or merged, the ArcInfo system looks to these policies to determine what values the resulting feature(s) have for a particular attribute.

An attribute for any given table, feature class, or subtype can have one of three split policies that control the value of an attribute in the output object:

- Default value: the attribute of the two resulting features takes on the default value for the attribute of the given feature class or subtype.

- Duplicate: the attribute of the two resulting features takes on a copy of the original object's attribute value.

- Geometry ratio: the attribute of resulting features is a ratio of the original feature's value. The ratio is based on the ratio in which the original geometry is divided. If the geometry is divided equally, each new feature's attribute gets half of the value of the original object's attribute. Geometry ratio policies only apply to domains for numeric field types.

In the parcel example, when a parcel is split, the Area attribute is automatically assigned as a property of the resulting geometry. The value for Owner is copied to the new objects (in this database, splitting a parcel does not affect its ownership). The PropertyTax is calculated based on the area, or size, of a parcel. To calculate the PropertyTax for each of the new objects, the split policy divides the PropertyTax of the original parcel proportionally among the new features according to their area.

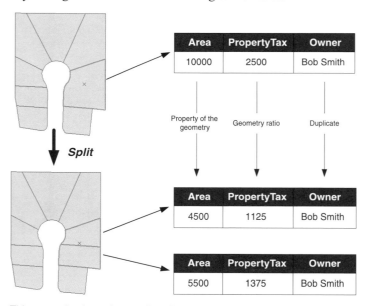

This example shows how split policies can be applied to attributes of a parcel object.

When two features are merged into a single feature, merge policies control the value of attributes in the new feature. An attribute for any given feature class or subtype can have one of three merge policies:

- Default value: the attribute of the resulting feature takes on the default value for the attribute of the given feature class or subtype. This is the only merge policy that applies to nonnumeric fields and coded value domains.

- Sum values: the attribute of the resulting feature takes on the sum of the values from the original features' attribute.

- Geometry weighted: the attribute of the resulting feature is the weighted average of the values of the attribute from the original features. This average is based on the original features' geometry.

In the parcel example, when two parcels are merged, the Area attribute is automatically assigned as a property of the resulting geometry. Owner is assigned its default value. As the PropertyTax for the merged feature is the sum of the original feature's PropertyTax, its merge policy is to sum the values.

This chapter shows you how to use ArcCatalog to create attribute domains for a geodatabase and how to create subtypes for a feature class or table. It then discusses how to create an attribute validation rule by associating an attribute domain to an attribute for a table, feature class, or subtype.

Schema locking

An exclusive lock is required on a feature class or table to modify its subtypes, default values, and attribute domains. For more information on exclusive locks and schema locking, see Chapter 3, 'Creating new items in a geodatabase'.

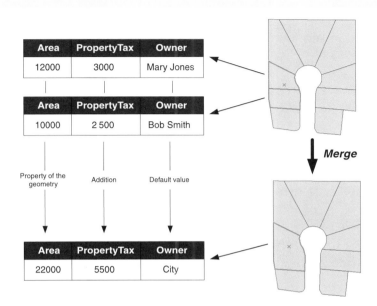

This example shows how merge policies can be applied to attributes of a Parcel object.

Working with attribute domain properties

The Domain Properties dialog box includes a list of all the domains that exist in a geodatabase. Each domain's name, description, properties, and valid set of values are displayed.

From this dialog box, you can also add, remove, and modify domains. An explanation of how to use this property page to manage your geodatabase's domains comes later in this chapter.

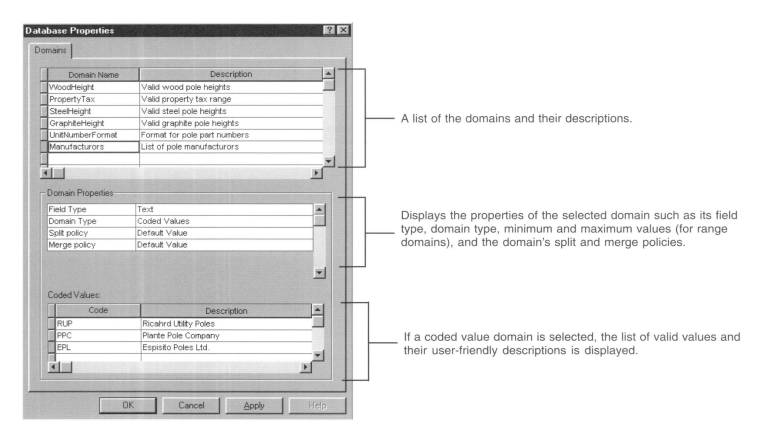

A list of the domains and their descriptions.

Displays the properties of the selected domain such as its field type, domain type, minimum and maximum values (for range domains), and the domain's split and merge policies.

If a coded value domain is selected, the list of valid values and their user-friendly descriptions is displayed.

Browsing the attribute domains of a geodatabase

Attribute domains are stored geodatabasewide. Once a user creates a new attribute domain, that user and all other users can view the properties of that domain and use the domain in a feature class or table.

Attribute domains are managed using the Domain properties dialog box. This dialog box can be displayed as part of the geodatabase's properties or from the feature class or table properties dialog box.

Attribute domains can be added, deleted, and modified with the Domain properties dialog box.

Browsing the domains of a personal geodatabase

1. In the ArcCatalog tree, right-click the personal geodatabase whose domains you want to browse.

2. Click Properties.

   The Attribute Domains properties dialog box appears.

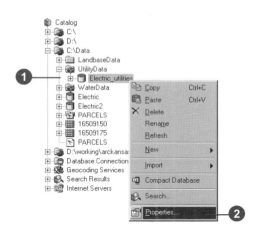

Browsing the domains of an ArcSDE geodatabase

1. In the ArcCatalog tree, right-click the ArcSDE connection for the geodatabase whose domains you want to browse.

2. Click Properties.

   The Attribute Domains properties dialog box appears.

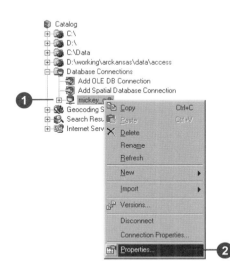

Browsing the attribute domains of a geodatabase from a feature class or table

1. In the ArcCatalog tree, right-click a feature class or table.

2. Click Properties.

3. Click the Subtypes tab.

4. Click Domains.

   The Attribute Domains properties dialog box appears.

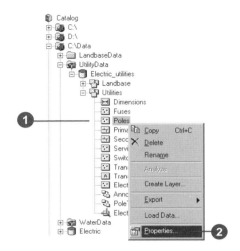

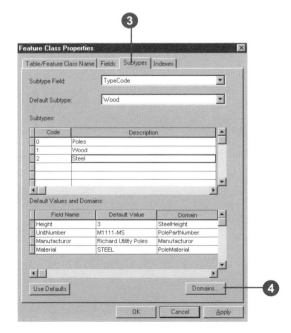

Creating new attribute domains

At any time in the life of a geodatabase, a new attribute domain can be created using the Domains properties dialog box.

You can create new attribute range domains, coded value domains, or string format domains.

See Also

To learn how to apply an attribute domain to a field in a feature class or table, see 'Associating default values and domains with tables and feature classes' in this chapter.

Creating a new attribute range domain

1. In the ArcCatalog tree, right-click the geodatabase and click Properties.

2. Click the first empty field under Domain Name and type a name for the new domain.

3. Press the Tab key or click the new domain's description field and type a description for the domain.

4. Click the field next to Field Type, click the dropdown arrow, and click the type of attribute field to which this domain will be applied. ▶

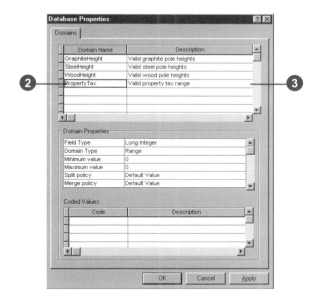

Range domains

Range domains can't be created for text fields. They can only be applied to numeric and date fields.

5. Click the field next to Domain Type, click the dropdown arrow, and click Range from the list of domain types.

6. Click the field with the minimum value for the range domain and type the minimum value. Do the same for the maximum value.

7. Click the field next to Split policy, click the dropdown arrow, and click the split policy for the new domain. Do the same for the merge policy.

8. Click Apply to create the new domain in the geodatabase or OK to create the domain and close the dialog box.

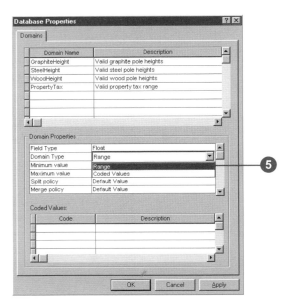

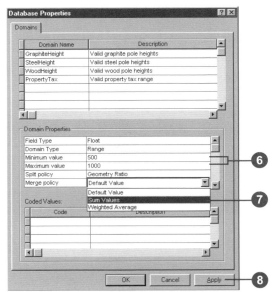

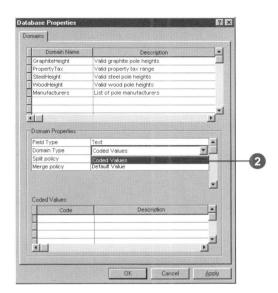

Tip

Coded value descriptions

When you add a new value to a domain's coded value list, you must also add a more user-friendly description. When you edit an attribute value for a field that has this domain, the user-friendly values appear in the ArcMap Editor. Descriptions help you select the right value.

Tip

Coded value split/merge policies

Coded value domains support only default value and duplicate split policies.

Coded value domains support the default value merge policy only.

Creating a new coded value domain

1. Follow steps 1 through 4 for creating a new attribute range domain.

2. Click the field next to Domain Type, click the dropdown arrow, and click Coded Values from the list of domain types.

3. Click the first empty field under Coded Values and type the first valid code.

4. Press the Tab key or click the new coded value's Description field. Type a user-friendly description for this coded value.

5. Repeat step 4 until all valid values and their descriptions have been typed.

6. Click the field next to Split policy, click the dropdown arrow, and click the split policy for the new domain. Do the same for the merge policy.

7. Click Apply to create the new domain in the geodatabase or OK to create the domain and close the dialog box.

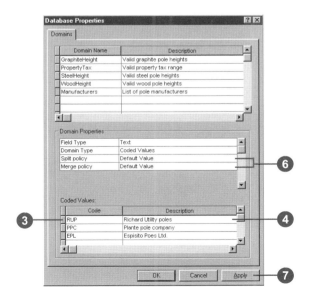

Modifying and deleting attribute domains

The Domains property page can be used to delete an attribute domain from the geodatabase or to modify an existing domain.

When a new domain is created, the owner of that domain—that is, the user who created it—is recorded. Only the owner of an attribute domain can delete or modify it.

As you will see later in this chapter, domains can be associated with particular fields for a feature class or table or for a subtype of a feature class or table. While a domain is being used by a table or feature class, it cannot be deleted or modified.

You can modify domains simply by selecting them on the domains properties dialog box and changing anything from their name to their type and valid values. This is done in the same manner as when you create a new domain.

1. In the ArcCatalog tree, right-click the geodatabase and click Properties.

2. Click the domain you want to delete by clicking the left-hand tab in the grid.

3. Press the Delete key.

4. Click Apply to delete the domain from the geodatabase or OK to delete the domain and close the dialog box.

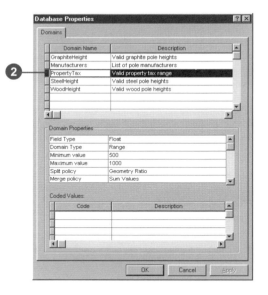

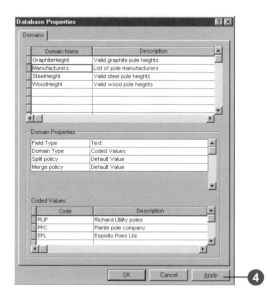

Associating default values and domains with tables and feature classes

Once you have created an attribute domain, or domains, you can associate them and their default values with fields in a table or feature class. Once a domain is associated with a feature class or table, an attribute validation rule is created in the database.

The same attribute domain can be associated with multiple fields of the same table, feature class, or subtype and can be associated with multiple fields in multiple tables and feature classes.

Tip

Subtypes

Not all of the objects in a table or feature class must have the same domains or default values applied to the same fields. To apply different domains and default values to the same field in a single table or feature class, you must create subtypes.

You'll learn how to create subtypes and associate domains and default values to a subtype's fields later in this chapter.

1. In the ArcCatalog tree, right-click the table or feature class with which you want to associate domains.

2. Click Properties.

3. Click the Fields tab.

4. Click the field for which you want to create a default value and associate a domain.

5. Click the field next to Default Value and type the default value.

6. If you don't want to associate a domain to the field, skip to step 9.

7. Click the field next to Domain, click the dropdown arrow, and click the domain you want to associate with the field.

   Only those domains that apply to the field type are displayed in the list.

8. Repeat steps 4 through 7 until you have associated default values and domains for all fields that you want to have these properties.

9. Click Apply.

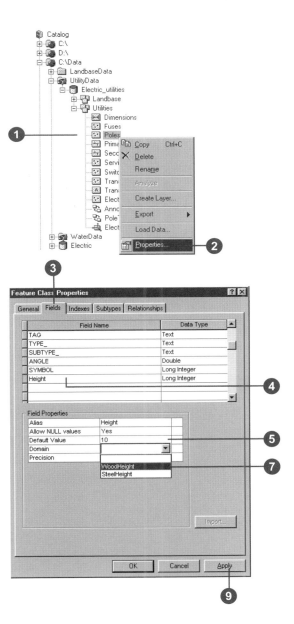

Creating subtypes

You can use ArcCatalog to add subtypes and to set default values and attribute domains for the fields of each subtype.

You can manage subtypes using the properties dialog box for each table or feature class. You can define the subtype field, add new subtypes, and remove or modify existing subtypes.

Creating new subtypes for a feature class or table

1. In the ArcCatalog tree, right-click the feature class or table to which you want to add subtypes.

2. Click Properties.

3. Click the Subtypes tab.

4. Click the dropdown arrow and click the subtype field from the list of available long integer and short integer fields. ▶

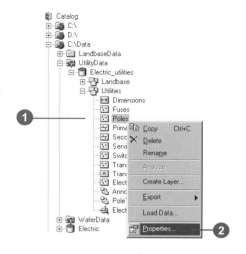

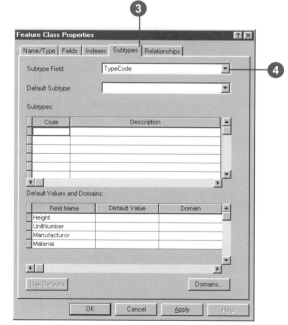

The default subtype

The default subtype serves two purposes. When you create a new subtype, click Use Defaults and the subtype will inherit all of the default values and domains for its fields from the default subtype. These can then be modified to meet the requirements for the new subtype. As you add additional subtypes, the default subtype can be changed at any time.

When you create a new feature in the feature class without specifying a subtype, it will automatically be assigned the default subtype.

5. To add a new subtype, click the first empty field under Code and type an integer value that will be the code for that subtype.

6. Press the Tab key or click the Description field and type a description for the subtype.

7. For each field, type a default value in the appropriate field in the table.

8. To associate an attribute domain with a field for the new subtype, click the Domain field, click the dropdown arrow, and click the domain from the list of domains.

   Only those domains that apply to the field type are displayed in the list.

9. To set this subtype as the default subtype, click the dropdown arrow and click it from the list of subtypes. ▶

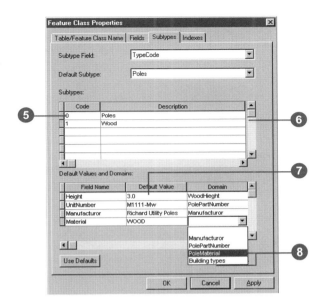

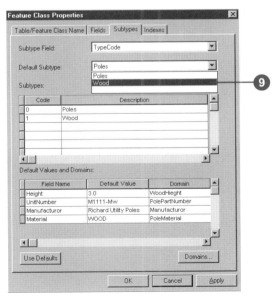

10. Repeat steps 5 through 8 to add additional subtypes. You can reset the default subtype at any time.

11. When adding a new subtype, click Use Defaults to have your new subtype take all of the default values and domains from the default subtype. You can then modify all or some of these.

12. When you are finished creating your subtypes and have selected the default subtype, click Apply to create the new subtypes in the geodatabase or OK to create the subtypes and close the dialog box.

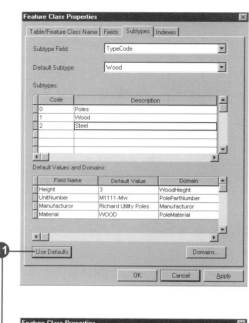

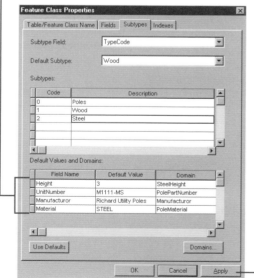

Modifying and deleting subtypes

Subtypes for a feature class or table can also be modified or deleted using the properties dialog box for the table or feature class. You can modify any aspect of a subtype including its description, its default values, and its domains. Modifying each aspect of a subtype is done the same way as creating a new subtype.

1. Follow steps 1 to 3 for adding subtypes.

2. Click the left-hand tab next to the subtype you want to delete.

3. Press the Delete key.

4. Click Apply to delete the subtype from the geodatabase or OK to delete the subtype and close the dialog box.

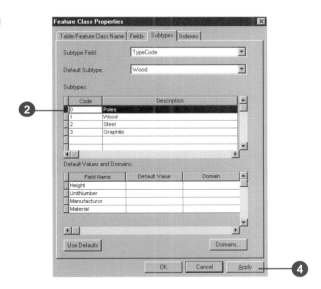

Defining relationship classes

6

IN THIS CHAPTER

- **What is a relationship class?**

- **Relationship classes in ArcCatalog and ArcMap**

- **Creating a simple relationship class**

- **Creating a composite relationship class**

- **Creating an attributed relationship class**

- **Creating relationship rules**

- **Managing relationship classes**

- **Exploring related objects in ArcMap**

- **Using related fields in ArcMap**

Objects in a real-world system often have particular associations with other objects in the database. These kinds of associations between objects in the *geodatabase* are called *relationships*. Relationships can exist between spatial objects (*features* in *feature classes*), nonspatial objects (rows in a *table*), or spatial and nonspatial objects. While spatial objects are stored in the geodatabase in feature classes and nonspatial objects are stored in tables, relationships are stored in *relationship classes*.

ArcCatalog contains tools to create, modify, and manage relationship classes in your geodatabase, while ArcMap provides tools to create, delete, and use relationships to find objects that are associated with other objects in the geodatabase. This chapter describes how to use ArcCatalog to manage these relationship classes and how to use relationships in ArcMap.

Chapter 12, 'Editing your geodatabase', discusses how to create and delete relationships.

What is a relationship class?

Objects in a real-world system, such as an electrical network or a parcel database, often have particular associations with other objects in the database. For example, in an electrical network, poles support transformers. In a parcel *database*, a parcel will have one or many owners.

These kinds of associations between objects in the geodatabase are called relationships. Relationships can exist between spatial objects (features in feature classes), nonspatial objects (rows in a table), or spatial and nonspatial objects. While spatial objects are stored in the geodatabase in feature classes and nonspatial objects are stored in tables, relationships are stored in relationship classes.

To store relationships between electric transformers and poles, you must create a relationship class. If in your geodatabase, transformers also have relationships to transformer attribute objects, then a second relationship class is required to store those relationships.

The anatomy of a relationship

Like any association, relationships have particular characteristics. One obvious characteristic is the notion of cardinality. Cardinality describes how many objects of type A are related to an object of type B. In the transformer–pole example, a single pole may support more than one transformer, but a transformer can only be mounted on a single pole. The relationship between transformers and poles is one to many: one pole, which is an object in the origin class of the relationship, to many transformers, which is an object in the destination class of the relationship.

In general, relationships can have one-to-one, one-to-many, many-to-one, and many-to-many cardinalities. As you will see later in this chapter, certain types of relationships support certain cardinalities, and you can control cardinalities for any relationship class when you define relationship rules.

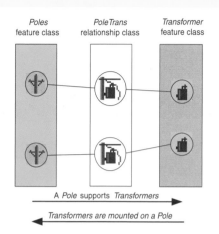

A relationship is an association between two or more objects in two feature classes or tables in a geodatabase. Relationships are stored in relationship classes.

A relationship between two objects is maintained through *attribute* values for key *fields*. In the transformer–pole example, the unit number of the pole that supports the transformer may be included in the attributes of the transformer object. This is an embedded foreign key. It tells us what object in the pole feature class this particular transformer is related to.

Relationship classes can have attributes. Any relationship class that has attributes must be stored as a table in the database and have a pair of foreign keys, each referencing the origin and destination classes of the relationship class. In this case, each relationship is stored as a row in the relationship classes table. Similarly, any many-to-many relationship classes require a table in the database to store at least the foreign keys.

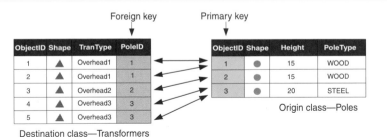

Foreign key   Primary key

ObjectID	Shape	TranType	PoleID
1	▲	Overhead1	1
2	▲	Overhead1	1
3	▲	Overhead2	2
4	▲	Overhead3	3
5	▲	Overhead3	3

Destination class—Transformers

ObjectID	Shape	Height	PoleType
1	●	15	WOOD
2	●	15	WOOD
3	●	20	STEEL

Origin class—Poles

A relationship between two objects is maintained through attribute values for key fields.

Relationship classes have path labels. Forward and backward path labels describe the relationship when navigating from one object to another. The forward path label describes the relationship navigated from the origin class to the destination class; the backward path label describes the relationship when navigating from the destination to the origin class. In the transformer–pole example, when navigating from the transformer to the pole, the relationship path label may be "is mounted on". The same relationship when navigated from the pole to the transformer may have a path label of "supports".

Relationship classes can also be used to propagate standard messages between related objects. Messaging is the mechanism that objects related to each other use to notify each other when they change. For example, in a relationship between poles and transformers, when the pole is deleted, it sends a message to its related transformer objects informing them it was deleted. As transformers can't exist without a pole to support them, these transformer objects could respond to the message by deleting themselves.

The geodatabase supports two kinds of relationships: simple or peer-to-peer relationships and composite relationships. Each is discussed briefly below.

Simple relationships

Simple, or peer-to-peer relationships, are relationships between two or more objects in the database that exist independently of each other.

In a relationship between object A and object B, if object A is deleted from the database, object B continues to exist. For example, in a railroad network you may have railroad crossings that have one or more related signal lamps. However, a railroad crossing can exist without a signal lamp, and signal lamps exist on the railroad network where there are no railroad crossings.

Simple relationships can have one-to-one, one-to-many, or many-to-many cardinality.

Composite relationships

The geodatabase also supports the notion of a composite relationship, where the lifetime of one object controls the lifetime of its related objects. The pole–transformer relationship is an example of a composite relationship. Once a pole is deleted, a delete message is sent to its related transformers, which are deleted from the transformer's feature class.

Composite relationships are always one to many but can be constrained to be one to one using relationship rules.

Attributed relationship classes

One-to-one and one-to-many relationship classes do not require a new table in the geodatabase to be created to store the relationships. However, many-to-many relationship classes do require a new table in the database to store the foreign keys from the origin and destination classes to make the relationship. This table can also have other fields to store attributes of the relationship itself that are not attributes of either the origin or destination class.

For example, in a parcel database you may have a relationship class between parcels and owners, where owners "own" parcels and parcels are "owned by" owners. An attribute of that relationship may be the percentage of ownership.

One-to-one and one-to-many relationship classes may also have attributes; in this case, a table would be created to store the relationships.

Relationship rules

Relationship classes can have an associated set of relationship rules. Relationship rules control which object *subtypes* from the origin class can be related to which object subtypes in the destination class. They can also be used to specify a valid cardinality range for all permissible subtype pairs.

For example, the subtype wood pole may be able to support from 0 to 3 transformers, whereas the subtype steel pole may support 0 to 5 transformers. In the first case, the cardinality range would be 0–3; in the second case, it would be 0–5.

You can establish a relationship between two or more objects in the geodatabase by using tools available in ArcMap. Once the relationship is established, use ArcMap tools to navigate it and symbolize features based on attributes in a related object. You can find all objects that have a relationship with a particular object through any particular relationship class.

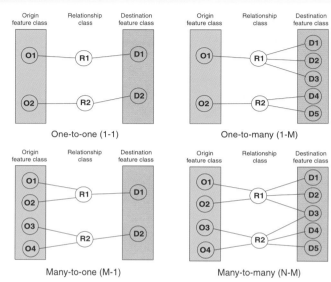

Relationships have cardinality. Cardinality describes how many objects of type A are associated with objects of type B. Relationships can have 1-1, 1-M, M-1, or N-M cardinality.

Performance considerations

When editing composite features, edits such as move, rotate, and delete also affect the related objects through the relationship class. There is a cost when navigating these relationships. The cost is minimized when indexes are maintained for the primary and foreign keys for the relationship class. When a new relationship class is created with ArcCatalog, the primary and foreign keys are automatically indexed if they do not already have indexes.

It is important to realize that when a feature class participates in a relationship class, that feature class utilizes messaging. When editing that feature class in ArcMap, the related class must be opened so it can respond to the message—either by moving, deleting itself, or implementing some custom behavior. If the related class is not already in the map you are working with, it will automatically be opened to respond to the message, then closed. Each time it responds to a message, it will need to be reopened.

In general, when working with a class in ArcMap, have all related classes also in the map. This way, the related classes are opened once when they are added to ArcMap. If they are not in the map, then each time you access related objects the class must be opened.

With many ArcInfo coverage data models, the feature-attribute table contained as few items as possible, and many of the attributes for a feature class were contained in a related table. This can be done with geodatabase feature classes; however, navigating a relationship in the geodatabase is a more costly operation than navigating relates in INFO. In the INFO environment, it was common to store the symbology for a feature in an external related table called a lookup table. This can still be done in the geodatabase using relationship classes; however, for large data, symbolizing this way will be slow, even with indexes on the primary and foreign keys. Try to keep attributes for symbolization on the feature class's table. For performance considerations, it is recommended that symbology information be stored in the feature class itself.

Schema locking

An exclusive lock is required when modifying a relationship class's relationship rules or when renaming or deleting a relationship class. An exclusive lock can only be aquired for a relationship class if the feature classes or tables that participate in the relationship can also be locked. Therefore, if a user has an exclusive or shared lock on either the origin, destination, or both classes, the properties of the relationship class cannot be edited.

For more information on exclusive locks and schema locking, see Chapter 3, 'Creating new items in a geodatabase'.

Relationship classes in ArcCatalog and ArcMap

Relationship classes in ArcCatalog

In ArcCatalog, you can automatically work with a relationship class in a geodatabase. Relationship classes can exist both inside feature datasets and at the root level of the geodatabase.

When you look at a particular relationship class in the ArcCatalog tree, it is not immediately evident how feature classes or tables are related. However, by examining the properties of both the feature class or table and the relationship class, you can achieve a clear picture of this.

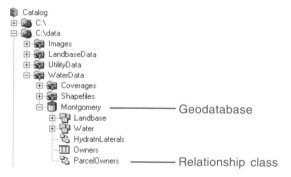

Relationship classes appear in the ArcCatalog tree either at the geodatabase level or inside a feature dataset.

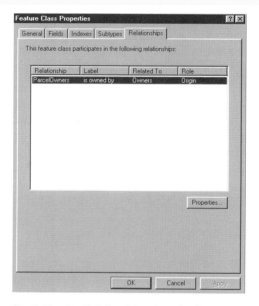

By clicking the Relationship tab on the Properties dialog box for a feature class or table, you can view what relationship classes the feature class or table participates in along with what role the feature class or table plays within the relationship class. To get more details about the relationship class, click the Properties button.

In the Feature Class Properties or Table Properties dialog box, the Relationships tab displays the relationship classes, if any, in which a feature class or table participates. For each relationship class, the Catalog tree displays the path label, the other feature class or table, and its role in the relationship. You can click Properties to view the properties for the selected relationship class.

The properties dialog box for each relationship class—whether opened from the Feature Class Properties or Table Properties dialog box tree—contains more detailed information about the

relationship class. It also lets you establish relationship rules. The procedure for creating and modifying relationship rules is discussed later in this chapter.

ArcCatalog also contains various tools to create, delete, and manage relationship classes. The tools will also be discussed in more detail in this chapter.

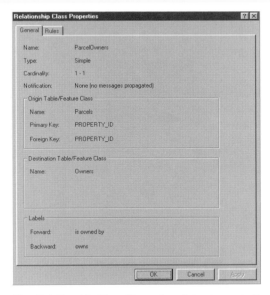

The Relationship Class Properties dialog box, whether opened from the feature class or table property page, contains detailed information about the relationship class.

Relationship classes in ArcMap

Once you have established a relationship class between feature classes or tables, you can use these relationships in ArcMap. For example, when you identify a feature in your map, you can see all of the objects related to that feature. When working with tables, you can open another table containing its related objects.

You may want to use fields on a related table or feature class to symbolize or label your map. Once you have added a feature class to your map that participates in a relationship class, you can do this by establishing a join between the feature class and its related feature class or table. You can use these joined fields like you use other fields in your feature *layer*.

For more information on maps, feature layers, symbolizing, and labeling your features, see *Using ArcMap*.

There are also a number of tools in ArcMap for editing relationships and related objects. For example, when you select a feature, you can edit the properties of its related objects. You can also use ArcMap to add new relationships and delete existing relationships. For more information on editing relationships, see Chapter 12, 'Editing your geodatabase'.

Creating a simple relationship class

You can create new relationship classes between any feature class or table within your geodatabase using tools in ArcCatalog. These tools can be used to create simple, composite, and attributed relationship classes.

Relationship classes appear in the Catalog tree, and you can inspect their properties as well as the relationships for any particular feature class.

The example in this task shows how to create a relationship class between a feature class that stores parcel objects and a table that stores owner objects. It is a simple, nonattributed relationship. In the database, a parcel can be owned by a single owner, and an owner can own a single parcel, so it is a one-to-one (1-1) relationship.

1. In the ArcCatalog tree, right-click the geodatabase or feature dataset in which you want to create the new relationship class.

2. Point to New.

3. Click Relationship Class.

4. Type the name for the new relationship class.

5. Click the origin table or feature class.

6. Click the destination table or feature class.

7. Click Next.

8. Click Simple (peer-to-peer) relationship.

9. Click Next. ▶

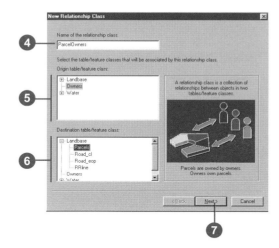

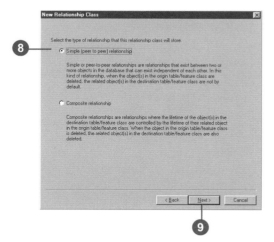

N-M relationship classes

Many-to-many (N-M) relationship classes require the relationship class to have its own table in the database. You can optionally add attributes to this table, or you can allow the ArcInfo system to manage the schema of the table for you.

Notification direction

By default, the notification direction for a simple relationship is None.

10. Type the forward and backward path labels.

11. Click the message notification direction.

12. Click Next.

13. Click the first cardinality option. In this example, an owner can own a single parcel and a parcel can be owned by a single owner, so this is a one-to-one (1-1) relationship.

14. Click Next. ▶

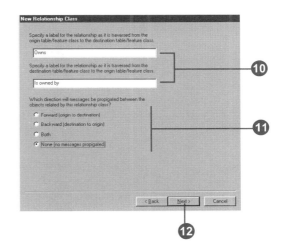

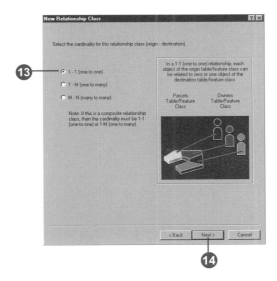

See Also

In this first example, you are not adding attributes to your relationship class, although any relationship class can have attributes. For more information on how to create an attributed relationship class, see 'Creating an attributed relationship class' in this chapter.

15. In this example, the relationship class does not require attributes. Click No.

16. Click Next.

17. Click the dropdown arrow to see a list of fields from the origin table or feature class. Click the primary key for this feature class or table.

18. Click the dropdown arrow to see a list of fields from the destination table or feature class. Only those fields that are the same type as selected in step 17 are displayed. Click the foreign key that refers to the primary key selected in step 17.

19. Click Next. ▶

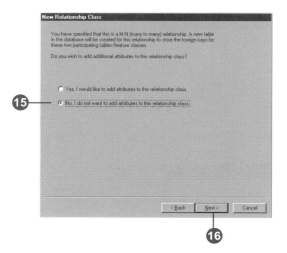

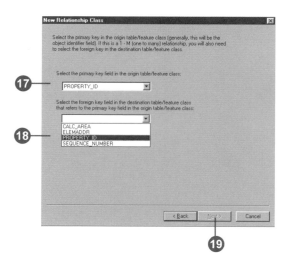

20. Review the options you specified for your new relationship class. If you want to change something, you can go back through the wizard by clicking Back.

21. Click Finish to create the new relationship class when satisfied with your options.

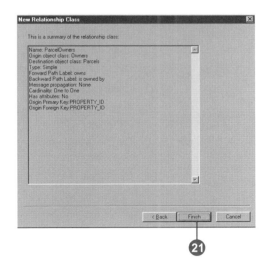

Creating a composite relationship class

You can use a wizard to create a composite relationship class. The example in this subtask shows how to create a relationship class between a feature class that stores transformer banks and one that stores transformer units.

The existence of a transformer unit in the database is dependent on the presence of a transformer bank. This relationship class is a composite relationship with the transformer bank as the origin feature class.

The relationship will be nonattributed; composite relationships are by definition one-to-many (1-M) relationships.

Creating a composite relationship involves many of the same steps used in the task for creating a simple relationship. The steps outlined here reflect the differences between the two tasks including using different origin and destination classes.

1. Follow steps 1 through 7 for creating a simple relationship class.

2. Click Composite relationship.

3. Click Next.

4. Type the forward and backward path labels.

5. Click the message notification direction.

6. Click Next. ►

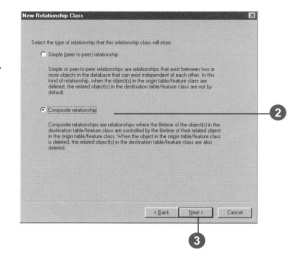

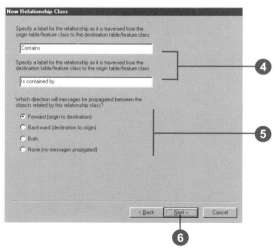

One-to-many relationships

When creating a one-to-many relationship, whether simple or composite, the one side must be the origin class. The many side must always be the destination class.

7. Click the first cardinality option. A composite relationship is, by definition, a 1-M or 1-1 relationship.

8. Click Next.

9. In this example, the relationship class does not require attributes. Click No.

10. Click Next. ▶

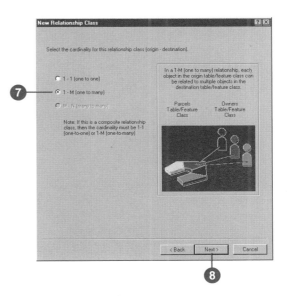

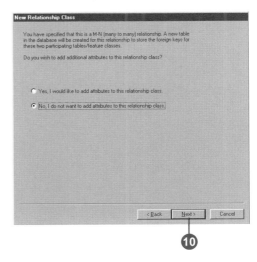

11. Click the dropdown arrow to see a list of fields from the origin table or feature class. Click the primary key for this feature class or table.

12. Click the dropdown arrow to see a list of fields in the destination table or feature class. Only those fields that are the same type as selected in step 10 are displayed. Click the foreign key that refers to the primary key selected in step 10.

13. Click Next.

14. Review the options you specified for your new relationship class. If you want to change something, you can go back through the wizard by clicking Back.

15. Click Finish to create the new relationship class when satisfied with your options.

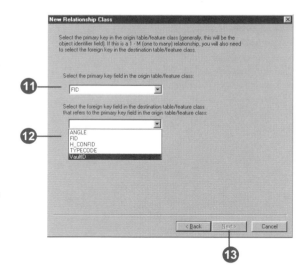

Creating an attributed relationship class

Any relationship class—whether simple or composite, of any particular cardinality—can have attributes. Relationship classes with attributes are stored in a table in the database. This table contains at least the foreign key to the origin feature class or table and the foreign key to the destination feature class or table.

An attributed relationship can also contain any other attribute. The example in this subtask shows how to create a simple relationship between a feature class that stores water laterals and a feature class that stores hydrants.

Water lateral objects have their own attributes, and hydrant objects have their own attributes. The relationship class in this example describes which water laterals feed which hydrants. Because you want to store some kind of information about that relationship, such as the type of riser connecting the two, you can store this information as attributes in the relationship class.

1. Follow steps 1 through 14 for creating a simple relationship class or steps 1 through 7 for creating a composite relationship class.

2. Click the first option to add attributes to the relationship class.

3. Click Next.

4. To add a field, click the next row in the Field Name column and type a name.

5. Click in the Data Type field next to the new field's name, then click its data type.

6. Set the new field's properties in the property sheet.

7. Repeat steps 4 through 6 until all the relationship class's fields have been defined.

8. Click Next. ▶

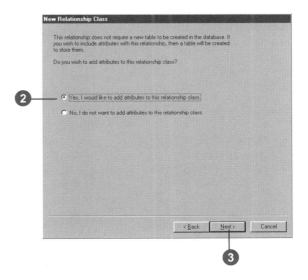

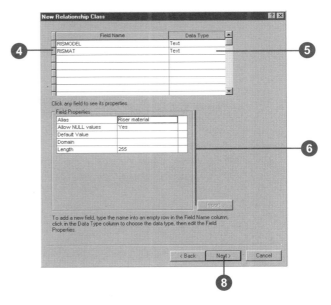

Relationship table foreign keys

In an attributed relationship, the relationship table must have fields that act as foreign keys to the origin and destination feature classes or tables.

These foreign keys relate to the primary keys on the origin and destination feature class or table primary keys.

9. Click the dropdown arrow to see a list of fields from the origin table or feature class. Click the primary key for this feature class or table.

10. Type the name of the foreign key field for the origin table or feature class.

11. Click the dropdown arrow to see a list of fields from the destination table or feature class. Click the primary key for this feature class or table.

12. Type the name of the foreign key field for the destination table or feature class.

13. Click Next.

14. Review the options you specified for your new relationship class. If you want to change something, you can go back through the wizard by clicking Back.

15. Click Finish to create the new relationship class when satisfied with your options.

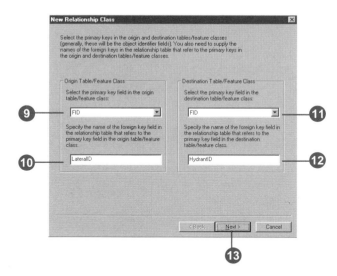

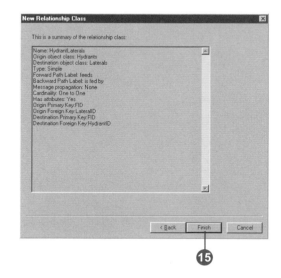

Creating relationship rules

Relationship rules let you restrict the type of objects in the origin feature class or table that can be related to a certain kind of object in the destination feature class or table.

Relationship classes are created with very general cardinalities such as one to many and many to many. In a real system, however, relationship cardinalities are more specific.

In this task, a relationship rule is being created between the hydrant laterals subtype on the water laterals feature class and the hydrants feature class. This rule says that it is valid for hydrants to be fed by hydrant laterals. Using the cardinality properties, you can specify exactly how many hydrants can be related to each hydrant lateral. In this example, it is invalid for a hydrant lateral not to feed a hydrant, and it is also invalid for a hydrant lateral to feed more than one hydrant. Therefore, the minimum and maximum cardinality will be 1.

1. Right-click the relationship class in the Catalog tree.

2. Click Properties.

3. Click the Rules tab.

4. If your origin class has subtypes, click the subtype that you want to associate with a relationship rule. If the origin class has no subtypes, the relationship rule will apply to all features.

5. If the destination class has subtypes, check the subtype that you want to make relatable to the selected subtype in the origin class. If the destination class has no subtypes, the relationship rule will apply to all features. ►

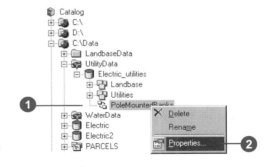

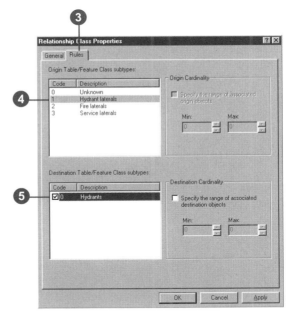

If one or both sides of the relationship class is a many, you can limit the specific range of cardinality. In this example, the origin side of the relationship is a 1, so you cannot modify its range. However, the destination side is a many, so you can modify its range.

6. Check the check box to specify the range of destination objects per related origin objects.

7. Click the up and down arrows to increase or decrease the minimum and maximum number of related destination objects.

8. Repeat steps 4 through 7 until you have specified all of the relationship rules for this relationship class. Click OK or Apply to create the rules in the database.

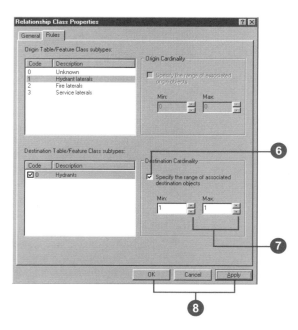

Managing relationship classes

Once created, a relationship class cannot be modified. You can only add, delete, or modify its rules.

Relationship classes can be deleted and renamed using ArcCatalog. Relationship classes are deleted and renamed in the same manner as any other object in the database.

Tip

Deleting the origin or destination relationship class

When you delete a feature class or table in ArcCatalog, if that feature class or table participates in a relationship class, the relationship class is also deleted.

Tip

Registering as versioned

If you register either the origin or destination class as versioned in ArcCatalog, then both the relationship class and the class that it is related to are also registered as versioned.

To learn more about versioning, see Chapter 13, 'Working with a versioned geodatabase'.

Renaming a relationship class

1. Right-click the relationship class that you want to rename.
2. Click Rename.
3. Type the new name and press Enter.

Deleting a relationship class

1. Right-click the relationship class you want to delete.
2. Click Delete.

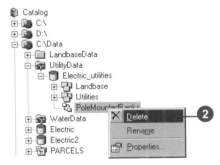

Exploring related objects in ArcMap

In ArcMap, you can explore what objects are related to any particular object in your geodatabase. When identifying features, the Identify Results dialog box allows you to navigate to a feature's related objects. When working with tables, you can navigate to a table of related objects.

Tip

Stacked relationships

If the related object that you navigate to in the Identify Results dialog box has objects related to it through other relationships, you can continue to navigate to those related objects.

Exploring the related objects of a feature

1. In ArcMap, click the Identify tool.

2. In the Identify Results dialog box, click the Layers dropdown arrow and click the layer in your map whose features you want to identify.

3. Click the feature on the map.

4. Double-click the feature in the left panel of the Identify Results dialog box.

5. Double-click the relationship path label.

   The related objects are listed below the path label.

6. Click the related object whose properties you want to explore.

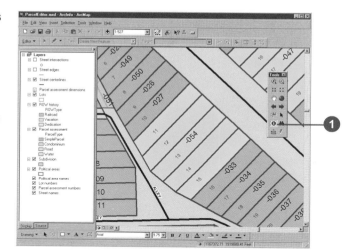

See Also

If you are not already familiar with how to add data to your map, please refer to Using ArcMap.

See Also

For more information on how to select records in a table, see Using ArcMap.

Exploring the related objects of an object in a table

1. On the ArcMap table of contents, click the Source tab.

2. Right-click to open the table that contains the objects whose related objects you want to explore.

3. Select the objects whose related objects you want to explore.

4. Click Options, point to Related Tables, and click the path label for the relationship. ▶

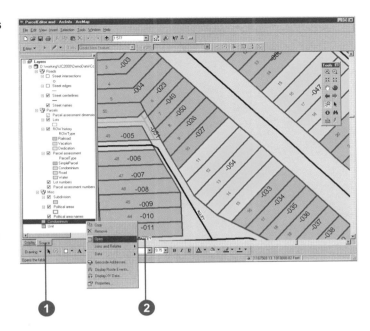

A new table dialog box opens for the related table.

5. Click Show Selected to display only those objects related to the selected objects in the first table.

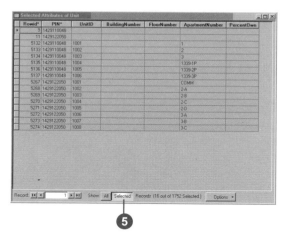

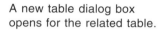

Using related fields in ArcMap

In order for fields from a related object to be used for symbolizing and labeling, you must create a join between the feature class and its related feature class or table. Once you have created this join, the fields from the related feature class or table are added to your feature layer. You can use these fields for labeling, symbolizing, and querying your features.

See Also

ArcMap has tools for editing relationships. To read more about relationships and editing in ArcMap, see Chapter 12, 'Editing your geodatabase'.

See Also

If are not already familiar with how to add data to your map, please refer to Using ArcMap.

1. Right-click the feature layer in the ArcMap table of contents.

2. Point to Joins and Relates and click Join.

3. Click the Join options dropdown arrow and click Join data based on a predefined relationship class. ▶

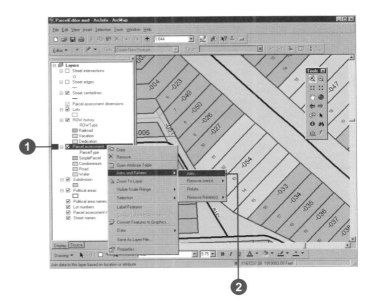

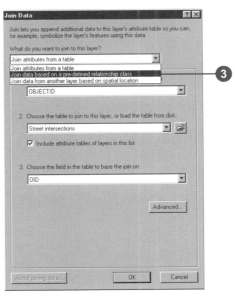

1-M and N-M relationships

If the relationship class is 1-M or N-M, each feature can have multiple related objects. In this case, the attributes of the first related object are joined to the feature.

See Also

For more information about joins and using joined data in ArcMap, see Using ArcMap.

4. Click the dropdown arrow to get a list of relationship classes, then click the relationship class.

5. Click OK.

   You can now use the related fields for labeling, symbolizing, and querying your features.

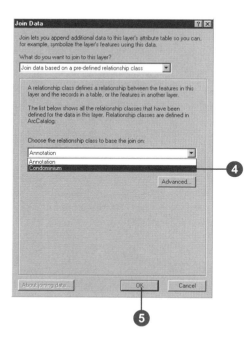

Managing annotation

7

IN THIS CHAPTER

- **Annotation in the geodatabase**

- **Annotation and ArcCatalog**

- **Creating annotation classes**

- **Converting labels to annotation**

- **Converting coverage annotation to geodatabase annotation**

In addition to geometry and location, geographic *features* may also have some descriptive text associated with them. For example, a *feature class* that contains streets may have text with the street's name associated with it. Annotation may also be a geographically located piece of text that exists independently of any other feature such as the name of a mountain range on a physical map.

Annotation refers either to the process of automating text placement or to the text itself. This chapter describes how to create annotation for your feature classes and how to convert annotation that you have in *coverages* to geodatabase annotation.

Annotation in the geodatabase

Annotation in the *geodatabase* is stored in special feature classes called annotation classes. Unlike points, lines, and polygons, which are stored as ESRI Simple Features, annotation is stored as ESRI Annotation Features.

What is geodatabase annotation?

Like other feature classes in the geodatabase, all features in an annotation class have a geographic location and *attributes* and can either be inside a *feature dataset* or a standalone annotation class. Each annotation feature has its own symbology including font, color, and so on. Annotation need not only be text—but can include shapes such as boxes and arrows, also.

There are two kinds of annotation in the geodatabase—feature-linked annotation and nonfeature-linked annotation. Nonfeature-linked annotation is geographically placed text strings that are not associated with features in the geodatabase. An example of nonfeature-linked annotation is the text on a map for a mountain range. No specific feature represents the mountain range, but it is an area you would want to mark.

Feature-linked annotation is associated with a specific feature in another feature class in the geodatabase. The text in feature-linked annotation reflects the value of a *field* or fields from the feature to which it is linked. The annotation feature class participates in a composite *relationship* with the feature class that it is annotating. The annotation feature class is the destination class in the relationship, while the feature class it is annotating is the origin class. This means the feature controls the location and lifetime of the annotation (see Chapter 6, 'Defining relationship classes').

As an example of feature-linked annotation, a hydrant in a water network may be annotated with its pressure, which is stored in a field in the feature class. In the same network, the water transmission mains may be annotated with their names.

As with other composite relationships, the origin feature controls the destination feature. Therefore, when the origin feature is moved or rotated, the linked annotation moves or rotates with it. When the origin feature is deleted from the *database*, its linked annotation feature is also deleted. If the value of a field from which the annotation text is derived changes in the feature, the annotation feature has special *behaviors* to respond to those changes and automatically update its text string.

In the water network example, a hydrant may be too close to a busy intersection and may need to be moved by 50 feet. When the hydrant is moved, its linked annotation moves with it. In the same network, the name of a transmission main may change. When the value in its name field is modified, the text stored in its linked annotation feature is automatically changed to reflect this.

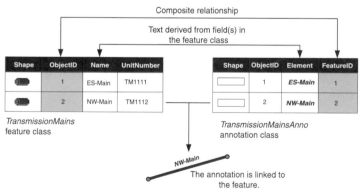

The link between a feature and its annotation is maintained through a composite relationship. Special behaviors in the ESRI Annotation Features allow you to derive an annotation feature's text from a field or combination of fields in the feature class.

Creating annotation

ArcCatalog contains tools to create both feature-linked and nonfeature-linked annotation classes. You have two options when creating feature-linked annotation classes. You can specify the field in the origin feature class on which to base your annotation. Alternatively, you can use more advanced labeling methods to derive the annotation from multiple fields and specify different labeling rules for different groups of features. Once you have created your annotation class, you can use ArcMap to populate it either on its linked feature or interactively with the drawing tools.

When a new feature is created in a feature class that has linked annotation, an annotation feature is automatically created in the annotation class and is linked to that feature. If the feature has default values associated with the fields from which the annotation is derived, its text will automatically be generated and placed.

Converting annotation

ArcMap also lets you convert labels and annotation stored in a coverage to a geodatabase annotation class. A geodatabase annotation class is created for the labels, and annotation features are inserted into it. When you convert labels to annotation, you can link them to the feature class that was used to create the labels, or you can convert them to nonfeature-linked annotation.

When converting coverage annotation, you must first create an annotation class in ArcCatalog. You must specify the symbology of the annotation that will be stored in the geodatabase annotation class by setting up symbology for the coverage annotation in ArcMap. You can specify a different annotation symbol for all the values of the $SYMBOL pseudo item in the coverage annotation class. During the process of setting the symbology, you should create test plots of your maps to ensure

that the symbology for the annotation is correct before you load the annotation features into the geodatabase. Once the symbology is set, you can then convert the coverage annotation class into the new annotation class.

Pseudo items in the coverage annotation class override the symbology properties you assign your annotation features in ArcMap. For example, if you set your annotation symbology in ArcMap to Arial 10 pt, but your $SIZE pseudo item for your features has a value of 14, then your text size will not be 10 pt in the resulting geodatabase annotation. Your text will not be 14 pt either since the value of $SIZE does not correspond to font size.

In general, when loading annotation from a coverage, to ensure that the symbology in the geodatabase annotation matches the symbology established in ArcMap for the coverage annotation layer, make sure your pseudo items have values of 0 in the coverage. To learn more about symbolizing map layers, see *Using ArcMap*.

You can make your coverage annotation feature-linked when you convert it to geodatabase annotation if you have an item in your coverage annotation's text attribute table (TAT) that relates to a field in the feature class you want to link them to. To create feature-linked annotation for annotations you import from a coverage, you must follow this sequence:

1. Create a new annotation class in ArcCatalog, linked to the feature class to which you want to link the annotations.

2. Add your coverage annotation class to ArcMap.

3. Adjust the text symbology, size, and scale. This should match the symbology you specified for the feature-linked annotation in ArcCatalog.

4. Use the Convert Coverage Annotation command in ArcMap, specifying the annotation class you created in step 1 as the target for the coverage annotation.

5. Use Structured Query Language (SQL) to link the features with the loaded annotation.

6. Register your data as versioned (if your geodatabase is stored in ArcSDE).

When creating annotation in an ArcSDE geodatabase by converting labels or converting coverage annotation, you should always try to convert the annotation before registering your data as versioned. Since the data is not versioned, all of the data will be loaded directly into the base tables, and a database compress will not be required. For more information about data loading strategies and their versioning impacts, see Chapter 4, 'Migrating existing data into a geodatabase'.

If you are creating annotation in an annotation class that is linked to a network feature class, you should create the annotation before building the geometric network. When features are snapped in the network building process, their geometry is modified at a level at which messages are not sent to linked annotation features to update themselves. So, after building the network, if a feature's geometry was changed in the snapping process, the feature and its linked annotation may be out of sync. To learn more about geometric networks, see Chapter 9, 'Geometric networks'.

Converting ArcSDE annotation to geodatabase annotation

Annotation stored in an ArcSDE layer that was not created with ArcGIS 8 can also be converted to geodatabase annotation. If you add the ArcSDE annotation layer to ArcMap, you can use the Convert Coverage Annotation command to convert ArcSDE annotation to geodatabase annotation in the same way that you convert coverage annotation to geodatabase annotation.

Performance considerations

Annotation features are both expensive to draw and expensive to retrieve from the database. When working with annotation classes, you should always apply a scale suppression so that the annotation features only draw when you are zoomed in enough to read their text. To learn more about applying scale suppression to map layers, see *Using ArcMap*.

Managing annotation classes

Annotation classes can be managed in the same way as other feature classes and tables. They can be renamed and deleted using ArcCatalog.

Similarly, the relationship class that links a feature-linked annotation class to its feature class is also managed like any other relationship class. For information on managing relationship classes, see Chapter 6, 'Defining relationship classes'.

It is important to note that if the relationship class that links the annotation to its features is deleted, the annotation will no longer be feature-linked but will behave as a nonfeature-linked annotation class. To learn how to re-create this relationship class, see Chapter 6, 'Defining relationship classes'.

Annotation and ArcCatalog

If you have access to an annotation class in a geodatabase, you can automatically acces it in ArcCatalog. Annotation classes can exist both inside feature datasets and at the root level of the geodatabase. Feature-linked annotation classes that are created inside a feature dataset must be linked to another feature class within the same dataset. Standalone nonfeature-linked annotation classes can be linked to other standalone feature classes.

A feature-linked annotation class can only be linked to a single feature class. However, a feature class can have any number of linked annotation classes.

When you look at the display of annotation classes in the ArcCatalog tree, it's not immediately evident which ones are feature-linked and which ones are nonfeature-linked. Moreover, simply looking at the Catalog tree won't tell you to which feature class the feature-linked annotation classes are linked to. However, examining the properties of the annotation class lets you determine if it is the destination class in a composite relationship. If it is, this indicates it is a feature-linked annotation class.

The Properties dialog box for a feature-linked annotation class displays special information about its default symbology, placement relative to the feature, and how its text is derived.

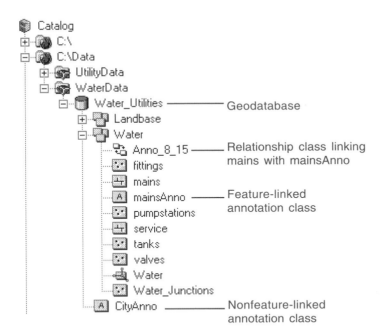

Annotation classes appear in ArcCatalog at either the database or feature dataset level. Feature-linked annotation classes also have a relationship class linking them to the feature class.

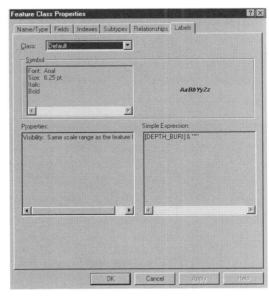

The Labels tab on the Properties dialog box displays feature-linked annotation information such as the default symbol and the expression used to derive the annotation text.

Creating annotation classes

Annotation is stored in annotation classes and can either be linked to features or not linked to features. Creating a nonfeature-linked annotation class is similar to creating a feature class that stores custom features.

When creating feature-linked annotation, however, you need additional information to create the composite relationship that links the annotation to the features. You must also describe how the annotation is derived based on the feature class's fields.

When you have created a feature-linked annotation class, you can use ArcMap to automatically populate the annotation class with annotation. This annotation is created and placed based on the features to which they are linked. The process of converting feature-linked annotation is described later in this chapter.

Nonfeature-linked annotation does not have a linked feature from which to derive its text and placement. You can still use ArcMap to interactively create and place annotations in the ▶

Creating a nonfeature-linked annotation class

1. Right-click the geodatabase or feature dataset in which you want to create the new annotation class.

2. Point to New.

3. Click Feature Class.

4. Type the name for the new annotation class. To create an alias for this annotation class, type the alias.

5. Click the second option to store custom objects in the feature class.

6. Click the dropdown arrow and click ESRI Annotation Feature.

7. Click Next. ▶

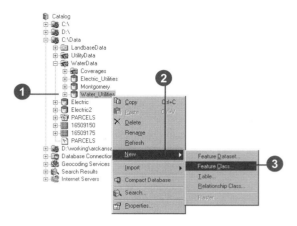

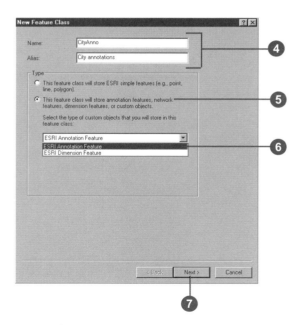

annotation class. For details on
how to create and edit individual annotation features, see
Chapter 12, 'Editing your
geodatabase'.

Tip

Required fields

*Annotation features require more
fields than simple features in order
to behave correctly. These
additional fields are Element and
FeatureID. Like any required field,
these cannot be modified or deleted.*

Tip

Reference scale

*The reference scale describes the
scale at which the annotation text is
displayed at the font size specified.
As you zoom out, the text will get
smaller, and as you zoom in, the
text will get larger.*

*The reference scale should always
be in the same units as the spatial
reference of the annotation class.*

8. Type the scale at which you
want the font size displayed.

9. Click the Map Units
dropdown arrow and click
the units for your data.

10. Click Next.

11. If you are creating this
annotation class inside a
feature dataset, follow
steps 6 through 14 for
creating a feature class in a
feature dataset in Chapter 3.
If you are creating a
standalone annotation class,
follow steps 2 through 12 for
creating a standalone
feature class in Chapter 3.

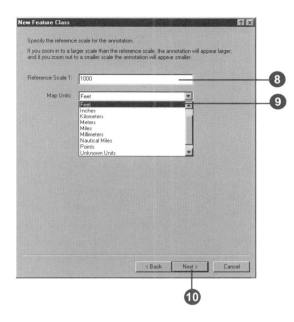

See Also

For a detailed discussion about labeling maps and the advanced labeling methods you can use, see Using ArcMap.

Creating a feature-linked annotation class

1. Right-click the geodatabase or feature dataset in which you want to create the new annotation class.

2. Point to New.

3. Click Feature Class.

4. Type a name for the new annotation class. To create an alias for this annotation class, type the alias.

5. Click the second option to store custom objects in the feature class.

6. Click the dropdown arrow and click ESRI Annotation Feature.

7. Check the check box to link the annotation to a feature class.

8. Click the dropdown arrow and click the feature class to which you want to link this annotation class.

9. Click Next. ►

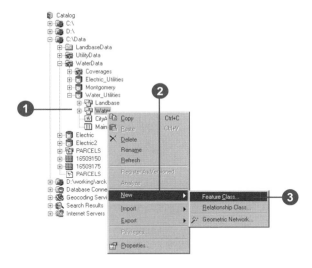

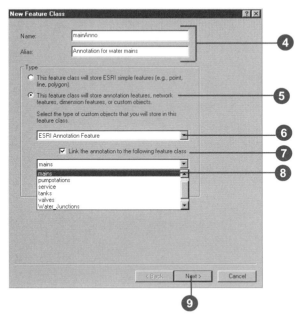

Relationship class

A relationship class will automatically be created to link the annotation class with the feature class it is annotating. The name of the relationship class will be Anno_<feature class ID>_ <annotation class ID>.

Reference scale

The reference scale describes the scale at which the annotation text is displayed at the font size specified. As you zoom out, the text will get smaller, and as you zoom in, the text will get larger.

The reference scale should always be in the same units as the spatial reference of the annotation class.

10. Click the Method dropdown arrow and click the method you want to use to create the annotation.

11. Click the dropdown arrow and click the field in the feature class from which you want to create the annotation text, or click Expression to create the annotation text from multiple fields.

12. Click Label Styles, Symbol, Label Placement Options, and Scale Range to set some more advanced parameters for your annotation.

13. Click Next.

14. Type the scale at which you want the font size displayed.

15. Click the Map Units dropdown arrow and click the units for your data.

16. Check the check box if you want an annotation feature to be created automatically every time a new feature is created in the feature you selected in step 8.

17. Click Next.

18. Follow steps 6 through 14 for creating a new feature class in a feature dataset in Chapter 3.

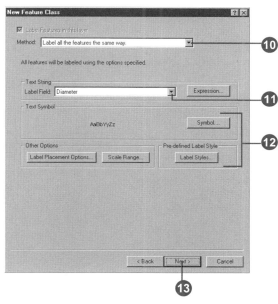

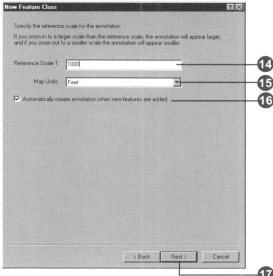

Generating feature-linked annotation

1. In ArcMap, click the Add Data button to add a feature class and its linked annotation class to your map.

2. Click the Select Features button to select the features for which you want to generate annotation. To create annotation for all of the features, select all of the features.

3. Right-click the feature class in the table of contents.

4. Point to Selection.

5. Click Annotate Selected Features.

6. Check the related annotation classes in which you want to store the annotation.

7. Check the check box to add unplaced labels to the overflow window.

8. Click OK.

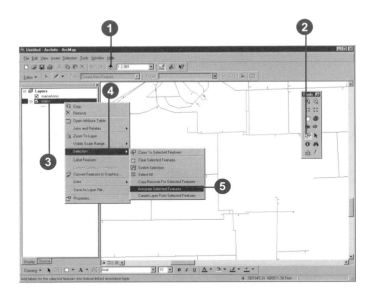

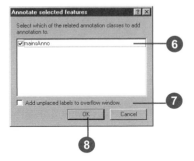

Converting labels to annotation

ArcMap lets you label features stored in a feature class. Once you have created labels, you can store them within the ArcMap document or as graphics in a database or convert them to annotation features.

If you choose to convert them to annotation features, ArcMap will create an annotation class to store the annotation. If you specify that you want them linked to the features, ArcMap will also create the relationship class to maintain the link.

The annotation class and relationship class are created inside the same feature dataset in which the feature class is stored or at the geodatabase level for a standalone feature class.

See Also

For a detailed discussion about labeling maps and the different advanced labeling methods you can use, see Using ArcMap.

1. In ArcMap, click the Add Data button to add the feature class for which you want to create annotation to your map.

2. Label the features in your map as described in *Using ArcMap*.

3. Right-click the feature class in the table of contents.

4. Click Convert Labels to Annotation. ▶

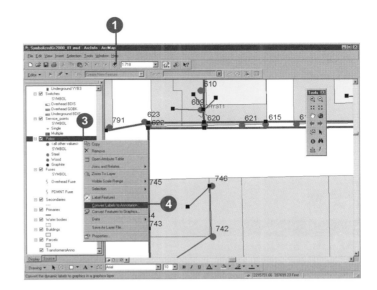

5. Click the feature class for which you want to save labels.

6. Click the third option.

7. Type a name for the new annotation class that will be created to store the annotation.

8. Click All features in the layer to create annotation for all of the features.

   Click Features displayed in the current extent to create annotation for features displayed in the current extent of the map.

   To create annotation for the selected features only, click Features currently selected.

9. Click Display overlapping labels in the overflow window to display annotation that cannot be created without overlapping others.

10. Click OK.

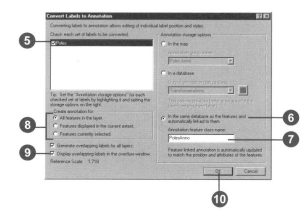

Converting coverage annotation to geodatabase annotation

ArcMap lets you convert annotation stored in a coverage annotation feature class to geodatabase annotation. You must convert the annotation into an existing annotation class in your geodatabase.

If the coverage annotation feature class contains attributes, when you convert it to geodatabase annotation, these attributes will automatically be converted, also.

The command to convert coverage annotation is available through the Customize dialog box in ArcMap.

See Also

For more information on how you can customize ArcMap, see Using ArcMap *and* Exploring ArcObjects.

Adding the Convert Coverage Annotation command to ArcMap

1. In ArcMap, click View, point to Toolbars, and click Customize.

2. Click the Commands tab in the Customize dialog box.

3. Click the Label category.

4. Drag the Convert Coverage Annotation command from the Commands list and drop it on the Standard toolbar.

   The command appears on the toolbar.

5. Click Close on the Customize dialog box.

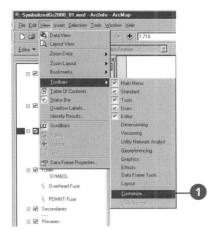

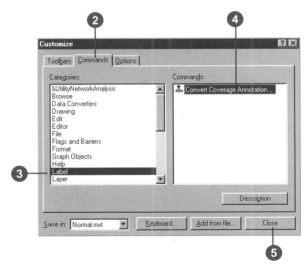

The command appears on the toolbar.

Annotation class

You can only convert coverage annotation into existing annotation classes. To create an annotation class, see the 'Creating a nonfeature-linked annotation class' and the 'Creating a feature-linked annotation class' tasks in this chapter.

Annotation storage

When storing geodatabase annotation in a DBMS, the row length is between 80 and 100 bytes.

Target annotation class

The annotation class into which you convert your coverage annotation must exist in the geodatabase before you perform the conversion. You can create a new annotation class using ArcCatalog.

For more information on using ArcMap to add feature classes to maps, symbolize annotation, and create plots, see Using ArcMap.

For more information on symbolizing layers in ArcMap, see Using ArcMap.

Converting coverage annotation

1. Add to your map the coverage annotation feature classes you want to convert.

2. Set the symbology for the coverage annotation feature class. Create test plots of your data to ensure the symbology is correct before continuing to step 3.

3. Click the Convert Coverage Annotation command.

4. Check the annotation classes that you want to convert. You can convert multiple coverage annotation classes into a single geodatabase annotation class.

5. Click the second option to convert the annotation into a database.

6. Click the Browse button to browse for an existing annotation class within your geodatabase.

7. Click Convert.

8. Click Close to close the Convert Coverage Annotation dialog box when your conversion is complete.

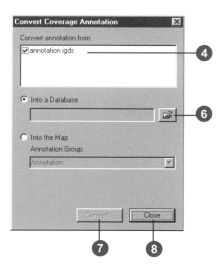

Dimensioning

8

IN THIS CHAPTER

- **Dimensions in the geodatabase**

- **Dimensions and ArcCatalog**

- **Creating dimension classes**

- **Creating and managing dimension styles**

For many applications, plotting a map that shows a feature's shape and some descriptive annotation isn't sufficient for showing precise measurements or distances. Dimensions are a special kind of map annotation for showing just that—specific lengths or distances. A dimension may indicate the length of a side of a building or land parcel, or it may indicate the distance between two features—for example, a fire hydrant and the corner of a building.

ArcInfo provides tools that allow you to store dimensions in your geodatabase. You can also create dimension styles to apply to your dimension features so they are consistent with your application standards. ArcInfo supports a number of dimension types and methods for creating dimensions. Dimensions can be created automatically from existing features, or you can use the rich set of construction tools available in ArcMap.

This chapter describes how to create *dimension feature classes* and *dimension styles*. Chapter 12, 'Editing your geodatabase', describes how to use the editing capabilities of ArcMap to create and modify *dimension features*.

Dimensions in the geodatabase

Dimensions are a special kind of map annotation that shows specific lengths or distances on a map. A dimension may indicate the length of a side of a building or land parcel, or it may indicate the distance between two features such as a fire hydrant and the corner of a building. Dimensions can be as simple as a piece of text with a leader line or as elaborate as the diagram shown opposite.

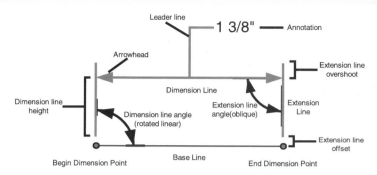

A dimension feature is composed of many parts. Each dimension feature can represent each part differently by using different symbology and placement rules. Dimensions may also display a subset of these parts.

Dimensions show specific lengths or distances on a map. For example, a dimension may indicate the length of a side of a building, the width of a street, or the length of a parcel.

A dimension feature is composed of several parts that may or may not be displayed, depending on the application. The following is an illustration of the anatomy of a dimension feature: Throughout this chapter, these parts will be referred to by the names in this diagram.

Dimension types

ArcInfo supports two types of dimensions: aligned and linear. *Aligned dimensions* run parallel to the baseline and represent the true distance between the begin and end dimension points.

Unlike aligned dimensions, *linear dimensions* don't represent the true distance between the begin and end dimension points. Linear dimensions can be vertical, horizontal, or rotated. A vertical dimension's line represents the vertical distance between the begin and end dimension points. A horizontal linear dimension's

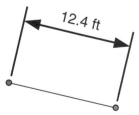

An aligned dimension has its dimension line parallel to the baseline, and its length represents the true distance between the begin and end dimension points.

line represents the horizontal distance between the begin and end dimension points. A rotated linear dimension is a dimension whose line is at some angle to the baseline and whose length represents the length of the dimension line itself, not the baseline.

All dimensions can be oriented either outward or inward. Outward dimensions have dimension lines pointing to the outside of the feature and represent the distance being measured. Inward dimensions have arrows pointing in from the outside of the

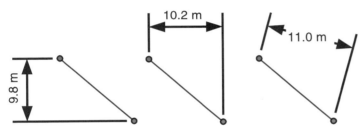

Linear dimensions may be vertical, horizontal, or rotated. In each case the dimension's length represents something other than the true distance between the begin and end dimension points.

feature and measure the distance between these two arrows. Whether a dimension is outward or inward is determined by the distance that the dimension represents and whether that distance on the map is sufficient to display all of the elements of the dimension between the extension lines.

You can create all of these types of dimensions using a number of tools and construction methods available while editing in ArcMap (see Chapter 12, 'Editing your geodatabase').

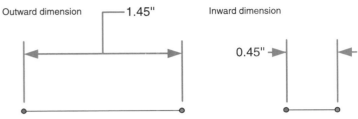

A dimension feature can be either outward or inward. Whether a dimension is inward or outward usually depends on its length and symbology.

Dimension feature classes

In the geodatabase, dimensions are stored in dimension feature classes. Like other feature classes in the geodatabase, all features in a dimension feature class have a geographic location and attributes and can either be inside or outside of a feature dataset. Like annotation features, dimension features are 'smart'; they act within the parameters of a predefined style and are able to determine their own symbology and how the dimension features themselves should be drawn.

Dimension styles

A collection of dimension styles is associated with a dimension feature class. A dimension feature's style describes its symbology, what parts of it are drawn, and how it is drawn. Every time you create a new dimension feature, it is assigned a particular style. All dimension features of a particular style share certain characteristics, some of which can be changed on a feature-by-feature basis. Styles for a dimension feature class are created, copied, and managed using ArcCatalog. Using the editing capabilities in ArcMap, styles are then assigned to individual dimension features.

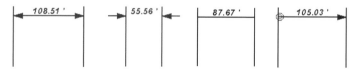

Dimension style examples. All dimension features are associated with a style. The style describes how the dimension feature is symbolized and the content of the dimension's text.

The following are the properties of a dimension feature that can be assigned based on a style:

- Dimension line symbol: the symbol used for the dimension line.

- Begin symbol: the symbol used for arrow at the end of the begin dimension line.

- End symbol: the symbol used for the arrow at the end of end dimension line.

- Dimension line display: indicates which of the dimension lines should be displayed—both, begin only, end only, or neither.

- Arrow display: indicates which dimension line arrows should be displayed—both, begin only, end only, or neither.

- Extension line symbol: the symbol used for the extension lines.

- Extension line display: indicates which of the extension lines should be displayed—both, begin only, end only, or neither.

- Offset and overshot: the distance that the extension lines are drawn from the dimension points and how far they extend beyond the dimension line, respectively.

- The value to display for the text: The actual string that is displayed for the dimension text. This may be derived from the feature itself or from a user-specified value or string. The value may be in map units or converted and displayed in other units.

- Arrow fit and text fit: The adjustment in the display of the arrows and text when the dimension's length is too short to show the arrows and text between the extension lines.

ArcInfo provides tools that allow you to store dimensions in your geodatabase. You can also create dimension styles to apply to your dimension features so they are consistent with your application standards. ArcInfo supports a number of dimension types and methods for creating dimensions. Dimensions can be created automatically from existing features, or you can use the rich set of construction tools available in the ArcMap editing environment.

Once a style is created in a dimension feature class, it cannot be modified. If you want to modify the properties of an existing dimension style, you must create a new style with the new properties. You can create new styles based on the properties of an existing style, or you can import styles from dimension feature classes in other geodatabases. For more information on ArcMap editing capabilities, see Chapter 12, 'Editing your geodatabase', and *Editing in ArcMap*.

Performance considerations

Dimensions are a type of map annotation. Like regular annotation, the information that dimension features convey is not very useful unless you are zoomed in to a scale in which you can visualize the dimension features clearly. Like annotation features, dimension features are costly to retrieve from the database and draw on the map display. When working with dimension feature classes in ArcMap, you should always apply scale suppression so that the dimension features only draw at scales in which they can be visualized. For more information on layers and scale suppression, see *Using ArcMap*.

Dimensions and ArcCatalog

In ArcCatalog, you can work with a dimension class in any accessible geodatabase. Dimension feature classes can exist both inside a feature dataset and at the root level of the geodatabase.

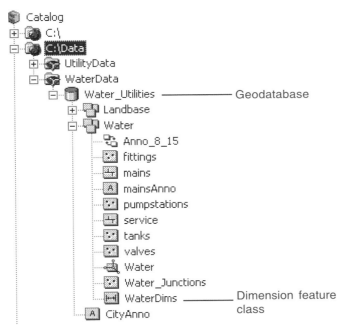

Dimension feature classes appear in ArcCatalog at either the database or feature dataset level.

You can use ArcCatalog to create and manage dimension feature classes. The Feature Class Properties dialog box displays special information about the dimension feature's styles and at what scale those styles are displayed with their specific symbol sizes. You can use the Feature Class Properties dialog box to create new styles, delete styles, and import dimension styles from other dimension feature classes.

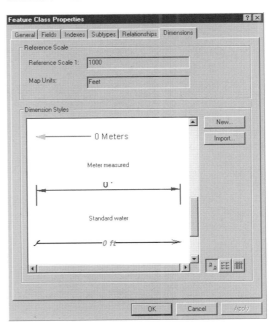

The Dimensions tab on the Feature Class Properties dialog box displays dimension information, such as the default style and the reference scale, for the dimension features.

Creating dimension feature classes

Dimension features are stored in dimension feature classes. When creating a dimension feature class, you must create at least one style for the dimension features you will create. You can specify the properties of the style yourself, import the style from another dimension feature class, or let the wizard create a default style for you.

Once you have created a dimension feature class, you can use ArcCatalog to create and import additional styles.

Creating a dimension feature class with the default style

1. Right-click the geodatabase or feature dataset in which you want to create the new dimension class.

2. Point to New.

3. Click Feature Class.

4. Type the name for the new dimension feature class. To create an alias for this feature class, type the alias.

5. Click the second option to store custom objects in the feature class.

6. Click the dropdown arrow and click ESRI Dimension Feature.

7. Click Next. ▶

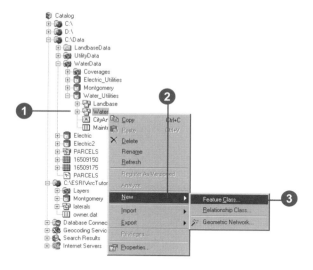

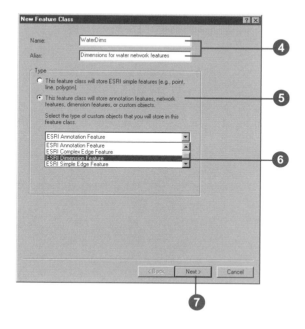

Reference scale

The reference scale describes the scale at which the symbology of the dimension feature is the same size as described in the style. For example, if your dimension text is Arial 12 pt and your reference scale is 1:1,000, then your text will be 12 pt at 1:1,000. As you zoom out from this scale, the text becomes smaller; and as you zoom in from this scale, the text becomes larger.

8. Type a reference scale. The reference scale units will automatically match the spatial reference's units if the dimension class is being created in a feature dataset. If this is a standalone dimension class, then you should pick the units for your spatial reference, which you will specify later in the wizard.

9. Click Next.

10. If you are creating this dimension feature class inside a feature dataset, follow steps 6 through 14 for creating a feature class in a feature dataset in Chapter 3, 'Creating new items in a geodatabase'. If you are creating a standalone dimension feature class, follow steps 2 through 19 for creating a standalone feature class in Chapter 3, 'Creating new items in a geodatabase'.

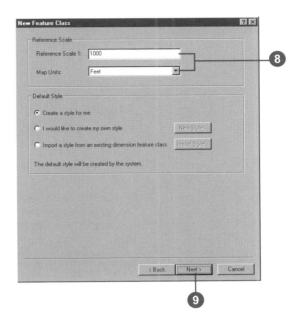

See Also

For more information on what each style element is and how to create styles, see 'Creating and managing dimension styles' later in this chapter.

Creating a dimension feature class with a custom style

1. Follow steps 1 through 8 for creating a dimension feature class with the default style.

2. Click the second option to create your own style.

3. Click New Style to open the style properties dialog box.

4. Use the Style Properties dialog box to set the characteristics of your dimension style.

5. Click OK.

6. Click Next.

7. If you are creating this dimension feature class inside a feature dataset, follow steps 6 through 14 for creating a feature class in a feature dataset in Chapter 3, 'Creating new items in a geodatabase'. If you are creating a standalone dimension feature class, follow steps 2 through 19 for creating a standalone feature class in Chapter 3, 'Creating new items in a geodatabase'.

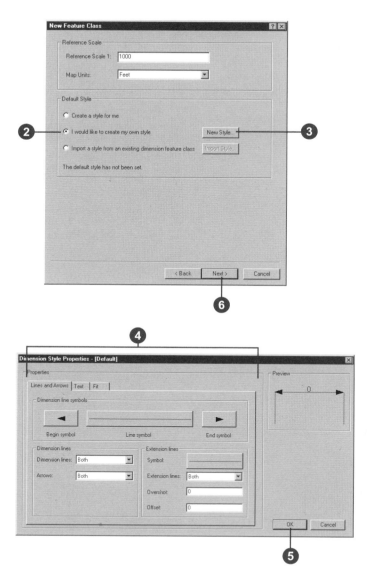

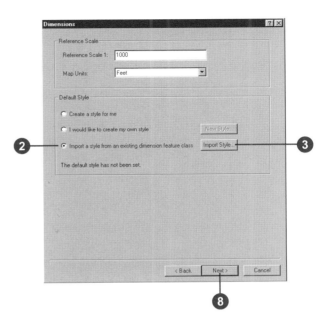

Tip

Browsing styles

You can browse styles by looking at an example dimension; or you can also click the View Options button at the bottom of the Import dialog box to switch the view to a list of the style names or the style names and style IDs.

Creating a dimension feature class by importing a style

1. Follow steps 1 through 8 for creating a dimension feature class with the default style.

2. Click the third option to import a style from an existing dimension feature class.

3. Click Import Style to browse for the dimension feature class from which you want to import a style. ▶

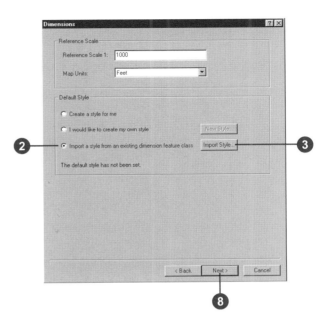

Tip

Importing more than one style

You can import multiple styles from multiple dimension classes by opening the property page for an existing dimension class. See 'Creating and managing dimension styles' later in this chapter.

4. Click the browse button to browse for a geodatabase. Once a geodatabase is selected, the dimension feature classes and feature datasets containing dimension feature classes are listed in the tree view.

5. Click the dimension feature class that contains the style you want to copy.

6. Click the dimension style that you want to copy.

7. Click OK.

8. Click Next.

9. If you are creating this dimension feature class inside a feature dataset, follow steps 6 through 14 for creating a feature class in a feature dataset in Chapter 3, 'Creating new items in a geodatabase'. If you are creating a standalone dimension feature class, follow steps 2 through 19 for creating a standalone feature class in Chapter 3, 'Creating new items in a geodatabase'.

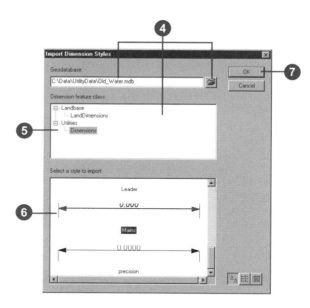

Creating and managing dimension styles

A dimension style describes how a dimension feature is displayed including its symbology, label font, and label text. Each dimension feature class has at least one style. Dimension features within the dimension feature class are associated with a particular style. All dimension features of a particular style have certain characteristics that are the same, while other characteristics can be overridden on a feature-by-feature basis.

Dimension styles are created and managed in ArcCatalog in the Feature Class Properties dialog box. You can create, delete, rename, and import dimension styles, and you can specify the default style for a dimension feature class.

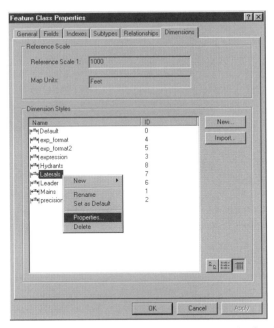

Dimension styles are created and managed in ArcCatalog in the Feature Class Properties dialog box.

The dimension styles properties are defined in the Dimension Style Property dialog box. This dialog box has three tabs: Lines and Arrows, Text, and Fit. The Lines and Arrows tab allows you to set the properties for the dimension lines, line arrows, and extension lines. The Text tab allows you to control the content of the dimension text as well as its symbology. The Fit tab allows you to define how the dimension and dimension text adjust when the dimension's length is too short to display the arrows and text between the extension lines. Each tab and property on the Dimension Style Properties dialog box is discussed in the following pages.

When creating dimension features and assigning them a style, some properties can be overridden on a feature-by-feature basis. The properties that you can override for each feature are:

- Dimension line display
- Dimension line arrow symbol display
- Dimension text value
- Extension line display

For more information on editing dimension features, see Chapter 12, 'Editing your geodatabase'.

Schema locking

An exclusive lock is required when creating, renaming, or deleting styles in a dimension feature class. For more information on schema locking, see Chapter 3, 'Creating new items in a geodatabase'.

Lines and Arrows tab

Symbology for the
extension lines.

Symbology for
the dimension
line and the
endpoints of the
dimension lines.

Setting for which
dimension lines
for dimension
features with this
style are
displayed.

Preview of the
dimension style.
The preview
updates as you
change elements
of the style.

Setting for which
extension lines
are displayed.

The extension
line overshot in
map units.

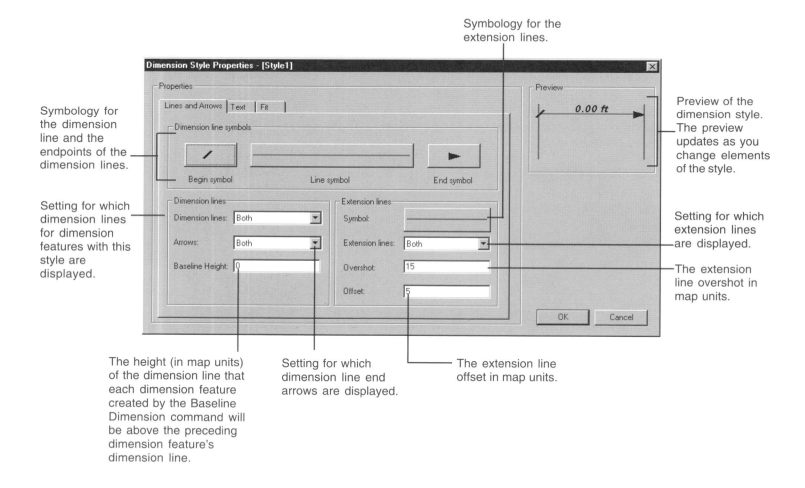

The height (in map units)
of the dimension line that
each dimension feature
created by the Baseline
Dimension command will
be above the preceding
dimension feature's
dimension line.

Setting for which
dimension line end
arrows are displayed.

The extension line
offset in map units.

Text tab

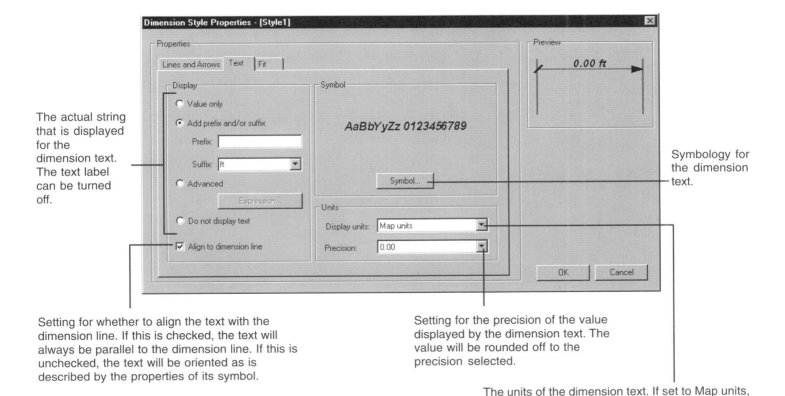

The actual string that is displayed for the dimension text. The text label can be turned off.

Symbology for the dimension text.

Setting for whether to align the text with the dimension line. If this is checked, the text will always be parallel to the dimension line. If this is unchecked, the text will be oriented as is described by the properties of its symbol.

Setting for the precision of the value displayed by the dimension text. The value will be rounded off to the precision selected.

The units of the dimension text. If set to Map units, the dimension text value will be in the units described by the dimension feature class's coordinate system. If a value other than map units is specified, then the dimension value will automatically be converted to those units at display time.

Fit tab

The behavior of the dimension when
its length is too short for the
dimension line arrows and the text
to fit between the extension lines.

Setting for how to resolve the case
where the dimension is too short for
the dimension text to fit between the
extension lines.

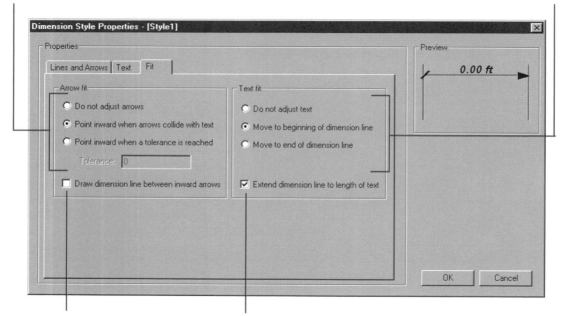

Setting for whether to draw the
dimension line between the arrows for
inward dimensions.

Setting for whether to extend the dimension
line to underline the dimension text when it
is moved to the outside of the dimension.

Creating a new dimension style

1. Right-click the dimension feature class.

2. Click Properties.

3. Click the Dimensions tab.

4. Click New. ▶

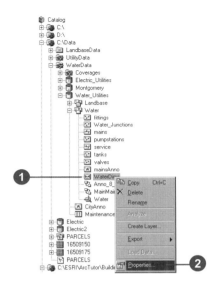

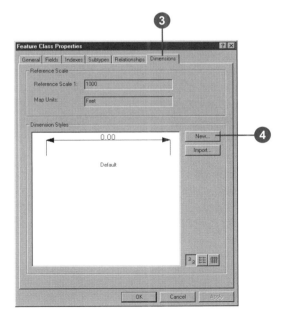

5. Type a name for the new style.

6. Click the dropdown arrow and click the style in the dimension feature class whose properties you want to copy into the new style.

7. In the Dimension Style Properties dialog box, modify those elements of the dimension style you wish to change.

8. Click OK.

9. Click Apply.

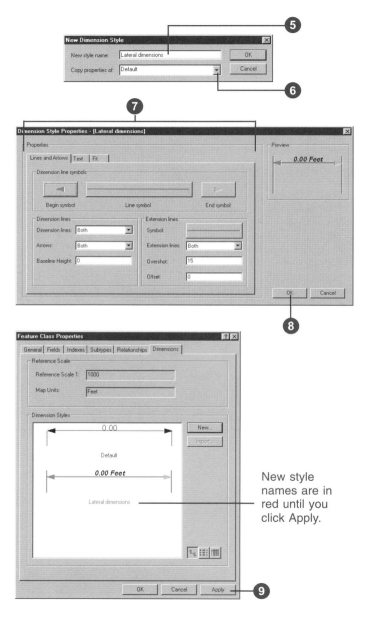

New style names are in red until you click Apply.

Importing dimension styles

1. Follow steps 1 through 3 for creating a new dimension style.

2. Click Import.

3. Click the browse button to browse for a geodatabase. Once a geodatabase is selected, the dimension feature classes and feature datasets containing dimension feature classes are listed in the tree view.

4. Click the dimension feature class that contains the styles you want to import.

5. Hold down the Ctrl key and click the dimension styles that you want to import.

6. Click Import.

7. A dialog box displays whether the import was successful.

8. Click OK.

9. Repeat steps 4 through 8 to import more styles from the same geodatabase or steps 3 through 8 to import styles from a different geodatabase.

10. Click OK.

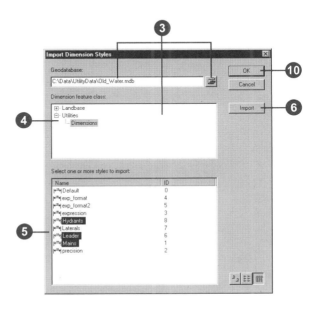

Tip

Dimension features

If dimension features that reference the style you want to rename already exist in your dimension feature class, they will not be affected. Those features will still reference the same style after it has been renamed.

Renaming a dimension style

1. Follow steps 1 through 3 for creating a new dimension style.

2. Right-click the dimension style you want to rename.

3. Click Rename.

4. Type the new name for the style and press Enter.

5. Click Apply.

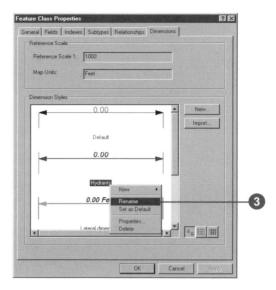

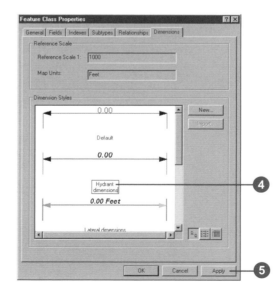

The default style

*Any style can be the default style.
The default style is the style that is
to be assigned to all new dimensions when they are created in
ArcMap, unless another style has
been selected in the Dimensioning
toolbar.*

*For more information on creating
dimension features and the
Dimensioning toolbar, see
Chapter 12, 'Editing your
geodatabase'.*

Setting the default dimension style

1. Follow steps 1 through 3 for creating a new dimension style.

2. Right-click the dimension style you want to set as the default.

3. Click Set as Default.

4. Click Apply.

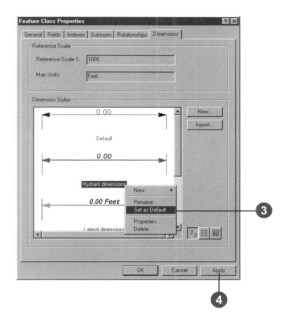

Deleting styles

All features that reference a style that has been deleted are symbolized as raw lines with a box for the text. You can use ArcMap to assign a different style to those dimension features.

For more information on editing dimension features, see Chapter 12, 'Editing your geodatabase'.

Deleting a dimension style

1. Follow steps 1 through 3 for creating a new dimension style.

2. Right-click the dimension style you want to delete.

3. Click Delete.

4. Click Apply.

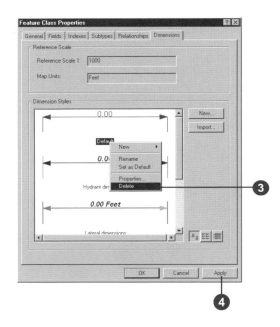

Geometric networks

9

IN THIS CHAPTER

- **What is a geometric network?**

- **Geometric networks and ArcCatalog**

- **Creating geometric networks**

- **Creating a new geometric network**

- **Building a geometric network from existing simple feature classes**

- **Adding new feature classes to your geometric network**

- **Network connectivity: defining the rules**

- **Establishing connectivity rules**

- **Managing a geometric network**

When you model automated mapping/facilities management (AM/FM) networks, or transportation networks, *features* have connectivity *relationships* with other features around them. This connectivity is maintained in the *geodatabase* through a topological association called a geometric network.

Geometric networks are created and managed using ArcCatalog. This chapter highlights the key tasks for creating and managing geometric networks.

What is a geometric network?

The movement of people, the transportation and distribution of goods and services, the delivery of resources and energy, and the communication of information all occur through definable network systems. In the geodatabase, networks are modeled as a one-dimensional nonplanar graph, or geometric network, that is composed of features. These features are constrained to exist within the network and can therefore be considered network features. The geodatabase automatically maintains the explicit topological relationships between network features in a geometric network. Network connectivity is based on geometric coincidence, hence the name geometric network.

A geometric network has a corresponding logical network. The *geometric network* is the actual set of *feature classes* that make up the network. The *logical network* is the physical representation of the network connectivity. Each element in the logical network is associated with a feature in the geometric network.

Once a geometric network is in place, ArcMap and ArcCatalog have tools that treat the network features in a special way. Editing and *tracing* on the network, as well as managing the feature classes participating in the network, are all handled automatically by the ArcGIS 8 system.

Network feature types

Geometric networks consist of edge network features and junction network features. An example of an edge feature is a water main, while a junction feature might be a valve. Edges must be connected to other edges through junctions. Edge features are related to *edge elements* in the network, and junction features are related to *junction elements* in the logical network.

There are two broad categories of network feature types: simple and complex. Simple network features correspond to a single network element in the logical network. A complex network feature corresponds to more than one network element in the logical network.

A simple edge feature corresponds to a single network edge element in the logical network. Simple edges are always connected to exactly two junction features, one at each end. If a new junction feature is snapped mid-span on a simple edge (thereby establishing connectivity), then that simple edge feature is physically split into two new features.

Complex edges correspond to one or more edge elements in the logical network. Complex edges are always connected to at least two junction features at their endpoints but can be connected to additional junction features along their length. If a new junction feature is snapped mid-span on a complex edge, that complex edge remains a single feature. Snapping the junction does cause the complex edge to be split logically—for example, if it corresponded to one edge element in the logical network before the junction was connected, it now corresponds to two edge elements.

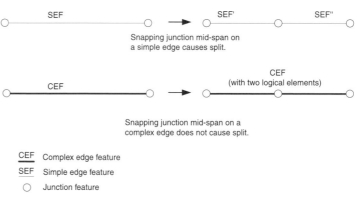

Simple edge features are connected to exactly two junction features. Complex edges can be connected to two or more junction features.

A complex junction is a single feature that corresponds to any number of edge and junction elements in the logical network. For example, a complex junction may be a water pump station in a water network. While the pump station feature itself is stored as a single complex junction feature in the geodatabase, its representation in the logical network may include a set of pipes, pumps, meters, and valves that all affect the flow through the pump station. The combination of these devices may be represented as a set of seven junction elements and six edge elements.

Complex junctions can be implemented as custom features only. To learn more about custom features, see *Exploring ArcObjects*.

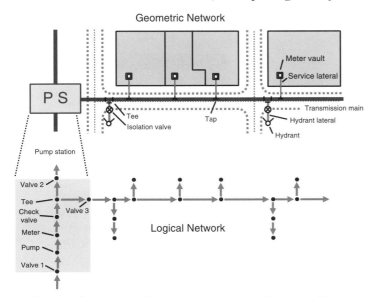

In this example, a pump station is a single polygon in the geometric network, but it represents a set of pipes, valves, meters, and pumps in the logical network. It is a complex junction feature.

Sources and sinks

Networks are often used to model real-world systems in which the direction of movement through the network is well defined. For example, the flow of electricity in an electrical network is from the power generation station to the customers. In a water network, the flow direction may not be as well defined as in an electric network, but the flow of water may be from a pump station to a customer or from customers to a treatment plant.

Flow direction in a network is calculated from a set of sources and sinks. In the above examples, electricity and water flow are driven by sources and sinks. Flow is away from sources, such as the power generation station or a pump station, and toward sinks such as a water treatment plant (in the case of a wastewater network).

Junction features in geometric networks can act as sources or sinks. When you create a new junction feature class in a network, you can specify whether the features stored in it can represent sources, sinks, or neither in the network. If you specify that these features can be sources or sinks, a field called AncillaryRole is added to the feature class to record if the feature is a source, sink, or neither a source nor a sink. When you calculate the flow direction for a geometric network in ArcMap, the flow direction will be calculated based on the sources and sinks in the network.

For example, you may have a tank in your water network that is down for maintenance, so its role in the network will be changed (temporarily) from source to none. The flow for the network is recalculated by the system; any traces on the network will be affected by the change in flow direction caused by the state of the tank. For more information on calculating flow direction and using flow direction in network analysis, see *Using ArcMap*.

Network weights

A network can also have a set of weights associated with it. A weight can be used to represent the cost of traversing an element in the logical network. For example, in a water network, a certain amount of pressure is lost when traveling the length of a transmission main due to surface friction within the pipe.

Weights are calculated based on some *attribute* of each feature. In the transmission main example above, an attribute that affects the weight would be the length of the feature.

A network can have any number of weights associated with it. Each feature class in the network may have some, all, or none of these weights associated with its attributes. The weight for each feature is determined by some attribute for that feature. Each weight can be associated with one attribute in a feature but, at the same time, can be associated with multiple features. For example, a weight called Diameter can be associated with the attribute Diameter in water main features and can also be associated with the attribute Dia in water lateral features.

Enabled and disabled features

Any edge or junction feature in a geometric network may be enabled or disabled in the logical network. A feature that is disabled in the logical network acts as a barrier. When the network is traced, the trace will stop at any barriers it encounters in the network including disabled network features.

The enabled or disabled state of a network feature is a property maintained by an attribute *field* called Enabled. It can have one of two values: true or false. When building a geometric network from simple feature classes, this field is automatically added to the input feature classes. When you use ArcCatalog to create a network feature class, Enabled is a required field for the feature class.

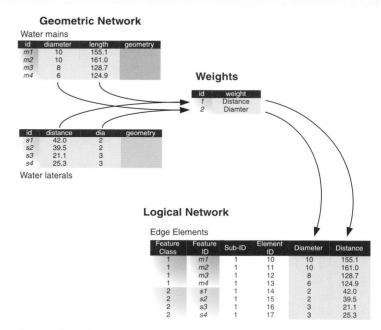

A network can have any number of weights associated with it. Each feature class in the network may have some, all, or none of these weights associated with its attributes. The weight for each feature is determined by some attribute for that feature.

For a discussion on required fields, see Chapter 3, 'Creating new items in a geodatabase'. When adding new features to a network, they are enabled by default. For more information on editing geometric networks, see Chapter 12, 'Editing your geodatabase'.

Values stored in the network weight, ancillary role, and enabled fields are the user's view of the state of the feature in the logical network. When analysis—such as tracing and flow direction calculation—is performed against a network feature, the value of these fields within the feature is not directly referenced to determine the enabled, ancillary role state of the feature or its weight. Instead, these states of the feature are stored in the logical network, which is queried during these operations. This is done for performance reasons.

When you edit a network feature and change the value of the enabled, ancillary role or a weight field, the state of the feature in the internal topology tables is modified to remain in sync with the field values of the feature.

Performance considerations

Geometric networks can be comprised of a number of edge and junction feature classes. When editing geometric networks in ArcMap, topological relationships between features are maintained while editing on the fly. The benefit of this model is that there is no need to perform a postediting process to build topology. The cost of continually maintaining network connectivity imposes overhead on the time it takes to add or modify features in network feature classes.

Topological connectivity in a network feature class is based on geometric coincidence. If a junction is added along an edge, the edge and junction will become topologically connected to one another. When a new feature is added to a network feature class, this geometric coincidence must be discovered. So, each feature class in the network must be analyzed by performing a spatial query against it to determine if the new feature is coincident with network features. If coincidence is discovered, then network connectivity is established.

When discovering connectivity, a separate spatial query must be executed on the server for each feature class in the network. If you use the edit cache while editing the network, these spatial queries do not need to go against the server and are much faster. You will not pay as much of a penalty in performance for having a large number of feature classes in your network if you use the edit cache. Using the edit cache when editing your network

features will significantly improve performance when adding new features or connecting and moving existing features. For more information on editing geometric networks and using the cache, see Chapter 12, 'Editing your geodatabase'.

Try to reduce the number of feature classes you have in your geometric network by lumping feature classes together using subtypes. If your feature classes carry different attributes, you can use relationships to manage subtype-specific attributes in different tables in the database; or you can keep all the attributes in the same table using nulls for those that don't apply to a particular subtype.

Geometric networks and ArcCatalog

In ArcCatalog, you can view and manage geometric networks in geodatabases that you have access to. Because all geometric networks must be inside a *feature dataset*, they appear in the ArcCatalog tree under their feature dataset.

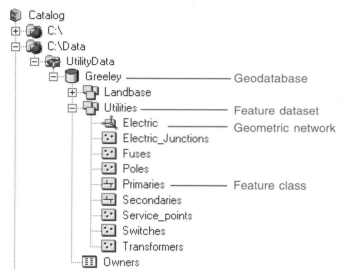

It is not immediately evident in the ArcCatalog tree which feature classes participate in the network, which feature classes participate in which network, and which participate in none. However, by examining the properties of both geometric networks and feature classes, the network feature classes can be determined.

ArcCatalog also contains various tools to create, delete, and manage both geometric networks and the feature classes that participate in geometric networks. These tools are discussed in more detail later in this chapter.

Creating geometric networks

A geometric network is a *topological* relationship between a collection of feature classes in a feature dataset. Each feature has a role in the geometric network of either an edge or a junction. Multiple feature classes may have the same role in a single geometric network.

The basic methodology for creating a geometric network is to determine which feature classes will participate in the network and what role each will play. Optionally, a series of network weights can be specified, as can other more advanced parameters.

Two different methods are available for creating a network. These are creating a new, empty geometric network and building a geometric network from existing simple features.

Creating a new, empty network

You can create a new geometric network with ArcCatalog from nothing and design and build up the network from scratch. You can then use editing tools in ArcMap or custom Visual Basic® (VB), Visual Basic for Applications (VBA), or C++ code to add features to the geometric network.

The process of creating a network can be summarized in the following steps:

1. Use ArcCatalog to create the feature dataset that will contain the geometric network and its feature classes.

2. Use ArcCatalog to create an empty geometric network in the feature dataset.

3. Use ArcCatalog to create new feature classes in the feature dataset and assign each a role in the geometric network.

4. Use ArcCatalog to establish *connectivity rules* for elements of the geometric network.

5. Use custom scripts or ArcMap editing tools to add features to the network.

Building a geometric network from existing data

You may already have data from which you want to create a geometric network in your geodatabase. ArcCatalog and ArcToolbox contain tools to create a geometric network from that data.

The process of building a geometric network from existing data can be summarized in the following steps:

1. Use ArcCatalog or ArcToolbox to convert and load your data into a geodatabase.

2. Use ArcCatalog or ArcToolbox to build a geometric network from existing simple feature classes.

3. Use ArcCatalog to add any additional empty feature classes to the geometric network.

4. Use ArcCatalog to establish connectivity rules for the geometric network.

How networks are built

Building networks from existing features is a computationally intense operation that may take a considerable amount of time and system resources, depending on the number of input features. If those features require snapping, the network building operation will spend most of its time in the feature snapping phase. The network building process proceeds in the following sequence:

1. If snapping is specified, snap simple features.

2. If snapping is specified, snap complex features.

3. Create an empty logical network.

4. Create the network schema in the database.

5. Extract attributes from the input feature classes for weight calculations.

6. Create the topology.

7. Create orphan junctions as required, add input junction features to the logical network, and initialize the junction-enabled values.

8. Set weight values for the junction elements.

9. Add edges to the logical network.

10. Set weight values for the edge elements.

11. Create all necessary indexes in the database.

Network snapping models

Ideally, your data should be clean before you build a network. Clean data means that all features that should be connected in the network are geometrically coincident—that is, no overshoots or undershoots. However, if this is not the case, the data may be snapped during the network building process.

It is important to understand how connectivity is established based on snapping during the network building process and how feature geometries are adjusted to establish that connectivity. The following is a series of examples of how connectivity is established in given scenarios. In these diagrams, use the key below to identify what types of features are illustrated in each scenario:

EF	Edge feature (simple or complex)
CEF	Complex edge feature
SEF	Simple edge feature
✕	Vertex
● ◔ ○	Junction features
⌒	Snapping tolerance

Simple edges: Connectivity against simple edges is established only at the ends of edge features. Mid-span connectivity will not be established, even if there is a vertex along the simple edge feature.

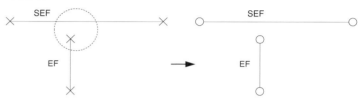

No connectivity is established.

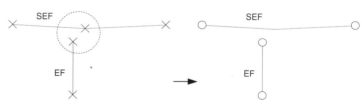

No connectivity established. Mid-span connectivity on simple edge features is not established in snapping.

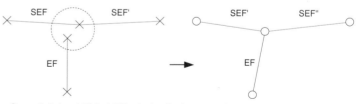

Connectivity is established. With simple edge features, only endpoint vertices are considered when establishing connectivity in snapping.

Simple edge connectivity models

Complex edges: Connectivity against complex edges is established both at the ends of features and mid-span. If there is no vertex along the complex edge where connectivity is established, a new vertex is created. When snapping complex edges, connectivity must be at the endpoint of at least one of the edges. Connectivity will not be established between the mid-span of one edge and the mid-span of another edge.

Vertex clustering: When snapping two features, if there is more than one vertex within the snapping tolerance, then those vertices are treated as a cluster. Snapping will occur to one of the vertices in the cluster, but not necessarily the closest.

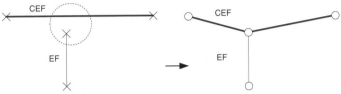

Connectivity established. Intersection detection is performed along complex edges, and new vertices are inserted as required.

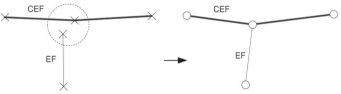

Connectivity established. Mid-span connectivity on complex edge features is established in snapping.

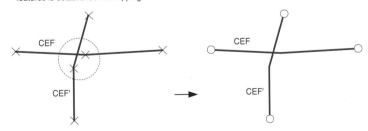

No connectivity established. Connectivity must be at an endpoint of one of the two edge features.

Complex edge connectivity models

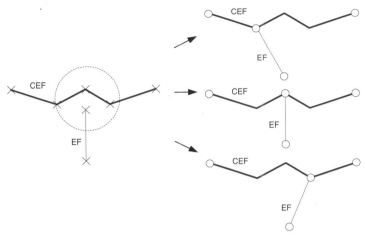

Connectivity established. One of the vertices within the snap tolerance is snapped to, but not necessarily the closest.

Network snapping vertex clustering does not guarantee the closest vertex is snapped to—it may be any of the vertices.

Connecting features to themselves: When the endpoints of a single edge feature come within the snapping tolerance of itself, the endpoint will not be snapped and no connectivity will be established. Connectivity is not established between a feature and itself.

Coincident junctions: When the network building process encounters coincident junctions, or when the snapping process results in coincident junctions, the resulting connectivity will be nondeterministic. That is, connectivity will only be established to one of the coincident junctions.

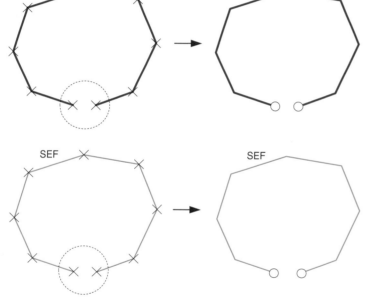

No connectivity established. Connectivity is not created between features and themselves.

Connectivity is not established between a feature and itself.

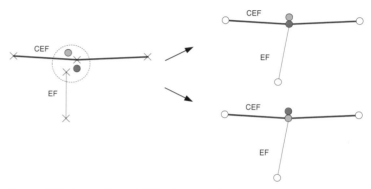

Connectivity is nondeterministic when coincident junctions are encountered.

Adjusting features

When snapping features during network building, it is important to understand how the geometry of features is adjusted when snapping. All or part of any feature in a feature class that was specified as being adjustable in the Build Geometric Network Wizard can potentially be moved. Those features that are in feature classes that are not adjustable will remain fixed throughout the network building process.

All features in all feature classes have equal weights when being adjusted during snapping. This means that if the endpoints for two edges need to be snapped and both features can be adjusted, then they will move an equal distance to snap together. If one of the features is not adjustable, then only the adjustable feature will move to snap to the static feature.

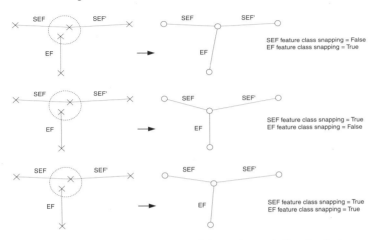

SEF feature class snapping = False
EF feature class snapping = True

SEF feature class snapping = True
EF feature class snapping = False

SEF feature class snapping = True
EF feature class snapping = True

How simple edge features are adjusted depends on whether the features they are snapping to can or cannot be adjusted.

Schema locking

An exclusive lock is required on all of the input feature classes when building a geometric network. If any of the input feature classes has a shared lock, the network will not be built.

If any of the feature classes in a network has a shared or exclusive lock, that lock is propagated to all of the other feature classes in the network. For more information on exclusive locks and schema locking, see Chapter 3, 'Creating new items in a geodatabase'.

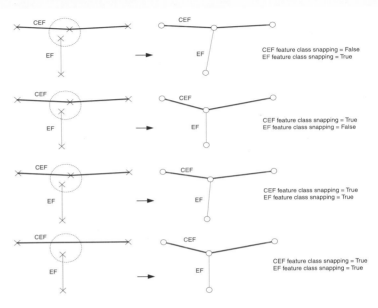

CEF feature class snapping = False
EF feature class snapping = True

CEF feature class snapping = True
EF feature class snapping = False

CEF feature class snapping = True
EF feature class snapping = True

CEF feature class snapping = True
EF feature class snapping = True

How complex edge features are adjusted depends on whether the features they are snapping to can or cannot be adjusted.

Creating a new geometric network

Geometric networks are created inside feature datasets. Once a geometric network has been created, you must add feature classes to the feature dataset and assign them roles in the network.

New feature classes can be added to a geometric network at any time.

See Also

For more information on creating feature datasets and feature classes, see Chapter 3, 'Creating new items in a geodatabase'.

1. Right-click the feature dataset that will contain the network.

2. Point to New.

3. Click Geometric Network.

4. Read the information on the first panel and click Next. ▶

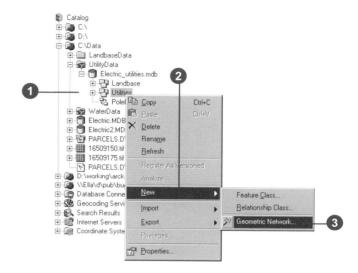

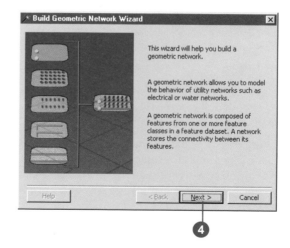

5. Click the second option to build an empty geometric network.

6. Click Next.

7. Type a name for the new geometric network.

8. Click Next. ▶

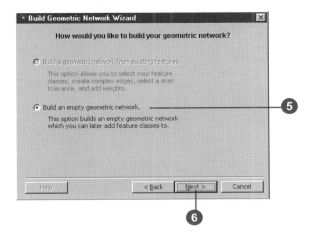

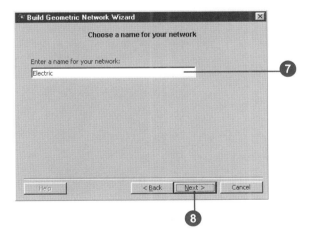

Tip

Network weights

Network weights apply to all elements in the network. You can assign which weights are associated with which field on each feature class when you create the network feature class.

You can't remove or add weights once the geometric network is created.

See Also

For more information on geometric networks and network weights, see Modeling Our World.

See Also

For details about using storage keywords with ArcSDE, see Managing ArcSDE Services.

9. Click Yes if you want to include weights in the network; otherwise, skip to step 13.

10. To add a new weight, click the New button and type a name.

11. Click the dropdown arrow and click the weight type.

12. Repeat steps 10 and 11 until all of the network's weights have been defined.

13. Click Next.

14. If your geodatabase is stored in an ArcSDE database, and you have a configuration keyword for the network storage, click Yes and type the name of the keyword. If not, skip to step 15.

15. Click Next. ►

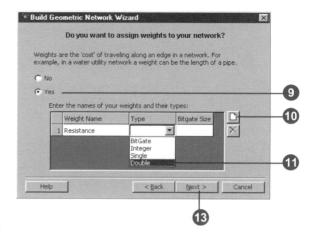

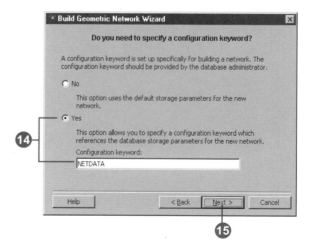

16. Review the options you specified for your new network. If you want to change something, you can go back through the wizard by clicking the Back button.

17. Click Finish to create the new geometric network.

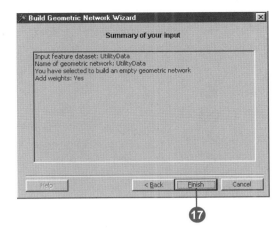

Build Geometric Network Wizard

Summary of your input

Input feature dataset: UtilityData
Name of geometric network: UtilityData
You have selected to build an empty geometric network
Add weights: Yes

Help   < Back   Finish   Cancel

Building a geometric network from existing simple feature classes

An alternative to creating and populating an empty geometric network is to build a geometric network from existing simple feature classes.

The Build Geometric Network Wizard discovers the connectivity for a group of feature classes in a feature dataset and promotes them from simple feature types (lines and points) to network feature types (edges and junctions).

When you build a geometric network, the feature classes must already exist in the feature dataset. However, they can be empty. After the network has been built, you can add new empty network feature classes.

Geometric networks can be built using either ArcCatalog or ArcToolbox.

Building a geometric network using ArcCatalog

1. Right-click the feature dataset that will contain the network.

2. Point to New.

3. Click Geometric Network.

4. Read the information on the first panel and click Next. ▶

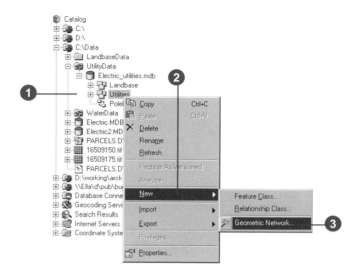

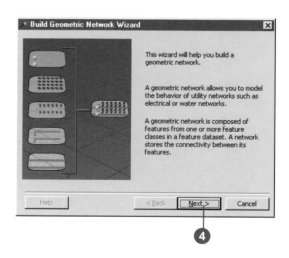

5. Click the first option to build a geometric network from existing features.

6. Click Next.

7. Click the feature classes that you wish to include in this geometric network.

8. Type a name for the new geometric network.

9. Click Next. ▶

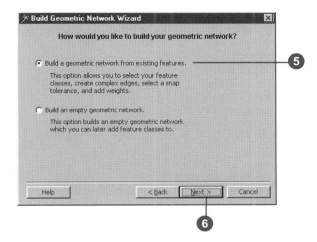

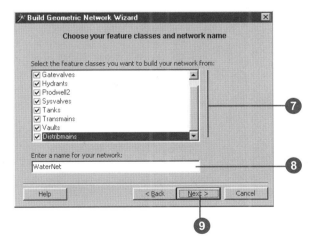

Complex edges

When you build a geometric network from existing simple feature classes, the line feature classes become simple edges by default. However, you can specify that you want some of the line feature classes to be complex edges in the geometric network.

Snapping features

The geometric network builder can automatically adjust features in the input feature classes to correctly snap to connecting features. The default snapping tolerance is 1.5 * 1/XY scale of the feature dataset's spatial reference.

If snapping, you cannot use a value smaller than the default. Very large snapping tolerances may cause unanticipated results. For best results, examine your data and provide an appropriate tolerance.

Snapping (geometry changes) cannot be undone.

10. Click Yes if you want some of the input line feature classes to become complex edges; otherwise, skip to step 12.

11. Check the line feature classes that you want to become complex edges. Those that are not selected will become simple edges.

12. Click Next.

13. Click Yes if you want features in some of the input feature classes to be automatically adjusted and snapped during the network building process; otherwise, skip to step 16.

14. Type a *snapping tolerance* if you don't want to use the default tolerance.

15. Check the feature classes whose features you want automatically adjusted and snapped. Feature classes that are not selected are not adjusted.

16. Click Next. ▶

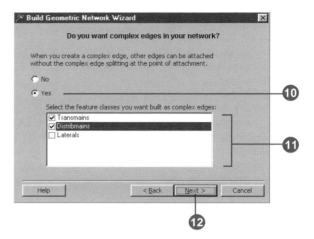

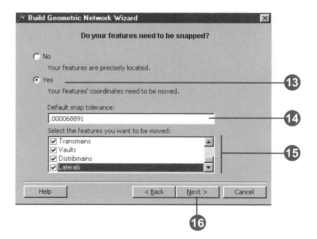

Tip

Sources and sinks

If you specify that you want to store sources and sinks in a junction feature class, a field called AncillaryRole will automatically be added to the feature class.

Tip

Network weights

Once the geometric network is built, no additional weights can be added to it. Also, the feature classes with which each weight is associated can't be altered.

When you add a new feature class to the geometric network, it can be associated with the existing network weights.

17. Click Yes if you want features in some of your junction feature classes to be able to act as sources or sinks; otherwise, skip to step 19.

18. Check those junction feature classes that you want to store sources and sinks.

19. Click Next.

20. Click Yes if you want to add weights to your network. Otherwise, skip to step 24, then skip over steps 25 through 29.

21. To add a new weight, click the New button.

22. Type a name for the new weight, click the dropdown arrow, and click a weight type.

23. Repeat steps 21 and 22 until all of the network's weights have been defined.

24. Click Next. ▶

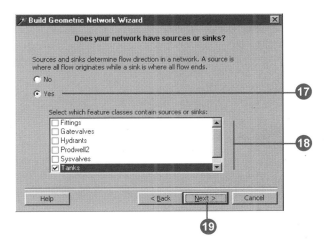

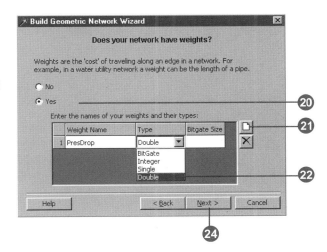

Tip

Building progress

You will be notified of the building progress with a series of progress bars indicating the progress of each step along the way.

See Also

For details about using storage keywords with ArcSDE, see Managing ArcSDE Services.

25. If you added weights, you can assign these weights to specific fields in each feature class.

26. Click the dropdown arrow and click the network weight to which you will assign an attribute.

27. Click the dropdown arrow and click the field you want associated with this weight.

28. Repeat step 27 for each feature class that you want to associate with this weight.

29. Repeat steps 26 through 28 until you are finished associating network weights with feature class attributes.

30. Click Next.

31. If your geodatabase is stored in an ArcSDE database, and you have a configuration keyword for the network storage, click Yes and type the name of the keyword. If not, skip to step 34.

32. Click Next. ►

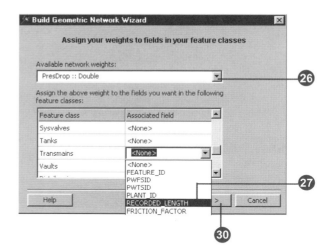

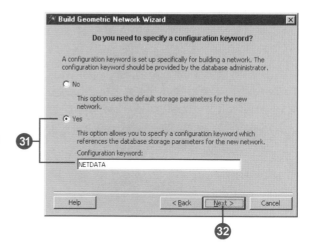

Aborting

At any time during the building process, you can abort by clicking Abort on the Progress dialog box.

When you abort the build, the system deletes any network tables created and sets the database to the state it was before the build started.

If snapping was already complete, that change is permanent and will not be restored.

33. Review the options you specified for your new network. If you want to change something, you can go back through the wizard by clicking the Back button.

34. Click Finish to create the new geometric network.

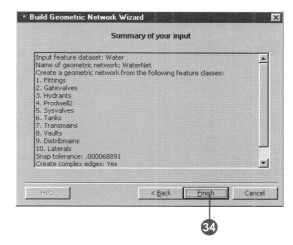

See Also

For more information on starting and using ArcToolbox, see Using ArcToolbox.

Building a geometric network using ArcToolbox

1. Start ArcToolbox from the Start menu.

2. Double-click Data Management Tools.

3. Double-click GeoDatabase.

4. Double-click Build Geometric Network Wizard.

5. Click Next. ▶

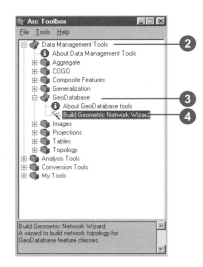

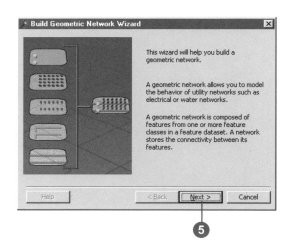

Tip

Input feature dataset

An alternative to browsing for the input feature dataset is to drag it from ArcCatalog and drop it in the feature dataset text box.

See Also

For more information on using the minibrowser to select data, see Using ArcCatalog.

6. Click the Browse button to browse for the feature dataset that contains the feature classes from which you want to build your network.

7. Check the feature classes that you wish to include in the geometric network.

8. Type a name for the new geometric network.

9. Click Next.

10. Follow steps 10 through 34 for building a geometric network using ArcCatalog.

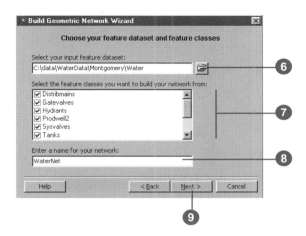

Adding new feature classes to your geometric network

At any time in a geometric network's life, you can add new edge and junction feature classes. These new feature classes are empty—you cannot add populated feature classes to an existing geometric network. Adding a new feature class to a geometric network is similar to the task of creating a new feature class to store *custom features* (see Chapter 3, 'Creating new items in a geodatabase').

When creating a new network feature class, you must specify a feature type other than simple as well as specify the geometric network in which that feature class will participate. The new feature class must be created in the same feature dataset as the geometric network.

If you create a new junction feature class, you can specify if you want its features to be able to act as sources or sinks.

All network feature classes have the same required fields as simple feature classes—OBJECTID and Shape. In addition to this, network ▶

Creating a new network edge feature class

1. Right-click the feature dataset that contains the network.

2. Point to New.

3. Click Feature Class.

4. Type a name and an *alias* for the new feature class.

5. Click the second option to store network objects in the feature class.

6. Click the dropdown arrow and click ESRI Simple Edge Feature to create a feature class that stores simple edges. Click ESRI Complex Edge Feature to create a feature class that stores complex edges.

7. Click the dropdown arrow and click the geometric network in which this feature class will participate.

8. Click Next. ▶

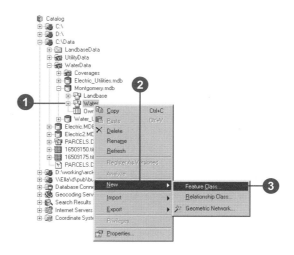

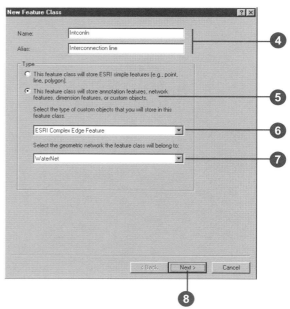

features have a required field called Enabled.

The Enabled field records whether or not a feature in the feature class is enabled or disabled in the logical network. This field has a fixed *attribute domain* automatically associated with it.

Junction features can also act as sources and sinks in the network. To record whether or not a junction feature is a source or a sink, a required field called AncillaryRole is created for the feature class. Like the Enabled field, the AncillaryRole field has a fixed attribute domain automatically associated with it.

For more information on how sources, sinks, and enabled and disabled features affect flow in a network, see *Using ArcMap*.

9. Follow the steps for creating a simple feature class (see Chapter 3, 'Creating new items in a geodatabase'). You will be presented with an additional dialog box where you can associate the network's weights with fields in the feature class.

10. To associate a weight in the network with a field in this new feature class under Field, click the field next to the weight you want to associate.

11. Click the name of the field in the dropdown list to associate with this weight.

12. Repeat steps 10 and 11 until you have associated the weights in the network with fields. You do not have to associate all of the weights with fields.

13. Click Finish.

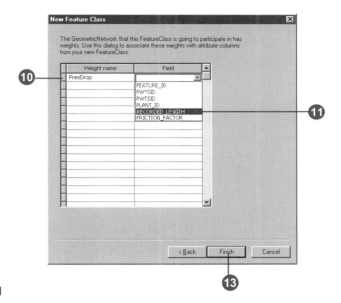

Sources and sinks

If you specify that you want to store sources and sinks in a junction feature class, a field called AncillaryRole will automatically be added to it. If not, then the AncillaryRole field will not be included in the feature class.

Creating a new network junction feature class

1. Follow steps 1 through 5 for creating a new network edge feature class.

2. Click the dropdown arrow and click ESRI Simple Junction Feature to create a feature class that stores network junctions.

3. Click the dropdown arrow and click the geometric network in which this feature class will participate.

4. Check the box to allow the junctions in this feature class to be able to act as sources or sinks in the network.

5. Click Next.

6. Follow steps 9 through 12 for creating a new network edge feature class.

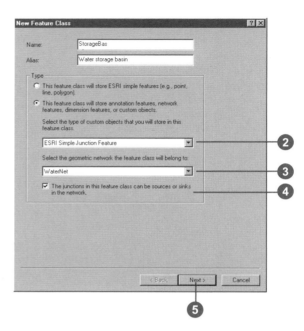

Network connectivity: defining the rules

In most networks, you do not want all edge types to be able to logically connect to all junction types. Similarly, not all edge types can logically connect to all other edge types through all junction types. For example, in a water network, a hydrant can connect to a hydrant lateral, but not to a service lateral. Similarly, in the same water network, a 10-inch transmission main can only connect to an 8-inch transmission main through a reducer.

Network connectivity rules constrain the type of network features that may be connected to one another and the number of features of any particular type that can be connected to features of another type. By establishing these rules, along with other rules such as attribute domains, you can maintain the integrity of the network data in the database. At any time, you can selectively validate features in the database and generate reports as to which features in the network are invalid—that is, are violating one of the connectivity or other rules.

There are two types of connectivity rules: edge–junction rules and edge–edge rules. An *edge–junction* rule is a connectivity rule that establishes that an edge of type A may connect to a junction of type B. An *edge–edge rule* is a connectivity rule that establishes that an edge of type A may connect to an edge of type B through a set of junction types. Edge–edge rules always involve a set of junctions.

You can establish and modify the connectivity rules for a network from within ArcCatalog by modifying the geometric network properties. You can establish connectivity rules between two feature classes, a feature class and the *subtype* of another feature class, or a subtype of one feature class and a subtype of another. In the water network example above, a connectivity rule would be established between two subtypes of the same edge feature class and a subtype of a third junction feature class (10-inch and 8-inch transmission mains and reducer valves).

Default junctions

Both edge–edge and edge–junction connectivity rules can have default junctions associated with them. Default junctions are automatically inserted by ArcMap when creating connectivity in a network.

When an edge pair has an edge–edge connectivity rule defined in the database, and you create a new edge that connects to an existing edge, the default junction is automatically inserted. For an edge–junction connectivity rule, ArcMap automatically inserts the default junction at the free end of new edges that are created in the network.

Establishing connectivity rules

Connectivity rules are established and modified using the geometric network's Properties dialog box in ArcCatalog.

The two examples given here describe how to establish an edge–junction rule and an edge–edge rule. For simplicity, each is done separately, but any number of rules can be established or modified for the network at a single time.

Tip

Junction rules

If an edge–junction rule does not yet exist between one of the edge subtypes or feature classes and one of the junction subtypes or feature classes, a rule is automatically created.

Tip

Default junction type

To set a default junction type, right-click the junction subtype or feature class in the Junction subtypes list, then click Set as default.

Adding an edge–edge rule

1. Right-click the geometric network.

2. Click Properties.

3. Click the Connectivity tab.

4. Click the dropdown arrow and click the feature class for which you want to create a rule.

5. Click the subtype of the feature class if your feature class has subtypes.

6. Navigate to and check the edge feature class or subtype you want to make connectable to this edge subtype or feature class.

7. Browse for and check the junction feature classes and subtypes through which these edge feature classes or subtypes will be permitted to connect.

8. Click OK to create the rule in the database.

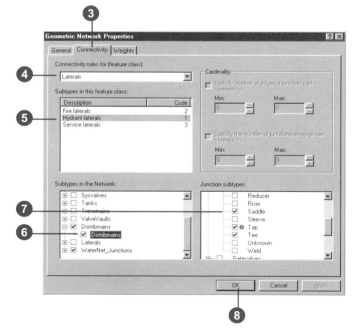

<table>
<tr><td>

Tip

Default junction type

To set a default junction type, right-click the junction subtype or feature class in the Junction subtypes list, then click Set as default.

</td><td>

Adding an edge–junction rule

1. Follow steps 1 and 2 for adding an edge–edge rule.

2. Click the Connectivity tab.

3. Click the dropdown arrow and click the feature class for which you want to create a rule.

4. Click the subtype of the feature class if your feature class has subtypes.

5. Navigate and check the junction feature class or subtype you want to make connectable to this edge feature class or subtype.

6. If you want to restrict the number of edges of this type that can connect to a single junction of this type, click the check box and enter the minimum and maximum number of permissible edges.

7. If you want to restrict the number of junctions of this type that can connect to a single edge of this type, check the check box and type the minimum and maximum number of permissible junctions.

8. Click OK to create the rule in the database.

</td></tr>
</table>

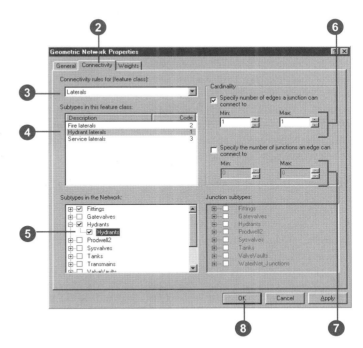

Managing a geometric network

You can manage geometric networks using ArcCatalog. Unlike most items that appear in ArcCatalog, the geometric network does not represent a single entity, such as a table, *shapefile*, or feature class. A geometric network is actually an association among several feature classes and is represented by several tables in the database. Managing a geometric network is different from managing other items in ArcCatalog.

Managing the geometric network itself

Some of the standard operations on the geometric network are handled the same way as with other items in ArcCatalog. A geometric network can be renamed or deleted. Renaming the geometric network doesn't affect any of its member feature classes or the topology of the network itself. However, deleting the geometric network does affect both.

You can delete a geometric network in two ways. The first is to delete the entire feature dataset that contains the network. This action deletes from the geodatabase all of the participating feature classes, all of the network topology tables, and any other objects stored inside that feature dataset. The second method is to simply delete the geometric network itself and leave the rest of the feature dataset intact.

All of the feature classes participating in a network store network feature types. A feature class can't store network features if it's not participating in a network. This means that when the network is deleted, all of the feature classes in the network are demoted to simple feature types. Edge feature classes become simple feature classes with line geometry, and junction feature classes become simple feature classes with point geometry. Deleting the network will also delete all of the related topology tables from the geodatabase.

Managing network feature classes

Managing network feature classes is more restrictive than managing simple feature classes. Although you can easily rename a network feature class, deleting one is more difficult. To delete the network feature class, you must first delete the geometric network; this action converts the network feature class to a simple feature class that can then be deleted. The alternative is to delete the entire feature dataset, which deletes the network and all of the feature classes.

Schema locking

An exclusive lock is required to modify a geometric network's connectivity rules or to rename or delete a geometric network. An exclusive lock can only be aquired for a geometric network if the feature classes that participate in the network can also be locked. Therefore, if another user has an exclusive or shared lock on any of the feature classes in a geometric network, then the properties of the geometric network cannot be edited.

For more information on exclusive locks and schema locking, see Chapter 3, 'Creating new items in a geodatabase'.

Geocoding services

10

IN THIS CHAPTER

- **Geocoding services**

- **Geocoding services in ArcCatalog and ArcMap**

- **Preparing reference data for a geocoding service**

- **Creating a geocoding service**

- **Maintaining geocoding indexes**

- **Preparing address data for geocoding**

When you want to map the locations of addresses, you need to create spatial descriptions of these locations from the textual descriptions contained in the address. This process is known as *geocoding*. ArcGIS uses geocoding services to perform the task of creating geometry from textual descriptions of locations.

Geocoding services are created and maintained in ArcCatalog. You can use geocoding services to geocode addresses in both ArcCatalog and ArcMap. This chapter describes the key concepts of creating and maintaining geocoding services inside a geodatabase.

Geocoding services

What is a geocoding service?

A feature is an object that has geometry. In most cases, this geometry is captured by digitization or scanning of paper maps. In many cases, however, geographic data exists that indirectly captures geometry by describing locations such as street addresses, city names, or even telephone numbers. While humans understand what these descriptions mean and how they relate to locations on the earth's surface, computers do not. In order to display these locations on a map and perform analyses with them, a computer must be given geometric representations (such as point features) of these locations.

Geocoding (also commonly known as address matching) is the process of creating geometric representations for descriptions of locations. A geocoding service defines a process for converting alphanumeric descriptions of locations into geometric shapes.

ArcGIS 8 provides tools and a framework for creating, managing, and using geocoding services. In ArcGIS 8, a geocoding service defines paths to *reference data*, algorithms for standardizing alphanumeric descriptions of places and matching them to the reference data, and parameters for reading address data, matching the address data to the reference data, and creating output.

Clientside and serverside geocoding services

In ArcGIS 8, you can create and use both clientside and serverside geocoding services. Clientside geocoding services are stored on the same machine as the ArcGIS desktop installation that created them. Serverside geocoding services are stored in an ArcSDE geodatabase on a server.

Clientside geocoding services do not require an ArcSDE server. They are created and used through the ArcCatalog and ArcMap interfaces or the ArcObjects™ application programming interface

(API). By default, clientside geocoding services are not shared among users.

Serverside geocoding services do require an ArcSDE server and are easily shared among users in an organization. Serverside geocoding services can be created and used through the ArcCatalog and ArcMap desktop applications, the ArcObjects API, or the ArcSDE API.

Geocoding reference data

In order to find the geographic location of an address, a geocoding service must refer to at least one data source that has both address information (attributes) and spatial information (geometry). A feature class is an example of a data source that includes both types of information. When geocoding an address, a geocoding service searches through the features in the reference data feature class to find the feature with address attributes that most closely match the address. The geometry of the matching feature is then used to create geometry for the address.

Geocoding services can use other types of reference data such as alternate street name tables and place name alias tables. For more information about these types of reference data, see 'Preparing reference data for a geocoding service' in this chapter.

Input address tables

You can use a geocoding service to geocode an entire table of addresses. Address tables can be in any format supported by ArcGIS 8, such as INFO, dBASE, or Geodatabase tables. Address tables store one address in each record, and the components of each address are contained in several fields in each record.

Output feature classes

When you geocode a table of addresses, ArcGIS creates a feature class for the geocoded features. This feature class contains the geometry for the geocoded features, the status of the geocoded address (whether it was matched or not), and the score with which the address was matched to a feature in the reference data and, for geocoding service styles that can match an address to a particular side of a street, the side of the street to which the address was matched. Optionally, the geocoding service can create attributes in the output feature class for the x,y coordinates of the geocoded feature, the standardized form of the input address, the feature ID from the geocoding reference data to which the address was matched and, for geocoding reference data with line geometry, the percent along the reference feature at which the geocoded feature is located.

When you geocode a table of addresses and create your output feature class in the same geodatabase as the input address table, you can choose to create a relationship between the address table and the output feature class. When you choose to create this relationship, ArcGIS creates a relationship class in the geodatabase that relates features in the output feature class to records in the input address table. After geocoding the table of addresses, this relationship class maintains the geocoded feature class to reflect any edits you make to the input address table. If you add or delete rows in the address table, the corresponding features are added or deleted in the geocoded feature class. If you edit the address information in a row of the address table, the corresponding feature in the geocoded feature class is updated to reflect the new address.

Alternatively, you can copy the attributes from the input address table to the output feature class. In this case, no relationship is created between the address table and the geocoded feature class, and edits made to the address table are not reflected in the geocoded feature class.

Geocoding services in ArcCatalog and ArcMap

Geocoding services in ArcCatalog

You can use ArcCatalog to create geocoding services, modify the properties of geocoding services, and geocode tables of addresses.

In the ArcCatalog tree, geocoding services are stored in Geocoding Services folders. Clientside geocoding services are stored in the top-level Geocoding Services folder. In addition, each ArcSDE database connection contains a Geocoding Services folder that contains the geocoding services that are stored on that ArcSDE server.

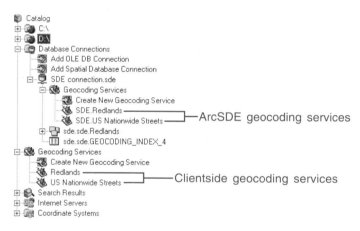

Geocoding services appear in the ArcCatalog tree.

The Geocoding Services folder also contains an item called Create New Geocoding Service. You can click this item to create a new geocoding service in the Geocoding Services folder.

The Geocoding Service Properties dialog box contains information about the reference data used by the geocoding service, parameters for matching addresses, and options for

writing output to geocoded feature classes. The Geocoding Service Properties dialog box can be opened by right-clicking a particular geocoding service in ArcCatalog and clicking Properties.

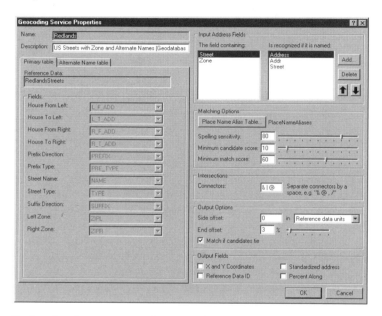

In ArcCatalog, you can also geocode tables of addresses using a geocoding service. For more information about geocoding tables of addresses, see *Using ArcCatalog*.

Geocoding services in ArcMap

Once you have created geocoding services in ArcCatalog, you can use them in ArcMap to find addresses and to geocode tables of addresses. In order to use a geocoding service in ArcMap, it must be added to the ArcMap document. The Geocoding Services Manager dialog box is used to manage the set of geocoding services that are loaded in an ArcMap document. For more information on finding addresses in ArcMap, see *Using ArcMap*.

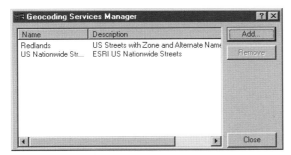

The Geocoding Services Manager dialog box lets you manage the set of geocoding services that are loaded in an ArcMap document. It is accessed by clicking the Tools menu in ArcMap, clicking Geocoding, then clicking Geocoding Services Manager.

Preparing reference data for a geocoding service

ArcGIS 8 comes with several predefined geocoding service styles that you can use immediately to create geocoding services. These geocoding service styles cover some of the most common styles of addresses that you might want to geocode. Each geocoding service style has specific requirements for the reference data that it can use to match addresses.

You can use ESRI StreetMap™ data, feature classes, and tables as reference data for geocoding services. When you use feature classes and tables as reference data, they may contain some common pieces of information that can be used for geocoding. This information includes:

* Prefix direction (a direction that precedes the street name), as in "W. Redlands Blvd."

* Prefix type (a street type that precedes the street name), as in "Avenue B"

* Street name

* Street type (a street type that follows the street name), as in "New York St."

* Suffix direction (a direction that follows the street name), as in "Bridge St. W."

* Zone (additional information used to resolve ambiguity between addresses by identifying a region in which the address is located), as in a ZIP Code or city name

Each geocoding service style has its own requirements for reference data that it can use. Each geocoding service style that is provided with ArcGIS 8 is discussed in this section.

StreetMap

ArcGIS 8 can use StreetMap data as a reference data source for geocoding. ArcSDE includes a StreetMap license so that you can create serverside geocoding services that use StreetMap data as reference data. However, if you want to create clientside geocoding services that use StreetMap data as reference data, you need to purchase a StreetMap license. Refer to the StreetMap installation guide for information on installing StreetMap for serverside and for clientside geocoding.

The Streets directory on the StreetMap CD contains one .edg file for each state. To create a StreetMap geocoding service for a single state, you can use the state's .edg file as reference data for your geocoding service. To create a geocoding service for the entire United States, use the usa.edg file as your reference datafile.

Single Field

The Single Field geocoding service style lets you create geocoding services for addresses that contain the address information in a single field. You could use a Single Field geocoding service style to geocode addresses such as place names, city names, and state names.

Although Single Field geocoding services can use feature classes with any type of geometry, they typically use feature classes with point or polygon geometry as reference data. In addition to an

ObjectID field and SHAPE field, feature classes that you can use as reference data for a Single Field geocoding service must have a key field that contains the unique "address" for that feature.

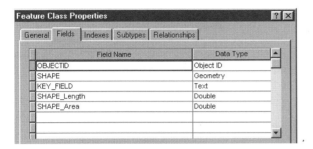

US One Address

The US One Address geocoding service style lets you create geocoding services for US addresses. US One Address geocoding services can use feature classes with polygon or point geometry as reference data. Each feature in the reference data corresponds to a single address. For example, you could use a feature class containing parcel polygons or parcel *centroids* (the

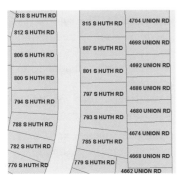

center points of parcel polygons) as reference data for a US One Address geocoding service.

To use a feature class as reference data for a US One Address geocoding service, it must have fields that contain street number and street name information, in addition to an ObjectID field and a SHAPE field. Optionally, you can use fields that contain the street's prefix direction, prefix type, street type, suffix direction, or zone.

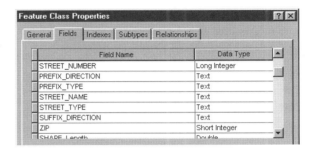

US One Range

The US One Range geocoding service style lets you create geocoding services for U.S. addresses. This geocoding service style can use feature classes with any type of geometry but typically uses feature classes with line or polyline geometry. Each feature in the reference data represents a street segment with a range of addresses that fall along that street segment.

To use a feature class as reference data for a US One Address geocoding service, it must have fields that contain from address, to address, and street name information, in addition to an ObjectID field and a SHAPE field. In addition, you can optionally specify fields that contain the street's prefix direction, prefix type, street type, suffix direction, or zone.

Feature Class Properties

General | Fields | Indexes | Subtypes | Relationships

Field Name	Data Type
FROM_ADDRESS	Long Integer
TO_ADDRESS	Long Integer
PREFIX_DIRECTION	Text
PREFIX_TYPE	Text
STREET_NAME	Text
STREET_TYPE	Text
SUFFIX_DIRECTION	Text
ADDRESS_ZONE	Text

US Streets

The US Streets geocoding service style lets you create geocoding services for U.S. addresses. This geocoding service

style can use feature classes with any type of geometry but typically uses feature classes with line or polyline geometry. Each feature in the reference data represents a street segment with two ranges of addresses that fall along that street segment, one for each side of the street.

To use a feature class as reference data for a US Streets style of geocoding service, it must have fields that contain from address and to address information for each side of the street, street name information, and an ObjectID field and SHAPE field. Optionally, you can specify fields that contain the street's prefix direction, prefix type, street type, suffix direction, or zone.

Feature Class Properties

General | Fields | Indexes | Subtypes | Relationships

Field Name	Data Type
LEFT_FROM_ADDRESS	Long Integer
LEFT_TO_ADDRESS	Long Integer
RIGHT_FROM_ADDRESS	Long Integer
RIGHT_TO_ADDRESS	Long Integer
PREFIX_DIRECTION	Text
PREFIX_TYPE	Text
STREET_NAME	Text
STREET_TYPE	Text

Alternate street names

For the US One Address, US One Range, and US Streets geocoding service styles, you can use a table to define alternate street names for the features in your reference data feature class. Using alternate street names allows you to match an address to a feature using one of many names for the feature. For example, if "Bridge Street" is also known as "Slash Road", then you can also find the address "266 Bridge St" using "266 Slash Road".

Tables that you use to specify alternate street names must have an ID field, a JOIN_ID that specifies the feature in the reference data to which the alternate name applies, and an alternate street name field. Optionally, the table can contain fields that contain prefix direction, prefix type, street type, or suffix direction information. You can specify multiple alternate names for the same feature in your reference data by creating records in the alternate street name table with the same JOIN_ID, referencing the same feature in the reference data feature class.

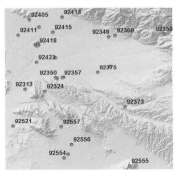

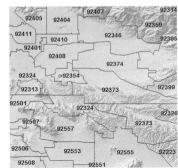

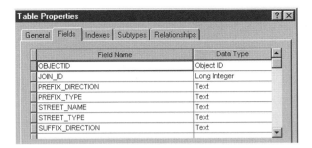

Each record in an alternate street name table applies to only one feature in your reference data feature class. In order to specify an alternate street name for all features that make up a particular street in your reference data feature class, you must create a record in the alternate street name table for each feature in your reference data feature class.

ZIP

The ZIP geocoding service style lets you create geocoding services for U.S. ZIP Codes. This geocoding service style can use feature classes with point or polygon geometry. Each feature in the reference data represents a ZIP polygon or its centroid.

To use a feature class as reference data for a ZIP style geocoding service, it must have a field that specifies the five-digit ZIP for the feature, in addition to an ObjectID field and a SHAPE field.

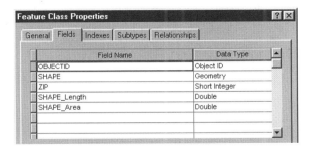

ZIP+4

The ZIP+4 geocoding service style lets you create geocoding services for US ZIP+4 codes. This geocoding service style can use feature classes with point or polygon geometry. Each feature in the reference data represents a ZIP+4 polygon or its centroid.

To use a feature class as reference data for a ZIP+4 style of geocoding service, it must have fields that specify the five-digit ZIP for the feature and the four-digit add-on code for the feature, in addition to an ObjectID field and a SHAPE field.

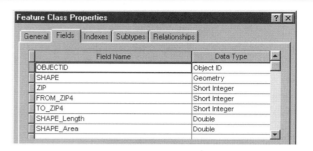

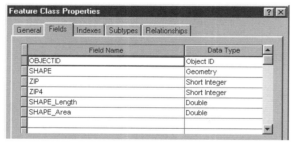

ZIP+4 Range

The ZIP+4 Range geocoding service style lets you create geocoding services for US ZIP+4 codes. This geocoding service style can use feature classes with point or polygon geometry. Each feature in the reference data represents a contiguous block of ZIP+4 codes.

To use a feature class as reference data for a ZIP+4 Range style of geocoding service, it must have fields that specify the five-digit ZIP for the feature and lower and upper bounds for the four-digit add-on code, in addition to an ObjectID and a SHAPE field.

Place name aliases

For all geocoding services, you can specify a place name alias table. Using a place name alias table, you can geocode addresses by their common names (for example, "Town Hall") instead of by their street addresses.

In order to use a place name alias table for a geocoding service, it must contain an alias field that contains the common name by which an address is referred, in addition to all of the required fields for the particular geocoding service style. Optionally, the place name alias table can use any or all of the optional address information fields for the particular geocoding service style.

Creating a geocoding service

You can create new geocoding services using ArcCatalog. Geocoding services appear in the ArcCatalog tree either in the top-level Geocoding Services folder (clientside geocoding services) or in the Geocoding Services folder in an ArcSDE database connection (serverside geocoding services). You can also view and modify the settings for a geocoding service in ArcCatalog.

1. In the ArcCatalog tree, click on a Geocoding Services folder.

2. Double-click the Create New Geocoding Service item.

3. Click the geocoding service style that you want to use to create the new geocoding service.

4. Click OK. ►

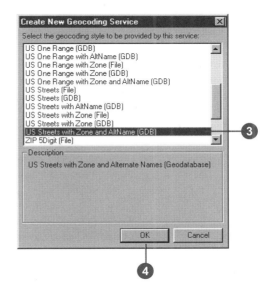

5. In the Name text box, type a name for the new geocoding service.

6. Click the Primary table tab and click the Browse button to navigate to the feature class that the geocoding service will use as reference data. Click Add.

7. Choose the column name from each dropdown list that contains the specified address information.

   The names of the required address attributes are shown in bold.

8. Click the Alternate Name table tab if your geocoding service will use an alternate street name table.

9. Click the Browse button to navigate to the table that the geocoding service will use as an alternate street name table, then click Add.

10. Choose the column name from each dropdown list that contains the specified alternate street name information.

    The names of the required address attributes are shown in bold.

11. Click Place Name Alias Table if your geocoding service will use a place name alias table. ▶

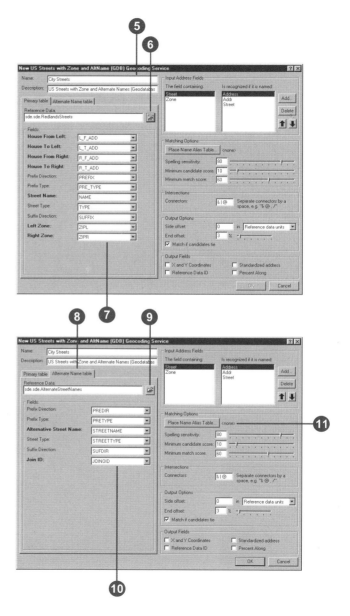

12. Click the Browse button to navigate to the table that the geocoding service will use as a place name alias table, then click Add.

13. Choose the column name from each dropdown list that contains the specified place name alias information.

    The names of the required address attributes are shown in bold.

14. Click OK.

15. Review the other settings for the new geocoding service, then click OK to create the new geocoding service.

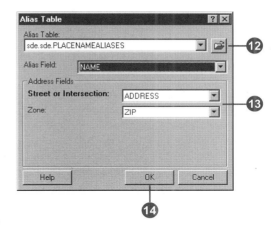

Maintaining geocoding indexes

Geocoding indexes

When you create a new geocoding service, ArcGIS creates *geocoding indexes* for the reference data that the new geocoding service uses. These geocoding indexes allow ArcGIS to quickly find features that may match the addresses that you geocode using the geocoding service. Which information is contained in the geocoding indexes is determined by the style on which the geocoding service is based. By default, the geocoding service styles that are provided with ArcGIS build geocoding indexes on fields containing street name information, both for the primary reference data feature class and the alternate street name table, if any.

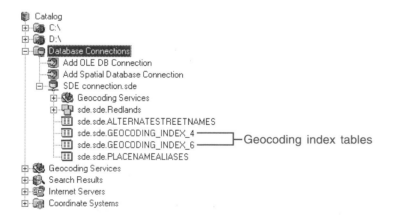

If your geocoding service uses feature classes and tables in a geodatabase as reference data, then the geocoding indexes are implemented as tables in the same geodatabase.

Maintaining geocoding indexes manually

In order to be able to geocode addresses, there must be a one-to-one correspondence between rows in an index table and features in the primary reference data feature class, or between rows in the index table and rows in the alternate street name table. If you add or delete features or rows from the primary reference data feature class or alternate street name table, or if you edit the street names of the features or rows, then the geocoding index needs to be updated.

By default, ArcGIS does not update your geocoding index tables for you when you edit your geocoding reference data. In order to keep geocoding indexes current with your geocoding reference data, you can delete the geocoding index tables from the geodatabase and re-create the geocoding service. Alternatively, you can use ArcObjects to rebuild the geocoding indexes without re-creating the geocoding service. A developer sample is provided with ArcGIS that demonstrates how to do this.

Maintaining geocoding indexes automatically

If you want ArcGIS to maintain your geocoding indexes when you edit your geocoding reference data, you can take advantage of relationship classes within the geodatabase. A relationship class between your geocoding reference data and your geocoding index table can be used to add or update rows in your geocoding index table when you add or update features or rows in your geocoding reference data. A composite relationship class will delete rows in the geocoding index table when features or rows are deleted from the geocoding reference data.

ArcGIS provides two objects that you can use to automatically maintain your geocoding indexes. One is the geocoding index object, which responds to edits to the geocoding reference data through the relationship class. When you register your geocoding index table as an object class containing geocoding index objects, the geocoding index objects respond to edits to features or rows in the geocoding reference data by recalculating their index values based on the values of attributes in the geocoding reference data.

The other object that is provided with ArcGIS for helping you maintain your geocoding indexes is the geocoding index class extension object. When you register this custom object class extension with your geocoding index object class, this object adds new geocoding index objects to your geocoding index when you add features or rows to the geocoding reference data.

The process for setting up your geocoding indexes so that they are maintained automatically is as follows:

- Register the geocoding index table as an object class.

- Register the geocoding index object class as containing custom geocoding index objects.

- Set the geocoding index object class to use a custom geocoding index object class extension.

- Create a relationship class between the geocoding reference data and the geocoding index object class.

A developer sample is provided with ArcGIS that demonstrates how to set up your geocoding indexes to be maintained automatically. For more information on the developer sample, see 'Maintaining geocoding indexes' in this chapter.

Maintaining geocoding indexes

By default, geocoding indexes are not maintained if you edit your geocoding reference data. When you make edits to your geocoding reference data (either by adding or deleting features or rows, or by editing the street names that they contain), you need to update your geocoding indexes.

ArcGIS provides two developer samples that demonstrate how to maintain geocoding indexes. The first sample is a command that rebuilds the geocoding indexes for a geocoding service. The second sample is a command that sets up geocoding indexes so that they are maintained automatically by the geodatabase.

Manually rebuilding geocoding indexes

1. In ArcCatalog, click Tools and click Customize.

2. Click the Toolbars tab and check Context Menus.

   The Context Menus toolbar displays. ►

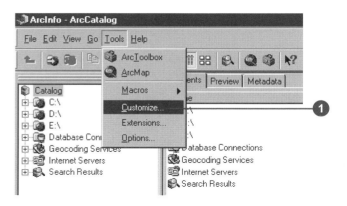

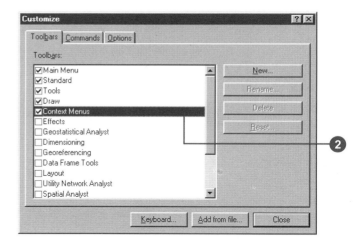

3. Click the Commands tab and click Add from file.

4. Navigate to the GCIndexManagement.dll library in the Developer Samples folder and click Open.

5. Click OK.

6. Scroll through the Categories list and click Menus.

7. Click the Context Menus toolbar and locate the Locator Context Menu. Click and drag Geocoding Indexes onto the Locator Context Menu.

8. Click Close. ▶

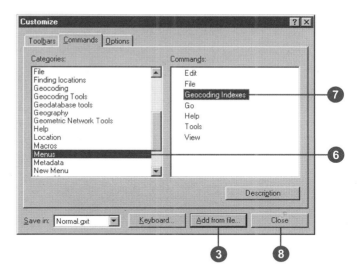

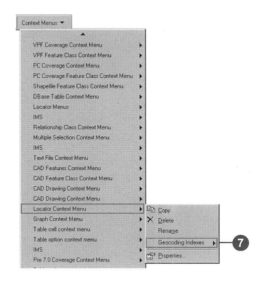

9. Right-click a geocoding service for which you want to rebuild the geocoding indexes, click Geocoding Indexes, and click Rebuild Geocoding Indexes.

10. Check the names of the indexes that you want to rebuild and click OK.

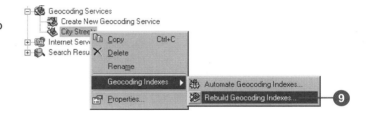

Automatically maintaining geocoding indexes

1. In ArcCatalog, click Tools and click Customize.

2. Click the Toolbars tab and check Context Menus.

    The Context Menus toolbar displays. ▶

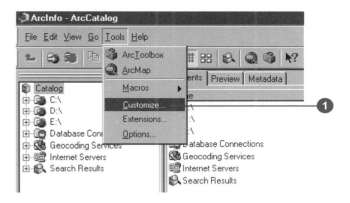

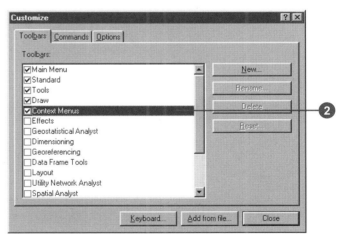

3. Click the Commands tab and click Add from file.

4. Navigate to the GCIndexManagement.dll library in the Developer Samples folder and click Open.

5. Click OK.

6. Scroll through the Categories list and click Menus.

7. Click the Context Menus toolbar and locate the Locator Context Menu. Click and drag Geocoding Indexes onto the Locator Context Menu.

8. Click Close. ▶

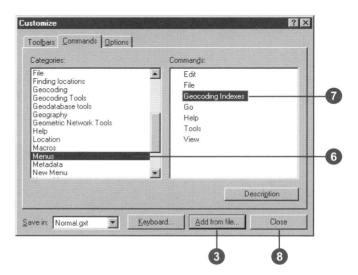

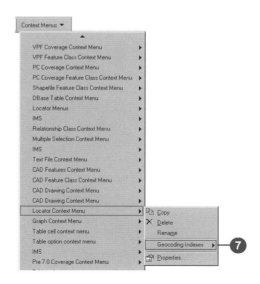

9. Right-click a geocoding service for which you want to automatically maintain the geocoding indexes, click Geocoding Indexes, and click Automate Geocoding Indexes.

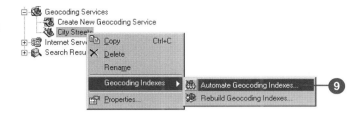

10. Check the names of the indexes that you want automatically maintained and click OK.

Preparing address data for geocoding

Just as each style of geocoding service has different requirements for the attributes of the reference data that it uses, each style also has different requirements for the information that tables of addresses must contain in order to be geocoded. For each style of geocoding service provided with ArcGIS 8, the requirements for address data are described below.

StreetMap

A StreetMap style of geocoding service allows you to geocode addresses anywhere in the United States. Tables of addresses that these geocoding services can match must include the following attributes:

- Address—includes the street number and street name and the street's prefix direction, prefix type, street type, or suffix direction, if any; intersection descriptions (for example, "Hollywood Blvd. & Vine St.") can also be included in this field.

- City—the city in which the address is located.

- State—the state in which the address is located.

- ZIP—the address's five-digit ZIP Code.

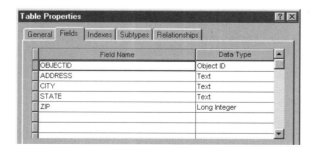

Single Field

A Single Field style of geocoding service allows you to geocode addresses using only a single item of information such as a state name or place name. Tables of addresses that can be geocoded using these geocoding services must contain a field with this information that can be used to find the locations.

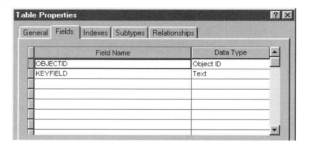

US One Address, US One Range, and US Streets

Each of the U.S. address geocoding service styles, while having different requirements for reference data, has the same requirements for input address data. Tables of addresses that can be geocoded using these geocoding services must contain a field that has an address (as described for the StreetMap geocoding service style). Optionally, if the geocoding service reference data

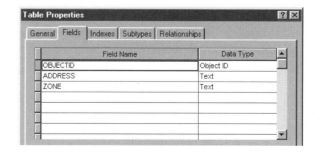

contains zone information, the table of addresses may contain a field having zone information (for example, city name or ZIP Code) that corresponds to the type of zone information in the reference data feature class.

ZIP

A ZIP style of geocoding service allows you to geocode addresses that contain five-digit ZIP Code information. Tables of addresses that can be geocoded using these geocoding services must contain a field that has five-digit ZIP Code information.

ZIP+4 and ZIP+4 Range

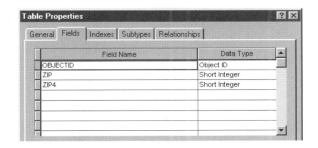

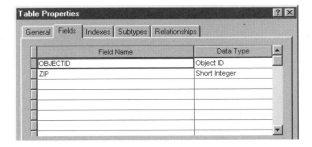

The ZIP+4 geocoding service styles allow you to geocode addresses that contain ZIP+4 code information. Tables of addresses that can be geocoded using these geocoding services must contain fields that have five-digit ZIP and four-digit add-on code information.

Building geodatabases with CASE tools 11

IN THIS CHAPTER

- **What are CASE tools?**

- **Creating UML packages and static structure diagrams**

- **Creating feature datasets**

- **Creating feature classes**

- **Creating relationship classes**

- **Creating domains**

- **Creating subtypes**

- **Creating geometric networks**

- **Creating connectivity rules**

- **Extending classes with custom behavior**

- **Exporting your UML model to the repository**

- **Generating schema from the repository**

Computer-Aided Software Engineering (CASE) tools allow you to create *custom objects* and *features* that extend the *geodatabase* model. Object-oriented design tools that support the Unified Modeling Language (UML) and the Microsoft Repository can be used to create designs for your objects. Once exported to the Microsoft Repository, the CASE tools subsystem will help you create a Component Object Model (COM) object that implements the *behavior* of your custom object and the *database schema* where these objects are stored.

This chapter discusses how you can use Visio® Enterprise to construct your UML and how you can use CASE tools in ArcCatalog to generate the schema for your geodatabase.

What are CASE tools?

As discussed in Chapter 1, there are three general strategies to creating geodatabases. So far, this book has dealt with the first two: migrating existing *databases* to the geodatabase and using tools in ArcCatalog and ArcToolbox to create the schema for your geodatabase design.

This chapter will discuss the third strategy: using UML and the CASE tools subsystem of ArcGIS to generate the schema for your geodatabase.

The geodatabase brings the physical representation of geographic features closer to their actual real-world counterparts. It is possible to create hydrants, mains, and valves and to define a number of characteristics, such as fields, validation rules, relationships, and subtypes, for each. The CASE tools subsystem lets you create blueprints of the structure of the geodatabase using a graphical language. Using class diagrams, you can represent geodatabase elements such as feature datasets or geometric networks and clearly see the relationships among them. To learn more about object modeling and geodatabase design, see *Modeling Our World*.

Based on a UML model, you can generate code to create the geodatabase schema where features are stored as well as custom feature behavior. Through the use of feature classes, subtypes, domains, rules, and relationships, you can create customized geodatabases without writing a line of code. The creation of custom features is optional, and the CASE tools can be used for the sole purpose of creating geodatabase schemas.

This chapter gives an explanation of how to model different aspects of the geodatabase using UML and the steps to construct such models in Visio Enterprise. Using the CASE tools to create custom features is discussed in detail in *Exploring ArcObjects*.

Using CASE for schema design and generation

The general strategy for using UML and CASE tools to design and create your geodatabase involves using UML to define all of the schema for the geodatabase, generating that schema, and then populating the schema with data. The steps for accomplishing this are outlined below:

1. Create your geodatabase design in UML.

2. Export your UML model to a Microsoft Repository.

3. Use the Schema Wizard in ArcCatalog to create the schema in your geodatabase from your UML model.

Once you have generated the schema, you may want to start directly editing that schema to build your database, but typically you will have existing data with which you want to populate that schema. There are a number of things that can impact perfor-

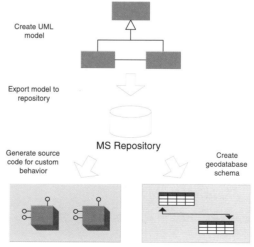

The general strategy for using UML and CASE tools to design and create your geodatabase involves using UML to define all of the schema for the geodatabase, generating that schema, and then populating the schema with data.

mance when loading data into a geodatabase schema, especially when working with network data.

There is more than one strategy for loading data into an existing database schema. Each strategy has its limitations and affects performance of the database. The different strategies for loading your existing data into that schema, and the performance considerations of each, are outlined in Chapter 4, 'Migrating existing data into a geodatabase'.

Modeling database structure

Geodatabase elements, such as tables, feature classes, and relationship classes, follow certain rules that dictate where these elements are stored in the geodatabase relative to each other. For example, feature datasets are defined under the geodatabase, while geometric networks are defined inside feature datasets. Some elements, such as feature classes and relationship classes, can be inside or outside feature datasets.

These aspects of a geodatabase's structure are defined in UML through the use of packages to represent the geodatabase and feature datasets. The UML classes that are used to define feature classes, relationship classes, tables, and geometric networks are defined under these packages.

Tagged values

Tagged values are used to set additional properties of UML elements. For example, you can set the length (in characters) of a string field by using a tagged value.

Tagged values are recognized on several other UML elements: class, attribute, associations, and so on. The following is a table summarizing the tagged values used for geodatabase schema elements.

Table 1: Tagged values for geodatabase UML elements.

Tagged value name	Values/Remarks
Fields:	
Precision	Integer value
	Integer fields: number of digits
	Double fields: total number of digits
Scale	Integer value
	Number of decimal places in single
	and double fields
Length	Integer value
	Width of character fields
AllowNulls	True/False
Feature class/Object class:	
Geometry type	esriGeometryPoint
	esriGeometryPolygon
	esriGeometryPolyline
	esriGeometryMultipoint
	Valid only for feature classes
Ancillary role	esriNCARNone
	esriNCARSourceSink
	Valid only for junction feature classes
ConfigKeyword	String value

HasM	True/False	OriginForeignKey	Name of the foreign key field of the origin class
	Valid only for feature classes		*For 1-1 and 1-M relationship classes, this field lives in the destination class.*
HasZ	True/False		
	Valid only for feature classes		*For 1-M/attributed relationship classes, this field lives in the auxiliary <<RelationshipClass>> class.*
CLSID	GUID in registry format		
	If specified, the Schema Wizard will look for a COM class identified by the CLSID in the system registry.	DestinationPrimaryKey	Name of the primary key field of the destination class
	If not specified, the appropriate ESRI COM class will be used instead. This tagged value will be overwritten by the Code Generation Wizard if code is generated for the custom feature.		*Valid for M-M/attributed relationship classes only.*
		DestinationForeignKey	Name of the foreign key field of the destination class
	This tagged value can be specified for UML classes representing class extensions as well.		*Valid for M-M/attributed relationship classes only. This field lives in the auxiliary <<RelationshipClass>> class.*

Relationship class:

Notification	esriRelNotificationBackward esriRelNotificationBoth esriRelNotificationForward esriRelNotificationNone
IsAttributed	True/False
OriginPrimaryKey	Name of the primary key field of the origin class

Domain:

Description	String value

Feature datasets

Feature datasets are modeled in UML as stereotyped packages that you create under the geodatabase workspace package. A feature dataset package cannot be created under another feature dataset package; however, other packages created for organiza-

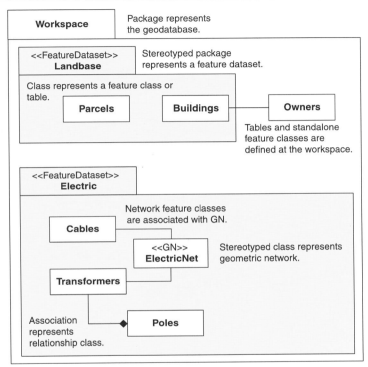

| Workspace | Package represents the geodatabase. |

<<FeatureDataset>>
Landbase — Stereotyped package represents a feature dataset.

Class represents a feature class or table.

Parcels   **Buildings**   **Owners**

Tables and standalone feature classes are defined at the workspace.

<<FeatureDataset>>
Electric

Network feature classes are associated with GN.

Cables

<<GN>>
ElectricNet — Stereotyped class represents geometric network.

Transformers

Association represents relationship class.   **Poles**

Geodatabase elements, such as tables, feature classes, and relationship classes, follow certain rules that dictate where these elements are stored in the geodatabase relative to each other. These aspects of a geodatabase's structure are defined in UML through the use of packages to represent the geodatabase and feature datasets.

tional purposes can. For example, a package to hold all of the subtypes for a particular class can be created under a feature dataset package.

Feature datasets have a spatial reference associated with them. Spatial references are not modeled in UML. Instead, the spatial reference for a feature dataset is set when generating the schema in ArcCatalog.

Tables, feature classes, and geometric networks

UML classes are used to model feature classes and tables. When schema is generated from the UML model, one table or feature class is created for each class in the model. Each property of the object is mapped to a field of the table or feature class. Required fields are included as properties of the base class and need not be repeated in any inherited classes. For example, you may have a class called Pipes that has the properties Material and Diameter. If you then create a new class called Mains that is inherited from Pipes, then Material and Diameter are also properties of the Mains class but do not need to be repeated in the Mains class in the UML model.

When schema is generated, each property is mapped as a field on the table or feature class. You can specify the length, scale, and precision of the fields that correspond with these properties in the UML diagram by setting tagged values. You can also use tagged values to set properties for feature classes, class extensions, relationship classes, and interfaces.

When generating schema, all feature classes the wizard creates use the coordinate system of the target feature dataset. Object classes (tables) are created at the workspace level.

The default grid size is 1,000. Grid size is not stored as part of the model because the coordinate system of target feature datasets might be different. You can specify a grid size for each feature class in the Schema Wizard.

Tables are created for those objects that inherit from the Object class, feature classes are created for those that inherit from the Feature class, and simple or complex network feature classes are created for those that inherit from the Network feature classes.

All network feature classes must be associated with a geometric network. Geometric networks are modeled in UML as special classes. The geometric network and its associated network feature classes must be created in the same feature dataset package. A junction feature class is created for all features that inherit from Simple Junction or Complex Junction. For more information on geometric networks, see Chapter 9, 'Geometric networks'.

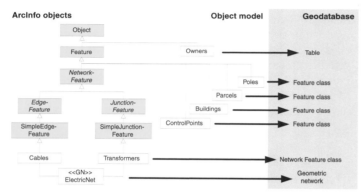

Tables are created for objects that inherit from the Object class, feature classes are created for objects that inherit from the Feature class, and network feature classes are created for objects that inherit from the Network feature class.

Subtypes and domains

Attribute domains are modeled in UML as special classes. When the CASE tool generates the schema from the UML model, these domain classes are stored in the geodatabase as domains. Coded value and range domains, along with their valid values, split policies, and merge policies, are all modeled in this way.

If your tables or feature classes require subtypes, these can also be modeled in UML and automatically generated when the tables or feature classes are created in the database. Subtypes are modeled in UML as classes related to the parent class through an association stereotyped as "Subtype". The subtype field is specified in the parent class as a stereotype of a UML attribute.

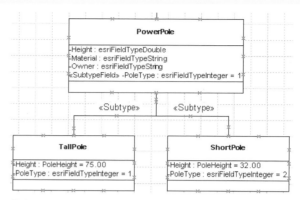

Subtypes are modeled in UML as classes related to the parent class through an association stereotyped as "Subtype". You can specify domains and default values for the fields for that subtype.

You can specify default values and domains for each field for a particular feature class or subtype. To associate a domain with a particular field, simply specify the name of the domain as the field type. Similarly, the field's default value can be supplied for feature classes or subtypes by setting the initial value in the UML attribute representing the field.

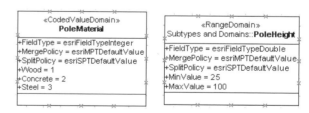

Attribute domains are modeled in UML as special classes.

If the feature class or table you are modeling does not have subtypes, but you still want to associate domains and default values to fields, you can do so directly on the class object itself.

Relationships

Associations between objects in your UML model are created in the geodatabase as relationship classes. The cardinality of those associations is reflected in the cardinality of the relationship class. The name of the relationship class is the name of the association. The primary and foreign keys are specified directly in the UML model as tagged values of the UML association.

Attributed *relationships* are modeled as classes with the same name as the relationship class, stereotyped as a relationship class. The fields for the relationship class's attributes are modeled in the same way as the attributes of any other class.

Notification direction—the direction messages are passed—for the relationship class can be modeled in UML using tagged values.

Relationship rules apply to subtypes in feature classes and tables. In UML, these relationship rules are modeled as associations between subtypes of the classes participating in the relationship class.

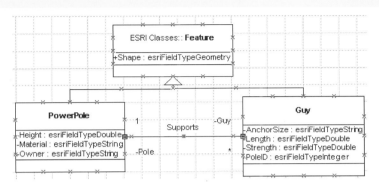

Relationship classes are modeled in UML as associations. The cardinality of the association is reflected as the cardinality of the relationship class. Attributed relationships are modeled as classes with the same name as the relationship class.

Composite relationships are modeled in UML as *aggregation*. In a composite relationship, the origin class is always the parent in the aggregation. Composite relationship classes are always one-to-many.

To learn more about relationship classes, see Chapter 6, 'Defining relationship classes'.

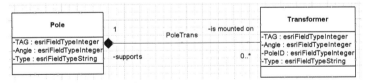

Composite relationship classes are modeled in UML as aggregations between classes.

Connectivity rules

Connectivity rules apply to network feature classes and subtypes of network features participating in the same geometric network. These connectivity rules are modeled in UML as a special association stereotyped as "*ConnRule*".

For *edge–junction connectivity rules,* the ConnRule association is between the edge subtype and the junction subtype. The junction in one of the edge–junction rules can be set as the default junction by stereotyping the association end as "Default". *Edge–Edge rules* are represented by a UML N-ary association that involves two edge subtypes and any number of junction subtypes. One of the junction subtypes must be marked as the *default junction* by stereotyping the association end as "Default".

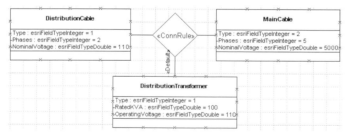

Edge–Edge rules are represented by a UML N-ary association. One of the junction classes or subtypes must be marked as the default junction by stereotyping the association end as "Default".

CASE tools

The CASE tools subsystem of ArcGIS 8 has two parts: the Code Generation Wizard and the Schema Wizard. The remainder of this chapter discusses how you can create each component of your geodatabase schema in UML using Visio Enterprise and how you can use the CASE tools in ArcCatalog to generate the schema for your UML design.

For more information on the ESRI object model and on generating code for your custom objects using the Code Generation Wizard, see *Modeling Our World* and *Exploring ArcObjects.*

The ArcInfo UML Model diagram

When you are ready to begin creating your UML model, you will start with one of the ArcInfo UML Model diagrams that were installed with ArcGIS. These diagrams are Visio Drawing templates—ArcInfo UML Model(Ent).vst for Visio Enterprise or the ArcInfo UML Model (Pro).vst for Visio Professional. These Visio Drawing templates are located under your ArcGIS installation in the casetools\UML Models directory.

The ArcInfo UML Model diagram contains the object model required for using UML to model your geodatabase. The object model has five packages:

- Logical View
- ESRI Classes
- ESRI Interfaces
- ESRI Network
- Workspace

These UML packages act as directories where different parts of the entire object model are maintained. The Logical View package is the root level and contains the other three packages. Database designers and developers can use the Workspace package to create their object and database designs. It is possible to create more packages if the complexity of the model requires you to do so.

The ESRI Classes package contains the portion of the GeoData Access Components necessary to create object models. Classes in this package represent components that are used to access spatial data sources including geodatabases. Feature classes and object classes in your object models will inherit from these classes. The ESRI Interfaces package contains the definition of the interfaces implemented by the components shown in the ESRI Classes package. The interfaces are used only for code generation when creating custom objects.

The tasks in this chapter demonstrate how you can use the ArcInfo UML Model diagram to model the pieces of your geodatabase design. All examples given are for Visio Enterprise 5; however, you may also use Visio Enterprise 2000.

Semantics checker

The CASE tools expect UML models to be created following a set of modeling rules. For example, a network feature class must be associated to a geometric network. The semantics checker can be used to verify that a model stored in the repository has been correctly defined. It will produce a report with the list of errors encountered in the model. You should use the semantics checker before running the CASE tools wizards. You can run the semantics checker from within Visio when the template diagram is loaded.

Applying your model to existing data

You can update the schema of a geodatabase with information stored in an object model. For example, you can import data to a geodatabase, then apply a model to add subtypes, relationships, and other elements. Alternatively, your current schema could have been created previously with the Schema Wizard based on a model. Since then, the model might have changed, and you may want to update the database.

You can use the Schema Wizard to modify an existing geodatabase, even if data has already been loaded. To do so, select the target geodatabase and run the Schema Wizard. When the wizard starts, some elements in the model are searched for and matched to objects in the database—feature classes and tables, for example. If found, the wizard will modify them. The Schema Wizard will show the matched elements with a red shadow in the tree view.

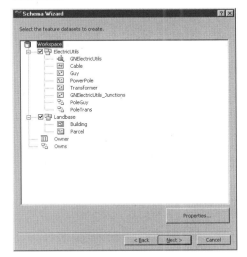

The Schema Wizard will show matched elements with a red shadow in the tree view.

For a number of reasons, your database may contain feature classes and fields whose names do not correspond exactly to the names in the UML model. Perhaps you have applications written previously that rely on the existing field's name being different. For example, a field could be named "Hgt" in the database and "Height" in the model. The geodatabase lets you assign a model name to feature classes and fields, and the CASE tools use the model name when matching them to UML elements. Some properties of the matched object may be read-only, for example, the spatial reference of an existing feature dataset.

Conversely, other properties of the existing object will be changed based on the information in the model such as the domain assigned to a field. In the former case, a locked database icon will appear in the form or tab displaying the particular property. In the latter case, a model icon will be used instead.

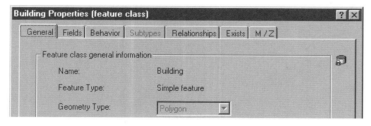

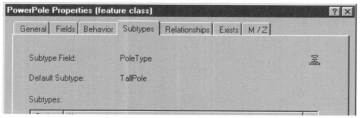

Those properties that cannot be changed when reapplying the model will have a locked database icon on their properties dialog box, while those that can be modified will have a model icon.

Since the schema of matched elements is modified when a model is applied, exclusive schema locks are acquired for the elements that will be modified. These locks can be established only if there are no other users connected to the database and the current user has the right permissions. Since the schema is modified, you should back up your database before applying the changes.

Each geodatabase element supported by the Schema Wizard follows a set of rules when the model is reapplied. The following is a description of these rules:

Feature datasets: The Schema Wizard uses the name of the UML package representing the feature dataset to search for an existing feature dataset in the target database. The spatial reference and spatial domain properties become read-only.

Other model elements are defined inside feature datasets such as geometric networks and feature classes. These elements will be found in the existing database only if the feature dataset itself is found.

Feature classes: The name of the UML class representing the table or feature class will be used to search for an existing object in the geodatabase. The comparison is first made against the model names of the existing feature classes. If no match is found, the comparison is made against the names of the existing feature classes. If still no match is found, you can manually set the match using the Exists tab in the feature class's properties dialog box.

Only feature classes with the same feature type can be used when matching manually. Also, only feature classes in the same location are available for matching—for example, the feature classes under the matched feature dataset.

When the Schema Wizard is run, it updates the model name of both existing and new feature classes and fields. This ensures the matching will occur automatically the next time the model is applied.

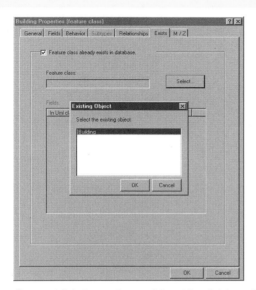

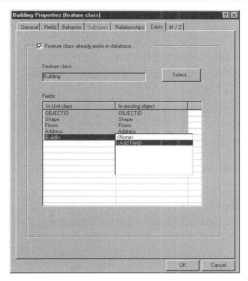

If no match between the model and the database is found for a feature class or table, you can manually set the match using the Exists tab in the feature class's properties dialog box.

If the UML class contains additional fields, these can be marked for addition in the Exists tab of the feature class properties dialog box.

Fields: Like feature classes, fields are matched based on model name, and a manual match can be done. The UML class may also contain additional fields. These can be marked for addition in the Exists tab of the feature class properties dialog box. Existing fields not matched are left untouched. Reapplying the model to existing data does not drop fields.

For matched fields, the field type, length, precision, and scale are read-only properties. However, the domain and initial value will be updated if they have been set in the model (the domain must have the same field type).

Domains: Domains are matched based on the name of the UML class and the existing domain. If found, the domain will be altered with modifications made to the UML class. For example, new codes can be added to a coded value domain.

Subtypes: Subtypes of matched feature classes are deleted and re-created using the subtypes in the model. Because connectivity and relationship rules are created among subtypes, they are deleted and re-created as well. Whenever you use ArcCatalog to add a subtype or rule, you should make sure the model is updated accordingly in case you ever reapply it.

Relationship classes: The name of the relationship class in the model will be used to search for an existing relationship class in the target database. Existing relationship classes that are not matched will be left untouched. The policies on modifying vary, depending on the type of relationship class.

Nonattributed relationship classes are deleted and re-created. Along with the relationship class, the relationship rules are deleted and re-created as well.

Internally, attributed relationship classes are implemented by creating an extra table in the database. This table holds attributes of the relationships and keys to the rows in the related tables. Because this table may be holding data already, only the relationship class's rules, not the relationship class itself, are deleted and re-created.

Geometric networks: The name of the class representing the network will be used to search for an existing geometric network in the target database. As mentioned before, a geometric network is matched only if the feature dataset it belongs to is matched as well. All existing connectivity rules are deleted and re-created.

Creating UML packages and static structure diagrams

Packages are a convenient way to organize your UML model. They act as folders where you can group model elements. Just like with folders on a disk, you can create a hierarchy of packages in your model.

You can create as many packages as you want. For example, you could have a model that has the following packages: Subtypes, Domains, and Connectivity Rules.

Before you begin, create a new diagram using the ArcInfo UML Model Visio templates. These templates are located under your ArcGIS installation in the casetools\UML Models directory.

All of the tasks for creating UML diagrams discussed are performed within the Visio Enterprise application.

See Also

Special packages are used to model feature datasets. See 'Creating feature datasets' later in this chapter.

1. In the UML Navigator tree, right-click Workspace, point to New, and then click Package.

2. Type the name of the package and Click OK.

3. Right-click the new package. Point to New and click Static Structure Diagram to create a new class diagram.

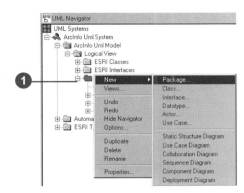

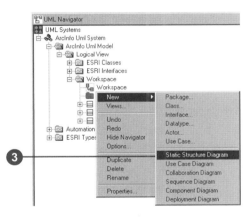

Setting tagged values

You use tagged values to set additional properties of UML elements. For example, you can set the length (in characters) of a string field by using a tagged value.

Tagged values are recognized on several other UML elements: class, attribute, associations, and so on.

1. In the Visio diagram, double-click the UML class.

2. Click the Attributes tab and double-click a string-typed attribute.

3. Click the Tagged Values tab.

4. Click New to create a new tagged value.

5. Type "Length" in the Tag text box and type the length of the field.

6. Click OK.

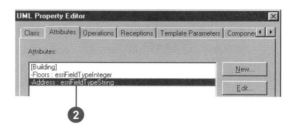

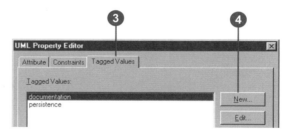

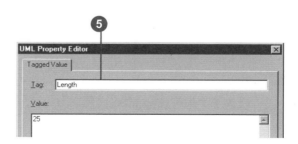

Creating feature datasets

Feature datasets are modeled in UML as stereotyped packages. Other geodatabase elements (feature classes, for example) defined under the package will be created under the feature dataset. The name of the UML package will become the name of the feature dataset.

The spatial reference of a feature dataset is set while running the Schema Wizard.

1. In the UML Navigator, double-click the Workspace diagram to open it.

2. In the UML Static Structure stencil, click Package and drag it onto the diagram.

3. Double-click the new package.

4. Type a name for the package.

5. Click the Stereotype dropdown arrow and click FeatureDataset.

6. Click OK.

   A new package and a new drawing are created in the UML Navigator.

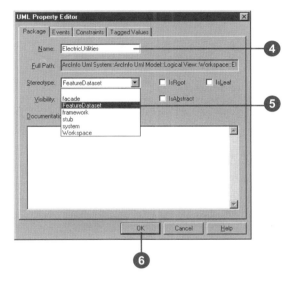

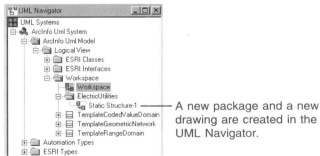

A new package and a new drawing are created in the UML Navigator.

Creating feature classes

Feature classes are represented by UML classes in the model. You can model fields, geometry type, and other characteristics of the feature class in the UML class.

Feature classes can be created in the Workspace UML package or in a feature dataset package.

You can add fields to a feature class by adding attributes to the UML class.

The field type is one of the values of the esriFieldType enumeration—for example, esriFieldTypeInteger.

A domain created beforehand can be used as the attribute type as well.

Creating a feature class

1. In the UML Navigator tree under ESRI Classes, click the parent class and drag and drop it onto the diagram.

2. In the UML Static Structure stencil, click Class and drag and drop a new UML class onto the diagram.

3. In the diagram, double-click the new class. ▶

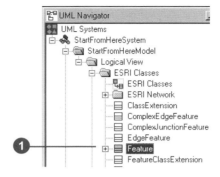

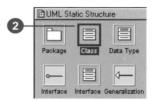

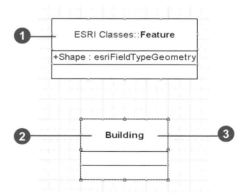

4. Type the name of the feature class.

5. To set tagged values, follow steps 2 through 5 for setting tagged values; otherwise, skip to step 6.

6. Click OK to accept the changes.

7. In the UML Static Structure stencil, click Generalization and drag and drop it onto the diagram.

8. Drag the ends of the generalization arrow and connect the new class with its parent.

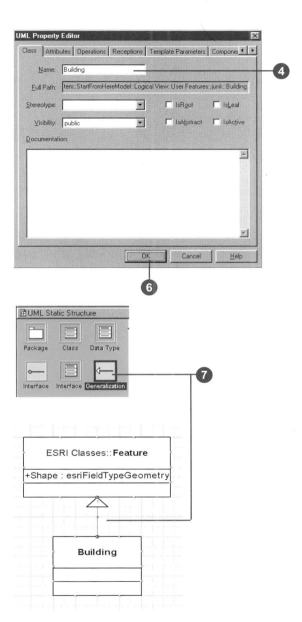

Adding fields to a feature class

1. In the diagram, double-click the class.

2. Click the Attributes tab.

3. Click New to add a new attribute. ▶

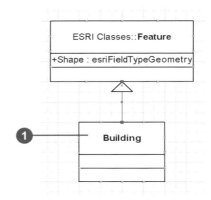

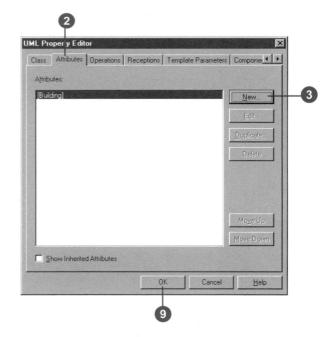

4. Type a name for the new field.

5. Click the Type dropdown arrow and click the field type.

6. To set tagged values, follow steps 2 through 5 for setting tagged values; otherwise, skip to step 7.

7. Click OK.

8. Repeat steps 3 through 7 until you have added all the fields for your new class.

9. Click OK.

The fields appear in the diagram as properties of the class.

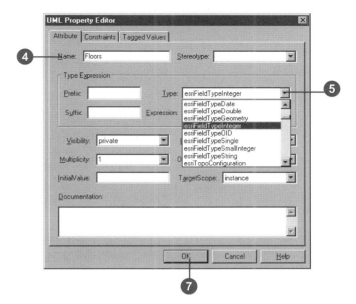

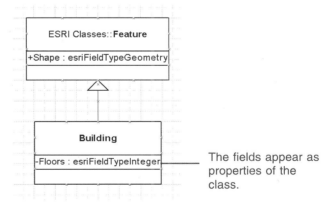

The fields appear as properties of the class.

Creating relationship classes

UML associations represent relationship classes among feature classes and object classes (tables).

Relationship classes can be created only among leaf classes. Primary and foreign key fields must be present in the classes.

Tagged values for relationship classes include:

- OriginPrimaryKey: the name of the primary key field in the origin class.

  Example:
  OriginPrimaryKey=OBJECTID

- OriginForeignKey: the name of the foreign key field in the destination class.

  Example:
  OriginForeignKey=PoleID ▶

Tip

Which one is the origin?
Make sure the first association end in the Association tab in the UML Property Editor dialog box corresponds to the origin class in your relationship.

Creating nonattributed relationship classes

1. In the UML Static Structure stencil, click Binary Association and drag and drop it onto the diagram.

2. Connect the two classes. The left end of the association is the origin class, and the right end is the destination class.

3. Double-click the association.

4. Type a name for the association.

5. Double-click one of the association ends. ▶

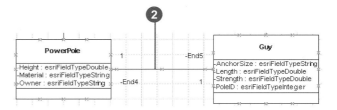

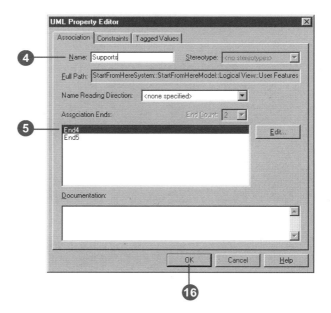

- Notification: one of the values of the esriRelNotification enumeration.

  Example:
  Notification=esriRelNotificationBoth

The cardinality of the relationship class is derived from the multiplicity of both association ends. Because the cardinality of a relationship class can be only 1-1, 1-M, or M-N, the only valid multiplicity values are 1 and * (many). The name of an association end becomes a relationship class path label.

A relationship class can have its own set of attributes. You can model such relationship classes by adding a UML class named after the relationship and stereotyped as "RelationshipClass". The fields of the relationship class are modeled in the same way as fields in any other class. Foreign keys must be included in the class representing the attributed relationship. Many-to-many relationships are always attributed.

The following tagged values are recognized for attributed relationship classes:

- IsAttributed: should be "True". ▶

6. Type the association end name.

7. Click the Multiplicity dropdown arrow and click the association end multiplicity.

8. Click OK.

9. Repeat steps 6 through 9 to set the name and multiplicity of the second end.

   The keys for the relationship class are set in UML using tagged values.

10. Click the Tagged Values tab.

11. Click New.

12. Type "OriginPrimaryKey" for the tag name.

13. Type the name of the origin primary key field.

14. Click OK.

15. Repeat steps 6 through 9 to set the origin foreign key and notification tags. ▶

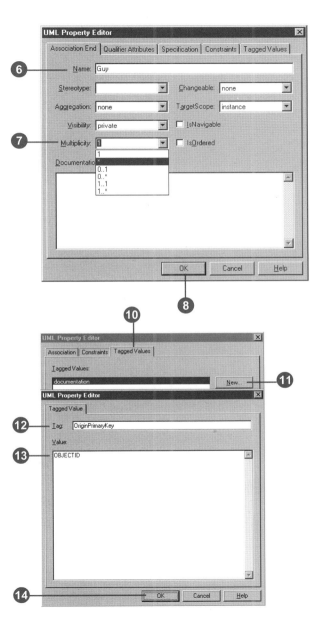

- OriginPrimaryKey: the name of the primary key field in the origin class.

  Example: OriginPrimaryKey=OBJECTID

- OriginForeignKey: the name of the foreign key field in the destination class.

  Example: OriginForeignKey=OwnerID

- DestinationPrimaryKey: the name of the primary key field in the destination class.

  Example: DestinationPrimaryKey=OBJECTID

- DestinationForeignKey: the name of the foreign key field in the attributed relationship.

  Example: DestinationForeignKey=BuildingID

- Notification: one of the values of the esriRelNotification enumeration.

  Example: Notification=esriRelNotificationBoth

Tip

Using OBJECTID as a key field

OBJECTID is defined in the Object class and is inherited by all other classes. If a field typed as OID is used as the primary key, then the foreign key must be typed as esriFieldTypeInteger.

16. Click OK.

The relationship class is shown as an association between two classes. The name of the association is the name of the relationship class.

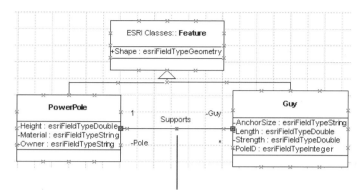

The relationship class is shown as an association between classes.

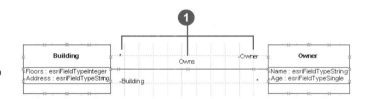

Tip

Composite relationships

In a composite relationship, one of the objects controls the lifetime of the associated objects. You can create a composite relationship by using a Composition instead of a binary association.

Creating attributed relationship classes

1. Create the UML association representing the relationship class by following steps 1 through 11 for creating nonattributed relationship classes.

2. In the UML Static Structure stencil, click Class and drag and drop a new UML class onto the diagram.

3. Double-click the new class.

4. Type the name of the association as the name of the new class.

5. Click the Stereotype dropdown arrow and click RelationshipClass.

6. Follow steps 1 through 8 for adding fields to a feature class to add fields to the relationship class.

7. Click OK.

   The keys for the relationship class are set in UML using tagged values. ►

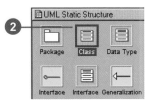

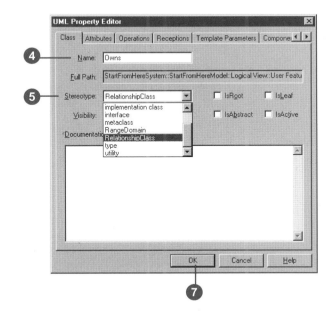

8. Double-click the association.

9. Click the Tagged Values tab.

10. Click New.

11. Type "OriginPrimaryKey" for the tag name.

12. Type the name of the origin primary key field.

13. Click OK.

14. Repeat steps 10 through 13 for the destination primary key, the origin and destination foreign keys, and the notification tags.

15. Click OK.

   The attributed relationship is represented by a class with the same name as the relationship association. Its attributes appear as properties of the class.

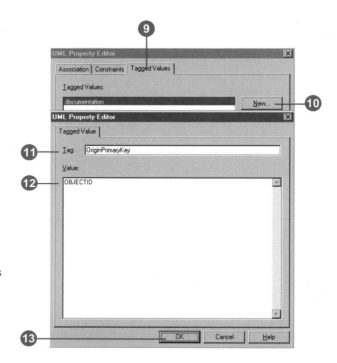

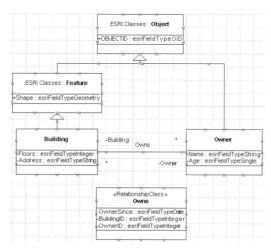

Creating domains

Domains are modeled in UML as stereotyped classes. Domains can be used as the type of a field to define the type and valid values for the field.

The first three attributes in the class define the field type, the *merge policy*, and the *split policy*. The type for any of these attributes is not important and can be left unspecified. The initial value, however, is the actual setting. For example, the following is a valid MergePolicy:

- Attribute name: MergePolicy

- Attribute type: <unspecified>

- Attribute Initial Value: esriMPTDefaultValue

The valid initial values for FieldType, MergePolicy, and SplitPolicy are taken from the esriFieldType, esriMergePolicy, and esriSplitPolicy enumerations, respectively.

In addition to the standard attributes of domains (FieldType, MergePolicy, and SplitPolicy), range domains have MinValue and MaxValue. ▶

Creating a range domain

1. In the UML navigator, under User Features package, right-click TemplateRangeDomain and click Duplicate.

2. A copy of the TemplateRangeDomain is created under the User Features package. Drag and drop it on the diagram.

3. Double-click the new class.

4. Type the name of the domain. ▶

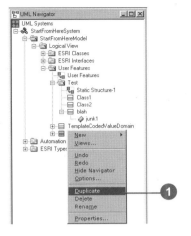

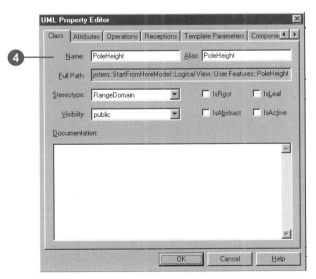

The initial values in MinValue and MaxValue define the actual range. The type of these attributes is not important and can be left unspecified.

Coded value domains can have any number of UML attributes representing the set of permissible values. The initial value defines the valid code, and the name of the attribute is the name of the code. The type of these attributes is not important and can be left unspecified.

5. Click the Attributes tab.

6. Double-click FieldType.

7. Type the type of field with which this domain will be associated in the InitialValue text box.

8. Click OK.

9. Double-click MergePolicy.

10. Type the merge policy in the InitialValue text box.

11. Click OK.

12. Double-click SplitPolicy.

13. Type the split policy in the InitialValue text box.

14. Click OK. ▶

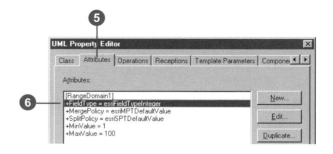

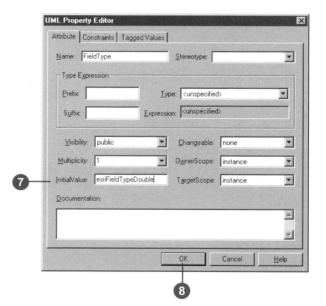

15. Double-click the MinValue attribute.

16. Type the minimum value for the range domain in the InitialValue text box.

17. Click OK.

18. Double-click the MaxValue attribute.

19. Type the maximum value for the range domain in the InitialValue text box.

20. Click OK.

21. Right-click the domain in the diagram and click Show Attribute Types to hide the attribute types.

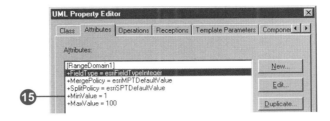

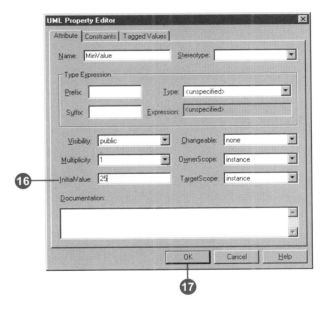

Creating coded value domains

1. In the UML Navigator, navigate to and right-click TemplateCodedValueDomain. Click Duplicate.

2. A copy of the TemplateCodedValueDomain is created under the User Features package. Drag and drop it on the diagram.

3. Double-click the domain in the diagram.

4. Click the Attributes tab.

5. Follow steps 6 through 14 for creating a range domain to set the field type and the split and merge policies.

6. Double-click the Code1 attribute. ▶

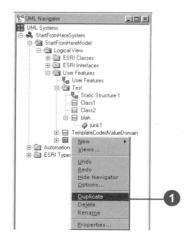

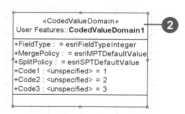

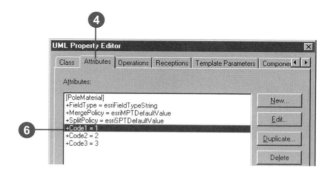

7. Type the code name.

8. Type the code in the InitialValue text box.

9. Click OK.

10. Repeat steps 6 through 9 for the other codes.

11. Click OK.

12. Right-click the domain in the diagram and click Show Attribute Types to hide the attribute types.

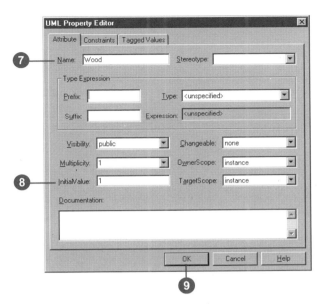

Creating subtypes

Subtypes are modeled in UML as classes related to the parent class through an association stereotyped as "Subtype". You can specify domains and default values for the fields in the subtype.

A field in the parent class must be stereotyped as "SubtypeField". Its initial value is the subtype code of the default subtype. The subtype field must be typed as "esriFieldTypeInteger" in the parent class.

All subtypes must have a unique value for the subtype field—this unique value is its subtype code. Fields in the subtype must match those of the parent class in name and type, but not all the fields of the parent class have to be present in the subtype. The subtype field, however, is a required field in the subtype.

Initial values must be type-compatible with the type of the field. The type of a field can be a domain previously created.

Defining the subtype field for the feature class

1. In the diagram, double-click the class for which you want to create a subtype.

2. Click the Attributes tab.

3. Double-click the attribute that will be the subtype field. ▶

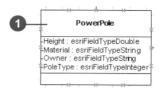

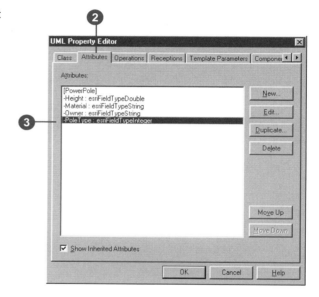

4. Click the Stereotype dropdown arrow and click SubtypeField.

5. Type the subtype code of the default subtype in the InitialValue text box.

6. Click OK.

   The subtype field appears as a property of the class with a stereotype of SubtypeField.

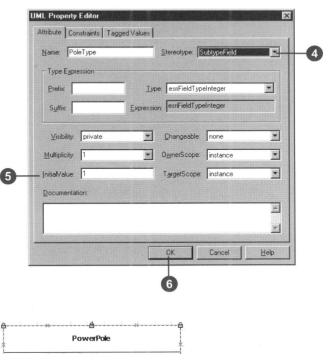

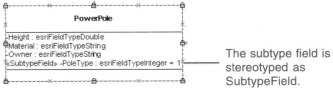

The subtype field is stereotyped as SubtypeField.

When to include a field in a subtype

A field should be included in a subtype only when you want to associate a default value or domain with it. Fields inherited from abstract classes can be included in subtypes.

Creating a subtype

1. In the diagram, copy the class for which you want to create a subtype. Paste it on the diagram.

2. Double-click the new class.

3. Type a name for the subtype.

4. Click the Attributes tab.

5. Click each field for which you don't want to associate a default value or domain for this subtype, then click Delete to remove each one. ▶

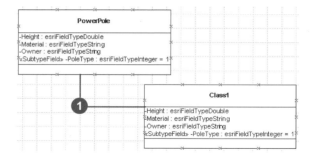

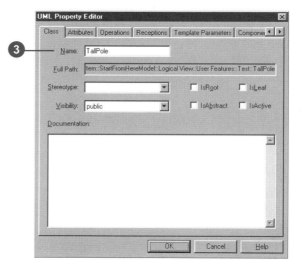

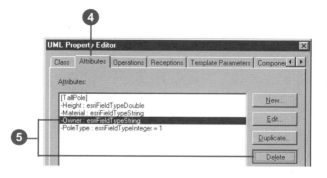

6. Double-click the subtype field.

7. Click the Stereotype dropdown arrow and click the blank stereotype to set its stereotype to nothing.

8. Type the code for this subtype in the InitialValue text box.

9. Click OK.

10. To set default values and domains for a field, double-click the attribute. ▶

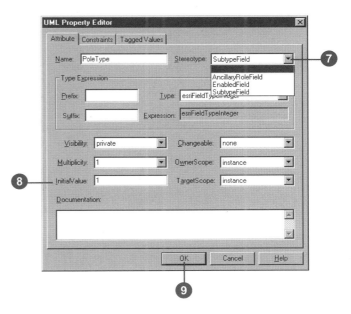

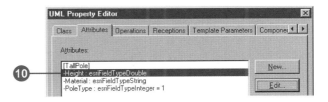

11. Click the Type dropdown arrow and click the domain you want to associate with the attribute as the type.

12. To associate a default value with this attribute, type the default value in the InitialValue text box.

13. Click OK.

14. Repeat steps 6 through 9 until you have associated default values and domains with all the attributes.

15. Click OK.

    The field appears in the class with its domain as its type and its default value as its initial value.

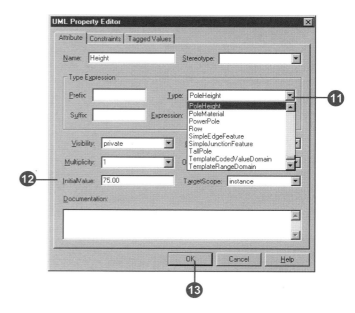

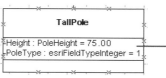

The domain is displayed as the field type and the default value as the initial value.

Setting the initial value for the subtype field

Be very careful when setting the initial value for the subtype field in your subtypes. Its value has to be unique across all the subtypes of a class.

Associating the subtype with its parent class

1. In the UML Static Structure stencil, click Binary Association and drag and drop it on the diagram. Connect the parent and subtype classes.

2. In the diagram, double-click the association. Click the Stereotype dropdown and click "Subtype".

3. Click OK.

4. In the diagram, right-click the association and click the menu commands to hide the ends and display the name.

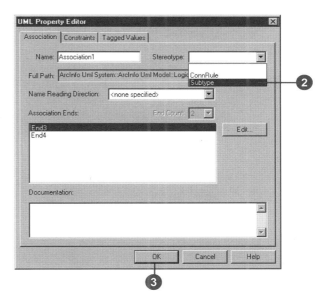

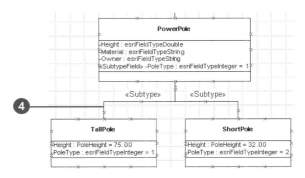

Creating relationship rules

Relationship classes can have a set of relationship rules. These rules control which subtypes of objects from the origin class can be related to which subtypes of the destination class.

Relationship rules are represented by a UML association between subtypes. Multiplicity in association ends is used to set the cardinality of the relationship rule.

A value of 1..3 means at least one and no more than three objects of this subtype can be related.

The cardinality range of both ends must be compatible with the cardinality of the parent relationship class (in the example, 1-1..3 is compatible with 1-M).

See Also

For more information on relationship rules, see Chapter 6, 'Defining relationship classes'.

1. In the UML Static Structure stencil, click Binary Association and drag and drop it on the diagram. Connect the two subtypes between which you want to create a relationship rule.

2. Double-click the association.

3. Type the name of the relationship between the parent classes as the name for this association.

4. Double-click one of the association ends. ▶

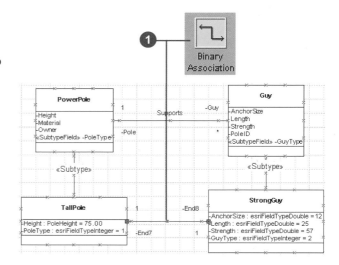

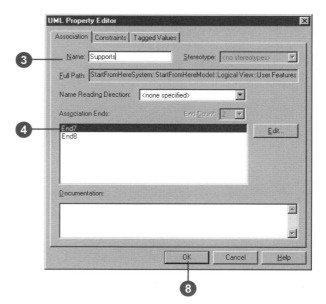

5. Type the valid cardinality as the multiplicity of the association end.

6. Click OK.

7. Repeat steps 4 through 6 for the other association end.

8. Click OK.

9. In the diagram, right-click the association and click the menu commands to hide the ends and display the name.

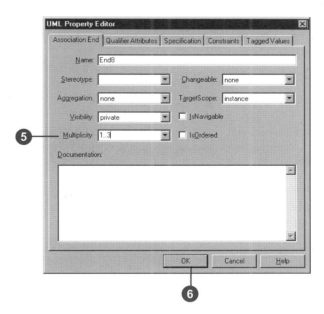

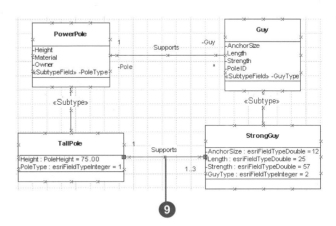

Creating geometric networks

A geometric network is modeled with a UML class stereotyped as GeometricNetwork. UML binary associations are used to associate the network feature classes in the model with the geometric network.

The geometric network UML class and all associated feature classes must be created under the same feature dataset UML package.

The only attribute in a geometric network class defines the network type. When you copy the template, the attribute is already in the class.

Tip

Feature datasets

Make sure you have created a feature dataset before creating a geometric network. A geometric network can exist only inside a feature dataset.

1. In the UML Navigator, under the Workspace package, right-click TemplateGeometricNetwork and click Duplicate.

2. A copy of the TemplateGeometricNetwork is created under the Workspace package. In the UML Navigator, drag and drop it inside the package representing the feature dataset. ▶

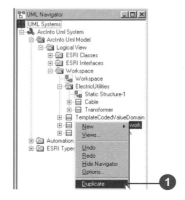

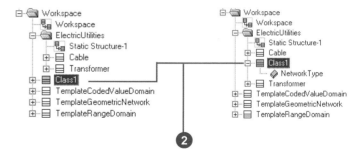

3. Double-click the feature dataset diagram to open it.

4. Drag and drop the new geometric network on the diagram.

5. Double-click the geometric network to open its properties.

6. Type a name for the geometric network.

7. In the UML Navigator, click Binary Association and drag and drop it on the diagram. Connect the network feature classes to the geometric network.

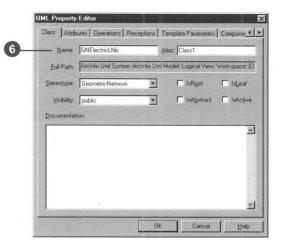

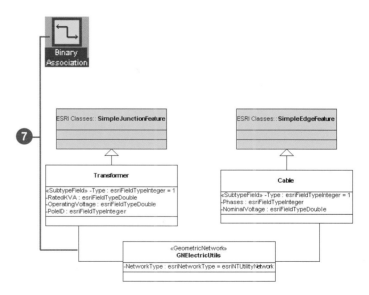

Creating connectivity rules

Connectivity rules can be defined among subtypes of network feature classes modeled in a geometric network. UML associations are used to define connectivity rules. Two types of connectivity rules can be created: edge–edge rules and edge–junction rules.

Edge–Junction connectivity rules can have specific cardinalities for each subtype involved. In this example, one power transformer can be connected to up to two main cables. One of the junction subtypes can be marked as the default junction by stereotyping the association end as "Default".

Edge–Edge rules are represented by a UML N-ary association that involves two edges and any number of junctions. One of the junction subtypes must be marked as the default junction by stereotyping the association end as "Default".

The rule in this example can be read as "Distribution cables can be connected to main cables through distribution transformers". ▶

Creating an edge–junction rule

1. In the UML Static Structure stencil, click Binary Association and drag and drop it on the diagram. Connect the edge subtypes and junction subtype.

2. Double-click the association.

3. Click the Stereotype dropdown arrow and click "ConnRule".

4. Double-click one of the association ends. ▶

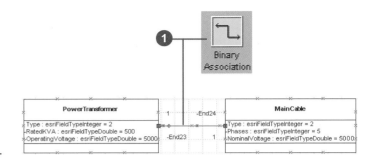

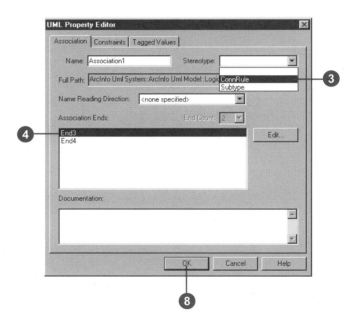

All geometric networks have a default or generic junction subtype, also called the orphan junction type. You can create connectivity rules that include the generic junction.

Both edge–junction and edge–edge rules can involve the generic junction.

5. Type the cardinality for the subtype.

6. Click OK.

7. Repeat steps 4 through 6 to set the cardinality for the second subtype.

8. Click OK.

9. In the diagram, right-click the association and click the menu commands to hide the ends and display the name.

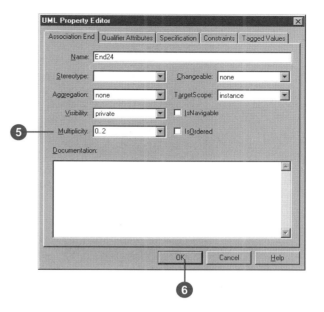

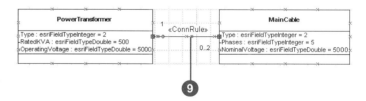

Creating an edge–edge rule

1. In the UML Static Structure stencil, click N-ary Association and drag and drop it on the diagram. Connect two edge subtypes and a junction subtype.

2. Double-click the association.

3. Click the Stereotype dropdown arrow and click "ConnRule".

4. If there is more than one junction subtype for this edge–edge rule, click the End Count dropdown arrow and click the number of junction subtypes.

5. Double-click one of the association ends. ▶

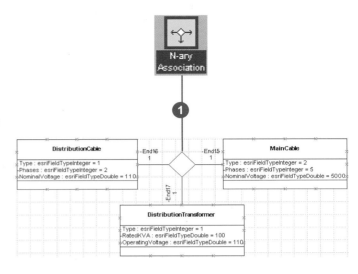

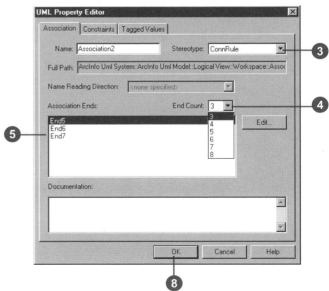

6. Click the Stereotype dropdown arrow and click Default to mark the junction subtype as the default junction subtype in the edge–edge rule.

7. Click OK.

8. Click OK.

9. Right-click the association and click the menu commands to show its name and stereotype and to hide the end names and cardinalities.

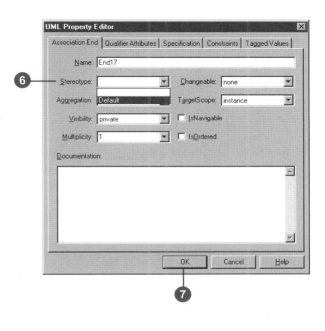

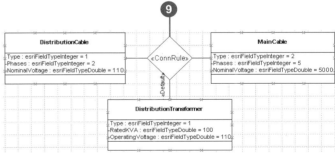

Using the generic junction subtype

1. In the UML Navigator, navigate to and click GenericJunctionST. Drag and drop it on the diagram.

2. Follow steps 1 through 9 for creating an edge–junction rule or steps 1 through 9 for creating an edge–edge rule, using the generic junction subtype.

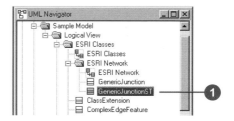

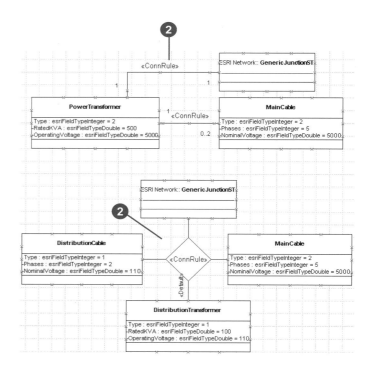

Extending classes with custom behavior

In addition to designing schema, you can use UML and CASE tools to generate code to create custom feature behavior. There are two modeling tasks associated with this: creating new interfaces and creating class extensions. It is important to understand that interfaces and class extensions in UML models are used only when code is generated for the model.

Interfaces are a set of related methods that a custom feature agrees to implement. A custom feature may implement any number of interfaces. Interfaces are inherited. An interface implemented by a parent class is also implemented by its children.

Types used in interfaces should be either other interfaces or automation-compatible types, such as long, double, DATE, and VARIANT_BOOL. UML attributes will become properties. They can be used as Object.Prop = value, or var = Object.Prop. ▶

Creating an interface

1. In the UML Static Structure stencil, click Class and drag and drop it on the diagram.

2. Double-click the class.

3. Type the name of the interface in the Name box.

4. Click the Stereotype dropdown arrow and click interface.

5. Check the IsAbstract check box. ▶

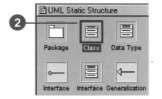

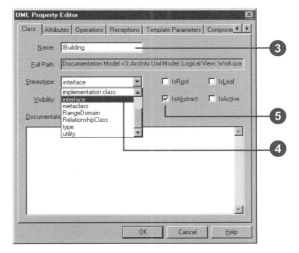

UML operations will become methods. They can be used as Object.Method(argument:type).

To create a read-only property, create an operation with the prefix "get_". Likewise, use the prefixes "put_" or "putref_" to create write-only properties.

You can model class extensions when you want custom behavior associated with the feature class. Class extensions require a naming convention. Its name must be formed by concatenating the name of the feature class or table with "ClassExtension".

Class extensions for tables are derived from ObjectClassExtension. Likewise, class extensions for feature classes are derived from FeatureClassExtension.

Class extensions may implement optional interfaces such as IObjectInspector. In addition, they may implement their own interfaces, for example, IBuildingClassExtension.

See Also

For a detailed explanation about creating custom features and class extensions, see Exploring ArcObjects.

6. Click the Attributes tab.

7. Click New to add a new attribute.

8. Type a name for the new property.

9. Click the Type dropdown and click the field type.

10. Click OK.

11. Repeat steps 7 through 10 until you have added all the properties of the new interface.

12. Click the Operation tab.

13. Click New to add a new method.

14. Type the name of the method.

15. Click the Return type dropdown and click the method type if it returns something

16. Click OK.

17. Repeat steps 13 through 16 until you have added all the methods of the new interface.

18. Click OK. ▶

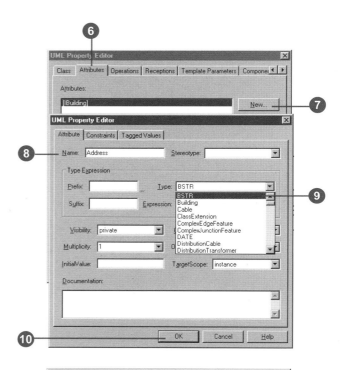

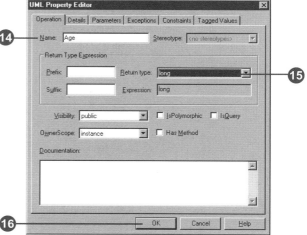

19. In the UML Static Structure stencil, click Refinement and drag and drop it on the diagram.

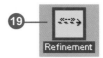

20. Connect the custom feature and the interface.

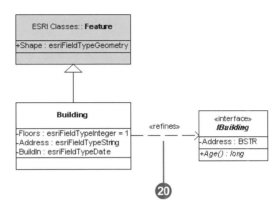

Creating a class extension

1. In the UML Navigator tree under ESRI Classes, click FeatureClassExtension and drag and drop it onto the diagram.

2. In the UML Static Structure stencil, click Class and drag and drop a new UML class onto the diagram.

3. In the diagram, double-click the new class.

4. Type the name of the class following the class extension naming convention.

5. Click OK. ▶

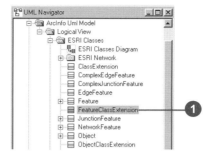

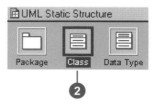

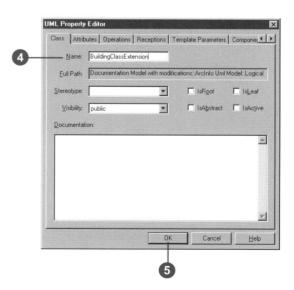

6. In the UML Static Structure stencil, click Generalization and drag and drop it onto the diagram.

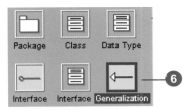

7. Drag the ends of the generalization arrow and connect the new class with its parent.

To add your own interfaces, follow the instructions for creating an interface. There are a number of predefined optional interfaces you can implement in your class extension. ▶

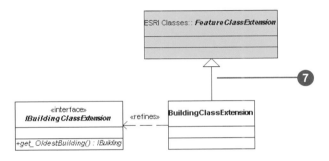

Tip

Optional interfaces

Your class extension can implement all or none of the optional class extension interfaces.

8. In the UML Navigator tree under ESRI Interfaces, click the optional interface and drag and drop it onto the diagram.

9. In the UML Static Structure stencil, click Refinement and drag and drop it onto the diagram.

10. Drag the ends of the refinement and connect the class extension with the interface.

11. Repeat steps 8 through 10 until you have added all of the optional interfaces you want to implement.

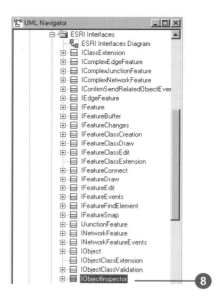

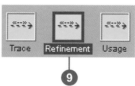

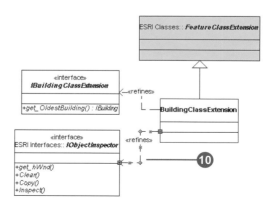

Exporting your UML model to the repository

Before you can generate your geodatabase schema from your UML model, you must first export it to a Microsoft Repository database. A repository database can be stored either in a Microsoft Access database or in an SQL Server database.

The tools to export your UML model to the repository are contained within Visio.

Tip

Existing models

If you select an existing repository to export your UML model to, you can click List Models to get a list of the models that are in the repository.

Exporting to a Microsoft Access repository

1. In Visio Enterprise, click UML and click Export.

2. Type the name of an existing or new access database or click Browse to navigate to it.

3. Type the name of the model as it will be stored in the repository.

4. Click OK to export the UML model.

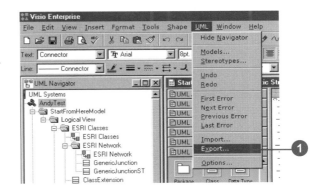

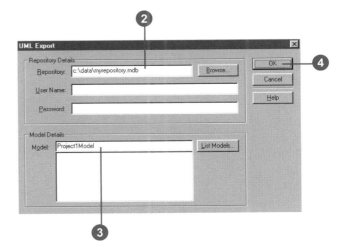

Exporting to an SQL Server repository

1. In Visio, click UML and click Export.

2. Type the name of the ODBC data source that stores the information describing how to connect to the SQL Server database.

3. Type the database *username* and *password*.

4. Type the name of the model as it will be stored in the repository.

5. Click OK to export the UML model.

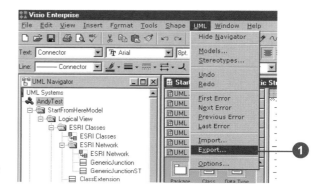

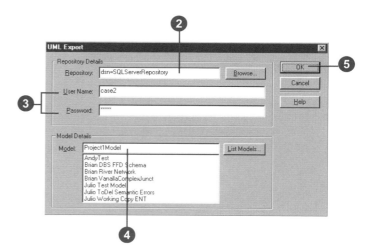

Checking your model for errors

The semantics checker can be used to make sure your models are valid. If errors are found, a report will be automatically created. The report can be printed or exported to a number of formats.

The semantics checker works on models already exported to the repository.

You should run the semantics checker before using the Schema Wizard or Code Generation Wizard.

Running the semantics checker

1. In Visio, click Tools, point to Macro, point to ESRI, then click Semantics_Checker.

2. Type the name of an existing repository or click Browse to navigate to it.

3. Click List Models to see the list of models in the repository.

4. Select the model you want to verify.

5. Click Check.

   If errors are found, a report is generated listing all of the modeling errors.

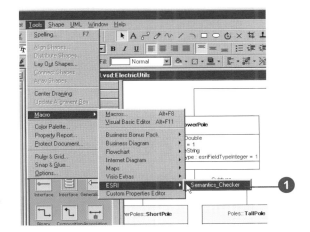

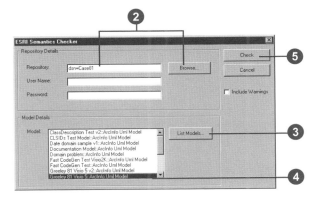

A report is generated listing all of the modeling errors.

Generating schema from the repository

ArcCatalog contains tools to read the Microsoft Repository database you created using the UML modeling software. The Schema Wizard guides you through the process of creating new feature classes, tables, and other pieces of your geodatabase.

Although all of the required information for the geodatabase schema can be read directly from the repository, you can change certain information. Once the wizard is finished, you will have the schema for your design ready to be populated with data.

During the schema generation process, you will be presented with a tree view of the feature datasets, tables, feature classes, network feature classes, and geometric networks in the model.

The examples here involve objects, features, and network features. Many of these objects and features contain subtypes with attribute domains and default values. The examples also include relationship classes between some of the ▶

Adding the CASE Tools wizard to ArcCatalog

1. In ArcCatalog, click Tools and click Customize.

2. Click the Commands tab in the Customize dialog box.

3. Click Case Tools.

4. Drag the Schema Wizard command from the Commands list and drop it on the Standard toolbar.

   The command appears on the toolbar.

5. Click Close on the Customize dialog box.

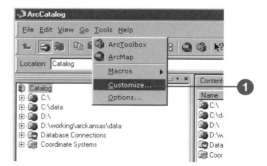

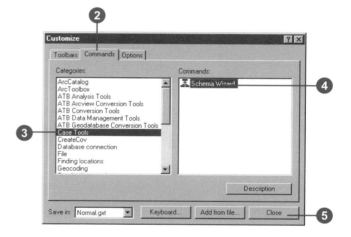

The command appears on the toolbar.

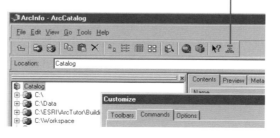

object and feature classes. However, a UML model can be as simple as containing a single feature or object class.

If the schema you are generating contains attribute domains, you can view the properties for these domains, but you cannot modify them.

See Also

For more information on how to customize ArcCatalog, see Using ArcCatalog *and* Exploring ArcObjects.

Connecting to the repository

1. In the ArcCatalog tree, click the geodatabase in which you will create the schema and click the Case Tools button.

2. Click Next. ▶

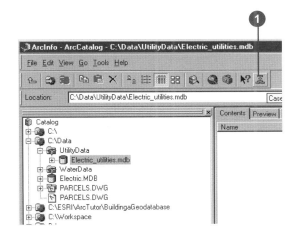

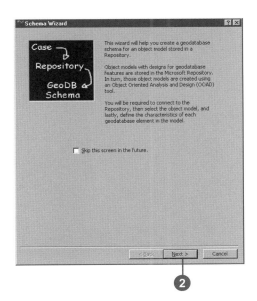

3. If you are connecting to a repository stored in a Microsoft Access database, type the name of the database, or click Browse to navigate to it, then skip to step 5.

   If you are connecting to a repository stored in SQL Server, type the name of the ODBC data source that stores the information describing how to connect to the SQL Server database.

4. Type the database username and password (SQL Server only).

5. Click Next. ▶

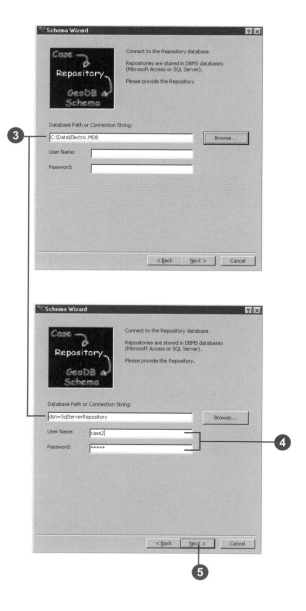

6. Click the name of the object model in the repository for which you want to generate schema.

7. Click Next.

A treeview of the schema represented in the model is displayed. Using this treeview, you will now select the object classes (tables), feature datasets, and feature classes from your UML model for which you want to generate schema.

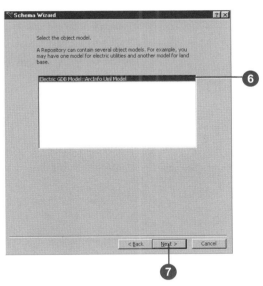

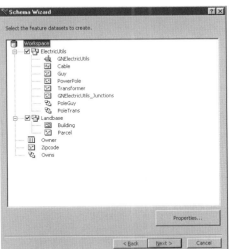

The geodatabase schema represented in the model is displayed in a treeview.

Selecting feature datasets

After connecting to the repository and selecting your model, you must select the feature datasets from your model for which you want to create schema.

Tip

Selecting feature datasets

When you select a feature dataset for which to generate schema, the schema for all of the feature classes, geometric networks, and relationship classes contained in that feature dataset is also created.

Tip

Spatial reference

When you select a feature dataset and assign it a spatial reference, all of the feature classes within that feature dataset share the same spatial reference.

The exception is the M-domain. Feature classes in the same feature dataset may have different M-domains.

See Also

For a detailed explanation of spatial references and how to set them for objects in a geodatabase, see Chapter 3, 'Creating new items in a geodatabase'.

1. Check the feature dataset for which you want to generate schema.

2. Click the Properties button to set the properties for this feature dataset.

   Since you cannot model spatial references in UML, you will have to set the spatial reference for this feature dataset.

3. Click Edit to modify the spatial reference of the feature dataset.

4. Click OK once you have set the spatial reference.

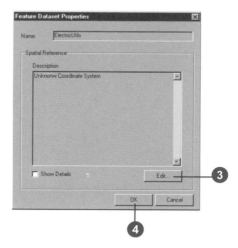

Setting properties for object classes (tables)

After connecting to the repository and selecting your model, you can set properties for the object classes (tables) from your model.

1. Click the table whose properties you want to set.

2. Click Properties.

   Since this class does not store features, a number of properties are unavailable.

3. If generating schema for an ArcSDE geodatabase, click the dropdown arrow and click a storage configuration keyword. If you do not select a keyword, DEFAULTS will be used. ►

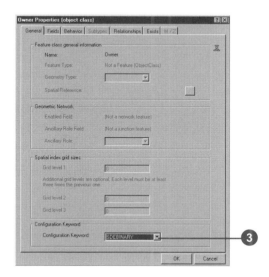

4. If the table in which you want to store this class does not already exist in the database, click the Fields tab. If the table does exist, skip to step 10.

5. Click a field in the list of fields. If you used tagged values in your UML model to set the field properties, skip to step 8.

6. Type its precision if it is an integer field, its precision and scale if it is a float field, or its length if it is a text field.

7. Check Allow Null Values if you want *null values* to be permitted in this field.

8. Repeat steps 5 through 7 for each field in the table, then skip to step 13.

9. Click the Exists tab if the table in which you want to store this class already exists in the database.

10. Check the check box to indicate that the table already exists.

11. Click Select to select the table from a list of tables in the database.

12. For each property in the UML class, click the field in the existing table that will store that property. ▶

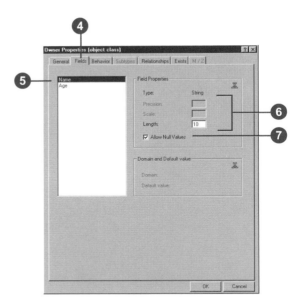

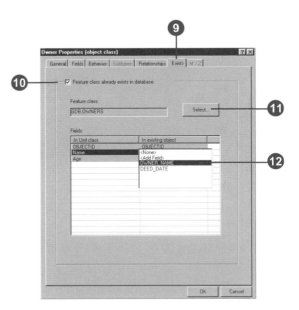

13. If you chose to use ESRI-provided components for all of your classes, skip to step 17.

14. Click the Behavior tab.

15. Click the dropdown arrow to see a list of COM classes that are registered on your system. Click the COM class that implements the behavior for this table.

16. If this table has subtypes or relationship classes associated with it, examine their properties by clicking the Relationships and Subtypes tabs.

17. Click OK.

18. Repeat steps 2 through 17 for the rest of your tables.

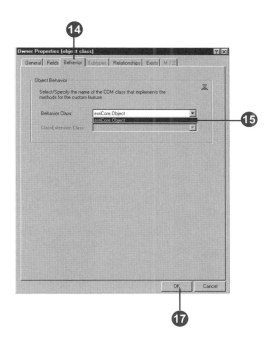

Setting properties for feature classes in a feature dataset

Once you have completed setting the properties for the object classes in your model, you must do the same for the feature classes in your model.

Tip

Spatial reference

When you select a feature dataset and assign it a spatial reference, all of the feature classes within that feature dataset share the same spatial reference.

The exception is the M-domain. Feature classes in the same feature dataset may have different M-domains.

Standalone feature classes have their own spatial reference.

1. Click the feature class whose settings you want to modify.

2. Click the Properties button to set the properties for this class.

3. Click the Geometry Type dropdown arrow and click the geometry type for this feature class.

4. Type the grid levels for the feature class. Personal geodatabase feature classes can have only one grid level.

5. If generating schema for an ArcSDE geodatabase, click the dropdown arrow and click a storage configuration keyword. If you do not select a keyword, DEFAULTS will be used.

6. Follow steps 5 through 18 for setting properties for object classes.

7. Repeat steps 1 through 6 for the rest of the feature classes in your feature dataset.

See Also

For a detailed explanation of spatial references and how to set them for objects in a geodatabase, see Chapter 3, 'Creating new items in a geodatabase'.

Setting properties for standalone feature classes

1. Click the feature class whose settings you want to modify.

2. Click the Properties button to set the properties for this class.

3. Click the button next to Spatial Reference to set the spatial reference for the feature class.

4. Click the Geometry Type dropdown arrow and click the geometry type for this feature class.

5. Type the grid levels for the feature class. Personal geodatabase feature classes can have only one grid level.

6. If generating schema for an ArcSDE geodatabase, click the dropdown arrow and click a storage configuration keyword. If you do not select a keyword, DEFAULTS will be used.

7. Follow steps 5 through 18 for setting properties for object classes.

8. Repeat steps 1 through 6 for the rest of the standalone feature classes in your model.

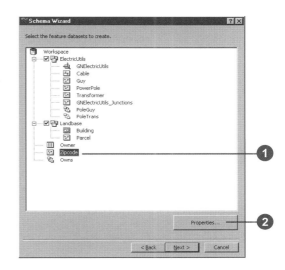

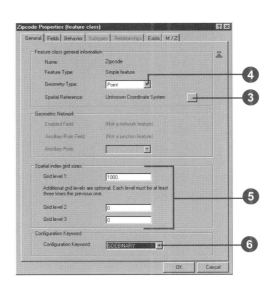

Setting properties for a geometric network

1. Click the geometric network whose settings you want to modify.

2. Click the Properties button to set the properties for this network.

3. If generating schema for an ArcSDE geodatabase, click the dropdown arrow and click a storage configuration keyword.

4. Click OK.

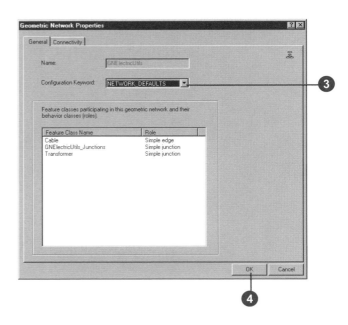

Setting properties for relationship classes

If you did not use tagged values for the properties of relationship classes in your UML model, you can set them in the Schema Creation Wizard.

See Also

For a detailed discussion of primary and foreign keys and relationship messaging, see Chapter 6, 'Defining relationship classes'.

1. Click the relationship class for which you want to set the properties.

2. Click the Properties button.

3. Click the dropdown arrow and click the notification direction for the relationship class.

4. Click the dropdown arrows and click the origin primary and foreign keys. ▶

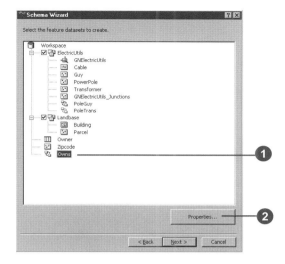

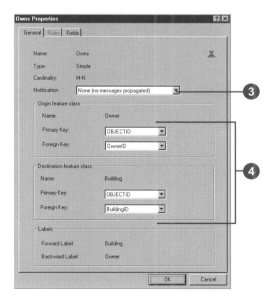

5. If your relationship class is not modeled as a class with attributes, skip to step 11.

6. Click the Fields tab.

7. Click a field in the list of fields. If you used tagged values in your UML model to set the field properties, skip to step 11.

8. Type its precision if it is an integer field, its precision and scale if it is a float field, or its length if it is a text field.

9. Click Allow Null Values if you want null values to be permitted in this field.

10. Repeat steps 1 through 9 for each field in the relationship class.

11. Click OK.

12. Repeat steps 1 through 11 for the rest of your relationship classes.

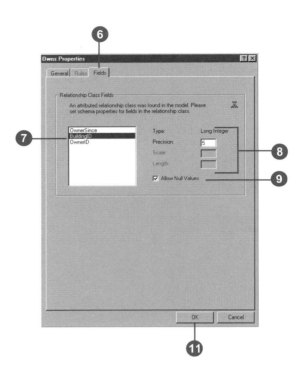

Creating the schema

Once you have connected to the repository and selected the classes from your UML model for which you want to generate schema, the last part of the Schema Wizard is to actually create the schema in the geodatabase.

1. Click Next.

2. Review the options you specified in the Schema Wizard. If you want to change anything, click Back and change the appropriate parameters.

3. Click Finish to generate the schema in the geodatabase.

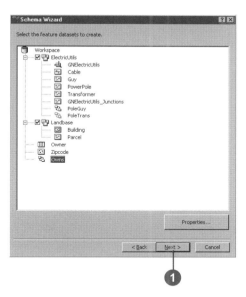

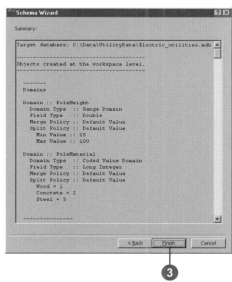

Editing your geodatabase

12

IN THIS CHAPTER

- **Editing in ArcMap and your geodatabase**

- **Editing with default values and attribute domains**

- **Editing relationships and related objects**

- **Editing annotation**

- **Editing network features**

- **Editing dimension features**

- **Loading objects from other feature classes**

Once you have finished creating your *geodatabase schema*—whether you imported existing *coverage* and *shapefile data*, created your geodatabase items with ArcCatalog, used CASE tools, or a combination of all three—it is ready to be edited.

Throughout the process of designing and creating your geodatabase schema, you had to make decisions about whether your data needed *validation rules*, *relationships*, and so on. This chapter shows you how all of these aspects come into play to make editing and maintaining the accuracy of your geodatabase easier.

Editing in ArcMap and your geodatabase

So far, this book has guided you through the process of creating all aspects of your geodatabase, from importing data to specifying complex relationships and rules. Now you are ready to edit your data.

The beginning of each chapter in this book describes the theory behind each of the special geodatabase abstractions. ArcMap editing capabilities are tightly integrated with the various special aspects of the geodatabase, such as *geometric networks* and validation rules. While each component of the geodatabase can act independently, the true power of the geodatabase becomes evident when you bring all of these things together.

In this chapter, you will learn how editing in ArcMap takes advantage of the aspects of a geodatabase that help you maintain a valid *database*.

This chapter assumes that you are already familiar with ArcMap and editing in ArcMap. To learn about these, see *Using ArcMap* and *Editing in ArcMap*.

Validation rules

The geodatabase supports three broad types of validation rules: attribute validation rules, network *connectivity rules,* and relationship rules. It is important to understand that these validation rules can be broken; in certain cases, a geodatabase permits invalid *objects* to be stored in the database.

For example, if you have an attribute rule stating that the valid pressure range for a water distribution main in your water network is between 50 and 75 psi, the geodatabase won't prevent you from storing a value outside of that range. However, a distribution main with a water pressure outside of this range will be an invalid object in the geodatabase. ArcMap has many editing tools that help you identify invalid features so that you can correct them.

The exceptions are *edge–edge connectivity rules*, *edge–junction connectivity rules*, and coded value attribute rules. In these cases, ArcMap takes a more active role when editing features with these rules associated with them. You will learn how editing in ArcMap behaves in these contexts later in this chapter.

The general approach to the issue of validating features is that the validation process should not result in valid features being flagged as invalid (false negatives); it is, however, allowable to have features that are invalid being reported as valid (false positives). If the geodatabase did not enforce any validation, every feature would effectively be valid. When performing validation on a particular feature, the validation occurs in five steps:

1. Validate the subtype.

2. Validate the attribute rules.

3. Validate the network connectivity rules (if network feature).

4. Perform custom validation (using optional class extension).

5. Validate the relationship rules.

This strategy means the least expensive validation is performed first. The validation process stops once a feature is found to be invalid. So, for example, if a feature fails the validity test for check number 1, then checks 2, 3, 4, and 5 are never executed.

When checking connectivity and relationship rules, all associated rules must be valid. With network connectivity rules, if you specify one rule, you must specify them all. Thus, if a type of connectivity exists that doesn't have an associated connectivity rule, the network feature is deemed invalid.

To learn more about attribute validation rules, see Chapter 5, 'Subtypes and attribute domains'. To learn more about connectivity rules, see Chapter 9, 'Geometric networks'.

Relationships

If you have created *relationship classes* between feature classes and tables in your geodatabase (see Chapter 6, 'Defining relationship classes'), you can use ArcMap editing tools to take advantage of the relationships. Using ArcMap editing tools, you can find all of the objects related to a particular object and edit them. For example, you can select a parcel and find the owner of that parcel, then edit some of the *attributes* of that owner without ever having to add the *table* that stores the owners to your ArcMap session.

You can also use ArcMap editing tools to establish a new relationship between objects or to break existing relationships between objects. For example, if a parcel changes ownership, you can delete the relationship between the parcel and its original owner, then establish a new relationship to its new owner.

To learn more about relationship classes, see Chapter 6, 'Defining relationship classes'.

Annotation

You can use the tools in ArcMap to edit features that have feature-linked *annotation* associated with them and to edit individual annotation *features*. Editing features with linked annotation is much the same as editing any other feature, except that when you edit such a feature, you also affect the annotation that is linked to it.

Editing a feature affects its linked annotation because of the composite relationship between them. If you move the feature, the annotation moves with it. If you delete the feature, its annotation is also deleted. However, feature-linked annotation is also affected if the values for *fields* from which its text is derived change. When you create a new feature, its linked annotation is also automatically created.

Annotation features themselves can also be edited. For example, you may want to adjust the location of a particular annotation relative to its linked feature, or you may want to edit nonfeature-linked annotation. In both cases, you use a combination of the ArcMap Editor and the drawing tools in ArcMap.

To learn more about annotation, see Chapter 7, 'Managing annotation'. For more information on composite relationships, see Chapter 6, 'Defining relationship classes'.

Network features

Editing geometric network *feature classes* is one of the most tightly integrated geodatabase editing tasks. When you create new network features, *topology* is maintained on the fly and is continuously updated as you make modifications to your network features.

When snapping network edges together, the editing tools in ArcMap use the connectivity rules you have defined for the network to determine the correct junction type for connecting the two features. Using the Network Analysis tools with the editing tools in ArcMap helps you ensure that you maintain correct connectivity while editing your geometric network features.

To learn more about geometric networks, see Chapter 9, 'Geometric networks'.

Integrated feature datasets

Topologically associated feature classes in a geodatabase are stored in an *integrated feature dataset*. You can use the topological editing tools in ArcMap to maintain the topological associations of features in an integrated feature dataset.

For information about integrated feature datasets, see Chapter 3, 'Creating new items in a geodatabase'. For information about how to use the topological editing tools in ArcMap and how to edit data in an integrated feature dataset, see Chapter 8, 'Editing topological features', in *Editing in ArcMap*.

Dimension features

Creating and editing *dimension features* are also tightly integrated into the editing environment. Standard editing tools are used for creating and editing dimension features; however, these tools behave in a much different way than when editing other features.

To facilitate the creation of dimension features, the *Dimensioning toolbar* contains a set of controls and tools to help you create the right type of dimension feature with the standard editor tools. Using a combination of the Editing toolbar and the Dimensioning toolbar, you can create aligned, simple aligned, horizontal linear, vertical linear, or rotated linear dimension features in a variety of styles. These dimension features can be based on points that you input with the Sketch tool, or you can use one of the auto-dimensioning tools to create dimension features from existing dimension features and other features.

To learn more about dimension feature classes and dimension styles, see Chapter 8, 'Dimensioning'.

Loading objects from other feature classes

When you create a new feature class using ArcCatalog, CASE tools, or a shapefile or coverage you have imported, you will often want to insert data stored in a shapefile, coverage, or geodatabase into that feature class. The ArcMap Object Loader lets you do this.

To run the Object Loader, you must be editing. To edit ArcSDE geodatabase data, it must be *versioned;* therefore, when you are working with an ArcSDE geodatabase, the target feature class or table must be versioned. When you insert data into an ArcSDE geodatabase, you insert features into the active version of the geodatabase in ArcMap. The Object Loader can be used to load multiple feature classes that have the same *schema* and can take advantage of the ArcMap Editor *snapping* environment by snapping the new features to existing features in your map. To learn more about how to work with a versioned database in ArcMap, see Chapter 13, 'Working with a versioned geodatabase'.

The Object Loader can be used to insert features into a network feature class, a simple feature class, or a feature class that stores custom objects. If the feature class has validation rules associated with it, the inserted features are validated.

Using the edit cache

When editing data in an ArcSDE geodatabase, whether it is network data or other types of data, one of the most important tools to use to improve performance is the edit cache. The edit cache will do exactly what its name implies—cache data from the server on the client. This caching of data cuts down on the number of queries that the client needs to execute on the server during editing. In general, when editing data in a geodatabase, especially network data, you should always use the edit cache. Using the edit cache can make your edits five times faster than without the cache.

The edit cache not only makes editing faster but also expedites drawing, selecting, and identifying features that are cached. Only spatial queries take advantage of the cache, so any attribute queries, or navigating to related objects outside the cache, will not benefit from the cache. Undo is slower when using the edit cache.

You must build the edit cache by clicking the Build Edit Cache command on the Edit Cache toolbar. This command will cache those features in the current map extent that you have the required privileges to edit—it will not cache read-only features. If you pan or zoom out of that area, you must rebuild the edit cache. The edit cache will also be cleared any time an edit operation is aborted for any reason or when you stop editing. In general, if everything suddenly slows down while you are editing, you probably need to rebuild your edit cache.

Updating data using SQL

After loading a large amount of data into your geodatabase, you may want to bulk update some values for some of the attributes. In the case of an ArcSDE geodatabase, you can do this by versioning the data, then editing in ArcMap to perform the update. The problem with this approach is that all of the updated features will be in the delta tables; you should compress your database to move the updated features into the base tables.

Another approach is to bulk attribute updates that can be done using SQL before the data is versioned. Using this approach means that these bulk updates are done before the database is versioned, and all of the features remain in the base tables. In the case of a personal geodatabase, you will not get the versioning impact described here.

There are some rules that apply to performing updates with SQL. It is important to understand your data models so the attributes you update don't affect other objects in the database through relationships or other behavior. Using SQL for this operation without a thorough understanding of your data model may result in data corruption. For example, if you use SQL to modify the attributes of a feature from which text is derived for feature-linked annotation, the annotation features will not be messaged to update themselves, so the annotation and feature will be out of sync. When these attributes are updated in ArcMap, all necessary behavior is executed.

The following is a list of some important guidelines when doing this kind of operation:

- Never update records in SQL after your data has been versioned.

- When updating data using SQL, do not modify attributes that, through geodatabase behavior, affect other objects in the database.

- Never update the ObjectID field with SQL.

- Never update the Enabled or AncillaryRole field, or a weight field for a network feature class using SQL. When these fields are updated through ArcInfo, it results in changes to the geometric network topology tables that SQL will not trigger.

For more information on loading existing data into a geodatabase, see Chapter 4, 'Migrating existing data into a geodatabase'.

Managing the edit cache

Using the edit cache when editing data stored in an ArcSDE geodatabase will greatly improve performance. Since the edit cache caches features on the client, it cuts down on the number of queries that the client needs to execute on the server during editing.

This improves the performance of your edit session and also reduces the load on the server itself in a multiuser environment. When editing network features or when using the shared geometry editing tools on ArcSDE geodatabases, you should always use the edit cache.

ArcMap has tools to build and help you work with the edit cache. These tools are found on the Edit Cache toolbar.

Tip
Adding the toolbar
You can also add the toolbar by clicking the View menu, pointing to Toolbars, then clicking Dimensioning.

Adding the Dimensioning toolbar

1. Right-click the Main menu.

2. Click Dimensioning.

3. Dock the toolbar to the ArcMap window. Now each time you start ArcMap, the toolbar will be displayed.

Tip

Using the edit cache

You can't build or use an edit cache unless you have started editing.

Tip

Edit cache tools

Click the Show Edit Cache command on the Edit Cache toolbar to display the extent of the current edit cache. This command will only be enabled if your map's extent intersects the extent of the current edit cache.

Click the Zoom To Edit Cache command on the Edit Cache toolbar to zoom to the extent of the current edit cache.

The Show Edit Cache and the Zoom To Edit Cache commands are enabled only when you have built an edit cache.

Tip

Read-only features

In an ArcSDE geodatabase, the features that you do not have write privileges to are not cached, nor are features in feature classes that are not registered as versioned.

Building an edit cache

1. Pan and/or zoom to the area of your map where you will be performing your edits.

2. Click the Build Edit Cache command on the Edit Cache toolbar.

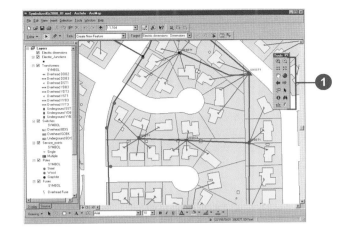

Editing with default values and attribute domains

Default values and *attribute domains* help you maintain realistic values for the attributes of the features in your database. For example, in a water network database you may have a feature class that stores water transmission mains. Transmission mains have rules that state their valid pressure range is between 40 and 100 psi. This is an example of a range domain. Another rule states that water transmission mains can have a diameter of 10, 24, or 30 inches. This is an example of a coded value domain.

When you create a new feature, default values associated with the feature are added automatically. When you modify the *subtype* of a feature, the new subtype takes on the field values of the feature as default values.

While the editing tools in ArcMap don't actively help you modify fields with range domains, they do actively help you modify fields with coded value domains. When you edit a field with a coded value ▶

Creating new features

1. Click the Current Task dropdown arrow and click Create New Feature.

2. Click the Target layer dropdown arrow and click the layer with the type of features you want to create.

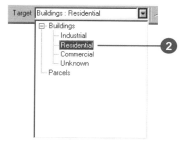

3. Click the Tool Palette dropdown arrow and click the Sketch tool.

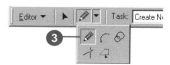

4. Click the map to digitize the feature's vertices. ▶

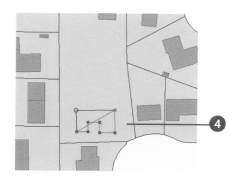

domain, a dropdown list of all of the domain values appears. When you choose one of the values from this list, you know that you are assigning the field a valid value.

5. Double-click the last vertex to finish the feature.

6. Click the Attributes button.

   The Attributes dialog box appears. Notice that some of the fields already have values. These are the default values you specified when creating this feature class.

   Also notice that the field aliases are displayed, not the true field names.

7. Click the fields whose values you want to modify and type the new values.

8. Click the Close button to close the Attributes dialog box.

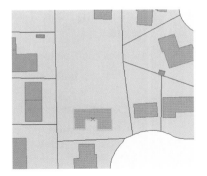

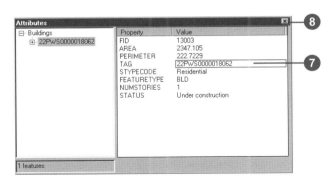

Modifying coded value fields

1. Click the Edit tool.

2. Click the feature whose attributes you want to edit.

3. Click the Attributes button.

4. Click the value of the coded value field you want to modify.

   A dropdown list of all the coded value descriptions in the domain appears.

5. Click the value you want for the field.

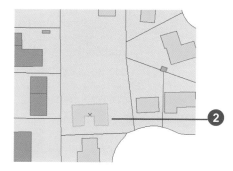

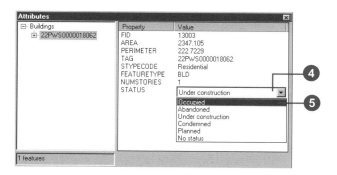

See Also

To learn more about subtypes and attribute domains, see Chapter 5, 'Subtypes and attribute domains'.

Changing a feature's subtype

1. Click the Edit tool.

2. Click the feature whose subtype you want to change.

3. Click the Attributes button.

4. Click the value of the subtype field.

   A dropdown list with all the available subtypes appears.

5. Click the subtype you want. ▶

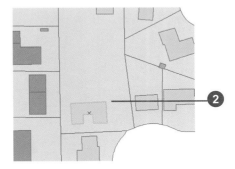

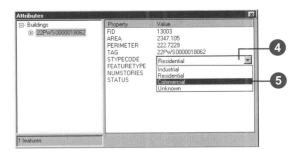

Default values

When you change a feature's subtype, the fields will take on the default values for the new subtype. If a field does not have a default value associated with it for the new subtype, its value remains unchanged.

The feature's symbology changes to match the new subtype. The fields with default values assume the default values for the new subtype.

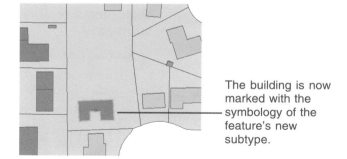

The building is now marked with the symbology of the feature's new subtype.

Validating features

1. Click the Edit tool.

2. Click the features that you want to validate.

3. Click Editor and click Validate Selection. ▶

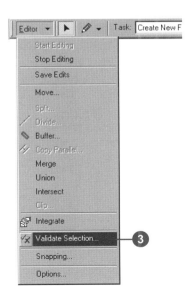

If your selection contains any invalid features, a message box appears with the number of invalid features. Only invalid features remain selected.

4. Click OK.

5. Click one of the invalid features.

6. Repeat step 3.

7. A message box appears telling you why the feature is invalid.

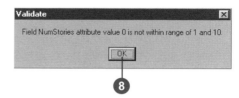

8. Click OK.

9. Click the Attributes button to view the attributes of the invalid feature.

10. Click the values that are invalid and change them.

11. Close the Attributes dialog box.

12. Repeat steps 5 through 11 for all of the invalid features.

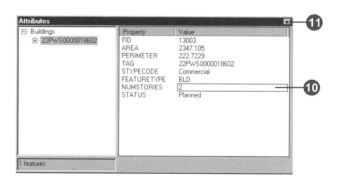

13. Repeat steps 2 and 3. You should see a message box informing you that all the features are valid.

14. Click OK.

Editing relationships

Relationship classes allow you to maintain associations between objects in your geodatabase. These relationships can be simple and passive, or they can be composite. Composite relationships imply parent/child relationships, or composition, and therefore have behavior, which is triggered through changes to objects on one side of the relationship to objects on the other side.

Relationships in a relationship class can be stored using primary and foreign keys in the object classes on either side of the relationship class. Alternatively, in the case of many-to-many relationship classes (M-N) and attributed relationship classes, the relationships are rows stored in a separate table.

You can use the Attributes dialog box or the table dialog box to find all objects related to any selected object. Once you have navigated to the related object, you can edit its attributes. You can also use the editing tool in ArcMap to break the relationship between any two objects or create new relationships between objects. When you edit objects and relationships in this way, all referential integrity is maintained.

Creating and deleting relationships

You can use the Attributes dialog box to create and delete relationships between two objects. If the relationship is managed by primary and foreign keys, the foreign key in the destination object is populated with the value of the primary key from the origin object. If a relationship between two objects is deleted, then the value for the foreign key in the destination object is replaced with a null.

If the relationship class is M-N or is attributed, then the relationships are stored on a separate table in the database. When a new relationship is created between two objects in this type of relationship class, a new row is added to that table. This new row is populated with the values from the primary keys in the origin and destination objects. If a relationship between two

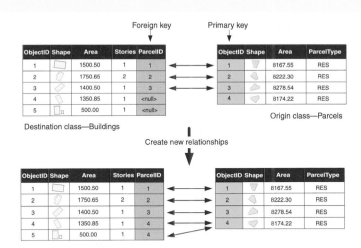

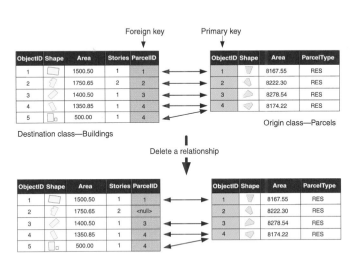

If the relationships in a relationship class are managed by primary and foreign keys (nonattributed 1-1 or 1-M relationships), creating and deleting relationships populate and null out the foreign key in the destination class objects.

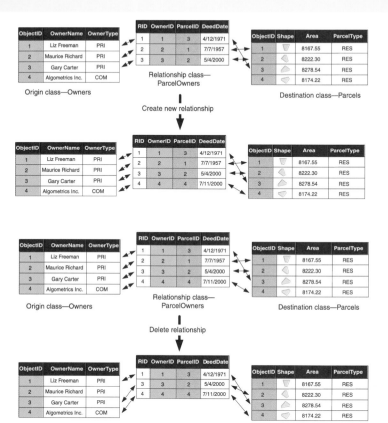

Origin class—Owners

ObjectID	OwnerName	OwnerType
1	Liz Freeman	PRI
2	Maurice Richard	PRI
3	Gary Carter	PRI
4	Algometrics Inc.	COM

Relationship class—
ParcelOwners

RID	OwnerID	ParcelID	DeedDate
1	1	3	4/12/1971
2	2	1	7/7/1957
3	3	2	5/4/2000

Destination class—Parcels

ObjectID	Shape	Area	ParcelType
1		8167.55	RES
2		8222.30	RES
3		8278.54	RES
4		8174.22	RES

Create new relationship

ObjectID	OwnerName	OwnerType
1	Liz Freeman	PRI
2	Maurice Richard	PRI
3	Gary Carter	PRI
4	Algometrics Inc.	COM

RID	OwnerID	ParcelID	DeedDate
1	1	3	4/12/1971
2	2	1	7/7/1957
3	3	2	5/4/2000
4	4	4	7/11/2000

ObjectID	Shape	Area	ParcelType
1		8167.55	RES
2		8222.30	RES
3		8278.54	RES
4		8174.22	RES

Origin class—Owners

ObjectID	OwnerName	OwnerType
1	Liz Freeman	PRI
2	Maurice Richard	PRI
3	Gary Carter	PRI
4	Algometrics Inc.	COM

Relationship class—
ParcelOwners

RID	OwnerID	ParcelID	DeedDate
1	1	3	4/12/1971
2	2	1	7/7/1957
3	3	2	5/4/2000
4	4	4	7/11/2000

Destination class—Parcels

ObjectID	Shape	Area	ParcelType
1		8167.55	RES
2		8222.30	RES
3		8278.54	RES
4		8174.22	RES

Delete relationship

ObjectID	OwnerName	OwnerType
1	Liz Freeman	PRI
2	Maurice Richard	PRI
3	Gary Carter	PRI
4	Algometrics Inc.	COM

RID	OwnerID	ParcelID	DeedDate
1	1	3	4/12/1971
3	3	2	5/4/2000
4	4	4	7/11/2000

ObjectID	Shape	Area	ParcelType
1		8167.55	RES
2		8222.30	RES
3		8278.54	RES
4		8174.22	RES

If the relationship class is M-N or is attributed, the relationships are stored as rows in the relationship class's table. Creating and deleting relationships adds and removes rows in the relationship class's table.

objects is deleted, then the row corresponding to that relationship is deleted from the relationship table.

Deleting objects with relationships

When an object that participates in relationships with other objects is deleted from the database, all of its relationships are also deleted. If the relationships are maintained using primary and foreign keys, and the object deleted is the origin object, then the foreign key in the destination object is nulled out. If the object deleted is the destination object, then the origin object is not affected.

If relationships are maintained as rows in a relationship table (M-N relationships or attributed relationships) and either an origin or destination object and its relationships are deleted, then the rows corresponding to those relationships are also deleted from the relationship's table.

Creating new related objects

In ArcMap, you can select an object, then use the Attributes dialog box to create a new nonspatial object in a related class. When this new object is created, all of its attributes are populated with their appropriate default values (see Chapter 5, 'Subtypes and attribute domains'), and a relationship is created back to the object it was created from. You can only create nonspatial objects in this way; you cannot create new features.

If the relationships are maintained using primary and foreign keys, then the foreign key in the destination object is populated with the primary key of the origin object, regardless of whether the origin or destination object is created using the Attributes dialog box. If the relationships are maintained as rows in a

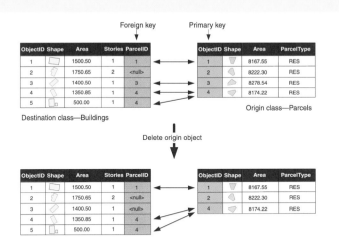

Destination class—Buildings

Origin class—Parcels

Delete origin object

When an object that participates in relationships with other objects is deleted from the database, all of its relationships are also deleted.

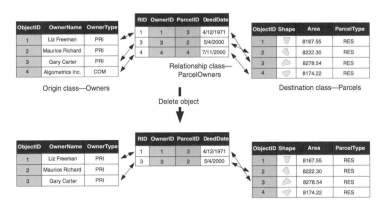

Origin class—Owners

Relationship class— ParcelOwners

Destination class—Parcels

Delete object

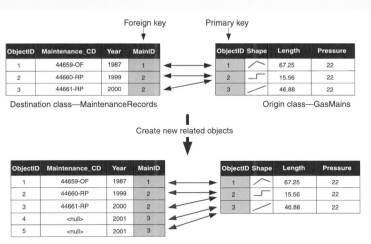

Destination class—MaintenanceRecords

Origin class—GasMains

Create new related objects

When you use the Attributes dialog box to create new related objects, a relationship is created back to the object from which it was created. If the relationships are maintained using primary and foreign keys, then the foreign key in the destination object is populated with the primary key of the origin object.

relationship table (M-N relationships, attributed relationships), then a new row is added to the relationship class's table.

Editing composite relationships

Composite relationships have some specialized behavior. When editing the objects that participate in a composite relationship, this behavior carries over to the editing process. Edits made to the origin object in a composite relationship often directly affect its related destination objects. This behavior is partially dependent on relationship class messaging.

By default, composite relationship classes have forward messaging (see Chapter 6, 'Defining relationship classes')—that is, when the origin object in a composite relationship is edited, it sends messages to its related destination objects. The related objects will respond to that messaging in a standard way: if the destination objects are nonspatial objects, then they will not change. However, if the destination objects are features when the origin object is moved, then the destination objects will also move the same distance. If the origin object is rotated, then the destination objects will also be rotated by the same angle.

Like simple relationships, composite relationships also maintain referential integrity when objects are deleted, but they do this in a different way. When the origin object in a composite relationship

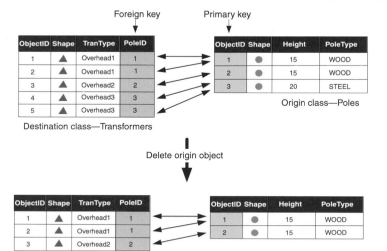

Destination class—Transformers

Origin class—Poles

Delete origin object

When an origin object in a composite relationship is deleted, all destination objects related to it through a composite relationship are also deleted.

is deleted, all of the objects related to it through that composite relationship are also deleted. This cascade deletion will happen whether messaging is set to forward, back, both, or none. When a destination object is deleted, the relationship between it and the origin object is deleted; the origin object itself is not deleted or modified.

Splitting features that participate in relationships

Splitting a single geodatabase feature into two separate features is actually a delete and create operation—that is, the original feature is deleted and two new features are created. This has implications when the feature being split has relationships with other objects in the database.

With simple relationships, when an origin feature is split the relationships between the original feature and its related

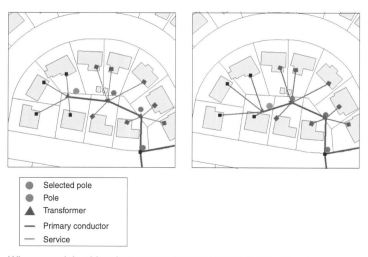

- ● Selected pole
- ● Pole
- ▲ Transformer
- — Primary conductor
- — Service

When an origin object in a composite relationship is moved and messaging is set to forward or both, if the related objects are features, they will move the same distance to follow the feature. In this example, the selected pole is the origin object and the transformer is the destination object.

destination objects are deleted. When the new features are created from the split operation, new relationships are created between the new feature with the larger portion of the original feature's geometry and the destination objects that were related to the original feature.

In the case of a composite relationship, the behavior is different. When an origin feature in a composite relationship is split, any objects related to it through that composite relationship are deleted before the two resulting new features are created from the split.

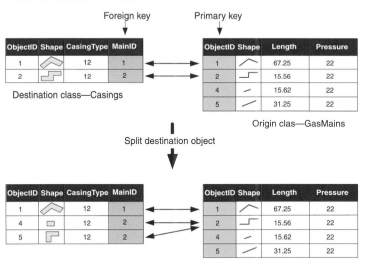

When splitting a destination feature in either a simple or composite relationship, the relationships between the original feature and the related origin objects are deleted and the new relationships are created between the origin objects and both new features that result from the split.

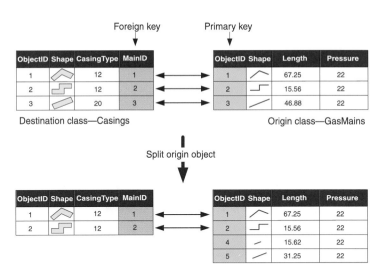

When an origin object in a composite relationship is split, its destination objects are deleted.

When splitting a destination feature in either a simple or composite relationship, the relationships between the original feature and the related origin objects are deleted and the new relationships are created between the origin objects and both new features that result from the split.

The behavior of splitting objects with relationships described here is the default behavior. You can override this behavior at the class level by writing a class extension that implements the IFeatureClassEdit interface. The IFeatureClassEdit interface has a property called CustomSplitPolicyForRelationship that allows you to specify how relationships are handled when features are split. To learn more about class extensions and how to implement them, see *Exploring ArcObjects*.

Editing relationships and related objects

The tasks presented here are all examples of editing relationships between water laterals and hydrants in a water network. The rules of this relationship class state that a hydrant lateral must have a hydrant related to it and that hydrants cannot be related to other lateral types.

Editing a related object

1. Click the Edit tool.

2. Click the hydrant lateral whose related hydrant you want to modify.

3. Click the Attributes button.

4. Double-click the lateral in the left panel of the Attributes dialog box.

5. Double-click the relationship path label.

   The related hydrant objects are listed below the path label.

6. Click the ID number of the related hydrant whose attributes you want to modify.

7. Modify the attributes of the hydrant object by clicking the value and typing a value or clicking the value and choosing the new value from the list.

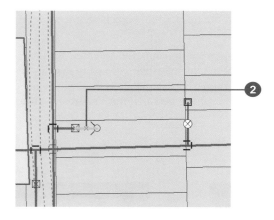

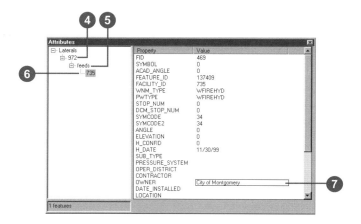

Selecting a related object

1. Click the Edit tool.

2. Click the hydrant lateral whose related hydrant you want to modify.

3. Click the Attributes button.

4. Double-click the lateral in the left panel of the Attributes dialog box.

5. Double-click the relationship path label.

   The related hydrant objects are listed below the path label.

6. Right-click the related hydrant you want to add to the map's selection and click Select. ▶

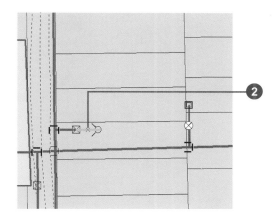

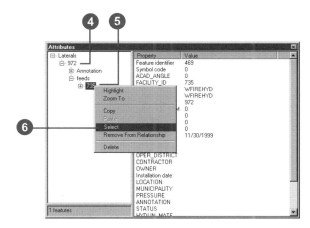

The hydrant is added to the
selection.

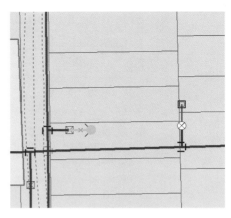

The hydrant is added to the selection.

Relating objects

Before adding a relationship between two objects, you must first create a relationship class between the feature classes or tables containing the objects you want to relate. To learn more about how to create relationship classes, see Chapter 6, 'Defining relationship classes'.

Creating a new relationship between features

1. Click the Edit tool.

2. Click the features between which you want to create relationships.

3. Click the Attributes button.

4. Double-click one of the features in the left panel.

5. Right-click the relationship path label and click Add Selected. ►

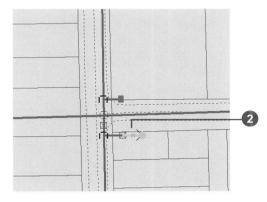

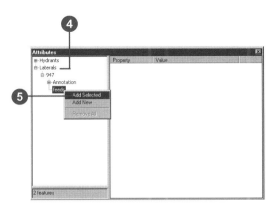

The selected object or objects are now added to the list of selected objects under the relationship class path label.

Relationships to the selected objects are added.

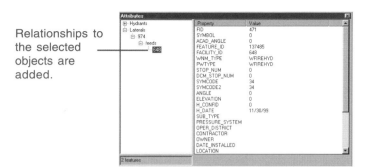

Creating a new relationship between a feature and a nonspatial object

1. Click the Edit tool.

2. Click the feature to which you want to create a relationship.

3. In the table of contents, right-click the table that contains the objects that you are relating to. Click Open. ▶

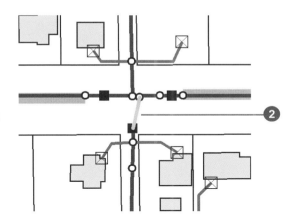

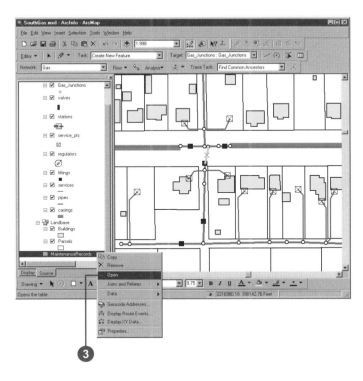

4. Click the object in the table with which you want to create a relationship to the selected feature.

5. Click the Attributes button.

6. Double-click the feature in the left panel.

7. Right-click the relationship path label and click Add Selected.

The selected object or objects are now added to the list of selected objects under the relationship class path label.

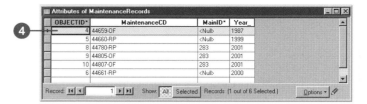

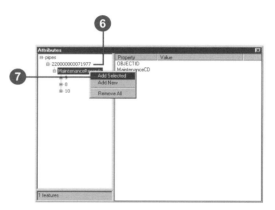

The object is listed under the relationship path label.

Deleting a relationship

1. Click the Edit tool.

2. Click the feature from which you want to delete a relationship.

3. Click the Attributes button.

4. Double-click the feature in the left panel.

5. Double-click the relationship path label to see a list of related objects.

6. Right-click the object from which you want to delete the relationship and click Remove From Relationship. ▶

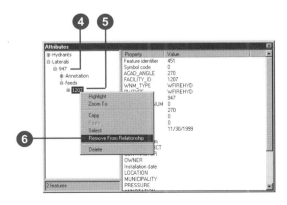

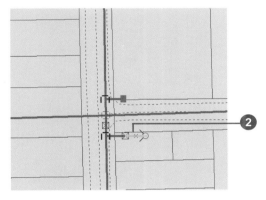

The object is no longer listed under the relationship path label.

7. Click the Close button to close the Attributes dialog box.

The object is no longer listed under the relationship path label.

Creating new related features

You cannot use the Add New command in the Attributes dialog box to create new related features. See 'Creating new related features', later in this chapter, to learn how to create new related features.

Creating new related nonspatial objects

1. Click the Edit tool.

2. Click the feature for which you want to create a new related object.

3. Click the Attributes button.

4. Double-click the feature in the left panel. ▶

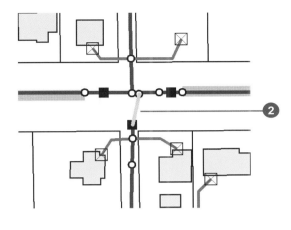

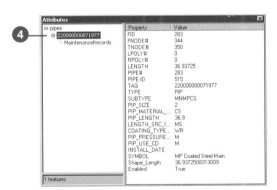

5. Right-click the relationship path label and click Add New.

A new object is created and related to the selected feature.

6. Click the new object in the left panel to see its attributes.

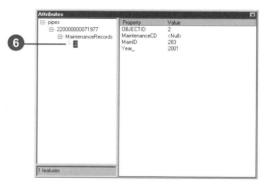

A new object is created in the related class, and a relationship is created between it and the selected feature.

See Also

To learn more about ArcMap sketch tools and how to create new features, see Editing in ArcMap.

Creating new related features

1. Use ArcMap sketch tools to create the new feature.

2. Click the Edit tool.

3. Hold down the Shift key and click the feature for which you want to create a relationship to the new feature.

   Both the new feature and the feature you are relating it to should be selected. ▶

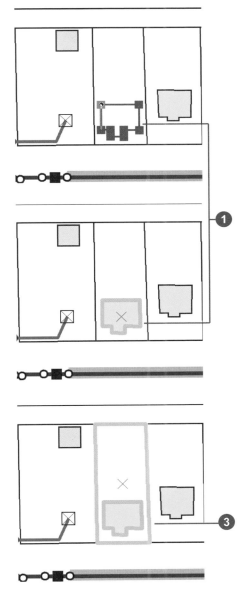

4. Click the Attributes button.

5. Double-click the feature in the left panel.

6. Right-click the relationship path label and click Add Selected.

   The selected object or objects are now added to the list of selected objects under the relationship class path label.

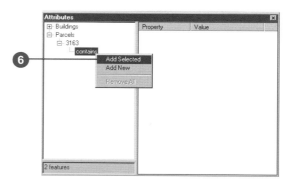

A relationship to the selected object is added.

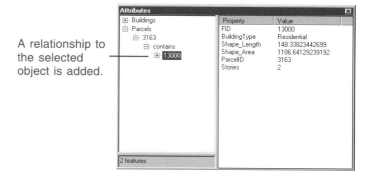

Deleting related objects

1. Click the Edit tool.

2. Click the feature whose related object you want to delete.

3. Click the Attributes button.

4. Double-click the feature in the left panel.

5. Double-click the relationship path label to see a list of related objects.

6. Right-click the object you want to delete and click Delete.

   The object is deleted and no longer listed under the relationship path label.

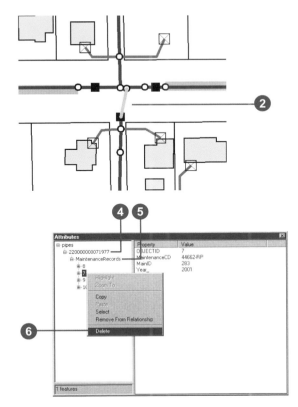

The object is no longer listed under the relationship path label.

The Attributes dialog box

The Attributes dialog box behaves the same way with composite relationships as it does with creating or deleting new features or relationships.

Editing features with composite relationships

1. Click the Edit tool.

2. Click the origin feature in the composite relationship you want to edit.

3. Click and drag the feature to a new location.

   The related features move the same x,y distance as the origin feature you moved. ▶

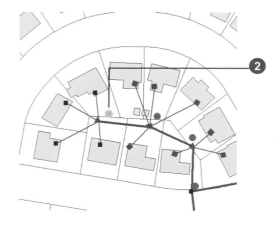

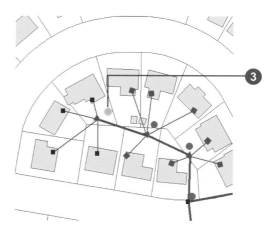

The related features move the same distance as the feature you moved.

4. Click the Rotate tool.

5. Click anywhere on the map and drag the pointer to rotate the feature to the desired location.

   The related features rotate with the feature.

6. Click the Edit tool and click a destination feature in a composite relationship.

7. Click and drag the feature to a new location.

   The origin feature in the relationship doesn't move. ►

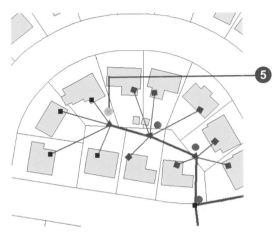

The related features rotate with the features.

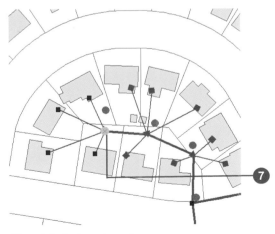

The origin feature doesn't move.

8. Click the origin feature again and click Delete.

   Both the feature and its related feature are deleted.

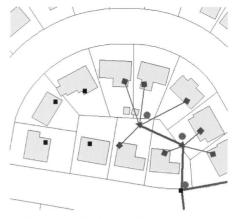

Both the origin feature and its related feature are deleted.

Relationship rules

Relationship rules can be broken in two ways: when a feature is related to a subtype of the related class for which no valid rule applies or when a cardinality rule is broken.

To learn more about relationship rules, see Chapter 6, 'Defining relationship classes'.

Validating relationships

1. Click the Edit tool and click the feature(s) you want to validate.

2. Click Editor and click Validate Selection.

   If there are any invalid features, a message box appears telling you how many features are invalid. Only invalid features remain selected. ▶

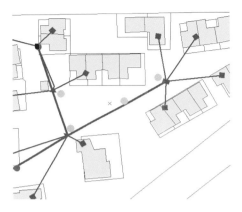

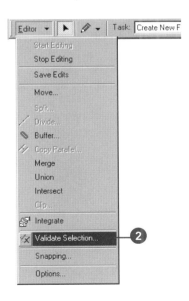

3. Click OK.

4. Click one of the invalid features.

5. Repeat step 2.

   A dialog box appears informing you why the selected feature is invalid.

6. Click OK.

7. Make the necessary edits to the relationships or the related objects to make the feature valid. This may involve adding and deleting relationships or altering the subtype of one or all of the features.

8. Repeat step 2—a message box appears informing you that all the features are valid.

9. Click OK.

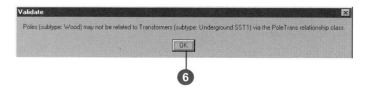

Editing annotation

You can use the editing tools in ArcMap to edit both feature-linked annotation and nonfeature-linked annotation. While you can perform the same edit operations on both kinds of annotation, a feature with linked annotation has special *behaviors* when edited. The annotation feature will respond to changes in its linked feature such as attribute updates.

You can use the drawing tools in ArcMap to edit the string, the symbology, or the location of any annotation feature. You can also use the drawing tools to create new annotation features.

When you edit features with linked annotation, all of the behaviors that apply to editing features with composite-related objects apply—for example, move and delete. In addition, when you edit the attributes of the feature, the linked annotation is also modified to reflect the changes.

You can use the same tools for editing related objects and breaking and creating new relationships; see 'Editing relationships and related objects' in this chapter.

Creating new nonfeature-linked annotation

1. Add your annotation feature class to ArcMap and add the Editor toolbar and the Draw toolbar.

2. Click Editor and click Start Editing.

3. On the Draw toolbar, click Drawing, point to Active Annotation Target, then check the feature class name of the annotation you want to create.

4. Use the font settings buttons on the Draw toolbar to set the properties of the annotation text you want to create.

5. Click the Create a new text element button.

6. Click the map where you want to add the new annotation feature.

7. Type the annotation's text string and press Enter. ▶

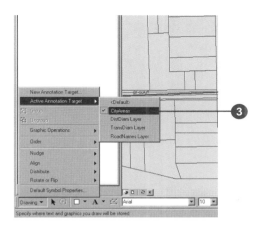

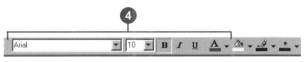

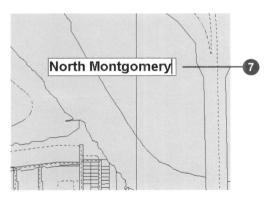

See Also

To learn more about geodatabase annotation, see Chapter 7, 'Managing annotation'.

Nonfeature-linked annotation is added to your *map*.

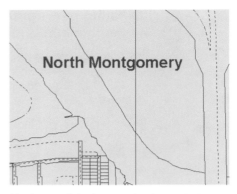

Nonfeature-linked annotation is created.

See Also

The ability to add and edit annotation features with ArcMap is extensive and cannot be fully covered here. If you want to learn more about this tool, see Using ArcMap.

Editing an existing annotation feature

1. Click the Select Graphics tool.

2. Click the annotation that you want to edit.

3. Right-click the annotation string you want to change and click Properties.

4. Edit the text string as desired.

5. Click OK. ►

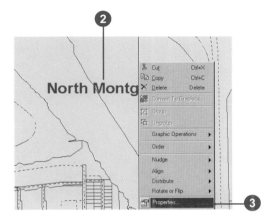

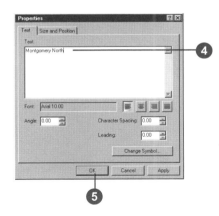

The text is updated on the map.

6. To move the annotation string, click and drag it to a new location.

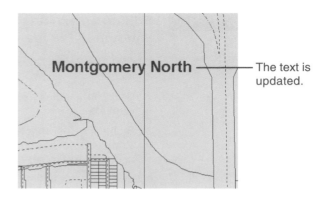

The text is updated.

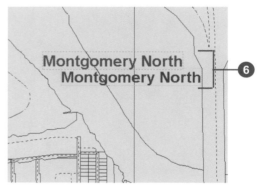

6

Creating new features with linked annotation

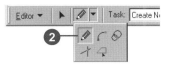

1. Zoom to the area where you want to add the new feature.

2. Click the Tool Palette dropdown arrow and click the Sketch tool.

3. Click the Current Task dropdown arrow and click Create New Feature.

4. Click the Target Layer dropdown arrow and click the type of feature you want to create.

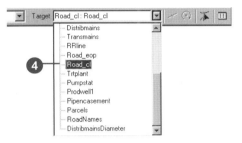

5. Click the map to create the new feature's vertices. ►

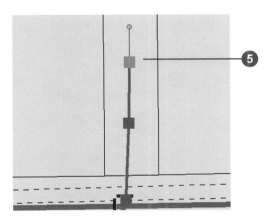

6. Double-click the last vertex to finish the feature.

An annotation feature is automatically created and linked to the new feature.

If your feature has default values for the field from which the annotation is derived, the annotation appears and reflects the values from those fields.

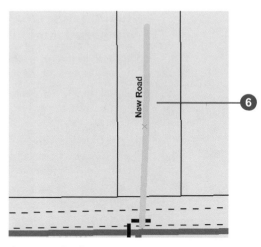

An annotation feature is created along with the new feature.

Modifying features with linked annotation

1. Click the Edit tool.

2. Click the feature you want to edit.

3. Click the Attributes button.

4. Click the value from which the annotation is derived and type the changes.

   The annotation is automatically updated to reflect these changes.

5. Click the Close button to close the Attributes dialog box. ►

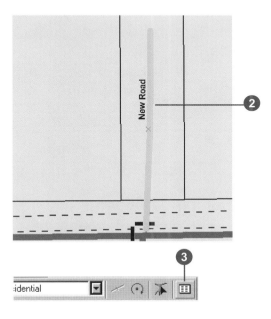

6. Click and drag the feature to a new location.

The linked annotation feature moves the same x,y distance as the feature you moved. ▶

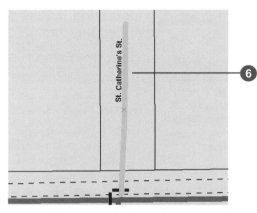

The linked annotation is automatically updated.

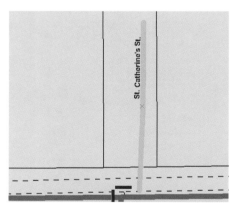

Linked annotation and feature move together to the new location.

7. Click the Rotate tool.

8. Click anywhere on the map and drag the pointer to rotate the feature to the desired location.

The annotation rotates with the feature.

9. Click the Delete tool.

The feature you selected, along with its linked annotation, is deleted from the database.

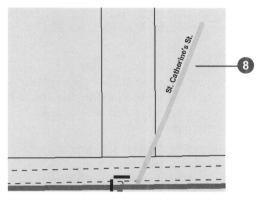

The feature is deleted along with its linked annotation.

Editing network features

Geometric network features store various mechanisms and behaviors that maintain the topological connectivity between them. ArcMap editing capabilities are tightly integrated with the geodatabase when it comes to editing network features.

Creating connectivity

Topological connectivity in a network feature class is based on geometric coincidence. If a junction is added along an edge, or one edge is added along another edge, they will become topologically connected to one another.

By using the ArcMap *snapping* environment, you can create new edge and junction features while maintaining network connectivity on the fly. The ArcMap snapping functionality will guarantee geometric coincidence when adding new network features along existing network features.

Simple and complex edges

An edge in a geometric network can be either simple or complex. A simple edge in a geometric network has a 1-1 relationship with edge elements in the logical network. A complex edge has a 1-M relationship with edge elements in the logical network. So one complex edge in the geometric network can represent multiple edges in the logical network.

If you snap a junction or edge along a simple edge, then the edge being snapped to is split both in the logical network and in the geometric network, giving you two edge features. If you snap a junction or an edge along a complex edge, then that edge is split in the logical network but remains a single feature in the geometric network. It will remain a single feature; however, a new vertex is created at the point where the new junction or edge connects to it.

Default junctions

When you snap an edge to another edge where there is no junction, a junction is automatically inserted to establish connectivity. If a default junction type has been specified as part of the connectivity rules for the network, that default junction type is used. If there is no edge–edge rule between these edge types, an orphan junction is inserted, which is stored in the <network>_Junctions feature class.

Similarly, if you create a new edge in the network that is not snapped to an existing junction or edge at both ends, a junction is automatically created and connected to the free end of the new edge. If there is a connectivity rule in place that defines a default junction type for the type of edge that is being added, that default junction type is the junction that is added to the free end of the new feature. If an edge type does not have a default junction type associated with it through a connectivity rule, then an orphan junction is inserted, which is stored in the <network>_Junctions feature class.

Junction subsumption

When you snap a junction to an existing junction, the old junction is subsumed by the new junction. That is, the original junction is deleted from the network and the new junction is inserted in its place. All network connectivity is maintained.

When you create a new edge feature in the network that has an end that does not connect to anything, and there is not a connectivity rule stating what type of junction to put at its free end, the network orphan junction type is inserted. This orphan junction can be replaced by snapping another junction to it.

Moving existing network features

When a network edge or junction is moved, the network features to which it is connected respond by rubber-banding and adjusting themselves to maintain connectivity. When you move a network feature and snap it to another network feature, the features may become connected (see below).

Connectivity models

Edit operations that involve adding, deleting, moving, and subsuming network features can all affect the connectivity of a geometric network. Each type of operation may or may not create connectivity, depending on the type of network features involved. The following set of diagrams illustrates various editing scenarios and their resulting connectivity or lack thereof. In these diagrams, use the key below to identify what types of features are illustrated in each scenario:

○   Orphan Junction

◉   Standard Junction

SEF   Simple Edge

CEF   Complex Edge

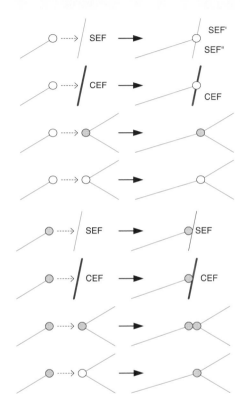

Connectivity behavior when stretching and moving network features

Stretching and moving: When stretching or moving junctions, any edges connected to them rubber-band to remain connected. When you snap these junctions to other network features, the following illustration summarizes the network connectivity that results:

Deleting: Deleting network features can affect those features connected to them. When you delete an edge feature, the edge is physically deleted from the geometric network and logically deleted from the logical network; however, its connected junction features will not be deleted. When deleting junction features, if the junction being deleted is not of an orphan junction type, it will not be physically deleted from the geometric network. Rather than being deleted, the junction will become an orphan junction. When you delete an orphan junction, it is physically deleted from the geometric network. When this happens, depending on what type it is and how many edges are connected to it, some edges may also be deleted. The following illustration summarizes the results of deleting network junctions:

Disconnecting features: The following illustration summarizes how connectivity is affected when disconnecting network edge features and junction features using the Disconnect command in ArcMap:

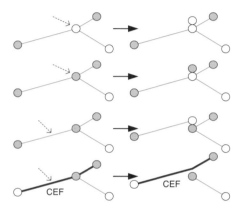

Connectivity behavior when disconnecting network features

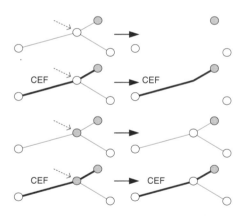

Connectivity behavior when deleting network features

Connecting features: The following illustration summarizes how connectivity is affected when connecting network features use the Connect command in ArcMap:

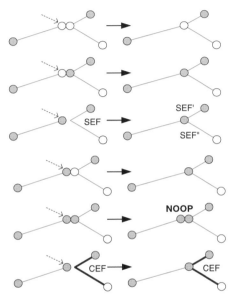

Connectivity behavior when connecting network features. NOOP indicates that the Connect command resulted in no edit operation.

Creating new network features: When creating new network features and snapping them to other network junction and edge features, the resulting connectivity and the effects on the features you connect them to are summarized below:

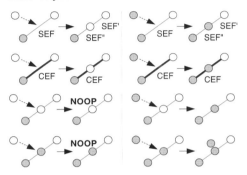

Connectivity behavior when creating new network features. NOOP indicates that the new feature was not created.

Repairing network topology

Connectivity between network features is maintained on the fly as you create, delete, and modify network features. In some circumstances, the association between some network features and their logical elements may become out of sync. This can happen, for example, when using a custom tool that does not correctly handle aborting edit operations.

This kind of network corruption is localized to a collection of features in the network. You will be able to see what features have corrupt topology in two ways: (1) when moving a network feature, if rubber-banding does not occur with other network features it is connected to and the edit operation fails, the topology is corrupt, and (2) reconciling a version with corrupt network features will result in an error (see Chapter 13, 'Working with a versioned geodatabase', to learn more about reconciling versions).

The Rebuild Connectivity tool in ArcMap rebuilds connectivity for a set of network features in an extent by re-creating their logical elements. Connectivity is established based on geometric coincidence using the same rules as described in 'Creating geometric networks' in Chapter 9.

Performance considerations

Connectivity is established for new network features based on geometric coincidence. When you add or move a feature in a network, each feature class in the network must be analyzed so connectivity can be established. Performing a spatial query against each network class will determine if the new feature or moved feature is coincident with other network features at any point.

If the network is in an ArcSDE geodatabase, then analyzing for connectivity requires a number of spatial queries against the server. By using the edit cache while editing the network, these spatial queries don't go against the server, are much faster, and are not as much of a load on the server. When editing network data in an ArcSDE geodatabase, always use the edit cache. Using the edit cache can make your edits five times faster than without the cache, and it is not as much of a load on the server.

See Also

For more information on the ArcMap snapping environment, see Editing in ArcMap.

Creating a new network edge at an existing junction

1. Add your network feature classes to ArcMap and add the Editor toolbar.

2. Click Editor and click Start Editing.

3. Zoom to the area where you want to add the new feature.

4. Click the Tool Palette dropdown arrow and click the Sketch tool.

5. Click the Current Task dropdown arrow and click Create New Feature.

6. Click the Target layer dropdown arrow and click the type of edge feature you want to create. ▶

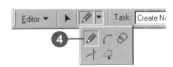

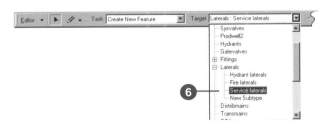

7. Check the appropriate boxes in the Snapping Environment window to set snapping to the vertex of the junction feature class to which you want to snap the new edge.

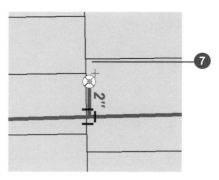

8. Move the pointer near the junction to which you want to snap this edge until the pointer snaps to it.

9. Click the map to create the new feature's vertices.

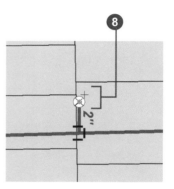

10. Double-click the last vertex to finish the feature. ▶

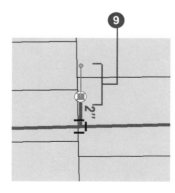

Default junction

You can specify what type of junction is placed at the free end of new edges by creating an edge–junction rule. For more information on connectivity rules, see Chapter 9, 'Geometric networks'.

You have now created a new network edge. Since you snapped it to an existing network junction, it is automatically connected to the network.

If there is an edge–junction rule for the new edge with a default end junction type specified, this junction type will be placed at the free end of the new edge. If there is not an edge–junction rule that specifies a default junction, an orphan junction will be placed at the end of the new edge. For information on how to replace the orphan junction with another junction type, see 'Subsuming network junctions' later in this chapter.

The network junction or orphan junction is added to the end of the edge.

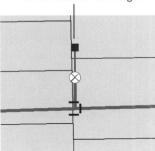

Creating a new network edge along a complex edge

1. Follow steps 1 through 6 for creating a new network edge at an existing junction.

2. Check the appropriate boxes in the Snapping Environment window to set snapping to the edge of the complex edge feature class to which you want to snap the new edge.

3. Move the pointer over the complex edge where you want the edge to snap until the pointer snaps to it.

4. Click the map to create the new feature's vertices.

5. Double-click the last vertex to finish the feature. ▶

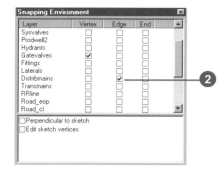

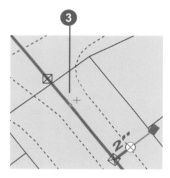

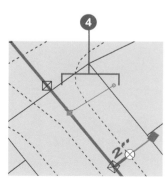

You have now created a new network edge. Since you snapped it to the edge of an existing edge, if there is an edge–edge connectivity rule between these edges, a new junction is created—the default junction type for that rule. If there is no edge–edge rule, then the new junction is the default network junction.

If there is an edge–junction rule for the new edge that has a default end junction type specified, this junction type will be added. If there is no edge–junction connectivity rule, an orphan junction is added.

Since the edge that was snapped to is a complex edge, it remains as a single feature but is split in the logical network.

6. Click the Edit tool.

7. Click the complex edge to which you snapped your new edge.

   The entire edge is selected even though another edge and junction are connected along it. It remains a single feature.

The default junction for the edge–edge rule is added.

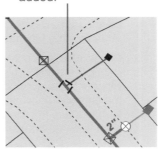

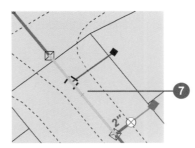

Creating a new network edge along a simple edge

1. Follow steps 1 through 6 for creating a new network edge at an existing junction.

2. Check the appropriate boxes in the Snapping Environment window to set snapping to the edge of the simple edge feature class to which you want to snap the new edge.

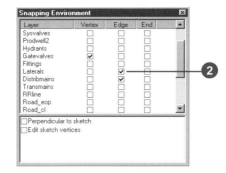

3. Move the pointer near the simple edge to which you want to snap this edge until the pointer snaps to it.

4. Click the map to create the new feature's vertices.

5. Double-click the last vertex to finish the feature. ▶

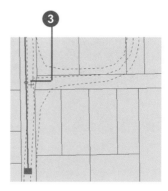

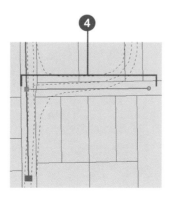

Tip

Adding junctions along simple edges

You can also snap a junction along a simple edge. Similar to snapping an edge, the junction is connected to the network. The simple edge is split into two new features.

Tip

Default junction

You can specify what type of junction is placed at the free end of new edges by creating an edge–junction rule. For more information on connectivity rules, see Chapter 9, 'Geometric networks'.

See Also

For more information on split policies and how they affect attribute values, see Chapter 5, 'Subtypes and attribute domains'.

You have now created a new network edge. Since you snapped it to the edge of an existing edge, if there is an edge–edge connectivity rule between these edges, a new junction is created, which is the default junction type for that rule. If there is no edge–edge rule, then the new junction is the default network junction.

If there is an edge–junction rule for the new edge with a default end junction type specified, this junction type will be added. If there is no edge–junction connectivity rule, an orphan junction is added.

Because the edge that was snapped to is a simple edge, it is split into two new edge features. The value of the attributes in the new features is determined by their split policies.

6. Click the Edit tool.

7. Click the simple edge to which you snapped your new edge.

   There are now two edges split at the new junction.

The default junction for the edge–edge rule is added.

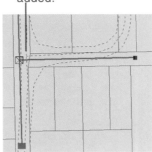

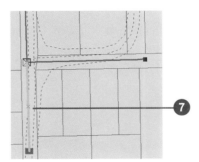

Subsuming network junctions

1. Follow steps 1 through 4 for creating a new network edge at an existing junction.

2. Click the Target layer dropdown arrow and click the type of junction feature you want to create.

3. Check the appropriate boxes in the Snapping Environment window to set snapping to the vertex of the junction feature class that you want to subsume.

4. Move the pointer near the junction you want to subsume with a new junction until the pointer snaps to it. ▶

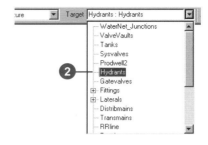

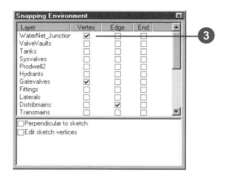

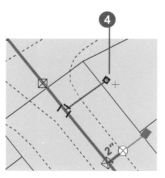

5. Click once to subsume the junction.

   The original junction is deleted and replaced with the new junction; network connectivity is maintained.

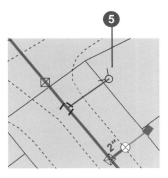

The original junction is deleted and replaced with the new junction.

Undoing network edits

If you move a network feature, other network features also move. Clicking the Undo button will undo the edits to all the affected features. To learn more about undoing edits, see Editing in ArcMap.

Moving existing network features

1. Follow steps 1 and 2 for creating a new network edge at an existing junction.

2. Click the Edit tool.

3. Click the network junctions and edges that you want to move.

4. Click and drag the features to the new location.

   Other network elements that are connected to the features rubber band. This shows how other network elements are affected by moving the selected features.

   All of the features that rubber-banded while you dragged your selected features are automatically updated to maintain network connectivity.

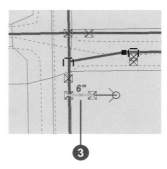

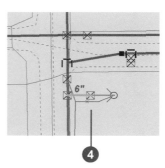

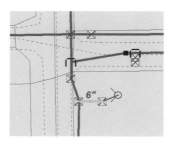

Altering a junction's ancillary network role

1. Click the Edit tool.

2. Click the network junction whose ancillary role you want to change.

3. Click the Attributes button.

4. Click the value for the AncillaryRole.

5. If you want this junction feature to act as a sink in the network, click Sink.

   If you want this junction feature to act as a source in the network, click Source.

   If you don't want this junction feature to be either a source or a sink, click None.

6. Repeat steps 3 through 5 until all the junctions whose ancillary roles you want to change are updated.

7. Use the tools found in the Network Analysis toolbar to recalculate the flow direction of the network.

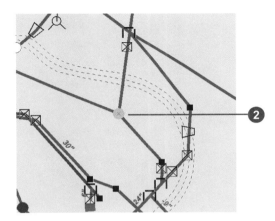

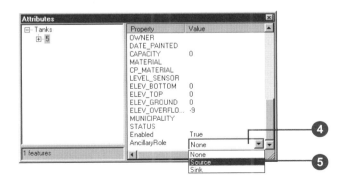

Enabling and disabling network features

1. Click the Edit tool.

2. Click the network feature you want to enable or disable.

3. Click the Attributes button.

4. Click the value for Enabled.

5. Click True if you want to enable the feature in the network.

   Click False if you want to disable the feature in the network.

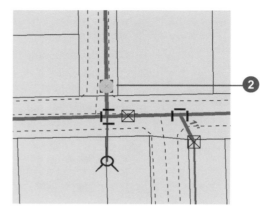

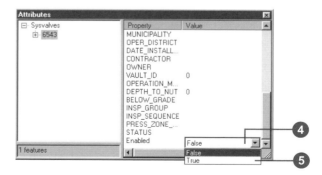

Repairing network topology

1. Click View, point to Toolbars, and click Customize.

2. Click the Commands tab.

3. Click Editor.

4. Click and drag the Rebuild Connectivity command from the Commands list and drop it on the Editor toolbar.

    The command appears on the toolbar.

5. Click Close. ▶

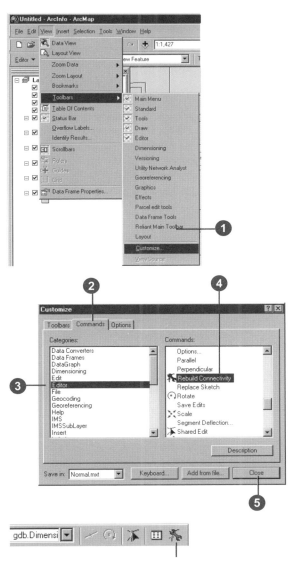

The command appears on the toolbar.

See Also

For more information on how network connectivity is established when building topology, see Chapter 9, 'Geometric networks'.

6. Click one of the feature classes in the geometric network in the ArcMap table of contents.

7. Click the Rebuild Connectivity tool.

8. Click and drag a box around the network features whose topology you want to rebuild.

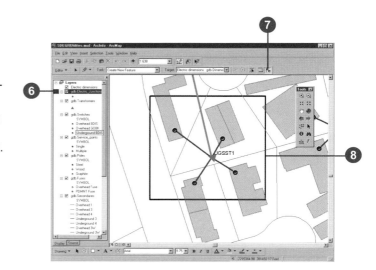

See Also

For more information on how to create and modify connectivity rules, see Chapter 9, 'Geometric networks'.

Validating network features

1. Click the Edit tool.

2. Click the network features you want to validate.

3. Click Editor and click Validate Selection. ►

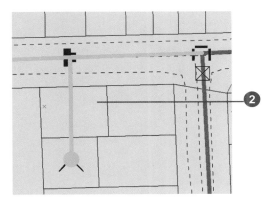

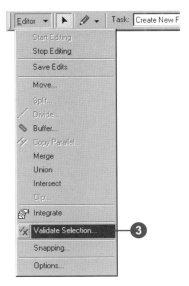

Validation rules

Network features may have connectivity rules as well as attribute and relationship validation rules associated with them. To learn more about validating attribute and relationship rules, see the tasks outlined earlier in this chapter.

If there are any invalid features, a message box appears telling you how many of the features are invalid. Only those features that are invalid remain selected.

4. Click OK.

5. Click one of the invalid network features.

6. Repeat step 3.

   A dialog box appears informing you why the selected feature is invalid.

7. Click OK.

8. Make the necessary edits to the network to make the feature valid. This may involve performing some of the network editing tasks described earlier in this chapter.

9. Repeat step 3—you should see a message box informing you that all the features are valid.

10. Click OK.

Editing dimension features

Dimension features, unlike simple features, know how they are created. A dimension feature requires a specific number of points to be entered into the edit sketch to describe its geometry. The standard edit tools can be used to manually input the points required for these *construction methods*. In addition to the manual construction methods, there are several tools that allow you to create new dimension features from existing dimension features and other features. These tools are collectively called the Auto-dimension tools.

You can assign a style to a dimension feature when you create it or change an existing dimension feature's style. Dimension features draw and symbolize themselves based on the properties of their assigned style.

Construction methods

The type of dimension feature you are creating will dictate the number of points that are required as input.

The following is a list of dimension types and the number of points required for their construction:

- Simple aligned: two points

- Aligned: three points

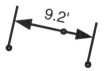

- Linear (horizontal and vertical): three points

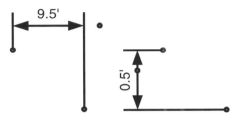

- Rotated linear: four points

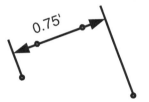

You can specify what type of construction method to use with which to create your dimension feature. The construction method dictates the type of dimension that is created. Each construction method knows how many points are required to create a specific kind of dimension feature. When using these methods, Finish Sketch is automatically called once you have input the correct number of points. The exception is the free construction methods.

The free construction methods also know how many points are required for input; however, they do not call Finish Sketch automatically. With the free construction methods, you can add as many points into the edit sketch as you need to construct your dimension feature. When you call Finish Sketch, the type of dimension feature that is created will depend on the number of points in your sketch.

The following summarizes the different construction methods:

- *Simple aligned:* creates simple aligned dimension features. It requires two points as input: the begin dimension point and the end dimension point. Finish Sketch is automatically called after the second point is input.

- *Aligned:* creates aligned dimension features. It requires three points as input: the begin dimension point, the end dimension point, and a third point describing the height of the dimension line. Finish Sketch is automatically called after the third point is input.

- *Linear:* creates horizontal and vertical dimension features. It requires three points as input: the begin dimension point, the end dimension point, and a third point describing the height of the dimension line. The location of the third point relative to the begin and end dimension points will dictate whether the dimension feature is horizontal or vertical. Finish Sketch is automatically called after the third point is input.

- *Rotated linear:* creates rotated linear dimension features. It requires four points as input: the begin dimension point, the end dimension point, a third point describing the height of the dimension line, and a fourth point describing the extension line angle. Finish Sketch is automatically called after the fourth point is input.

- *Free aligned:* creates simple aligned and aligned dimension features. It requires either two or three points as input. If you call Finish Sketch with two points in the edit sketch, a simple aligned dimension feature is created. If you call Finish Sketch with three points in the edit sketch, an aligned dimension feature is created. If you call Finish Sketch with less than two or more than three points in the edit sketch, the edit operation will fail.

- *Free linear:* creates horizontal linear, vertical linear and rotated linear dimension features. It requires either three or four points as input. If you call Finish Sketch with three points in the edit sketch, a horizontal or vertical linear dimension feature is created. If you call Finish Sketch with four points in the edit sketch, a rotated linear dimension feature is created. If you call Finish Sketch with less than three or more than four points in the edit sketch, the edit operation will fail.

The Auto-dimension tools

The Auto-dimension tool palette contains three tools for automatically creating dimension features: Dimension Edge, Baseline Dimension, and Continue Dimension. Using these tools, you can create new dimension features based on existing dimension features as well as other features.

Dimension Edge works on any type of feature. The Dimension Edge tool will automatically create a dimension whose baseline is described by a line segment of an existing feature. The Dimension Edge tool creates only horizontal and vertical linear dimension features.

Baseline Dimension and Continue Dimension are both used only on existing dimension features. Baseline Dimension creates a new dimension feature whose begin dimension point is the same as the existing dimension feature that is being baselined. The Continue Dimension tool creates a new dimension feature whose begin dimension point is the same as the end dimension point of the existing dimension feature being continued. The Baseline Dimension and Continue Dimension tools create the same type of dimension as the existing dimension they are applied to and assign it the style selected in the Style dropdown list in the Dimensioning toolbar.

Dimension styles

All dimension features are associated with a *dimension style.* When you create a new dimension feature, you must assign it a dimension style. This dimension style must exist in the dimension feature class in which you are creating your new dimension feature. Once a dimension feature is created, it assumes all of the properties of its style. You can use the Attributes dialog box to modify some of those properties; however, some properties (such as the symbology of the dimension feature elements) cannot be modified.

To learn more about dimension styles and how to create them, see Chapter 8, 'Dimensioning'.

The Dimensioning toolbar

The Auto-dimension tools and the controls for setting the construction method and assigning a dimension style are located on the Dimensioning toolbar. The controls on the Dimensioning toolbar are only active when you are editing, and the feature class selected in the Editor toolbar's Target dropdown list is a dimension feature class.

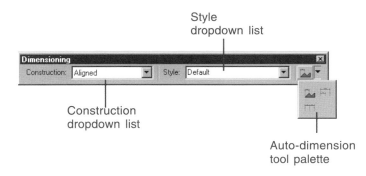

Style dropdown list

Construction dropdown list

Auto-dimension tool palette

The Construction dropdown list contains all of the methods for constructing dimension features. The construction method dictates the number of points required to construct a dimension feature and the type of dimension feature that is created.

The Styles dropdown list contains all of the styles in the dimension feature class that are selected in the Target dropdown list in the Editor toolbar. New dimension features are created and assigned the style that is selected in the Style dropdown list.

It is important to remember that the Baseline Dimension and Continue Dimension tools will only be active if a dimension feature is selected. The Dimension Edge tool will be active when any feature is selected.

Modifying a dimension feature's geometry

Dimension features not only draw and symbolize themselves based on their assigned style but are also able to regulate the modification of their geometry. By using the editing tools in ArcMap that you use to modify the geometry of other types of features, you can modify a dimension feature's geometry while maintaining the correct configuration of points for a valid dimension feature.

When you are modifying a dimension feature, there are a series of vertices you can pick up and move with the Edit tool and move to alter the dimension feature's geometry. You can't add additional vertices or delete any of the existing vertices. The following diagram illustrates what aspect of a dimension feature is modified when one of these vertices is moved:

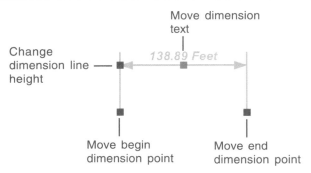

Change dimension line height

Move dimension text

138.89 Feet

Move begin dimension point

Move end dimension point

A dimension feature's geometry can be modified by moving a set of vertices while maintaining a valid dimension feature.

You can move a dimension feature's text away from its dimension line. The way the text is shown is dependent on the style chosen for the dimension feature. Some styles have line decoration including a leader line. For these styles, if you move the dimension feature's text far enough from the dimension line that it surpasses the leader line tolerance, then that leader line will automatically be displayed.

138.89 Feet

If a dimension feature's style has a text symbol with a leader line, that leader line is drawn when the text is moved farther away from the dimension line than the leader tolerance for the text symbol.

The extension line angle and the other properties of a dimension feature's geometry can be modified by altering the values of some of its fields. The following is a list of the fields you can modify for a dimension feature and how they correspond to its geometry:

Field	Property
BEGINX	x-coordinate of the begin dimension point
BEGINY	y-coordinate of the begin dimension point
ENDX	x-coordinate of the end dimension point
ENDY	y-coordinate of the end dimension point
DIMX	x-coordinate of the dimension line height
DIMY	y-coordinate of the dimension line height
TEXTX	x-coordinate of the text point (null if the text hasn't been moved relative to the dimension feature)
TEXTY	y-coordinate of the text point (null if the text hasn't been moved relative to the dimension feature)
EXTANGLE	Extension line angle

For more information on editing a feature's geometry, see Chapter 7, 'Editing existing features', in *Editing in ArcMap*. For more information on text symbols and text decoration, see Chapter 7, 'Labeling maps with text and graphics', in *Using ArcMap*.

Modifying a dimension feature's properties

A dimension feature gets most of its properties from its style. However, you can override some aspects of a dimension feature's style. The following are the properties that can differ between a dimension feature and its style:

- Dimension line display
- Dimension line arrow symbol display
- Extension line display

For more information about dimension styles, see Chapter 8, 'Dimensioning'.

In addition to overriding these style properties, you can also change a dimension feature's style, specify a custom value to use for the dimension text instead of the length of the dimension feature, and change the extension line angle.

Dimension features can be modified using the Attributes dialog box. Dimension features have a special Attributes dialog box to allow you to easily modify their various properties. However, you can also use the standard Attributes dialog box to modify the properties of a dimension feature or to modify the values of fields that you have added to your dimension feature class.

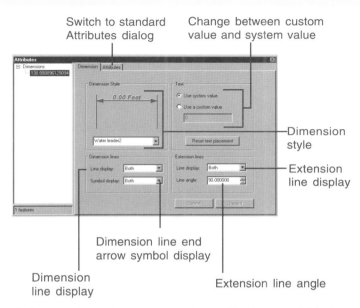

A dimension feature's properties can be modified by a special Attributes dialog box or by using the standard Attributes dialog box.

Each property of a dimension feature that you can change in the dimensioning Attributes dialog box can also be changed by altering the values of some of its fields. A list of the fields that you can modify for a dimension feature and how they correspond to its properties is illustrated below:

Field	Property
STYLEID	ID of the dimension style.
USECUSTOMLENGTH	0 indicates that the feature's length is used for the dimension text; 1 indicates a custom value is used for the dimension text.
CUSTOMLENGTH	Value used for the dimension text if USECUSTOMLENGTH is 1.
DIMDISPLAY	Null indicates both dimension lines are displayed; 1 indicates only the begin dimension line is displayed; 2 indicates only the end dimension line is displayed; 3 indicates none of the dimension lines are displayed.
EXTDISPLAY	Null indicates both extension lines are displayed; 1 indicates only the begin extension line is displayed; 2 indicates only the end extension line is displayed; 3 indicates none of the extension lines are displayed.
MARKERDISPLAY	Null indicates both dimension line end arrow markers are displayed; 1 indicates only the begin dimension line end arrow marker is displayed; 2 indicates only the end dimension line end arrow marker is displayed; 3 indicates none of the dimension line end arrow markers are displayed.

For more information on using the Attributes dialog box in ArcMap, see Chapter 9, 'Editing attributes', in *Editing in ArcMap*.

Adding the toolbar

You can also add the toolbar by clicking the View menu, pointing to Toolbars, then clicking Dimensioning.

Adding the Dimensioning toolbar

1. Right-click the Main menu.

2. Click Dimensioning.

3. Dock the toolbar to the ArcMap window. Now each time you start ArcMap the toolbar will be displayed.

Creating a simple aligned dimension feature

1. Add your dimension feature class to ArcMap, then add the Editor toolbar and the Dimensioning toolbar.

2. Click Editor and click Start Editing.

3. Zoom to the area where you want to add the new feature.

4. Click the Tool palette dropdown arrow and click the Sketch tool.

5. Click the Current Task dropdown arrow and click Create New Feature.

6. Click the Target layer dropdown arrow and click the dimension feature class. ▶

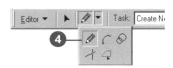

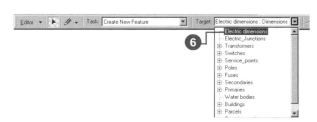

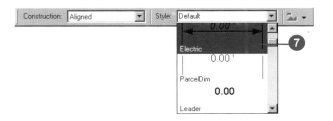

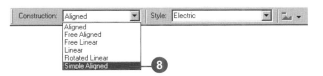

Tip

Edit sketch display

When creating dimension features, the edit sketch will actually show you how the resulting dimension feature will look as you move your mouse.

The exceptions are the free dimension construction methods. With these construction methods, the edit sketch display is the same as that for creating simple features.

7. Click the Style dropdown arrow and click the style you want your new dimension feature to have.

8. Click the Construction dropdown arrow and click Simple Aligned.

9. Click the map at the begin dimension point to start the edit sketch.

   As you move the mouse, you will see that the new dimension dynamically draws itself with your mouse location as the end dimension point. ▶

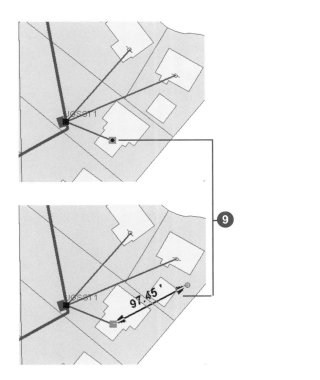

10. Click the map at the end
dimension point.

The sketch is automatically
finished and the new simple
aligned dimension feature is
created with the style you
selected.

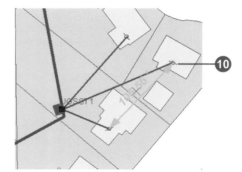

Aligned dimension features

An aligned dimension feature's dimension line is always parallel to its baseline.

To learn more about the different types of dimension features, see Chapter 8, 'Dimensioning'.

Creating an aligned dimension feature

1. Follow steps 1 through 7 for creating a simple aligned dimension feature.

2. Click the Construction dropdown arrow and click Aligned.

3. Click the map at the begin dimension point to start the edit sketch.

   As you move the mouse, you will see that the new dimension dynamically draws itself with your mouse location as the end dimension point. ▶

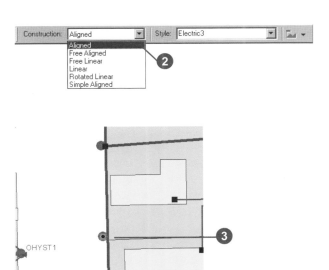

4. Click the map at the end dimension point.

   The new dimension continues to dynamically draw itself; now, however, the begin and end dimension points are fixed, and the height of the dimension line changes as you move your mouse.

5. Click the map where you want the dimension line to be.

   The sketch is automatically finished, and the new aligned dimension feature is created with the style you selected.

   Since you selected Aligned as your construction method, the dimension line is parallel to the baseline.

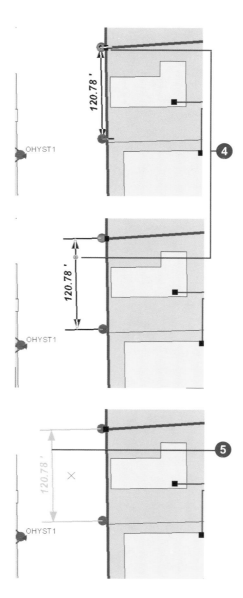

Linear dimension features

*A linear dimension feature's
dimension line is generally not
parallel to its baseline. Therefore,
the distance represented by a linear
feature is not the length of the
baseline.*

*To learn more about the different
types of dimension features, see
Chapter 8, 'Dimensioning'.*

Creating a linear dimension feature

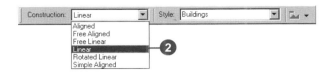

1. Follow steps 1 through 7 for creating a simple aligned dimension feature.

2. Click the Construction dropdown arrow and click Linear.

3. Click the map at the begin dimension point to start the edit sketch.

   As you move the mouse, you will see that the new dimension dynamically draws itself with your mouse location as the end dimension point. ▶

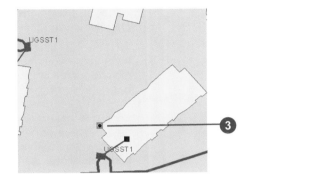

4. Click the map at the end dimension point.

   The new dimension continues to dynamically draw itself; now, however, the begin and end dimension points are fixed, and the height of the dimension line changes as you move your mouse.

   If you move your mouse to the left or right of the baseline, you will see a vertical linear dimension feature. If you move your mouse above or below the baseline, you will see a horizontal linear dimension feature. ▶

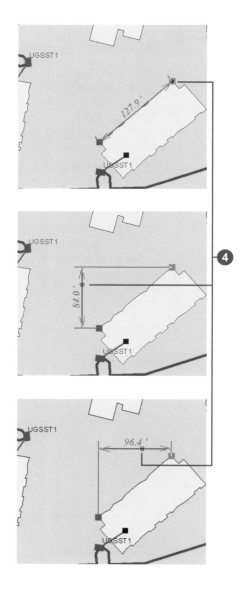

5. Click the map where you want the dimension line to be.

   The sketch is automatically finished, and the new linear dimension feature is created with the style you selected.

Creating a rotated linear dimension feature

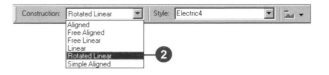

1. Follow steps 1 through 7 for creating a simple aligned dimension feature.

2. Click the Construction dropdown arrow and click Rotated Linear.

3. Click the map at the begin dimension point to start the edit sketch.

   As you move the mouse, you will see that the new dimension dynamically draws itself with your mouse location as the end dimension point. ▶

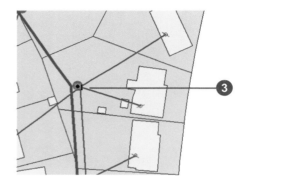

4. Click the map at the end dimension point.

   The new dimension continues to dynamically draw itself; now, however, the begin and end dimension points are fixed, and the height of the dimension line changes as you move your mouse.

   If you move your mouse above or below the baseline, you will see a horizontal linear dimension feature. If you move your mouse to the left or right of the baseline, you will see a vertical linear dimension feature. ▶

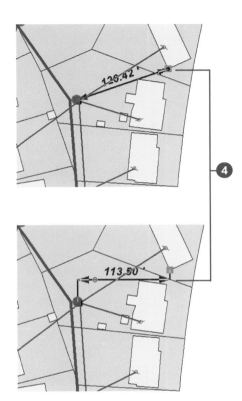

5. Click the map where you want the dimension line to be.

The new dimension continues to dynamically draw itself; now, however, the begin and end dimension points and dimension line height are fixed, and the angle of the extension lines changes as you move your mouse.

6. Click the map at the angle you want the extension lines to be.

The sketch is automatically finished, and the new rotated linear dimension feature is created with the style you selected.

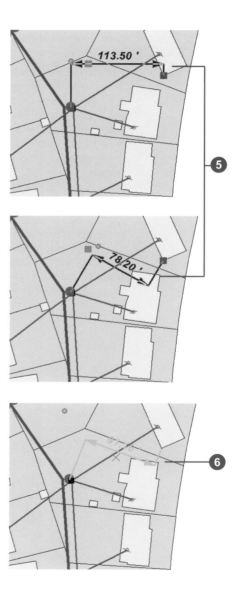

Creating a dimension feature with the free aligned construction method

1. Follow steps 1 through 7 for creating a simple aligned dimension feature.

2. Click the Construction dropdown arrow and click Free Aligned.

3. Click the map at the begin dimension point to start the edit sketch.

   As you move the mouse the dimension feature won't dynamically draw itself.

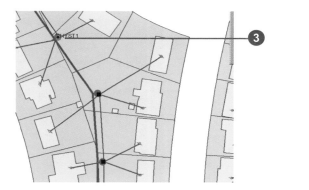

4. Use ArcMap sketch tools and construction methods to enter the end dimension point.

   If you are creating a simple aligned dimension feature, skip to step 6. ▶

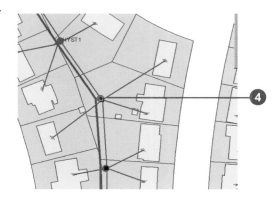

5. Use ArcMap sketch tools and construction methods to enter the point where you want the dimension line to be.

6. If your sketch has more than three vertices or has any vertices that do not represent the begin or end dimension point or dimension line height, you must delete them before continuing to step 7. ▶

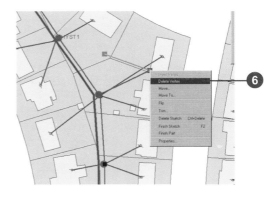

7. Right-click the sketch and click Finish Sketch.

The new dimension feature is created with the style you selected. If the edit sketch has two points, then a simple aligned feature is created. If the sketch has three points, then an aligned dimension feature is created.

The dimension feature points that the vertices represent will be determined by the order in which you entered them into the edit sketch. The vertex first entered will be used as the begin dimension point. The second vertex entered will be used as the end dimension point. If the edit sketch has three vertices, the third vertex will be used as the dimension line height point.

Creating a dimension feature with the free linear construction method

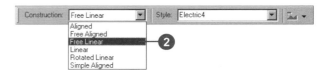

1. Follow steps 1 through 7 for creating a simple aligned dimension feature.

2. Click the Construction dropdown arrow and click Free Linear.

3. Click the map at the begin dimension point to start the edit sketch.

   As you move the mouse the dimension feature won't dynamically draw itself.

4. Use ArcMap sketch tools and construction methods to enter the end dimension point. ▶

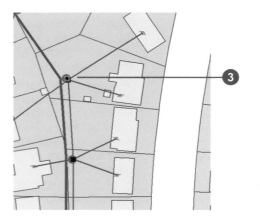

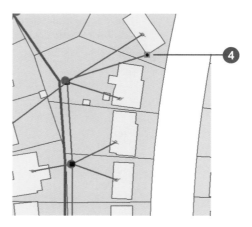

Tip

Extension line angle

When creating rotated linear dimensions, the extension line angle is calculated such that the dimension line is parallel to the line between the third and fourth construction points.

5. Use ArcMap sketch tools and construction methods to enter the point where you want the dimension line to be.

   If you are creating a horizontal or vertical linear dimension feature, skip to step 7.

6. Use ArcMap sketch tools and construction methods to enter the point that describes the extension line angle. ▶

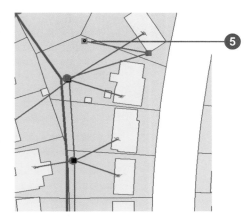

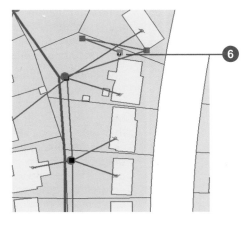

7. If your sketch has more than four vertices or has any vertices that do not represent the begin or end dimension point, dimension line height, or extension line angle, you must delete them before continuing to step 8.

8. Right-click the sketch and click Finish Sketch.

   The new dimension feature is created with the style you selected. If the edit sketch has three points, then a vertical or horizontal linear dimension feature is created. If the sketch has four points, then a rotated linear dimension feature is created.

   The dimension feature points that the vertices represent will be determined by the order in which you entered them into the edit sketch. The vertex first entered will be used as the begin dimension point. The second vertex entered will be used as the end dimension point. The third vertex will be used as the dimension line height point. If the edit sketch has four vertices, the fourth vertex will be used to describe the extension line angle.

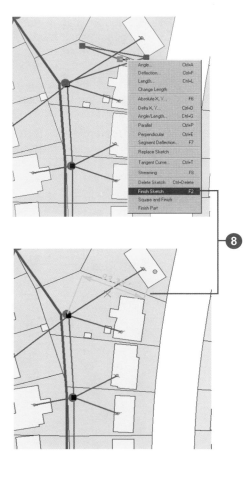

Auto-dimension tools

The Dimension Edge tool only creates linear dimension features by automatically using vertices on existing features for their begin and end dimension points.

Creating a dimension feature with the Dimension Edge tool

1. Follow steps 1 through 7 for creating a simple aligned dimension feature.

2. Select the feature whose edge you want to use as the baseline for your new dimension feature.

3. Click the Tool Palette dropdown arrow and click the Dimension Edge tool.

4. Click the edge you want to use as the baseline for your dimension feature.

   As you move your mouse, the new dimension dynamically draws itself with the begin and end dimension points fixed at the ends of the edge you clicked; the height of the dimension line changes.

   If you move your mouse to the left or right of the baseline, a vertical linear dimension feature is shown. If you move your mouse above or below the baseline, a horizontal linear dimension feature is shown.

5. Click the map where you want the dimension line to be.

   The sketch is automatically finished and a new linear dimension feature is created with the style you selected.

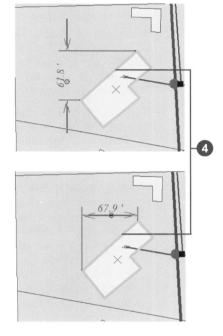

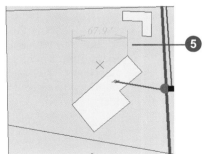

Creating a dimension feature with the Baseline Dimension tool

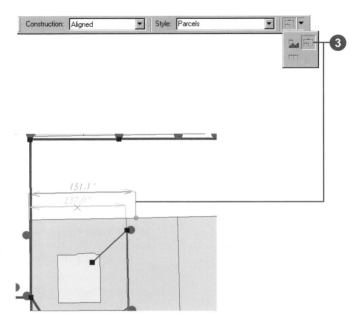

1. Follow steps 1 through 7 for creating a simple aligned dimension feature.

2. Select the dimension feature whose begin dimension point you want to use as the begin dimension point for your new dimension feature.

3. Click the Tool Palette dropdown arrow and click the Baseline Dimension tool.

   As you move your mouse, the new dimension feature dynamically draws itself with the begin dimension point fixed at the begin dimension point of the dimension feature you selected in step 2. The height is fixed at the height of the dimension feature you selected, plus the baseline height for the style you selected in step 2.

   The end dimension point changes as you move your mouse, keeping the baseline for the new dimension feature parallel to the baseline of the dimension feature you selected in step 2. ▶

Baseline height

For a dimension feature created with the Baseline Dimension tool, the height of the dimension line will be controlled by the baseline height property of its style.

The baseline height is only used for creating dimension features. If you change an existing dimension feature's style to a style with a different baseline height, the height of the dimension line will not change.

For more information about styles and how to set the baseline height property, see Chapter 8, 'Dimensioning'.

4. Click the map where you want the end dimension point to be.

   The sketch is automatically finished, and a new dimension feature is created with the style you selected. The dimension type will be the same as the dimension feature you selected in step 2.

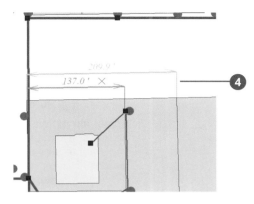

Creating a dimension feature with the Continue Dimension tool

1. Follow steps 1 through 7 for creating a simple aligned dimension feature.

2. Select the dimension feature whose end dimension point you want to use as the begin dimension point for your new dimension feature.

3. Click the tool palette dropdown arrow and click the Continue Dimension tool.

   As you move your mouse, the new dimension feature dynamically draws itself with the begin dimension point fixed at the end dimension point of the dimension feature you selected in step 2. The height is also fixed at the height of the dimension feature you selected in step 2.

   The end dimension point changes as you move your mouse, keeping the baseline for the new dimension feature parallel to the baseline of the dimension feature you selected in step 2. ▶

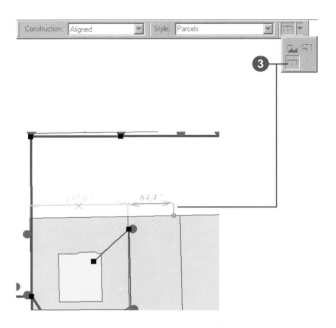

4. Click the map where you want the end dimension point to be.

The sketch is automatically finished, and a new dimension feature is created with the style you selected. The dimension type will be the same as the dimension feature you selected in step 2.

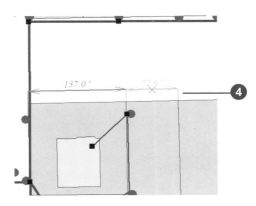

Tip

Modifying a dimension feature's geometry

In addition to modifying the dimension line height, you can also modify the begin dimension point, the end dimension point, and the dimension text placement.

Tip

Modifying a dimension feature's geometry

The move and rotate tools also work with dimension features. To learn more about these and other editor tools, see Editing in ArcMap.

Modifying a dimension feature's geometry

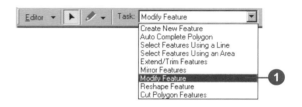

1. Click the Current Task dropdown arrow and click Modify Feature.

2. Click the Edit tool and click the dimension feature whose geometry you want to modify.

3. Position the pointer over the vertex that corresponds to the aspect of the dimension's geometry you want to modify.

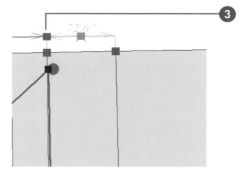

4. Click and drag the vertex to the desired location.

    As you move your mouse, the dimension feature dynamically updates itself so you can see how the feature will look after you have modified its geometry. ▶

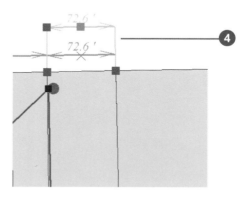

**Modifying a dimension
feature's geometry
attributes**

*In addition to using the Modify tool,
you can also use the Attributes
dialog box to modify the dimension
feature's geometry.*

5. Right-click over any part of
the sketch and click Finish
Sketch.

The dimension feature's
geometry is updated.

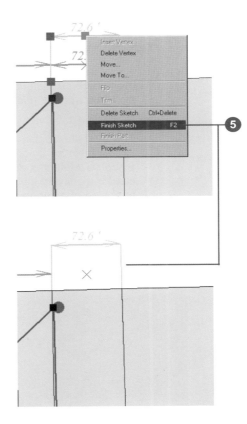

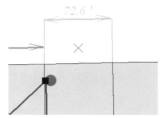

Tip

The Attributes dialog box

In addition to modifying the style for a dimension feature, you can use the Attributes dialog box to modify

- *Dimension line display*
- *Dimension line arrow symbol display*
- *Extension line display*
- *Extension line angle*
- *Dimension text value*

Modifying a dimension feature's style

1. Click the Edit tool and click the dimension feature whose style you want to modify.

2. Click the Attributes button.

   The Attributes dialog box appears. Notice that there is a special Attributes dialog box for modifying the attributes of a dimension feature.

3. Click the Dimension Style dropdown list and click the dimension style you want to assign to this feature. ▶

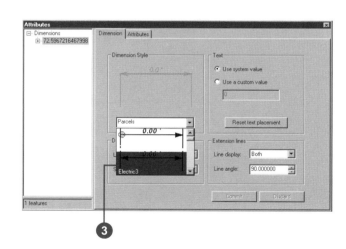

4. Click Commit.

   The dimension feature updates itself to reflect the new style.

5. Close the Attributes dialog box.

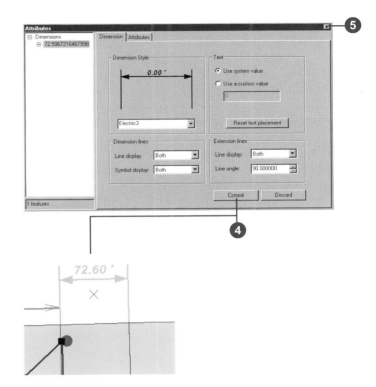

Loading objects from other feature classes

Chapter 4, 'Migrating existing data into a geodatabase', describes a number of tools for converting CAD, shapefile and coverage features, and INFO and dBASE tables to your geodatabase. These tools and wizards require that each shapefile and coverage feature class be loaded into a new feature class and each INFO and dBASE table be loaded into a new table. The feature class or table cannot exist before you begin the import process. The Simple Data Loader, also described in Chapter 4, can be used to load data into existing simple, nonversioned feature classes and tables.

Feature classes and tables that are versioned, or that store custom or network features, require an edit session to insert new records into the table or feature class. This ensures that the network connectivity and version information is managed correctly. The Object Loader Wizard in ArcMap lets you do this.

There are several things to consider before you use the Load Objects command. First, loading data into network feature classes is a slow process—several seconds per feature. This performance hit may make large data loads into network feature classes impractical.

If you use the Load Objects command to load data into versioned ArcSDE feature classes, once all of the data is loaded it will be in the delta tables, not the base tables for the feature classes. If you use this method, you should run Compress on your database once the data is loaded to push all the records from the delta tables to the base tables. Having your data in the base tables will result in better query speed than if you have large amounts of data in your delta tables. For more details on compressing your database to improve performance, see Chapter 13, ' Working with a versioned geodatabase'.

If you need to append large amounts of data to your database but want to avoid the performance hit associated with loading data into network feature classes or versioned feature classes, you should consider one of the data appending strategies outlined in Chapter 4, 'Migrating existing data into a geodatabase'.

Adding the Load Objects command to ArcMap

1. Click View, point to Toolbars, and click Customize.

2. Click the Commands tab.

3. Click Data Converters.

4. Click and drag the Load Objects command from the Commands list and drop it on the Editor toolbar.

   The command appears on the toolbar.

5. Click Close.

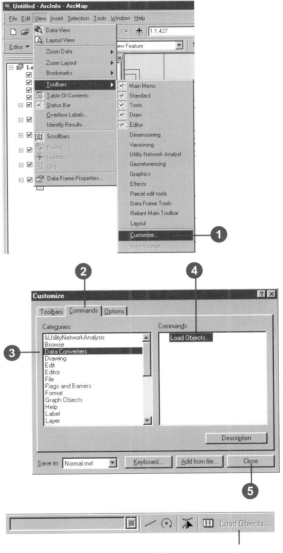

The command appears on the toolbar.

Tip

The subtype field

If you choose to load data into a specific subtype, you will not be able to match a field from the source data to the subtype field in the target data. The subtype field in this case is automatically populated.

Tip

Versioned data

When you load data into a versioned feature class, the new features are only visible in the version you are working with.

Loading data with the Load Objects command

1. Add your data to ArcMap, click Editor, then click Start Editing.

2. Click the Target layer dropdown arrow and click the feature class or subtype into which you want to load data.

3. Click Load Objects. ▶

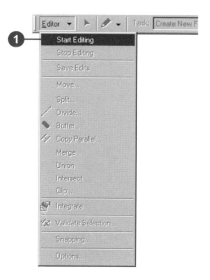

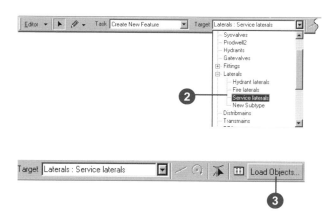

4. Browse to the source feature class.

5. Click Add to add it to the list of source data.

6. Repeat steps 4 and 5 until you have specified all of the source data.

7. Click Next.

8. To match a source field with a field in the target feature class or table, click the dropdown arrow in the Matching Source Field list and click the field from the source data you want to match to the target field.

9. Repeat step 8 until you have matched the fields you want loaded from your source data to the target fields.

10. If you don't want data from a field in the source data to be loaded into the target data, leave the Matching Source Field blank.

11. Click Next. ▶

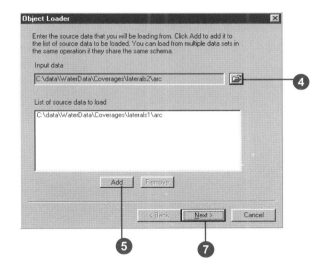

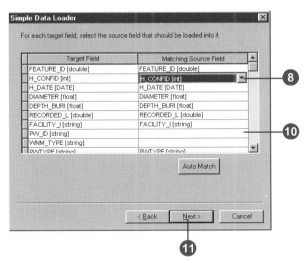

See Also

To learn more about using the Query Builder to query your data, see *Using ArcMap.*

12. If you want to load all of the source data, click the first option, then skip to step 16.

13. If you want to limit the features from the source data to load into the target using an attribute *query,* click the second option.

14. Click Query Builder to open the Query Data dialog box.

15. Create a query to limit the features or rows from the source data to be loaded into the target.

16. Click OK.

17. Click Next. ▶

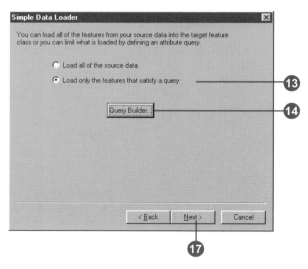

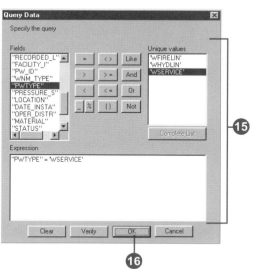

Network features

When loading data into an edge network feature class, the network connectivity is maintained, and default junctions are used as described earlier in this chapter.

For more information on the ArcMap snapping environment, see Editing in ArcMap.

18. Click No if you don't want your features to be snapped to existing features in your edit session.

    Click Yes if you want to use the current Editor snapping environment to snap the new features as they are loaded.

19. Click No if you don't want your new features to be validated after they are loaded.

    Click Yes if the feature class or subtype into which you are loading data has rules associated with it and you want any new invalid feature to be selected after the loading process.

20. Click Next.

21. Review the options you have specified for loading your data. If you want to change something, go back through the wizard by clicking Back.

22. When satisfied with your options, click Finish to load your data.

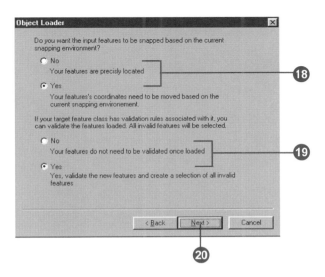

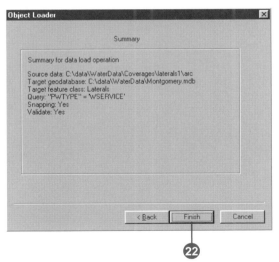

Working with a versioned geodatabase 13

IN THIS CHAPTER

- **Integrating versioning with your organization's work flow**

- **Registering data as versioned**

- **Creating and administering versions in ArcCatalog**

- **Working with versions in ArcMap**

- **Editing and conflict resolution**

- **Editing a version**

- **Versioning scenarios**

With ArcGIS 8, multiple users can access geographic *data* in a *geodatabase* through *versioning*. Versioning lets users simultaneously create multiple, persistent representations of the *database* without data replication. Users can edit the same *features* or rows without explicitly applying locks to prohibit other users from modifying the same data.

An organization can use versioning to manage alternative engineering designs, solve complex "what if" scenarios without impacting the corporate database, and create point-in-time representations of the database.

Primarily, versioning simplifies the editing experience. Multiple users can directly modify the database without having to extract data or lock features and rows before editing. If, by chance, the same features are modified, a *conflict* resolution dialog box guides the user through the process of determining the feature's correct representation and *attributes*.

Integrating versioning with your organization's work flow

The geodatabase and versioning provide organizations with advanced data storage techniques that revolutionize the *work flow* process in many applications where spatial information is used. Engineers can generate design alternatives using the entire database. Spatial analysts can perform complex "what if" scenarios without affecting the current representation of the database. Database administrators can create "historical" snapshots of the database for archiving or database recovery.

In the long run, an organization benefits from implementing a versioned database. The data is centrally located in one corporate database. There is never a need to extract units of the database to update, or lock, map sheets or individual features. These factors simplify the administration process.

The work flow process

The evolution of the work flow process—how projects or *work orders* transpire over time—varies greatly from organization to organization and throughout each sector of the business community. Therefore, the geodatabase's versioning process has been designed to be flexible enough to accommodate the most basic of work flow processes as well as the most complex and to be sufficiently restrictive with or without additional application customization.

Common work flow processes usually progress in discrete stages. At each stage, different requirements or business rules may be enforced. Typically, during each stage of the process, the project or work order is associated by a named stage. For example, within the utility domain, common stages include "working", "proposed", "accepted", "under construction", and "as built". The process is essentially cyclical. The work order is initially generated and assigned to an engineer and then modified over time as it progresses from stage to stage, and finally the changes are "posted" or applied back to the corporate database.

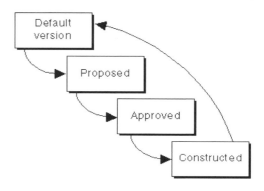

A common work flow process evolving through each stage of a project

This is one example of how versioning can help simplify the work flow process. Because the work flow process may span days, months, and even years, the corporate database requires continuous availability for daily operations. If a work order applied restrictive locks to the data involved in the process, other database users might not be able to perform their daily work assignments.

To implement your work flow in the geodatabase, versions can be created to correspond with each stage of the work flow process. Alternatively, you may want to create one version for each work order and modify the version's name to represent the current stage as the process proceeds through each step.

The current structure of your organization's work flow significantly influences how the geodatabase's versioning process is implemented to manage your spatial transactions. The flexibility and openness of the system allows you to determine the best solution to meet the requirements of your business processes.

The remaining sections of this chapter will help illustrate how to use ArcCatalog and ArcMap to perform various versioning tasks. In particular, the last section provides examples of how an organization can implement work flow processes using the geodatabase's versioning capabilities. For additional details on managing your organization's work flow with versions, read *Modeling Our World*.

Registering data as versioned

Before editing *feature datasets, feature classes,* and *tables,* you must first register the data as versioned in ArcCatalog.

Making a feature class or table multiversioned requires a unique integer *field.* Only the owner of the data may register or unregister the object as versioned.

When unregistering a dataset or feature class as versioned in ArcCatalog, a warning dialog box may appear informing you that outstanding edits still remain in existing versions. Therefore, unregistering the class as versioned will remove all the edits. To preserve the edits, you must compress the database.

Tip

Registering data as versioned

Registering a feature dataset as versioned registers all feature classes within the feature dataset as versioned.

1. In the ArcCatalog tree, right-click the feature dataset, feature class, or table you want to register as versioned.

2. Click Register As Versioned.

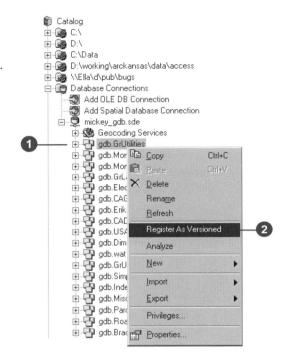

Creating and administering versions in ArcCatalog

ArcCatalog lets you create new versions, rename existing versions, delete versions, and modify version properties. These administrative tasks are accomplished using the Version Manager dialog box.

Initially, the database consists of one version named "DEFAULT", owned by the ArcSDE administrative user. The new versions that are created are always based on an existing version. When the new version is created, it is identical to the version from which it was derived. Over time, the versions will diverge as changes are made to the parent version and to the new version.

A version consists of several properties: an alphanumeric name, an owner, an optional description, the creation date, the last modified date, the parent version, and the version's permission.

A version's permission can only be changed by its owner. The available permission settings are: ▶

Creating a new version

1. In ArcCatalog, create a new connection to the database with the Add SDE Connection dialog box. (See Chapter 1, 'Introduction'.)

2. In the Catalog tree, right-click your database connection and click Versions. ▶

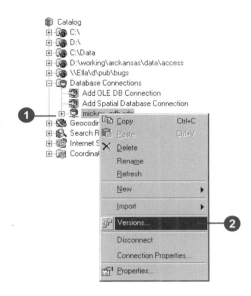

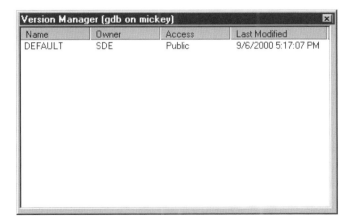

- Private—only the owner may view the version and modify available feature classes.

- Protected—any user may view the version, but only the owner may modify available feature classes.

- Public—any user may view the version and modify available feature classes.

Only the version's owner can rename, delete, or alter the version. A parent version cannot be deleted until all dependent child versions are first deleted.

To improve database performance, the database should be compressed periodically. Compressing the database removes all unreferenced database states and redundant rows. Only the ArcSDE administrator can perform this task. When the *Compress* command is executed, the database is unavailable until compression is completed. For additional details, see the versioning scenarios section at the end of the chapter.

Finally, after compressing the database or editing the data, the Analyze command should be executed to update the database statistics for each dataset or feature class. This will help ▶

3. Right-click a version and click New.

4. Type the new version's name.

5. Type a description.

6. Click the appropriate permission type; the default is Private.

7. Click OK.

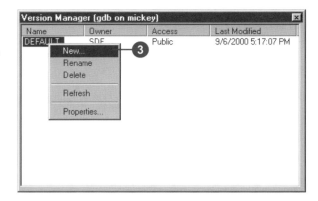

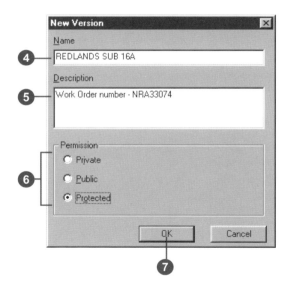

improve display and query performance.

Renaming a version

1. Right-click your database connection and click Versions.

2. Right-click the version you want to rename and click Rename.

3. Type a new name and press Enter.

Deleting a version

1. Right-click your database connection and click Versions.

2. Right-click the version you want to delete.

3. Click Delete or press Delete on your keyboard.

Tip

Refresh

Use the Refresh command to update the properties of each version with their current values.

Changing a version's properties

1. Right-click your database connection and click Versions.

2. Right-click a version.

3. Click Properties.

4. Type the new description.

5. Click the new permission type.

6. Click OK.

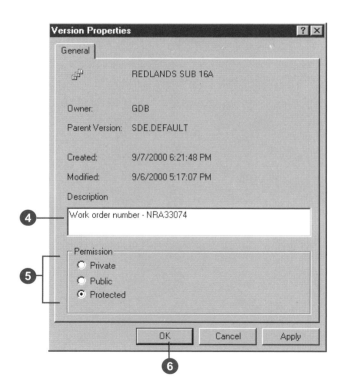

See Also

For more information on how to customize ArcCatalog, see Using ArcCatalog *and* Exploring ArcObjects.

Adding the Compress command to ArcCatalog

1. In ArcCatalog, click View, click Toolbars, and click Customize.

2. Check Context Menus in the list of toolbars. ▶

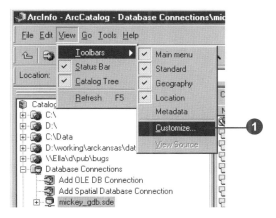

3. Click the Context Menus menu.

4. Click the arrow next to the Remote Database Context Menu.

5. Click the Commands tab in the Customize dialog box.

6. Click Geodatabase tools.

7. Click and drag the Compress Database command from the Commands list and drop it on the context menu.

   The command appears in the context menu.

8. Click Close on the Customize dialog box.

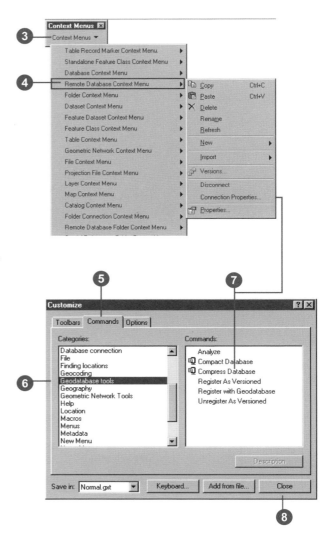

Compressing the database

1. In ArcCatalog, create a new database connection as the ArcSDE administrative user.

2. Right-click the new database connection and click Compress Database.

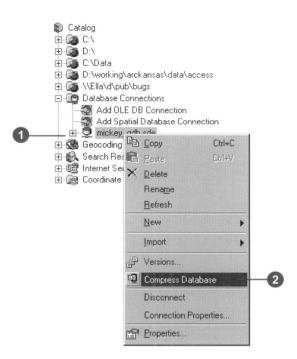

Working with versions in ArcMap

In ArcMap, you can view and work with multiple versions simultaneously, create new versions, and change the feature classes or tables from one version to another version. You can also use the version manager, refresh a version's *workspace* connection, and modify available feature classes in ArcMap.

To create a new version, at least one version must be present in the map. If multiple versions are present, you will need to specify the parent version. The newly created version will then be identical to the parent version.

Changing versions allows you to quickly navigate between two versions by changing the feature classes currently in the map. This simplifies the process of viewing the differences between feature classes or performing an analysis with two versions. ▶

Creating a new version in ArcMap

1. Add the Versioning toolbar to the map.

2. Click the Create New Version button. At least one version is required to be in ArcMap prior to the command becoming enabled.

3. Click the Parent Version dropdown arrow and click the parent version from which you want to create the new version.

4. Type the new version's name.

5. Optionally, type a description.

6. Click the appropriate permission type.

7. Optionally, if you are not currently editing, check the check box to switch the parent version to the new version.

8. Click OK.

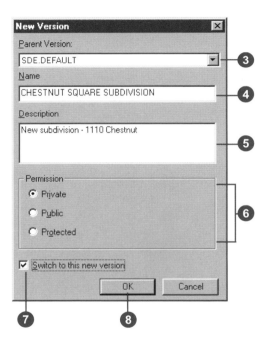

When a version workspace is changed to a different version, all feature classes present in the workspace will represent the "target" version.

Two methods are available in ArcMap for changing versions. You can change versions from the Versioning toolbar or in the table of contents.

When you work in a multiuser environment, the database may be modified by another user at the same time you're viewing the database. Therefore, the feature classes present in ArcMap may become outdated.

To update the feature classes in ArcMap, you can refresh one or all of the version workspaces present.

To refresh all the versions, click the Refresh button on the Versioning toolbar. To refresh an individual workspace, use the Refresh command on the table of contents context menu.

While you are editing, the Refresh button and the Refresh command for the version's workspace are unavailable. ▶

Tip

The Change Version command

Use the Change Version command instead of adding multiple version workspaces to your map document.

Changing versions

1. Click the Source tab at the bottom of the ArcMap table of contents to list the workspaces in your map.

2. Right-click a version workspace.

3. Click Change Version.

4. Click the version to which you want to change.

5. Click OK.

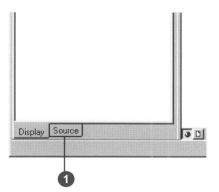

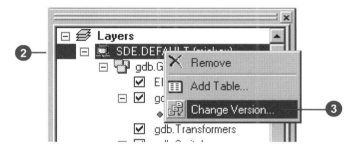

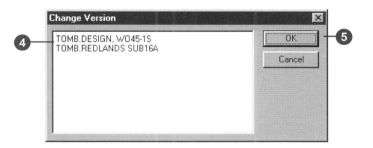

You can have as many versions in the map as needed, but you can only edit one version per *edit session*.

Tip

Preserving a version

If you need to preserve a current representation of the database, create a new version before refreshing.

Refreshing a workspace

1. Click Refresh on the Versioning toolbar.

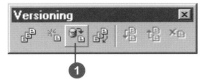

Editing and conflict resolution

The geodatabase is designed to efficiently manage and support long *transactions* using versions. The geodatabase also allows multiple users to edit the same version at the same time. Each edit session in ArcMap is its own representation of the version until you save. Saving the edit session applies your modifications to the version, making these changes immediately accessible in the database.

When multiple users simultaneously edit a version or *reconcile* two versions, *conflicts* can occur. Reconciling is the process of merging two versions. Conflicts occur when the same feature or topologically related features are edited by two or more users, and the database is unclear about which representation is valid. Conflicts are rare but can occur when overlapping geographic areas in the database are edited. To ensure database integrity, the geodatabase detects when a feature has been edited in two versions and reports it as a conflict. ArcMap provides the necessary tools for conflict resolution, but your interaction is still required to make the final decision as to the feature's correct representation.

ArcMap provides tools to resolve conflicts, as well as the necessary tools to reconcile and *post* versions. The next sections explain these capabilities in more detail.

Reconcile

The Reconcile button in ArcMap merges all modifications between the current edit session and a target version you select. Any differences between the features in the target version and the features in the edit session are applied to the edit session. Differences can consist of newly inserted, deleted, or updated features. The reconcile process detects these differences and discovers any conflicts. If conflicts exist, a message is displayed, followed by the conflict resolution dialog box. Reconciling happens before posting a version to a target version. A target

version is any version in the direct ancestry of the version such as the parent version or the DEFAULT version.

In addition, the reconcile process requires that you are the only user currently editing the version, and you are the only user able to edit the version throughout the reconcile process until you save or post. If another user is simultaneously editing the version or attempts to start editing since you have reconciled, an error message will inform you that the version is currently in use.

The reconcile process requires that you have full permissions to all the feature classes that have been modified in the version being editied. If a feature class is modified in the version for which you do not have update privileges, an error message appears. You will not be able to reconcile the versions; a user with adequate permissions to perform the reconcile must do this for you.

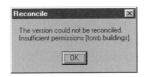

An error message appears when you do not have permission to a feature class to reconcile versions.

For example, suppose you have completed your changes in a version and need to post the version to the database. You must first reconcile the version with a target version you select, resolve any conflicts if necessary, and then post.

Autoreconciliation

When multiple users are simultaneously editing the same version and one user has already saved his or her edit session, ArcMap can notify you when you save that the edit session has been reconciled with the version's current representation. You also have the option to explicitly perform the reconcile and save without notification. You may want the notification to allow further inspection of the results from the reconciliation. It's an opportunity to review the difference introduced from the reconciliation between the edit session and the current version's representation. If conflicts are detected, you will be informed with a warning message, and the save process will fail.

The Notification dialog box appears when an edit session could not be saved because another user has modified and saved their edit session prior to the current user saving his or her edit session.

Post

You can post a version after you have first performed a reconcile. Once the edit session has reconciled with a target version, clicking the Post button synchronizes the edit session with the reconciled version and performs a save. Posting cannot be undone, as you are applying changes to a version that you are not currently editing. If the reconciled version is modified between reconciling and posting, you will be notified to reconcile again before posting.

This message indicates that the target version has been modified since the reconciliation; reconcile again before posting.

Conflicts

Conflicts occur when the same feature, or topologically related features or relationship classes, is modifed in two versions—the current version being edited and a target version. Conflict detection only occurs during the reconciliation process. If conflicts are detected, a message appears, followed by the conflict resolution dialog box.

There are three categories of conflicts: when the same feature has been updated in each version, when the same feature has been updated in one version and deleted in the other or vice versa, and when the same feature has been deleted in one version and updated in the other version.

When conflicts are detected, the parent version's feature representation takes precedence over the edit session's representation. Therefore, all conflicting features in the current edit session are replaced by their representation in the parent version. If multiple users are editing the same version and conflicts are detected, the feature that was first saved, the current version's representation, is preserved by replacing the edit session's feature representation. ArcMap ensures database integrity by forcing you to interactively inspect each conflict and resolve the conflict by replacing the feature in the current version with your edit session's representation.

Conflict resolution

Once conflicts are detected, a conflict resolution dialog box appears, containing all the conflict classes and their features or rows in conflict. The conflict resolution dialog box allows you to interactively resolve conflicts at the level of the feature class or individual feature. Resolving the conflict implies that you will make a decision as to the feature's correct representation; this could mean doing nothing at all if you are satisfied with the current feature's representation.

You can choose from three representations of the conflicting feature or row to resolve the conflict. The preedit version is the feature's representation when you initially started editing, before making any changes. The edit session version represents the feature as it existed before you performed the reconcile. The last representation is the conflict version, the feature's representation in the conflicting version.

Selecting a feature class or individual feature displays any of the three representations of the feature in the map. The preedit's version is displayed in yellow, the edit session's version is displayed in green, and the conflict's version is displayed in red. You can also optionally enable or disable the display settings for each version (preedit, edit session, and conflict) by clicking the Display command on the context menu and checking or unchecking the corresponding version.

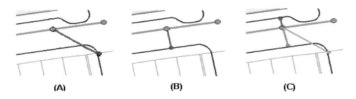

(A) (B) (C)

The lateral in blue as it existed prior to editing (A), the lateral after being modified (B), and the three representations during conflict resolution (C).

When you select a feature in the conflict resolution dialog box, each version's representation of the feature's or row's attributes is listed in the bottom half of the box. A red dot to the left of the field name identifies why the feature is a conflict. For example, if the feature's geometry was edited in each version, a red dot appears next to the shape field. The same principle holds true for attribute conflicts. If a feature has been deleted in either version, "<deleted>" appears for that version's attribute value. Therefore,

a red dot marks each column, signifying that each column is an update/delete or a delete/update conflict.

Resolving a conflict implies that you made a conscious decision about the feature's correct representation. You can select the feature in the conflict resolution dialog box and replace the current feature in the map with any of the three representations of the feature. This allows you to quickly update and replace conflicting features. If further modifications are required, you can simply use any of the ArcMap editing tools to update the feature.

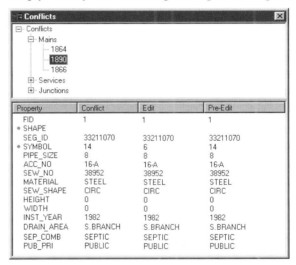

This conflict resolution dialog box shows three feature classes with conflicts and a feature with each of its version's attributes.

Conflicts with geometric networks, feature-linked annotation, and relationships

Resolving conflicts with features that are related to other features through *geometric networks*, feature-linked *annotation*, and *relationship classes* is different than resolving conflicts with simple feature classes. Because each of these feature classes has specific geodatabase behaviors that can impact other feature classes, resolving a feature conflict may impact related features.

When you edit network features, changes to the geometric network and to the logical network may create conflicts. For example, when you add a service to a main, the main will not be physically split in the geometric network but will be split in the *logical network*. Therefore, while you have not directly edited the main's geometry, it has been edited logically. If the target version you are reconciling has also modified the main, then the new service you inserted will create a conflict with the main.

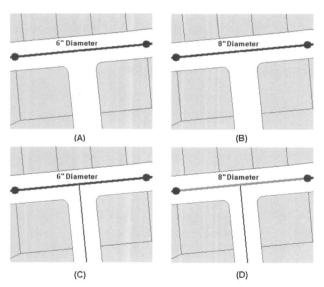

The original water main (A), the water main changed to an 8-inch diameter in the first edit session (B), a new service inserted in the second edit session (C), and the water main in red as a conflict (D).

Resolving a conflict involving geometric network feature classes requires understanding how the Replace With command in the conflict resolution dialog box will update the existing network topology present in the edit session.

In the previous example, two users modified the water main—one by changing an attribute and the second by connecting a new service. Resolving the conflict would merely require investigating the differences and seeing that the conflict is valid and no further resolution is required. Since the main contains the correct attribute for the diameter, the new service is correctly connected to the main. But there are cases when resolving conflicts involving a junction feature class will also update the connected network edge.

Working with feature-linked annotation requires remembering one rule: when replacing a feature that has feature-linked annotation, both the feature and the annotation are replaced with the new feature and annotation. You may have to further edit the new annotation. For example, you may encounter a conflict in which you have moved a feature and repositioned its annotation. The conflict version has performed the same edit, moving the feature and rotating the annotation. Your decision is to replace the feature with the conflict version's feature. This action deletes the existing feature-linked annotation, inserts the conflict feature, and creates a new annotation. You will then need to further edit the new annotation by moving and rotating it as necessary.

Relationships have similar dependencies to feature-linked annotation. Deleting a feature from an origin relationship class may trigger a message to delete a feature from the destination relationship class. Therefore, be aware of the ramifications of simply replacing conflicts involving feature classes that participate in relationship classes.

An example of when a conflict can arise between relationship classes is if you were to update the origin class primary field, breaking the relationship in version A. At the same time, in version B, the destination class-related feature is also updated. When you reconcile the versions, since the destination class is dependent on the origin class, a conflict is detected. A similar example is if you were to delete a pole that has a relationship to a transformer, the transformer is also deleted. But in the conflict version, the transformer's attributes are edited. An update/delete conflict would be detected when reconciled.

Editing a version

The ArcMap editing toolbar provides the arena for editing versions, reconciling versions, resolving conflicts, and posting versions.

When you start editing, if multiple versions are present in the map, you will have to select one version. Starting an edit session on a version creates a new, unnamed, temporary version that exists until you save or end the edit session. You are the only user who can see your changes until you explicitly save.

When saving an edit session, you have an option to enable or disable autoreconciliation. If enabled, autoreconciliation will automatically reconcile your edit session with the version's current database state and save, making your changes available to others using the database. If autoreconciliation is not enabled, then when you save, your edit session will be reconciled with the version's current database state. A message will inform you that the edit session has been reconciled but has not been saved. This will only occur if a second user has also edited the version and saved since you ▶

Enabling and disabling autoreconciliation

1. Click Editor and click Start Editing.

2. Click Editor and click Options.

3. Click the Versioning tab.

4. Check the check box to enable autoreconciliation or uncheck the check box to disable autoreconciliation.

5. Click OK.

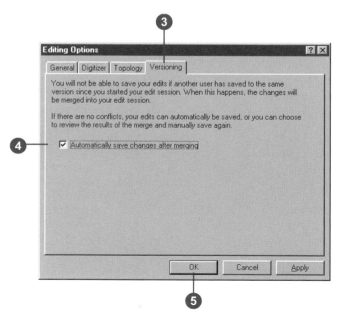

started editing. You will need to save again to make your changes available to others using the database.

Based on your organization's work flow, you may eventually need to reconcile two versions. Reconciliation is the process of merging features from a target version into the current edit session. Reconciliation must be done before posting changes to another version.

During reconciliation, conflicts may be discovered. Conflicts arise when the same feature is updated in each version or updated in one and deleted in the other.

When conflicts arise, an interactive conflict resolution dialog box will provide the tools necessary to resolve the conflicts. For each conflict, you can choose whether to replace the feature in your edit session with the conflict version, the version from your edit session, or the version as it existed at the beginning of your edit session.

Once you have successfully completed the reconciliation, you can post the version. The post operation synchronizes your edit session with the target version. They are then identical.

Reconciling

1. Click the Reconcile button on the Versioning toolbar.
2. Click the target version.
3. Click OK.

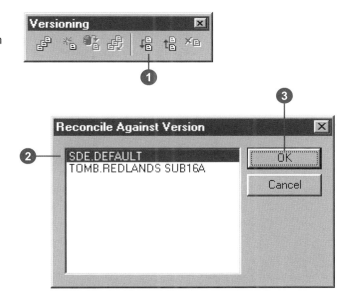

Posting

1. Click the Post button on the Versioning toolbar.

Displaying conflicts

1. Click the Conflicts button on the Versioning toolbar.

2. Right-click Conflicts and click Display.

3. Click the appropriate check box to display each conflict category.

4. Click OK.

5. Click the Close button to close the Conflicts dialog box.

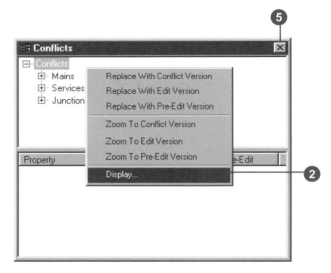

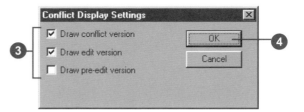

Resolving conflicts

1. Click the Conflicts button on the Versioning toolbar.

2. Click a feature class.

3. Click a feature and right-click to display the context menu.

4. Click the appropriate Replace With command to resolve the conflict.

5. Click the Close button to close the Conflicts dialog box.

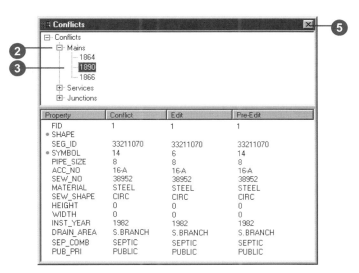

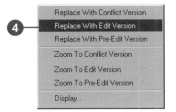

Versioning scenarios

The following scenarios show how an organization can implement its work flow process using a versioned database. These examples demonstrate several techniques available for performing long transactions in a multiuser environment. It is likely that organizations will, in some manner, use each of these techniques depending on the task.

Scenario 1: Simple database modifications

Task: Multiple users are concurrently editing the database, performing common map sheet changes such as inserting new features, updating attributes, and removing out-of-date facilities.

Solution: Each user can simply connect to the DEFAULT version (simultaneously), start editing, and save their changes when their work is complete. Users do not have to create new versions to modify the database. If another user has edited the DEFAULT version since the current user has started editing, the user saving is notified that the version has been changed and therefore the version will need to be saved again. Users may bypass this warning message by enabling autoreconciliation in the ArcMap Options dialog box. Also, if two users modify the same feature during their edit sessions, the second user to save encounters a conflict. The user then has to decide what the feature's correct representation is and save the edit session.

Scenario 2: Transactions spanning multiple days

Task: Update the database to incorporate new and updated facilities in the field, which will likely require multiple edit sessions and a couple of days to complete.

Solution: A user creates and switches to a new version derived from the DEFAULT version. The user starts editing the new version and begins modifying features and saving as required. The user can resume the edit session, as appropriate, the following day or possibly the following week. When the changes are complete and ready to be posted to the DEFAULT version, the user must first click the Reconcile button on the Versioning toolbar. If conflicts are detected, the user can resolve the differences and complete the transaction by clicking the Post button. The posting process applies all the changes in the user's version to the DEFAULT version. The user can then delete the version.

Scenario 3: A work flow process

Task: Create individual versions for each step or stage of the work order and work flow process and post the work order to the database.

Solution: A user or supervisor creates a new version derived from the DEFAULT version. The user starts editing the new version and begins modifying features or creating a new design. When the user has completed the design or proposed modifications, the work order can be submitted to a supervisor for review. At this time, a new version can be created to ensure the preservation of the initial design. The new version can then be further modified or adjusted as required. Once the work order has been approved for construction, another version can be created. The purpose of this version is to reflect any changes that may occur while the work order is being constructed in the field. Finally, as the construction is completed and the new facilities are in service, the work order must be posted to the database. A user can then start editing the work order, perform a reconcile with the DEFAULT version, resolve any conflicts if necessary, and post.

The solution allows the organization to create new versions of the work order for each step of the project—the initial design or proposed version, a working or accepted version, and a version for the construction phase. Each version is preserved and available to look back on for historical purposes. The final step is to post the constructed version to the database. The project completes a full circle from start to finish, creating individual versions at each step.

Scenario 4: Restricting permissions to the database

Task: The organization's supervisor has restricted write access to the DEFAULT version, requiring managerial review of each user's edits prior to posting the changes to the database.

Solution: To restrict write permissions to the database (the DEFAULT version), the ArcSDE administrative user can set the permission of the DEFAULT version to "protected" using the version manager. This allows users to continue to view the DEFAULT version but does not allow users to start editing the version. Therefore, users will need to create new versions for editing the database, similar to Scenario 2. When a user has completed and saved the edit session, the ArcSDE administrator can reconcile the version with the DEFAULT version. To accomplish this task, the manager who connects to the database as the ArcSDE administrator starts editing the user's version and clicks the Reconcile button. The process will merge all the changes in the user's version and the DEFAULT version. If conflicts are detected, the manager can resolve the conflicts and save the edit session. Once the edits are acceptable to the manager, the version is ready to be posted to the DEFAULT version. The ArcSDE administrative user can then start editing the version, perform a reconcile, and then post the version. The user's version can then be deleted.

Scenario 5: Compressing the database

Task: The geodatabase has been edited for an extended time, and the number of database states and rows in each feature classes' delta tables has significantly increased. How do we improve performance by running the Compress command?

Solution: The Compress command will remove all database states that are no longer referenced by a version and move all the rows in the delta tables, which are common to all versions, to the base table. To achieve the maximum benefit when running the Compress command, you will need to first reconcile, post, and delete each version with the DEFAULT version. Sometimes this may not be a reasonable option based on your organization's work flow. At minimum, to improve performance, simply reconcile each version with the DEFAULT version and save, then perform the compress. This will ensure that all the edits in the DEFAULT version will be compressed from the delta tables to the business table. Remember, the Compress command can still be executed without first reconciling, posting, and deleting each version, but the benefits may not be as noticeable.

Glossary

alias

Another name for a field in a table.

aligned dimension

A dimension that runs parallel to the baseline and represents the true distance between the begin and end dimension points.

annotation

The process of automating text placement or the text associated with a feature or an area on a map.

ArcSDE

A gateway to a multiuser commercial RDBMS—for example, Oracle, Microsoft SQL Server, Informix, and DB2. ArcSDE is an open, high-performance spatial data server that employs client/server architecture to perform efficient spatial operations and manage large, shared geographic data. Was known as SDE before 1999.

attribute

A characteristic of a map feature. Attributes of a river might include its name, length, average depth, and so on.

attribute domain

A named constraint in the database. An attribute constraint can be applied to a field of a subtype of a feature class or object class to make an attribute rule. Types of attribute domains include range and coded value domains.

behavior

Properties of an object in a geodatabase that describe how it can be edited and drawn. Behavior includes, but is not limited to, validation rules, subtypes, default values, and relationships.

CAD feature class

A feature class in a CAD dataset. A CAD feature dataset is composed of feature classes representing all the points, lines, polygons, or annotation in the CAD drawing. For example, a CAD drawing may contain two line layers representing roads and parcel boundaries, respectively. The CAD dataset's line feature class represents all features in both the road and parcel boundary layers.

centroid

The mathematical or geographical center point of a polygon or the midpoint of a line.

compress

Improves database performance by removing redundant rows shared by multiple versions. The process can only be run by the ArcSDE administrator.

conflict

In the versioning reconciliation process, if the same feature in the edit version and reconciliation version have both been edited, the feature is said to be in conflict. Resolving the conflict requires you to make the decision as to the feature's correct representation using the conflict resolution dialog box.

connectivity rules

Network rules that constrain the type of network features that may be connected to one another, and the number of features of any particular type that can be connected to features of another type. In most networks, not all edge types can logically connect to all junction types. Similarly, not all edge types can logically connect to all other edge types through all junction types. There are two types of connectivity rules: edge–junction and edge–edge.

constraints

In real-world databases, an object's attributes can't have any particular value based solely on what data types and ranges a particular field type in the database allows. In reality, the permissible values are a range or list of values.

coverage

A vector data storage format for storing the location, shape, and attributes of geographic features. One of the primary vector data storage formats for ArcInfo.

current task

A setting in the Current Task dropdown list that determines with which task the sketch construction tools (Sketch, Arc, Distance–Distance, and Intersection) will work.

The current task is set by clicking a task in the Current Task dropdown list. All tasks in the Current Task dropdown list work with a sketch that you create. For example, the Create New Feature task uses a sketch you create to make a new feature. The Extend/Trim Feature task uses a sketch you create to determine where the selected feature will be extended or trimmed. The Cut Polygon Feature task uses a sketch you create to determine where the polygon will be cut.

custom behavior

Behavior is the implementation of an object class method. ESRI-provided objects have a set of methods associated with them. A developer can choose to override one of these methods or create additional methods. In this instance, the object is said to have custom behavior.

custom feature

A feature with specialized behavior instantiated in a class by a developer.

custom object

Objects that have custom behavior provided by a developer.

data

A collection of related facts usually arranged in a particular format and gathered for a particular purpose.

database

A collection of related files organized for efficient retrieval of information. In the context of an ArcSDE geodatabase, some relational databases group data together in discrete named databases (for example, SQL Server, Sybase), while others do not (for example, Oracle).

dataset

A dataset is any feature class, table, or collection of feature classes or tables in the geodatabase.

default junction type

Two edge types may be connectable through more than one junction type. You can establish which of those junction types is the default for connecting the two edge types. This junction type is the default junction type.

dimension contruction methods

Dimension construction methods dictate what type of dimension feature is created and the number of points required to complete the feature's geometry. Construction methods include simple aligned, aligned, linear, rotated linear, free aligned, and free linear.

dimension feature

Dimension features are a special kind of map annotation that shows specific lengths or distances on a map. A dimension feature may indicate the length of a side of a building or land parcel, or it may indicate the distance between two features such as a fire hydrant and the corner of a building. Dimension features are stored in a dimension feature class.

dimension feature class

In the geodatabase, dimension features are stored in dimension feature classes. Like other feature classes in the geodatabase, all features in a dimension feature class have a geographic location and attributes and can either be inside or outside of a feature dataset.

dimension style

A dimension feature's style describes its symbology, what parts of it are drawn, and how it is drawn. Every time you create a new dimension feature, it is assigned a particular style. A collection of dimension styles is associated with a dimension feature class.

Dimensioning toolbar

A toolbar in ArcMap that facilitates the creation of dimension features.

direct connect

A two-tiered architecture for connecting to spatial databases. Direct connect does not require the ArcSDE application server to connect to a spatial database.

edge–edge rule

A connectivity rule that establishes that an edge of type A may connect to an edge of type B through a junction of type C. Edge–Edge rules always involve a junction type.

edge–junction cardinality

A rule may exist that allows an edge of type A to connect to a junction of type B. By default, any number of edges of type A can connect to a single junction of type B. You may want to restrict this. You can specify that between two and five edges of type A can connect to a junction of type B, but if there are less than two edges, or more than five edges, the connectivity rule is being violated. Similarly, you can restrict the number of junctions of type C that can connect to any junction of type D. This range of permissible connections is edge–junction cardinality.

edge–junction rule

A connectivity rule that establishes that an edge of type A may connect to a junction of type B.

edge element

See logical network.

edit cache

A setting used in spatial data editing in ArcMap that causes the features visible in the current map extent to be held in memory on your local machine. Designed to be used when working with large amounts of data, an edit cache results in faster editing because ArcMap doesn't have to retrieve the data from the server.

edit session

All editing takes place within an edit session. An edit session begins when you choose Start Editing from the Editor menu and ends when you choose Stop Editing.

Editor toolbar

A toolbar that lets you create and modify features and their attributes in ArcMap.

feature

A representation of a real-world object in a layer on a map.

feature class

An object class that stores features and has a field of type geometry.

feature dataset

A collection of feature classes that share the same spatial reference. Because the feature classes share the same spatial reference, they can participate in topological relationships with each other such as in a geometric network. Relationship classes can also be stored in a feature dataset.

field

A column in a table. Each field contains the values for a single attribute.

geocoding

The process of creating geometric representations for locations (such as point features) from descriptions of locations (such as addresses).

geocoding index

An index on geocoding reference data used by geocoding services.

geocoding reference data

Data that a geocoding service uses to determine the geometric representations for locations.

geocoding service

An object that defines a process for creating geometric representations for locations (such as point features) from descriptions of locations (such as addresses).

geodatabase

A geographic database that is hosted inside a relational database management system that provides services for managing geographic data. These services include validation rules, relationships, and topological associations.

geometric network

A geometric network can be thought of as a one-dimensional nonplanar graph, or logical network, that is composed of features. These features are constrained to exist within the network and can therefore be considered network features. ArcInfo will automatically maintain the explicit topological relationships between network features in a geometric network.

index

Created for an attribute, a group of attributes in a feature class or table to improve query performance. Feature classes also have spatial indexes that improve spatial query performance.

instance

The name of the process running on the ArcSDE server that allows connections and access to spatial data.

integrated feature dataset

Topologically associated feature classes in a geodatabase are stored in an integrated feature dataset. You can use the topological editing tools in ArcMap to maintain the topological associations of features in an integrated feature dataset.

IP address

The server's address on the network. The address consists of four numbers, each separated by a ".".

junction element

See logical network.

layer

A collection of similar geographic features—such as rivers, lakes, counties, or cities—of a particular area or place for display on a map. A layer references geographic data stored in a data source, such as a coverage, and defines how to display it. You can create and manage layers as you would any other type of data in your database.

linear dimension

A dimension whose length doesn't represent the true distance between the begin and end dimension points. Linear dimensions can be vertical, horizontal, or rotated. A vertical dimension's line represents the vertical distance between the begin and end dimension points. A horizontal linear dimension's line represents the horizontal distance between the begin and end dimension points. A rotated linear dimension is a dimension whose line is at some angle to the baseline and whose length represents the length of the dimension line itself, not the baseline.

logical network

A logical network is an abstract representation of a network. A logical network consists of edge, junction, and turn elements and the connectivity between them. You can ask a logical network which elements are connected, but you cannot ask it for the geometry of these elements. A logical network does not contain any coordinate data, so you cannot ask it for the location of its elements. For this you need a geometric network. In a logical network, an edge element is connected to two junction elements (a from-junction and a to-junction), and a junction can have zero or more edges connected to it. A turn has a from-edge, a junction, and a to-edge. Each element can also have many weights associated with it. Weights are typically used to describe the cost to traverse an edge or turn or the cost to pass through a junction.

map

A graphical presentation of geographic information. It contains geographic data and other elements such as a title, north arrow, legend, and scale bar. You can interactively display and query the geographic data on the map and also prepare a printable map by arranging the map elements around the data in a visually pleasing manner.

merge policy

All attribute domains have a merge policy associated with them. When two features are merged into a single feature in the ArcMap Editor, the merge policies dictate what happens to the value of the attribute to which the domain is associated. Standard merge policies are default value, sum, and weighted average.

network trace

In the most generic sense, a network trace means to navigate through the network following the connectivity of the network for some purpose.

null value

The absence of a value. A geographic feature for which there is no associated attribute information.

object

The representation of a real-world entity stored in a geodatabase. An object has properties and behavior.

object class

A collection of objects in the geodatabase that have the same behavior and the same set of attributes. All objects in the geodatabase are stored in object classes.

password

The password used for authentication when you log on to an ArcSDE geodatabase.

port number

The TCP/IP port number that an ArcSDE geodatabase instance is communicating on.

post

Posting is the process of applying the current edit session to the reconciled target version.

projection

A mathematical formula that transforms feature locations from the earth's curved surface to a map's flat surface. A projected coordinate system employs a projection to transform locations expressed as latitude and longitude values to x,y coordinates. Projections cause distortions in one or more of these spatial properties: distance, area, shape, and direction.

pyramids

In raster datasets, reduced resolution layers, or pyramids, record the original data in decreasing levels of resolution. The coarsest level of resolution is used to quickly draw the entire dataset. As you zoom in, layers with finer resolutions are drawn; performance is maintained because you're drawing successively smaller areas.

query

A question or request used for selecting features. A query often appears in the form of a statement or logical expression. In ArcMap, a query contains a field, an operator, and a value.

raster

Represents any data source that uses a grid structure to store geographic information.

reconcile

Reconciling is the process of merging all modified datasets, feature classes, and tables in the current edit session and a second target version. All features and rows that do not conflict are merged into the edit session, replacing the current features or rows. Features that are modified in each version are conflicts and require further resolution via the conflict resolution dialog box.

reference data

Tables or feature classes containing address information that geocoding services use to find the locations of addresses.

relationship

An association between two or more objects in a geodatabase.

relationship class

Objects in a real-world system often have particular associations with other objects in the database. These kinds of associations between objects in the geodatabase are called relationships. Relationships can exist between spatial objects (features in feature classes), nonspatial objects (rows in a table), or between spatial and nonspatial objects. While spatial objects are stored in the geodatabase in feature classes, and nonspatial objects are stored in object classes, relationships are stored in relationship classes.

schema

The structure or design of a database.

select

To choose from a number or group of features or records; to create a separate set or subset.

Selectable layers list

A list on the Selection toolbar that lets you choose from which layers you can select.

For example, suppose you wanted to select a large number of buildings by drawing a box around them but selected a parcel by mistake as you drew the selection box. To avoid this, you might uncheck the Parcels layer in the Selectable Layers list so that parcels cannot be selected.

selected set

A subset of the features in a layer or records in a table. ArcMap provides several ways to select features and records graphically or according to their attribute values.

server

The computer where the ArcSDE geodatabase you want to access is located.

shapefile

A vector data storage format for storing the location, shape, and attributes of geographic features.

simple feature

A feature that implements ESRI Simple Feature.

sketch

A shape that represents a feature's geometry. Every existing feature on a map has an alternate form, a sketch. A sketch lets you see exactly how a feature is composed with all vertices and segments of the feature visible. To modify a feature, you must modify its sketch. To create a feature, you must first create a sketch. You can only create line and polygon sketches, as points have neither vertices nor segments.

Sketches help complete the current task. For example, the Create New Feature task uses a sketch you create to make a new feature. The Extend/Trim Feature task uses a sketch you create to determine where the selected feature will be extended or trimmed. The Cut Polygon Feature task uses a sketch you create to determine where the polygon will be cut into two features.

snapping environment

The automatic intersecting of disjoint lines or nodes that arise when map data are being digitized or scanned.

snapping tolerance

The distance within which the pointer or a feature will snap to another location.

If the location being snapped to (vertex, boundary, midpoint, or connection) is within the distance you set, the pointer will automatically snap. For example, if you want to snap a power line to a utility pole and the snapping tolerance is set to 25 pixels, whenever the power line comes within a 25-pixel range of the pole it will automatically snap to it. Snapping tolerance can be measured using either map units or pixels.

spatial database

Any DBMS that contains spatial data.

spatial domain

Describes the range and precision of x,y coordinates and z- and m-values that can be stored in a feature dataset or feature class in a geodatabase.

spatial reference

Describes both the projection and spatial domain extent for a feature dataset or feature class in a geodatabase.

split policy

All attribute domains have a split policy associated with them. When a feature is split into two new features in the ArcMap Editor, the split policies dictate what happens to the value of the attribute to which the domain is associated. Standard split policies are duplicate, default value, and geometry ratio.

stream tolerance

The minimum distance the pointer must be moved from the last vertex before the next vertex will be created when using the Sketch tool in stream mode.

When streaming, vertices are automatically created at a defined interval as you move the mouse. For example, if the stream tolerance is set to 10 map units, you must move the pointer at least 10 map units before the next vertex will be created. If you move the pointer more than 10 map units, there may be more space between vertices, but there will always be a minimum interval of 10 map units. Stream tolerance is measured in map units.

subtypes

Although all objects in a feature class or object class must have the same behavior and attributes, not all objects have to share the same default values and validation rules. You can group features and objects into subtypes. Subtypes differentiate objects based on their rules.

table

Information formatted in rows and columns.

table of contents

Lists all the layers on the map and shows what the features in each layer represent.

tabular data

Descriptive information that is stored in rows and columns and can be linked to map features.

tagged values

Tagged values are used to set additional properties of UML elements. For example, you can set the length (in characters) of a string field by using a tagged value.

target layer

A setting in the Target dropdown list that determines to which layer new features will be added.

The target layer is set by clicking a layer in the Target dropdown list. For instance, if you set the target layer to Buildings, any features you create will be part of the Buildings layer. You must set the target layer whenever you're creating new features—whether you're creating them with the Sketch tool, by copying and pasting, or by buffering another feature.

topological feature

A feature that supports network connectivity that is established and maintained based on geometric coincidence.

topology

1. In geodatabases, relationships between connected features in a geometric network or shared borders between features in a planar topology.

2. In coverages, the spatial relationships between connecting or adjacent features (for example, arcs, nodes, polygons, and points). The topology of an arc includes its from- and to-nodes and its left and right polygons. Topological relationships are built from simple elements into complex elements: points (simplest elements), arcs (sets of connected points), areas (sets of connected arcs), and routes (sets of sections, which are arcs or portions of arcs). Redundant data (coordinates) is eliminated because an arc may represent a linear feature, part of the boundary of an area feature, or both.

tracing

The building of a set of network elements according to some procedure.

transaction

A group of atomic data operations that comprise a complete operational task such as inserting a row into a table.

username

The identification used for authentication when you log in to an ArcSDE geodatabase.

validation rule

Validation rules can be applied to objects in the geodatabase to ensure that their state is consistent with the system that the database is modeling. The geodatabase supports attribute, connectivity, relationship, and custom validation rules.

version

A version is an alternative representation of the database that has an owner, a description, a permission (private, protected, or public), and a parent version. Versions are not affected by changes occurring in other versions of the database.

vertex

A point that joins two segments of a feature.

For instance, a square building would have four vertices, one at each corner.

work flow

An organization's established processes for design, construction, and maintenance of facilities.

work order

One specific task that proceeds through each stage of an organization's work flow processes such as design, acceptance, and construction in the field.

workspace

A container of geographic data. This can be a folder that contains shapefiles, an ArcInfo workspace that contains coverages, a personal geodatabase, or an ArcSDE database connection.

Index

A

Address data. *See* Geocoding: address data
Address matching. *See* Geocoding
Alias
  defined 461
  described 21–23, 58–60
  feature class 21, 58, 71, 228
  field 22, 46, 57, 58, 63, 73, 335
  table 23, 58, 64
Aligned dimension
  defined 461
Alternate street names. *See* Geocoding services:
    reference data: alternate street names
AM/FM (Automated mapping/Facilities
    management) 205
Analyze command 88, 128
Angular unit 69
Annotation
  and versioning 451–452
  converting
    and geometric networks 174
    and versioning 174
    Convert Coverage Annotation command 183
    coverage 173, 183
    coverage pseudo items 173
    labels 173, 181
  creating 36, 39–40, 173–174, 176, 177, 181
  defined 171, 461
  described 172–174
  editing 177
  feature-linked
    converting from coverage 173
    creating 36, 180, 329
    described 172
    editing 47, 329, 365
    in ArcCatalog 175
  in ArcCatalog 19
  nonfeature-linked 172, 175, 176, 176–177, 365
  performance 174
  placement 175

Annotation (continued)
  reference scale 38–39
  string 368
Annotation class
  coverage annotation feature class 183
  creating 43, 176–177
  described 172
  in ArcMap 181, 365
  managing 174
  populating 176
  standalone 172
Annotation feature class 464. *See* Annotation class
Annotation features 88, 172, 181, 329, 367,
    370. *See also* Annotation
Appending data 92–94
ArcCatalog
  and versioning 437, 438, 439
  creating schema 5, 15–16, 53
  Customize dialog 312
  customizing 312
  getting help 14
  mini-browser 20
  previewing data 18–19
  schema locking 60
  tree 9, 18, 20
ArcInfo UML Model
  described 266
  ESRI classes 266–270
  ESRI interfaces 266–270
  ESRI network 266–270
  logical view 266–270
  user features 266–270, 274
ArcMap
  active annotation target 365
  and annotation 39, 176
  and default values 57
  and layers 41
  and relationships 147
  and versioning 437, 446–448, 449
  commands 391, 429

ArcMap (continued)
  converting annotation 173, 181
  Customize dialog 183
  customizing 183, 429
  document 181
  drawing tools 173, 329, 365
  network analysis 329, 389
  overflow window 180
  Selectable layers list 467
  table of contents 180, 181, 468
ArcSDE
  administration tools 94
  analyzing data 128
  ArcSDE for coverages 90
  defined 461
  described 1
  migrating data 94
  registering data with the geodatabase 127
ArcSDE for coverages. *See* ArcSDE
ArcSDE geodatabase. *See* SDE geodatabase
ArcStorm 5, 90
ArcToolbox
  building geometric networks 211
  data importing tools 83, 84
  data management tools 226
Area 59
Association 147, 148. *See also* Relationships
Attribute domains
  associating with a field 63, 73, 141
  associating with a subtype 142, 145,
    264, 288
  browsing in ArcCatalog. *See* Attribute
    domains: Domain properties dialog
  coded value domain
    code description 25, 50, 131, 134, 139
    codes 25, 131, 134, 139, 284
    creating 139
    described 24–25, 131
    in ArcCatalog 134
    in ArcMap Editor 50, 328, 334
    in UML 264, 284

Attribute domains (continued)
  creating 24, 137
  defined 461
  deleting 140
  described 24, 130–133
  domain description 137
  domain name 137
  Domain properties dialog 135, 137
  domain type 134, 138, 139
  field type 134, 137
  in UML 264–265, 274, 312, 313
  mentioned 6, 23, 57, 127, 129, 229, 328
  merge policy
    defined 465
    defining 138, 139
    described 24–25
    in UML 264, 283
  modifying 140
  properties 134, 140
  range domain
    creating 137–138
    described 24–25, 131–133
    editing in ArcMap 328
    in UML 264
    maximum value 134, 138, 283
    minimum value 134, 138, 283
  split policy
    defining 138, 139
    described 24–25
    editing in ArcMap 385
    in UML 264, 283
    mentioned 134
  valid values 24, 264, 283
Attribute validation rule 141. *See also*
    Attribute domains
Attributes
  and annotation 183
  and relationship classes 148, 150, 156,
    161, 172
  creating 56
  defined 461

Attributes (continued)
  editing in ArcMap 46, 50, 334, 385
  importing data 84
  in UML 279
  mentioned 5, 329, 435, 451, 458
  rules 130. *See also* Attribute domains
Automated mapping/Facilities management
    (AM/FM) 205

B

Barrier 208
Behavior 1, 14, 15–16, 20–23, 28, 35, 53,
    130, 172, 259, 319, 365, 452
  defined 461
Behavior class. *See* Behavior

C

CAD feature class
  defined 461
  field mapping (table) 87
  loading 114
Cardinality 148–151
CASE tools. *See also* UML model
  and data loading 89
  connecting to the repository 313
  mentioned 2, 6, 14, 327
  modeling database structure 261
  Schema Wizard
    described 260
    generating schema 325
    mentioned 312–313, 313
    selecting object classes 316
  semantics checker 267, 311
  spatial reference 316, 320
Centroid
  defined 462
Classification 42
COM (Component Object Model) 6, 60,
    84, 94, 127

COM class 319
Complex edge 32, 50, 206, 222. *See also* Network features
Complex junction 207, 264. *See also* Network features
Component Object Model (COM) 6, 60, 84, 94, 127
Composite relationships. *See* Relationships: composite
Compress 440
  defined 462
Configuration keyword 62, 72, 109–110, 113, 317, 320, 321, 322
Conflict 435, 449, 450–451, 454–455
  defined 462
Connection file 8
Connectivity rules
  creating 232
  default junctions 231
  defined 462
  described 231
  edge–edge rule
    creating 34–35, 232
    default junction 34–35, 49, 298, 383, 463
    described 231
    in ArcMap Editor 328, 374, 383
    in UML 266, 298
    junction type 329
  edge–junction rule
    cardinality 233, 298
    creating 33–34, 233
    defined 463
    described 231
    in UML 266, 298
  in ArcMap Editor 47, 49
  in UML 266–270
  mentioned 7, 26, 31, 130, 211, 234, 328
Constraints. *See* Attribute domains
  defined 462
Converting data 5, 428. *See also* Importing data; Loading data

Coordinate system
  and CASE tools 263
  and feature datasets 65
  and importing data 99
  custom 56
  defining 65, 69
  described 56
  geographic 69, 70
  projected 70
  saving 66
Copy/Paste geodatabase data 88, 121
Coverage
  annotation 88, 171
  data mapping 85
  data model 1
  defined 462
  items
    mapping (table) 86
    type 85
  loading data 428
  mentioned 2, 5–6, 15–16, 20, 43, 83, 327
  tics 85
Current task
  defined 462
Custom behavior. *See also* Behavior
  defined 462
Custom feature 78. *See also* Behavior
  defined 462
Custom object 3, 4, 6, 61, 64, 259, 330. *See also* Behavior
  defined 462
Custom rules 130. *See also* Validation rules
Customization 15. *See also* ArcCatalog: customizing; ArcMap: customizing

D

Data 435, 436
  defined 462
Data dictionary 21, 58
Data loading 90–92

Database 435, 436
  defined 462
Dataset 18–19
  defined 463
Datum 69
DB2 1
Default junction type
  defined 463
Default values
  and CASE tools 312
  and importing data 87, 111
  associating with a field 73, 141
  associating with a subtype 26–28, 142, 264, 288
  described 57, 130
  editing in ArcMap 370
  in UML 277
  mentioned 127
Dimension feature class
  and ArcCatalog 189
  creating 190, 190–191, 192, 193
  defined 187, 463
Dimension features
  auto-dimension tools 395, 396
    baseline dimension 396, 420
    continue dimension 396, 422
    dimension edge 396, 419
  baseline 187
  changing style 426
  construction methods
    aligned 396, 405
    defined 463
    described 395
    free aligned 396, 413
    free linear 396, 416
    linear 396, 407
    rotated aligned 396, 410
    simple aligned 396, 402
  creating 51, 185, 188
  defined 186, 463
  editing 395

Dimension features (continued)
mentioned 185, 190
modifying 397, 399, 424
performance 188
properties (table) 398, 400
types
aligned 51, 186
horizontal linear 186
rotated linear 186
vertical linear 186
Dimension styles
and ArcCatalog 189
arrow and text fit 188
arrow display 188
baseline height 421
begin symbol 188
creating 199–200
creating and managing 195
default style
mentioned 190
setting 203
defined 187, 463
deleting 204
dimension line display 188
dimension line symbol 188
end symbol 188
extension line display 188
importing 193, 201
lines and arrows 196
mentioned 185, 190
offset and overshot 188
overriding 195
renaming 202
style ID 199
text 197
text and arrow fit 198
text display 188
Dimensioning toolbar 51, 330, 397, 401
defined 463
Direct connect 8, 11, 12
defined 463

Drawing exchange format (DXF) 83
DXF (drawing exchange format) 83

E

Edge element 464. See Logical network
Edge feature class
creating 228–229
editing in ArcMap 382, 384
mentioned 232
Edge features. See Network features
Edge–Edge rule
defined 463
Edge–Junction cardinality
defined 463
Edge–Junction rule
defined 463
Edit cache
and geometric networks 209
defined 464
described 330
tools 333
using 332
Edit session. See also Editing; Editing in
ArcMap
and versioning 448, 449, 450, 454, 458
defined 464
mentioned 89, 123, 428
Editing 15–16, 19, 24, 43, 447. See also
Editing in ArcMap
Editing in ArcMap
and annotation
creating new 365, 365–366
creating new features with linked
annotation 369–370
described 329–331, 365
editing annotation features 367–368
editing features with linked annotation
371–373
and attribute domains
coded value domains 336

Editing in ArcMap (continued)
and attribute domains (continued)
described 334–335
validating 339–340
and attributes 346
and default values 334–335
and subtypes 130, 337, 338, 364
and validation rules 328–331
and versioning 449
Attributes dialog 46, 50, 335, 340,
341, 346, 347, 354, 360, 371, 426
creating new features 333, 334, 334–335
current task 334, 369, 379, 402, 462
deleting features 362, 373
edit sketch 49
Edit tool 45, 361, 363, 383, 385, 388,
390, 393
editing network features
ancillary roles 389
connectivity rules 329, 332, 393–394
creating a new network edge 374,
379–380, 382–383, 384–385
described 329–331
enabling and disabling network features
390
subsuming network junctions 374,
386–387
undoing edits 388
editing relationships
composite relationships 360–362
creating 349–350, 351–352
deleting 341, 353–354, 355–356,
357–358, 359, 364, 365
described 169, 329–331, 346
editing related objects 346
relationship rules 363
loading objects 430–433
mentioned 28
Rotate tool 361, 373
selection 394

Editing in ArcMap (continued)
   Sketch tool 48, 334, 369, 379, 402
   snapping environment 48, 329, 330, 374,
      380, 382, 384, 386, 433
   start editing 365
   Target layer 334, 369, 379, 386,
      402, 430, 468
   undo 388
   validate features 330
   validate selection 339, 363, 393
Editor toolbar. *See also* Editing in ArcMap
   defined 464
Embedded foreign key 148. *See also* Key field
ESRI Annotation Feature. *See* Feature type
ESRI Complex Edge Feature. *See* Feature type
ESRI Dimension Feature. *See* Feature type
ESRI Simple Edge Feature. *See* Feature type
ESRI Simple Feature. *See* Feature type
ESRI Simple Junction Feature. *See* Feature
   type
ESRI Simple Row. *See* Feature type

F

Feature. *See also* Feature class; Feature type;
   Object
   and data loading 123
   defined 464
   described 1
   editing 334. *See also* Editor toolbar
   mentioned 15–16, 147, 171, 176, 312,
      435, 449, 458
   selecting 153, 329
   simple 234, 467
   splitting and merging 132
Feature class
   and attribute domains 141
   and CASE tools 312–313
   and geometric networks 31, 206–209
   and importing data 20, 102, 111, 114
   and loading data 123, 428

Feature class (continued)
   and relationship classes 147
   and spatial reference 75–77
   and subtypes 24, 130
   as a template 72
   converting data 84
   creating
      described 56, 71–72
      New Feature Class Wizard 36–37
   custom 78
   defined 464
   in ArcCatalog 19
   in UML 263–265, 278
   labeling 181
   mentioned 5, 16, 55, 135, 140, 145, 334,
      431, 438, 446, 450
   registering with the geodatabase 94, 127
   simple 56, 87, 111, 208, 220, 330
   standalone 56, 71, 75–77, 84, 96,
      111, 114
Feature dataset
   and annotation classes 172, 175
   and CASE tools 313
   and creating 65
   and geometric networks 31, 210, 211
   and importing data 20, 96, 102, 111, 114
   and relationship classes 152
   converting data 84
   defined 464
   described 56, 59
   in ArcCatalog 19
   integrated 59, 330
   mentioned 5, 55, 71, 177, 191, 192, 194,
      216, 220, 228–229, 438
   modeling 59
Feature type 228
   custom 36, 71, 228, 259
   ESRI Annotation Feature 36, 172, 176, 178
   ESRI Complex Edge Feature 228
   ESRI Dimension Feature 190
   ESRI Simple Edge Feature 228

Feature type (continued)
   ESRI Simple Feature 84, 88, 172
   ESRI Simple Junction Feature 230
   ESRI Simple Row 84
   network 36. *See also* Network features
   simple 36, 56, 71, 220, 228
   topological 56, 469. *See also* Topology
Feature-linked annotation. *See* Annotation
Field
   and annotation 172, 176, 179
   and attribute domains 63, 140, 141
   and importing data 99, 108, 109–110, 113
   and indexes 79
   and loading data 124
   creating 61
   defined 464
   deleting 62, 99, 108, 110, 113
   described 57
   in UML 318, 324
   mapping 85
   mentioned 55, 438, 451
   properties
      data type 61, 85, 130, 161, 274
      default value 63
      length 263, 318, 324
      name 161
      precision 57, 263, 318, 324
      scale 57, 263, 318, 324
   related 153, 169
   required 39, 58, 61, 72, 177, 208,
      229, 263
Folder connection 18
Foreign key 30, 161, 162, 265

G

Geocoded feature classes
   attributes
      score 237
      standardized address 237
      status 237

Geocoded feature classes (continued)
  automatically maintaining 237
Geocoding
  address data
    Single Field 256
    StreetMap 256
    U.S. addresses 256–257
    ZIP 257
    ZIP+4 257
  defined 464
Geocoding index
  defined 464
Geocoding indexes
  automatically maintaining 248–249,
    253–255
  defined 248
  manually maintaining 248, 250–252
Geocoding reference data
  defined 464
Geocoding service
  defined 464
Geocoding service styles
  Single Field 240
  StreetMap 240
  US One Address 241
  US One Range 241–242
  US Streets 242
  ZIP 243
  ZIP+4 243
  ZIP+4 Range 244
Geocoding services
  clientside 236
  creating 245–247
  defined 236
  in ArcCatalog 238
  in ArcMap 238–239
  reference data
    alternate street names 236, 242–243, 246
    place name aliases 236, 244, 246
    preparing 240–244
  serverside 236

Geocoding Services folder 238, 245
Geodatabase
  and versions 435
  creating 9
  data model 1, 14, 129
  defined 464
  in ArcCatalog 8
  mentioned 436, 449
  three ways to create 4–5, 260
Geographic database 129
Geometric network
  and CASE tools 263, 296
  and connectivity rules 232
  and the edit cache 378
  and versioning 451
  appending data 93–94
  Build Geometric Network Wizard 31,
    220, 226
  building 31, 31–35, 211, 214, 220
  connectivity models 375
  copying data 121
  creating 211, 216
  defined 464
  deleting 234
  described 206
  editing 44, 328–331
  flow direction 32, 207, 389
  in ArcCatalog 210
  in UML 266
  loading data 90–92
  managing 234
  mentioned 3, 43, 56–60, 127, 205
  modeling 209
  network weights 33
  performance 209, 378
  properties 231, 232
  renaming 234
  repairing topology 377
  snapping models 212
  sources and sinks 207–209, 223

Geometry
  area and length 58
  importing data 84
  mentioned 56, 171, 451
Geometry field 71, 74
Geometry type
  and CASE tools 320, 321
  in UML 274
  mapping 85
  mapping (table) 85
  setting 74
Graphics 181

I

Importing data
  and CASE tools 90
  CAD feature classes 114
  coverages 20–22, 84–95, 102
  data mapping 85–87
  described 84–95
  geodatabase feature classes 87, 111
  in batch 97, 109, 111, 114
  mentioned 5, 44, 83, 327, 328
  raster 115
  shapefiles 84–95, 96
  tables 19, 22, 84–95, 109
Index
  attribute
    ascending 79
    creating 79
    deleting 80
    described 79–80
    unique 79
  defined 464
  spatial. See Spatial index
Instance
  defined 465
Integrated feature dataset. See Feature dataset:
    integrated
  defined 465

Invalid features 231, 328, 340, 363–364, 394
Invalid objects 328. *See also* Invalid features
IP address 10, 12
   defined 465

J

Junction element
   defined 465
Junction feature class
   and connectivity rules 232, 233
   and versioning 452
   creating 32, 228, 230
   described 207
   in ArcMap Editor 380, 386
   sinks 32
   sources 32
Junction features. *See* Network features

K

Key field 148, 156, 160, 452. *See also*
       Foreign key; Primary key

L

Labels
   converting to annotation 181
   creating 173
   expression 37, 179
   rules 173
Layer
   defined 465
Layer files
   adding layers to your map 44
   creating 41, 43
   described 41
   mentioned 40
Line 58
Linear dimension
   defined 465

Linear unit 70
Loading data
   and CASE tools 260
   described 89
   example 89–95
   mentioned 5, 83
   Object Loader 7, 89, 430–433
   Simple Data Loader 7, 89, 123, 123–124, 428
Logical network 206, 383. *See also* Geometric
       network
   defined 465

M

Map 44, 180, 446. *See also* ArcMap
   defined 465
Map LIBRARIAN 90
Merge policy. *See also* Attribute domains
   default value 133
   defined 465
   described 132–133
   geometry weighted 133
   sum values 133
Microsoft Access 309, 314
Microsoft Repository 6, 259, 309, 312, 316, 317
Multipoint 59
Multiuser database 60
Multiversioned. *See* Versioned data

N

Network connectivity 47, 89, 205, 206, 220, 375, 385, 388
Network elements 208, 388
Network feature class. *See also* Edge feature
       class; Junction feature class
   creating 220, 228
   editing in ArcMap 330
   in UML 263, 266, 298

Network features
   ancillary role 207, 389
   and CASE tools 312
   and versioning 452
   complex 1, 374
   described 206, 206–209
   edges 32, 206, 211, 220, 231
   editing in ArcMap 47, 393, 428, 433
   enabled and disabled 208
   junctions 49, 206, 211, 231, 264, 389
   mentioned 228, 234
   sources and sinks 228, 230, 389
Network trace
   defined 465
Network weights
   associating with a field 229
   creating 218, 223
   described 208–209
   mentioned 211
Nodes 85
Null values
   and CASE tools 318, 324
   defined 466
   in attribute domains 131
   mentioned 57, 73

O

Object
   and relationships 29, 56, 148, 154, 163, 341
   custom. *See* Custom object
   defined 466
   described 1
   invalid 130
   mentioned 3, 5, 24, 147
   simple 1, 61
   valid 130
Object class 3, 56
   defined 466
Object Loader. *See* Loading data

Object model 315
Object-oriented 1, 6, 259
ObjectID 57, 62, 63, 72, 127
ODBC 310, 314
Oracle 1, 8, 11

P

Password
  defined 466
Perimeter 59
Personal geodatabase 8, 9, 83, 98, 107, 110, 112, 135, 320, 321
Place name aliases. *See* Geocoding services: reference data: place name aliases
Point 59, 85
Polygon 58
Port number
  defined 466
Post 436, 449, 450, 454–455, 458
  defined 466
Precision. *See* Field: properties: precision
Primary key 30, 156, 160, 162, 265
Prime meridian 69
Privileges
  and versioning
    described 439, 449, 459
    private 440
    protected 440
    public 440
  delete 82
  described 82
  granting 55, 82
  insert 82
  mentioned 131
  revoking 55, 82
  select 82
  update 82
Projecting data 84
Projection 3, 70
  defined 466

Pyramids
  defined 466

Q

Query 124, 432
  defined 466
Query Builder 125, 432

R

Raster
  data compression 94
  defined 466
  importing 94
  mosaic 95
  pyramids 94
  tile size 94
RDBMS (relational database management system) 1, 21, 58, 79, 85, 88
Reconcile 449, 449–450, 454–455, 458
  defined 466
Reference data
  defined 466
Reference scale 177, 179, 191
Registering data 84, 127
Relational database management system (RDBMS) 1, 21, 58, 79, 85
Relationship class
  and annotation 175, 179, 181
  and CASE tools 312, 319
  and versioning 450, 451–452
  attributed
    and CASE tools 324
    described 149–151
    in UML 265
  cardinality 30, 161, 163, 265
  composite 149–151, 158, 161, 172, 265, 365
  creating 29–30, 161
  defined 467

Relationship class (continued)
  deleting 165
  described 147, 148–151
  destination class 29, 148, 150, 154, 158, 161, 162, 163, 172
  editing in ArcMap 47
  foreign key. *See* Foreign key
  in ArcCatalog 152, 154
  in ArcMap 153, 166, 169
  in UML 265, 294
  managing 165
  mentioned 19, 55, 56, 60, 129
  messaging 149, 155, 158, 265
  modeling 150
  origin class 29, 150, 154, 158, 161, 162, 163, 172, 265, 294
  path labels
    backward path label 29–30, 46, 155, 158
    described 149–151
    editing in ArcMap 166, 346, 347, 349, 352, 353, 356, 358
    forward path label 29–30, 155, 158
    in ArcMap Editor 359
  performance 150
  primary key. *See* Primary key
  renaming 165
  simple 149–151, 154, 158, 161
Relationship rules
  cardinality 150, 163, 164
  creating 163
  described 150–151
  in ArcMap Editor 363
  in UML 265
  mentioned 130, 152, 328
Relationships
  and annotation 40
  and versioning 452
  composite 176, 329, 371
  creating 153, 329
  creating and deleting 341
  creating new 342
  defined 466

Relationships (continued)
    deleting 153
    deleting objects 342
    described 148–151
    destination object 164, 172, 294, 361
    editing in ArcMap 328
    mentioned 1, 3, 7, 19, 84–95, 127, 147,
        205, 327
    navigating 44
    origin object 164, 172, 360
    related object 353, 359, 360, 452
    splitting features 344
    validating 363–364
Remote geodatabase. *See* SDE geodatabase
Row 61, 123, 147, 148, 312. *See also* Object

S

Scale. *See* Field: properties: scale
Schema
    and CASE tools 316
    and geometric networks 221
    and loading data 124, 330
    creation 5
    defined 467
    designing 3, 5, 14, 55, 131
    in UML 260, 309, 315
    mentioned 2, 14, 259, 327
    modifying 60
Schema locking
    and dimension styles 195
    and geometric networks 215, 234
    and relationship classes 151
    and subtypes 133
    described 60
    exclusive lock 60, 151, 195, 215, 234
    shared lock 60, 151, 215, 234
SDE. *See* ArcSDE
SDE connection 8, 10, 11, 12, 96, 135
SDE for coverages. *See* ArcSDE
SDE geodatabase 8, 9, 62, 72, 83, 98, 107,
        112, 317, 320, 321, 322, 330

SDE layers 94
SDE server 10, 12, 467
SDE service 10
Select
    defined 467
Selectable layers list
    defined 467
Selected set
    defined 467
Selection 180, 341, 383, 467
Server
    defined 467
Shape_Area 59
Shape_Length 59
Shapefile
    and data loading 123, 428
    as a template 56
    data mapping 86
    defined 467
    field mapping (table) 86, 87
    mentioned 2, 5–6, 83, 234, 327
Simple feature
    defined 467
Sketch
    defined 467
Sketch constraints 467
Snap tolerance 32, 222
    defined 467
Snapping agent 467
Snapping environment
    defined 467
Snapping features 222
Spatial database
    defined 468
Spatial domain
    defined 468
Spatial index
    creating 79–80, 81
    deleting 81
    described 56–57
    grid size 74, 81, 84, 98, 107, 112, 263,
        320, 321

Spatial reference
    and feature classes 71
    and feature datasets 65
    and importing data 84, 99
    defined 468
    defining 100, 106
    described 56
    importing 65–66
    precision 56, 67
    selecting 65–66
    spatial domain 56, 65, 66, 468
Split policy. *See also* Attribute domains
    default value 132
    defined 468
    described 132–133
    duplicate 132
    geometry ratio 132
SQL 331
SQL Server 8, 12, 309, 314
Standardized address. *See* Geocoded feature
        classes: attributes: standardized address
Stream tolerance
    defined 468
Subtypes
    and attribute domains 140, 141
    and CASE tools 312, 319
    and connectivity rules 231, 232, 298
    and data copying 121
    and data importing 87, 111
    and data loading 124
    and relationship rules 150, 163
    and symbology 42–43
    creating 26–28, 142
    default subtype 143
    defined 468
    deleting 145
    described 24, 130–133
    editing in ArcMap 334
    in UML 264–265, 266
    mentioned 3, 6, 15–16, 23, 56
    modifying 142, 145

Subtypes (continued)
    subtype code 26, 130, 143, 288
    subtype description 143, 145
    subtype field 124, 130, 142, 288, 430
Symbology 41, 153, 172, 175, 338, 365

T

Table
    and attribute domains 140, 141
    and CASE tools 312, 315
    and importing data 21–23
    and relationship classes 148, 148–151,
        152, 154, 155, 161, 278
    and subtypes 24, 130, 135, 145
    creating 61–62
    dBASE 5–6, 83, 87, 109, 123, 428
    defined 468
    designer 61
    editing in ArcMap 329
    in UML 234, 263–265
    INFO 5–6, 15–16, 19, 20–23, 29, 43,
        83, 109, 123, 428
    mentioned 5, 55, 56, 147, 438, 446
Table of contents
    defined 468
Tabular data
    defined 468
Tagged values
    defined 468
Target layer
    defined 468
TCP/IP 10
Topological features
    defined 469
Topology
    defined 469
    described 59
    integrated features 1, 5, 449, 450

Topology (continued)
    network topology 47, 205, 206, 211,
        234, 329, 374. *See also* Network
        connectivity
    tools 330
Tracing
    defined 469
Transaction 449, 458–459
    defined 469

U

UML
    applying to existing databases 267
    feature datasets 273
    mentioned 2
    tagged values 263, 272, 274, 318, 323
    tagged values (table) 261
UML model
    abstract class 275
    and CASE tools 313, 316, 317, 325
    attribute domains
        associating with a subtype 290–292
        codes 287
        creating 283–285
        description 287
        field type 284, 286
        maximum value 285
        merge policy 284, 286
        minimum value 285
        split policy 284, 286
        TemplateCodedValueDomain 286
        TemplateRangeDomain 283
    binary association 278, 294
    class 317
    class diagrams 273
    class extensions 303
    connectivity rules
        creating 298–299, 311
        default junction 301
        junction subtypes 300

UML model (continued)
    custom behavior 303–304
    default values 277, 290–292
    exporting to the repository
        Microsoft Access 309
        SQL Server 310
    feature class 274
    fields
        creating 276–277
        data type 277
        described 274
    generalization 275
    generating schema 312–313
    in Visio Enterprise 271
    interfaces 303
    relationship class
        attributed 279
        cardinality 279
        composite 281
        destination class 278
        foreign key 278
        origin class 278
        primary key 278
        stereotype 281
        tagged values 278–280, 281
    relationship rules 294, 295
    setting tagged values 261, 272, 468
    subtypes
        and relationship rules 294
        creating 290–292
        default subtype 289
        subtype field 288–289, 291
UML packages 266, 271
Username
    defined 469

V

Valid feature 364

Validation rules. *See also* Attribute domains;
    Connectivity rules; Relationship rules
  and importing data 84
  and loading data 433
  defined 469
  described 130
  editing in ArcMap 44, 327, 328
  mentioned 1, 3, 15–16
  validation order 328

Vector data 1

Version
  and editing 449–453
  conflict. *See* Conflict
  connecting to 13
  DEFAULT 9
  defined 435, 469
  described 436–437
  in ArcMap 446–448
  post. *See* Post
  reconcile. *See* Reconcile
  refresh 442, 447
  transaction. *See* transaction

Versioned data 89, 123, 131, 165, 221, 330,
    428, 430

Vertex
  defined 469

W

Work flow 436
  defined 469

Work order 436
  defined 469

Workspace 446
  defined 469